The Value Chain of Foreign Aid

Contributions to Economics

www.springer.com/series/1262

Further volumes of this series can be found at our homepage.

Carsten Schröder
Variable Income Equivalence Scales
2004. ISBN 978-3-7908-0183-5

Wilhelm J. Meester
Locational Preferences of Entrepreneurs
2004. ISBN 978-3-7908-0178-1

Russel Cooper/Gary Madden (Eds.)
Frontiers of Broadband, Electronic and Mobile Commerce
2004. ISBN 978-3-7908-0087-6

Sardar M. N. Islam
Empirical Finance
2004. ISBN 978-3-7908-1551-1

Jan-Egbert Sturm/Timo Wollmershäuser (Eds.)
Ifo Survey Data in Business Cycle and Monetary Policy Analysis
2005. ISBN 978-3-7908-0174-3

Bernard Michael Gilroy/Thomas Gries/Willem A. Naudé (Eds.)
Multinational Enterprises, Foreign Direct Investment and Growth in Africa
2005. ISBN 978-3-7908-0276-4

Günter S. Heiduk/Kar-yiu Wong (Eds.)
WTO and World Trade
2005. ISBN 978-3-7908-1579-5

Emilio Colombo/Luca Stanca
Financial Market Imperfections and Corporate Decisions
2006. ISBN 978-3-7908-1581-8

Birgit Mattil
Pension Systems
2006. ISBN 978-3-7908-1675-4

Francesco C. Billari/Thomas Fent/Alexia Prskawetz/Jürgen Scheffran (Eds.)
Agent-Based Computational Modelling
2006. ISBN 978-3-7908-1640-2

Kerstin Press
A Life Cycle for Clusters?
2006. ISBN 978-3-7908-1710-2

Russel Cooper/Gary Madden/Ashley Lloyd/Michael Schipp (Eds.)
The Economics of Online Markets and ICT Networks
2006. ISBN 978-3-7908-1706-5

Renato Giannetti/Michelangelo Vasta (Eds.)
Evolution of Italian Enterprises in the 20th Century
2006. ISBN 978-3-7908-1711-9

Ralph Setzer
The Politics of Exchange Rates in Developing Countries
2006. ISBN 978-3-7908-1715-7

Dora Borbély
Trade Specialization in the Enlarged European Union
2006. ISBN 978-3-7908-1704-1

Iris A. Hauswirth
Effective and Efficient Organisations?
2006. ISBN 978-3-7908-1730-0

Marco Neuhaus
The Impact of FDI on Economic Growth
2006. ISBN 978-3-7908-1734-8

Nicola Jentzsch
The Economics and Regulation of Financial Privacy
2006. ISBN 978-3-7908-1737-9

Klaus Winkler
Negotiations with Asymmetrical Distribution of Power
2006. ISBN 978-3-7908-1743-0

Sasha Tsenkova, Zorica Nedović-Budić (Eds.)
The Urban Mosaic of Post-Socialist Europe
2006. ISBN 978-3-7908-1726-3

Brigitte Preissl/Jürgen Müller (Eds.)
Governance of Communication Networks
2006. ISBN 978-3-7908-1745-4

Lei Delsen/Derek Bosworth/Hermann Groß/Rafael Muñoz de Bustillo y Llorente (Eds.)
Operating Hours and Working Times
2006. ISBN 978-3-7908-1759-1

Pablo Coto-Millán; Vicente Inglada (Eds.)
Essays on Transport Economics
2006. ISBN 978-3-7908-1764-5

Christian H. Fahrholz
New Political Economy of Exchange Rate Policies and the Enlargement of the Eurozone
2006. ISBN 978-3-7908-1761-4

Sandra Gruescu
Population Ageing and Economic Growth
2007. ISBN 978-3-7908-1905-2

Christian Schabbel

The Value Chain of Foreign Aid

Development, Poverty Reduction, and Regional Conditions

With 32 Figures and 22 Tables

Physica-Verlag
A Springer Company

Series Editors

Werner A. Müller
Martina Bihn

Author

Dr. Christian Schabbel
Research Assistant
Duisburg-Essen University
Department of Managerial Economics
Mercator School of Management - Faculty of Business
Lotharstraße 65
47057 Duisburg
Germany
christian.schabbel@uni-due.de

This publication was accepted as doctoral dissertation at Duisburg-Essen University, Germany (2006), under the title: Foreign aid, poverty reduction strategies and the impact of regional conditions.

Library of Congress Control Number: 2006939790

ISSN 1431-1933

ISBN 978-3-7908-1931-1 Physica-Verlag Heidelberg New York

Physica-Verlag is part of Springer Science+Business Media

springer.com

Production: LE-TEX Jelonek, Schmidt & Vöckler GbR, Leipzig
Cover-design: WMX Design GmbH, Heidelberg

SPIN 11949527 134/3100YL - 5 4 3 2 1 0 Printed on acid-free paper

Foreword

For more than 50 years industrialized countries and international organizations attempt to improve the lives of people in low-income countries. Many strategies and initiatives have been "tested" since then and, on the whole, the results were sobering. It became evident during the 1990s that conditional and standardized macroeconomic policy reform packages, known as structural adjustment programs, were in most cases not able to transform poor countries into high growth performers. Similarly, (even large) inflows of Official Development Assistance (ODA) proved to have little if any effect in promoting development, let alone in reducing poverty. To the contrary, poverty in most sub-Saharan African, Latin American and Asian countries (excluding China) remained high or even increased during the last two decades. In some cases, foreign aid financed local elites, strengthened undemocratic government structures, thwarted market forces and gave adverse incentives to the locals.

The case for aid began to flourish again in the late 1990s following a study by Craig Burnside and David Dollar that spurred immense interest among researchers and practitioners. The authors claimed that foreign aid does have a positive impact on growth in countries with a sound policy environment and provided empirical support for this hypothesis. Although a general consensus on this relationship is far from emerging, the appealing suggestion to select aid recipients based on their past performance in various (e.g., policy) indicators quickly made its way on the agendas of most high-level conferences. Aid practitioners and politicians pledged to scale-up official aid flows. Following their rhetoric, halving poverty until 2015 (as envisioned in the Millennium Declaration) seemed to be primarily a question of gathering enough official resources ('halving poverty by doubling aid"). Alongside, the World Bank shifted its analytical focus on pro-poor growth, i.e. growth specifically designed to benefit the poor. A detailed catalogue of objectives (Millennium Goals) should foster goal orientation, extended debt relief initiatives (HIPC) should give selected recipient countries a "fresh start" and poverty reduction strategy papers (PRSP) should serve as reference documents to guarantee donors and recipients act in concert.

Still, despite an improved analytical knowledge of poverty, a complex bilateral and multilateral transfer system of ODA and a list of clearly defined objectives, the problems of then are still the ones of today: The number of countries seeking assistance and the demands (of donors and recipients) increased, the conditions of success seem to be more heterogeneous and the respective solutions more homogenous. The overall track record of 50 years of foreign aid is disappointing.

Against this background, Christian Schabbel assesses the potential of ODA to reduce poverty. He analyzes the entire value chain of ODA, beginning with its provision over its allocation to its utilization. Into each of these components, region-specific conditions and influential factors are embedded. The horizontal interactions between donors and recipients as well as the vertical connections to local and regional conditions represent the heart of Christian Schabbel's approach. Chap. 2 analyzes supply-side aspects of ODA (actors and instruments, innovative development finance, donor coordination). In Chap. 3, optimal and factual ODA allocation, selectivity as well as allocation policies, motives and strategies are examined. Chap. 4 deals with the utilization of aid, the aid-growth-inequality-poverty nexus and the macroeconomic impacts of aid inflows. Finally, Chap. 5 investigates the role of regional conditions for ODA and poverty reduction and presents reform proposals.

Christian Schabbel's dissertation shows that catchy prescriptions and global plans to reduce poverty simply by accumulating enough official resources are misleading. Doubling or tripling ODA (with or without so-called innovative financing mechanisms) will not alleviate poverty in all countries. Planning economic development by applying outsiders' instructions (e.g., Western bilateral donors or multilateral organizations) is likely to fail in the complex and heterogenous societies of the developing world.

This does not imply that foreign aid should be abolished. Instead of a quantitative and planning approach, a demand-side oriented concept of aid-financed poverty alleviation is urgently needed. The future of foreign aid lies in finding (many) small-scale solutions specifically laid out for the poor's actual needs, which may be very different across societies, and execute them efficiently. The conditions under which aid works and the likelihood of transferring practical solutions to other countries and regions must be investigated further in order to alleviate poverty not only on a global scale, but also in every country and region.

Duisburg, October 19, 2006 Günter Heiduk

Acknowledgements

When I started my PhD dissertation at the Chair for International Economic Relations (University of Duisburg-Essen) in August 2002, the first conversation with my thesis advisor Prof. Dr. Günter Heiduk encouraged me to start researching on developing countries. Instead of having a predefined topic in mind, Prof. Heiduk gave me a high degree of academic freedom. When my academic search led me to the fields of foreign aid and poverty reduction, he was very supportive and assisted by asking the right questions. The discussions with him were always very rewarding. I would like to thank Prof. Dr. Günter Heiduk for a great time at his institute, an enjoyable work atmosphere and an exemplary "open door policy". He was always available for the exchange of thoughts, ideas and chapter outlines.

My two referees Prof. Dr. Günter Heiduk and Prof. Dr. Markus Taube graded the dissertation in a very short time despite their packed workload. The examining committee consisting of Prof. Dr. Günter Heiduk, Prof. Dr. Markus Taube, Prof. Dr. Peter Anker and Prof. Dr. Bernd Rolfes made it possible to hold my oral defense soon after submitting my thesis. I greatly appreciate their courtesy in this matter.

During the four years working for the Chair, I shared the office with my collegue and friend Dr. Kerstin Preß. I would like to thank her for joint research and classroom work, valuable discussions (on and off-topic) and her time to proofread and review major parts of my studies. It was always a great pleasure and fun working with her.

I also would like to thank my colleague Yiping Zhu (PhD), who I luckily got the chance to work with during my last year, for a very harmonious and mutually rewarding companionship at our institute.

The secretaries Marianne Appelt and Nicole Jaschinski as well as a number of student assistants were a great help throughout the last years. Once a student assistant myself I know that the research assistants usually outsource "the boring stuff" such as collecting and formatting data and copying endless amounts of articles and books. I am especially indebted to Sonja Fischer, Nadja Kremser, Stefanie Lenz and Andreas Eickel for providing great assistance to me in these issues.

The valuable feedback I got from staff members and research colleagues of the Department of Managerial Economics during the PhD research seminars and also at lunch talks supported me as well. I very much appreciated their help. Moreover, I would like to express my thankfulness to Dr. Nejc Jakopin for his suggestions and constant motivation, as well as my international friends Ania Nadgrodkiewicz, Drew Kompanek and Christine Svitlana Otsver for proofreading and critically questioning some ideas of my work.

I thank my parents Brigitte and Peter Schabbel for their love and support throughout my life, for encouraging me to pursue my own way and, of course, for asking the question PhD candidates like the most ("how is your thesis going, son?").

Finally, I would like to express my deepest gratitude to my girl-friend Yvonne Dalkowski who, especially in the final year of writing, endured many complaints and had to do without me a number of weekends. Having a much harder educator job than I have sitting in a bureau the entire day, I admire her durability and energy.

I thank you all for your support to make this thesis reality.

Duisburg, October 20, 2006 Christian Schabbel

Contents

List of abbreviations

ADB	Asian Development Bank
AfDB	African Development Bank
BMZ	Bundesministerium für wirtschaftliche Zusammenarbeit und Entwicklung
CAS	Country Assistance Strategies
CBCT	Cross-Border Capital Tax
CDF	Comprehensive Development Framework
CFF	Compensatory Finance Facility
Cif	Cost, inclusive insurance and freight
CIFA	Canadian Investment Fund for Africa
CPA	Country Policy Assessment
CPIA	Country Policy and Institutional Assessment
CPPA	Country Portfolio Performance Assessments
CTT	Currency Transaction Tax
DAC	Development Assistance Committee
DFID	UK Department for International Development
DSA	Debt Sustainability Analysis
EBRD	European Bank for Reconstruction and Development
EDF	European Development Fund
EEF	Extended Fund Facility
ENP	European Neighborhood Policy
ERND	Exchange Rate Normalization Duty
ESAF	Enhanced Structural Adjustment Facility
FDI	Foreign Direct Investment
Fob	Free on board (exclusive insurance and freight)
GAVI	Global Alliance for Vaccines and Immunization
GDP	Gross Domestic Product
GEF	Global Environment Facility
GEP	Growth Elasticity of Poverty
GNI	Gross National Income
GNP	Gross National Product
GTZ	Gesellschaft für Technische Zusammenarbeit
HD	Harrod and Domar
HIPC	Highly Indebted Poor Country

IADB	Inter-American Development Bank Group
IBRD	International Bank for Reconstruction and Development
IDA	International Development Association
IDPF	International Drug Purchase Facility
IFC	International Finance Corporation
IFF	International Finance Facility
IFFIm	International Finance Facility for Immunization
JSA	Joint Staff Assessment
KfW	Kreditanstalt für Wiederaufbau
LAMIC	Lower and middle-income country
LDC	Least Developed Country
LIC	Low-income country
LMIC	Lower Middle-Income Country
MCA	Millennium Challenge Account
MDB	Multilateral Development Bank
MDG	Millennium Development Goals
MDRI	Multilateral Debt Relief Initiative
MFI	Multilateral Financial Institutions
MIGA	Multilateral Investment Guarantee Agency
MPF	Multilateral Fund for the Implementation of the Montreal Protocol
NGO	Non-Governmental Organization
NPV	Net Present Value
OA	Official Aid
ODA	Official Development Assistance
ODF	Official Development Finance
OLIC	Other Low-Income Country
OOF	Other Official Flows
PFP	Policy Framework Paper
PFTT	Politically Feasible Tobin Tax
PPGI	Pro-Poor Growth Index
PPP	Private Public Partnership
PPP	Purchasing Power Parity
PRGF	Poverty Reduction and Growth Facility
PRSC	Poverty Reduction Support
PRSP	Poverty-Reduction Strategy Paper
RDB	Regional Development Bank
SAL	Structural Adjustment Loan
SAP	Structural Adjustment Policies
SDR	Special Drawing Right
SDRM	Sovereign Debt Restructuring Mechanism
SECAL	Sectoral Adjustment Loan

UMIC	Upper Middle-Income Country
UNDP	United Nations Development Program
UNESCO	United Nations Educational, Scientific and Cultural Organization
UNFPA	United Nations Populations Fund
UNICEF	United Nations International Children's Emergency Fund
USAID	United States Agency for International Development
VENRO	Verband Entwicklungspolitik deutscher Nichtregierungs-organisationen
WHO	World Health Organization

1 Introduction

1.1 Overview

The question how to alleviate poverty in low-income countries has been discussed broadly and with plenty of controversies in the literature on development economics. Traditional proposals are dominated by two major arguments: First, economic growth is regarded as the most important driver to reduce poverty, and second, an outward-oriented development strategy focusing on international trade and investment flows is claimed to lead to a higher domestic growth path. These ideas have been derived from classical economic theory, suggesting that the accumulation of capital is the central ingredient for increased savings and investment, which in turn results in a higher economic growth rate. An assumed trickle-down process then ensures that also poor social groups within the economy will receive a higher income.

Economic policy advice of multilateral institutions to low-income countries was formulated accordingly with macroeconomic stability, privatization and liberalization as the key prescriptions ("Washington Consensus"). In general, a market-based concept was regarded as the most efficient way to reduce poverty, whereas state-led development strategies with strong interventionist and distributional policies were rejected.

In cases of a lack of developed private capital markets, below-market loans and Official Development Assistance (ODA) by multilateral and bilateral creditors were approved to help countries close their financing gap and generate self-sustained growth. These financial contributions were combined with conditional and standardized policy reform packages known as structural adjustment policies.

The results have been disappointing. A reduction of poverty has only occurred in countries where certain strengths (i.e., favourable conditions) were already pre-existing. Although World Bank data indicates that the number of extremely poor people (living on less than $1 per day) has been reduced from 40.4 percent of the world's population in 1981 (1.45 billion poor) to 21.1 percent in 2001 (1.10 billion), this development can be traced back almost exclusively to poverty reduction in populous China (see Fig.

1.1 and Table 1.1). Without China, extreme poverty actually increased in absolute terms from 848 million to 877 million during this time period. In sub-Saharan Africa, extreme poverty nearly doubled from 164 million to 313 million, according to official information, representing an increase from 41.6% of the population to 46.4%. Poverty and inequality in South American and South Asian low-income countries also remain high. These countries were not able to transform the economic policy advice and financial support into economic growth and poverty reduction. Instead, their indebtedness increased to unsustainable levels, depressed their growth potential and led to complex and often politically-motivated deals to restructure and forgive debt. Therefore, international donors concluded in the late 1980s that foreign aid is a rather ineffective tool to assist in poverty alleviation and official aid flows stagnated until the end of the 1990s ("aid fatigue").

New empirical findings challenge this pessimistic view and argue that ODA has a positive impact on economic growth and poverty reduction in countries with "good policies". Although this standpoint does not remain undisputed, multilateral and bilateral donors began to adjust their policies and strategies. In many official documents, aid agencies called for "pro-poor growth", demanded country-owned poverty reduction strategies from recipient countries, introduced a goal-oriented global poverty-reduction plan (Millennium Development Goals), agreed to forgive multilateral debt of most highly indebted poor countries and to a greater extent based their aid allocation on the past performance of recipient countries (selectivity). Since these ambitious efforts are likely to demand much more financial resources in the future, there are frequent calls for a large and rapid scaling-up of ODA.

Table 1.1. Share of people living on less than $1 a day [in %]

	1981	1984	1987	1990	1993	1996	1999	2001
East-Asia and Pacific	57.7	38.9	28.0	29.6	24.9	16.6	15.7	14.9
China	63.8	41.0	28.5	33.0	28.4	17.4	17.8	16.6
Europe and Central Asia	0.7	0.5	0.4	0.5	3.7	4.3	6.3	3.6
Latin Am. and Caribb.	9.7	11.8	10.9	11.3	11.3	10.7	10.5	9.5
Middle East /N. Africa	5.1	3.8	3.2	2.3	1.6	2.0	2.6	2.4
South Asia	51.5	46.8	45.0	41.3	40.1	36.6	32.2	31.3
Sub-Saharan Africa	41.6	46.3	46.8	44.6	44.0	45.6	45.7	46.4
Total	40.4	32.8	28.4	27.9	26.3	22.8	21.8	21.1
Excluding China	31.7	29.8	28.4	26.1	25.6	24.6	23.1	22.5

Source: World Bank (2006a)

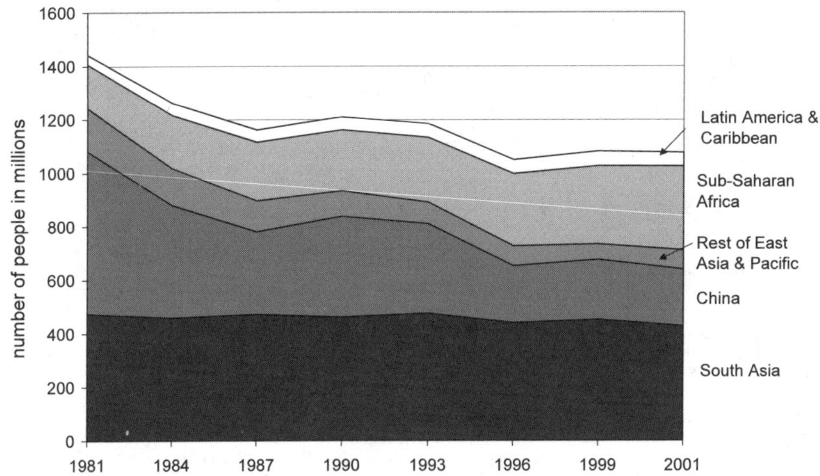

Fig. 1.1. Number of extreme poor people by region [$1 per day poverty line]

Source: Author based on World Bank data (2006a)
The regions Europe & Central Asia as well as Middle East & North Africa are not included in this figure. Their aggregate number of extreme poor people amounted to 25 million in 2001.

Adressing the question whether or not ODA leads to poverty reduction lies at the core of this book. Unlike in other contributions, the entire "value chain" will investigated here, beginning with the provision of ODA over its allocation to its utilization. In each step, theoretical, institutional and policy weaknesses which adversely affect the intended final outcome of poverty alleviation will be critically analyzed. Fig. 1.2 shows the complex interaction of donors, recipients and their transactions and the claim defended here states that accounting for regional conditions during ODA provision, allocation and utilization will improve ODA effectiveness and efficiency and therefore assist in poverty reduction efforts. Special emphasis will be put on the diverse regional conditions in low-income countries. The following sections expand on these ideas and present the overall framework of the thesis.

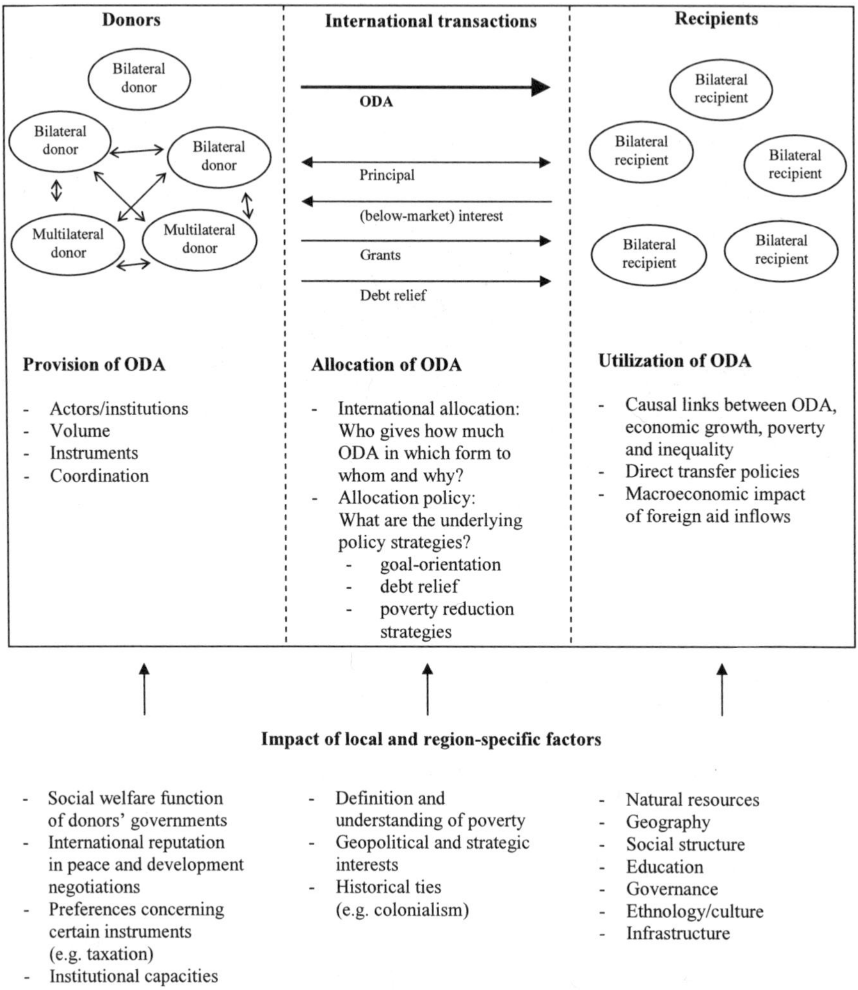

Fig. 1.2. Actors, recipients and transactions in official development finance

Source: Author

1.2 Provision of ODA

1.2.1 Actors and institutions

Negotiations and transactions regarding ODA between aid agencies and low-income countries calling for financial assistance involve different actors and institutions and take place simultaneously on multilateral, bilateral and non-governmental platforms. At the multilateral level, the United Nations (UN), the World Bank and the International Monetary Fund (IMF) are the most important donor agencies. Although they have – to a limited extent – harmonized their policies, each institution still essentially follows its own set of objectives, instruments and strategies, which in turn are heavily influenced by their individual shareholders (= bilateral donors).[1] Also subsumed under multilateral development institutions are Regional Development Banks (RDB) that focus on a specific geographic region and cooperate closely with the World Bank. At the bilateral level, governmental departments of development policy decide on the volume, channels, instruments and allocation of foreign aid. Although bilateral decision-making is harmonized within the G7/G8 group, there are major differences in ODA volume, disbursement patterns and objective functions across bilateral donors. At the non-governmental level, a patchwork of different aid agencies has evolved over time. Non-governmental organizations (NGOs) are progressively more capable of taking part in international efforts on poverty reduction. Due to their improved organization and coordination, NGO have also increased their ability to exert public pressure on the decision-making of multilateral and bilateral donors.

There is an inherent sanguinity in most aid agencies that foreign aid can assist in poverty reduction in every low-income country in the world. This confidence not only entails a tendency to over-estimate the external influence on low-income countries via a plain resource transfer, but also implicitly assumes that a complete cancellation of absolute poverty is feasible in every region in the world if only enough capital is accumulated to finance it. Critics note that the underlying assumptions, e.g. for analyses assessing the cost of reaching certain predefined objectives, are overly optimistic. For example, it is not uncommon to set required target annual GDP growth rates at five to seven percent while evidence shows that such a high growth rate has only been realized over a long period of time by a small

[1] In the case of the IMF, this influence is especially evident: the United States has a veto power in the decision-making on the reallocation of funds (special drawing rights) and voting rights.

number of newly industrialized economies in East Asia and just one country in Africa (Botswana).

International donors have agreed on an ambitious time schedule to reduce absolute poverty worldwide with the introduction of the Millennium Development Goals (MDG) in the year 2000. While such a goal-oriented approach may motivate aid agencies to increase aid efficiency and effectiveness of their work, it also entails the risk of loosing credibility in the case of (repeated) failure. It seems reasonable to make out increasing (public) pressure exerted on international donors, especially by NGOs and particularly in the debate on debt relief. This public pressure may spur enhanced cooperation among institutional and private donors, but so far it has predominantly led to heated and controversial discussions concerning international cooperation among donors and the (in)effectiveness of foreign aid.

1.2.2 ODA volume and instruments

The bandwidth of opinions on ODA reaches from massive scaling-up to complete abolition. The quantity-oriented discussion is dominated by asking how much "additional aid" is needed to reach certain internationally-agreed objectives. With "aid [...] back on the agenda"[2], many economists call for a rapid scaling-up of foreign aid flows to low-income countries. The conventional way of increasing financial assistance is to earmark a certain percentage of donor countries' budget for ODA. However, the budget constraints of bilateral donors alongside increased "demand" for financial aid in developing countries have induced researchers and policy-makers to shift their attention towards alternative ways of generating official resources. Such new proposed measures have been labelled "innovative sources of development finance" and most notably include taxation of international transactions or specific goods (e.g. airline tickets), setting up global funds for specific poverty-reducing purposes and "front-loading" official funds over private capital markets. The proposals vary in their revenue potential, technical and political feasibility and steering function. While some of them carry a "double dividend", i.e. fulfill more than one development goal, others inhabit (adverse) crowding out effects.

[2] Heller (2005), p. 9.

1.3 Allocation of ODA

1.3.1 International and national ODA allocation

The decision which country receives how much bilateral ODA (= international allocation) remains with the donor country's and agencies' officials. While some donor states supply a relatively large number of recipients, others concentrate their funding on selected countries. Some allocate parts of their funds according to minimum requirements, optimal rules or good policies. Others base their decision predominantly on ad-hoc negotiations. Finally, some donors pay more attention to political allies or partner countries with historical and cultural similarities. Even multilateral aid institutions favour some recipients over others.

National allocation refers to the distribution within the recipient country. Typically, ODA is granted to recipient governments, for instance as budgetary assistance, program aid or debt relief. If the government is incapable to manage foreign resources because of insufficient human capital skills or if it misallocates ODA (e.g., because of corruption), other actors may take over the function of domestic recipients. These include international NGOs active in the recipient country, domestic NGOs or private partners. Examples for ODA disbursed in this way are project assistance and emergency assistance.

1.3.2 Underlying allocation policies

As outlined in the opening section, the macroeconomic policies commonly prescribed by the international community of donors in the 1980s and 1990s comprised of relatively standardized stabilization programs and structural adjustment policies. In retrospect, these dirigiste approaches have rather undisputedly yielded disappointing results in alleviating poverty. One potential explanation is the tendency of multilateral and bilateral donors to generalize their economic allocation strategies: instead of modifying such strategies according to country- and region-specific contexts, donors applied them interchangeably in developing countries. The term "Washington Consensus" has evolved to describe this uniform macroeconomic policy advice. More recent contributions have elaborated on this point of view (e.g., post-Washington Consensus). Given the combination of globally-defined indicators of the MDG and limited staff capacity in most international aid agencies regarding the number of their "clients", the idea of a worldwide standardization of development strategies still gains momentum.

However,

> „[p]oor nations include an incredible variety of institutions, cultures and histories: millennia-old civilizations in gigantic China and India; African nations convulsed by centuries of the slave trade, colonialism, arbitrary borders, tropical diseases and local despots; Latin American nations with two centuries of independence and five centuries of extreme inequality; Islamic civilizations with a long history of technical advance relative to the West and then a falling behind; and recently created nations like tiny East Timor. The idea of aggregating all this diversity into a 'developing world' that will 'take off' with foreign aid is a heroic simplification."[3]

Nevertheless, there is growing support by many, most notably Jeffrey Sachs, leading the UN Millennium Project, for a global plan to end poverty. Recent initiatives led by Tony Blair, the G8 and others also follow such kind of "planning mentality", in which the major aim is to develop and transform countries by the use of ODA.

The allocation policies of international donors have seen a major move with influential studies by Craig Burnside, David Dollar and Paul Collier.[4] Burnside and Dollar have concluded "that aid has a positive impact on growth in developing countries with good fiscal, monetary, and trade policies, but has little effect in the presence of poor policies."[5] Based on these findings, Collier developed an "optimal, poverty-efficient allocation rule" allowing aid agencies to distribute their limited resources efficiently. The general and intuitive results of this research found many supporters among politicians and aid officials[6] who unfortunately often oversimplified, misinterpreted or exaggerated the findings. Soon after the publications, then, there seemed to be a convincing body of evidence and a prevailing sense among development researchers that good policies are nearly all that matters for poverty reduction. This conviction was subsequently translated into adjusting aid policies toward increased aid selectivity based on a country's past performance. The most prominent example thereof is the US Millennium Challenge Account, a bilateral aid program that pledges aid grounded in a given country's past performance in certain polica areas. As Easterly pointed out, "[here], we have an unusually clear link running from a growth regression in an economic study to a policy outcome."[7]

---

[3] Easterly (2003), p. 40.

[4] See Burnside and Dollar (2000) and Collier and Dollar (1999).

[5] Burnside and Dollar (2000).

[6] Easterly (2003), p. 24 illustrates vividly how the Burnside/Dollar results made their way to other official (Word Bank) reports, newspapers, media reports and finally UN conferences.

[7] Ibid., p. 25.

There are, however, no indications so far that this new selectivity approach has improved poverty reduction in low-income countries. On the contrary, the poverty focus of ODA is heavily disputed.

1.4 Utilization of ODA

1.4.1 Causal links between ODA, growth and poverty reduction

There are surprisingly few theoretical foundations that establish a direct link between foreign aid and poverty reduction. The subject literature contains two viewpoints: The first regards aid as additional capital from abroad that adds to national savings and thus promotes investment, which in turn leads to economic growth. This growth is assumed to eventually trickle down to the poor. The second approach highlights the role of direct transfer and distribution policies for poverty reduction in an attempt to allocate foreign aid directly to the poor. Although the two positions took turns during the last decades, the literature on foreign aid has been almost exclusively debated in a growth theory context. Based on early classical writings of Roy Harrod and Evsid Domar, so-called gap and trap models continue to dominate the theoretical underpinning of foreign aid. They assess how foreign aid can be employed to fill missing financing gaps or to provide a "big push" to escape from a trap-like economic situation. "The ghost of financing gap [...] still haunts development economics"[8] although to date there is no theoretical model that establishes a clear link between aid and economic growth. Easterly states that

> "[t]he 'financing gap' model in which aid increases investment and then that investment increases economic growth has dubious theoretical foundations and numerous empirical failings. Yet no other model of aid and growth has arisen to take its place. The financing model continues to be used today in the World Bank and other institutions making aid policy."[9]

Consequently, even though there have been a sizable number of studies analyzing the relationships between aid, savings, investment, economic growth and poverty reduction, the only relatively robust finding seems to be that additional investment spurs economic growth in the long-run.[10] The

[8] Easterly (1997).

[9] Easterly (2003), p. 33.

[10] Even here, though, the assumption of a stable linear relationship between investment and growth (i.e., a so-called fixed/incremental capital-output ratio) has been identified as a major constraint of the theory, because it does not allow for substitution of labor for capital or vice versa.

assumed positive link between foreign aid and savings is lacking because the former entails certain characteristics setting it apart from private capital. ODA is defined as having a grant element of at least 25 percent, i.e. a significant part of it is not subject to be paid back. This complicates the determination of the real (market) net present value of aid "investment", e.g. in the case of calculating the outstanding debt of a recipient country. Furthermore, official debt "dictates" private debt because of the preferred creditor status of international institutions.[11] The allocation mechanism of foreign aid is also different than that of private capital: Political objectives (promoting democracy and human rights, but also rewarding allies or securing repayment of outstanding loans) play a pivotal role and distort the market allocation rule. Moreover, aid is to a large extent consumed and not invested, leaving little impact on capital formation, which has been confirmed in many empirical studies that found only a limited impact of aid on investment. Even in the long run the correlation remains considerably weak and a model by Gong and Zou[12] goes as far as showing that a permanent rise in foreign aid in fact reduces the long-term capital accumulation. Finally, although the correlation between growth achieved through capital formation stemming from foreign aid and poverty reduction tends to be positive in the long-run, it is affected by a large number of additional economic and non-economic factors that seriously weaken any such interdependence. Consequently, it is not surprising that only very few studies have found a significant positive relationship between aid and poverty reduction.

Recently, several new approaches have been developed that combine distributional objectives with growth theory. Among them, the Pro-Poor-Growth approach deserves the most attention as it represents the World Bank's "new paradigm" on poverty reduction. Yet, a controversial discussion on what pro-poor growth actually means and on the "best" definition of pro-poor growth is ongoing. The question whether pro-poor growth can be treated as equivalent to poverty reduction has been debated to a much lesser extent.

1.4.2 Macroeconomic impact of ODA inflows

The discussion on scaling-up the quantities of international official assistance often omits the fact that foreign aid inflows may have a variety of

---

[11] Multilateral donors are given the right to be repaid first, so that official loans are preferred over private bank loans.

[12] See Gong and Zou (2001), p. 117.

macroeconomic effects in recipient countries, including diminishing returns, absorptive capacity constraints, aid dependency, crowding out, exchange rate effects and effects on corruption. Consequently, it is crucial to keep in mind that foreign aid has serious macroeconomic repercussions on recipient countries and the analysis thereof should have important impact on the volume and the optimal allocation of aid by international donors. This holds especially true for low-income countries that rely to a large degree on ODA.

1.5 Propositions and structure

The focus of this book is on the capability of official development finance to alleviate poverty in low-income countries. The following propositions will be made:

1. Even if ODA supply is doubled or tripled and innovative financing mechanisms are applied, global goals on poverty reduction will not be met in many low-income countries. On the contrary, a massive scaling-up of ODA is associated with a number of negative macroeconomic impacts.
2. Among other causes, ODA inefficiency is rooted in a misconception: Aid is understood as (often conditional) supplement to missing private capital, not as a mere subsidy.
3. In the present aid agency system, ODA is utilized in order to promote economic growth, not to minimize poverty, reducing its potential impact.
4. Policy advice by international and national aid agencies is dominated by generalized, one-fits-all strategies that do not take into account regional- and country-specific differences.

The foundation to tackle these issues is a detailed analysis of theoretical, institutional and policy aspects in the "ODA value chain", i.e. its provision, allocation and utilization. By doing so, the newly gained "aid optimism" will be justified against the evidence and it will be assessed whether a global plan to reduce poverty with ODA may fulfil its promises. The starting point for an own contribution to the existing literature is the notion that the current poverty reduction policies can be improved by paying more attention to region-specific conditions such as geographical, institutional and socio-economic factors. It is hypothesized that doing so will advance the allocation process, raise the quality of foreign aid and, most importantly, augment the poverty-focus of ODA. Current ODA aims at improving economic development, not immediate poverty reduction.

The structure of the thesis follows the main outline of this introductory chapter. Chap. 2 is concerned with the actors in the *provision* of ODA (Sect. 2.2), the present volume of ODA (Sect. 2.3), estimates of ODA requirements to meet international development objectives (Sect. 2.4), innovative sources of development (Sect. 2.5) and the coordination among donors (Sect. 2.6). Chap. 3 analyzes the present allocation of ODA (Sect. 3.1), discusses optimal allocation rules and selectivity (Sect. 3.2) and international allocation policies (Sects. 3.3 to 3.6). Chap. 4 examines the *utilization* of ODA and highlights the interdependencies between ODA and economic growth (Sect. 4.2) as well as ODA, inequality and poverty reduction (Sect. 4.3). Furthermore, this chapter studies the macroeconomic impacts of ODA (Sect. 4.4). In Chap. 5, *region-specific conditions* will be included in the analysis. Sect. 5.2 analyzes the origins of initial regional differences. Sect. 5.3 presents findings on the link between regional conditions, poverty reduction and ODA and Chap. 5.4 gives suggestions how to reform the current ODA system. Chap. 6 summarizes the main findings.

2 The provision of ODA

2.1 Halving poverty by doubling aid?

A variety of events in the new Millennium (international conflicts, terrorist acts, natural disasters) have altered the landscape for ODA. Not only did they pave the way for increased strategically directed foreign aid and emergency assistance. The recent years have also witnessed a substantial increase in ODA, after a decade of "aid pessimism", "donor fatigue" and almost continuous reductions in net disbursements. "Aid is back on the agenda".[13] The major bilateral donors have agreed at the International Conference on Financing for Development in Monterrey (2002) to expand their ODA in order to reach the Millennium Development Goals set by the UN for 2015. Under the motto "halving poverty by doubling aid", it has been proposed from various sides (multilateral organizations, bilateral donors, politicians, economists, NGOs, well-known individuals) to significantly increase ODA flows, especially to least developed countries (LDCs).[14] The development ministers of some donor countries demanded the year 2005 to be the turning year of development finance.[15]

If the donor countries were to meet UN targets, ODA would almost triple (compared to present levels) to $175 billion per year. Most donors, however, have been cautious in the past to increase their ODA budget despite repeatedly announced pledges. They are seeking different channels and instruments for disbursement. Consequently, the research focus of recent years has shifted towards finding alternative mechanisms to increase development assistance. They have been put under the headline "innovative sources of development finance". Yet, it is by far not uncontested that

---

[13] Heller (2005), p. 9.

[14] See, for example, the suggestions of the High-Level Panel on Financing for Development, also known as Zedillo-Report (UN 2001), the Conference on Financing for Development in Monterrey (UN 2002) and the United Nations Millennium Project (2005), also referred to as Sachs-Report. The High-Level Panel has estimated that an additional $50 billion is needed annually to meet the MDG in 2015; the Millennium Project proposes an additional $135 billion per year.

[15] See, for example, Wieczorek-Zeul (2005).

additional aid reduces poverty. Opponents of scaling up aid flows argue that additional financial resources will crowd out other investments, appreciate the domestic currency, enrich the elite and prolong corrupt and bad governments, thereby dampening or even outweighing the positive effects of more aid, a situation sometimes referred to a "leaky bucket". They also point out that coordination among donors should be improved first before scaling up aid flows.

This chapter is concerned with the supply side of ODA. First, Sect. 2.2 will present the multilateral, regional and bilateral actors engaged in bringing up ODA. Sect. 2.3 provides a detailed analysis of the present volume and type of ODA flows. In Sect. 2.4, cost estimates of how much additional aid is needed to meet certain international objectives will be discussed. Sect. 2.5 examines innovative sources of development finance by studying their revenue potential, technical and political feasibility and their steering function and side effects. The coordination efforts between different groups of donors will be addressed in Sect. 2.6 and Sect. 2.7 summarizes the main conclusions.

2.2 Actors in the provision of ODA

It is beyond the scope and aim of this chapter to review all organizations and institutional arrangements dealing with poverty reduction, debt relief and economic and social development in low-income countries. Instead, the intension is to provide the reader with the basic terms and programs currently applied within the "UN / World Bank / IMF / RDB" nexus in order to better understand the major policy initiatives and responsibilities, which will then be analyzed in later chapters.

2.2.1 Multilateral donor agencies

United Nations

Within the United Nations (UN) organization, two institutions play a central role for economic development and poverty reduction: The United Nations Development Programme (UNDP) and the United Nations Conference on Trade and Development (UNCTAD).

UNDP is the UN's network for global development and assists developing countries by providing analytical capabilities and financial resources as well as coordinating aid efforts of developed countries. The focus is on democratic governance, poverty reduction, crisis prevention, recovery from crisis, energy supply, environment issues and HIV/AIDS.

UNCTAD was established in 1964 and serves as the UN's arm for trade and development related issues in the fields of investment, finance, technology, enterprise development and sustainable development with the overarching objective of integrating developing countries into the world's global trading system. Its main functions are providing technical assistance to countries in transition and least developed countries as well as collecting, analyzing and exchanging data. The UNCTAD's highest decision-making body is a quadrennial conference, which is a subsidiary organ of the UN General Assembly. The conferences provide the platform for member states to assess current trade and development issues as well as discuss and formulate policy strategies. The most recent conferences were UNCTAD XI (2004, Sao Paulo/Brazil), UNCTAD X (2000, Bangkok/Thailand) and UNCTAD IX (1996, Midrand/South Africa).

World Bank Group

The World Bank Group provides financial and technical assistance, low-interest loans, interest-free credits and grants to developing countries for education, health, infrastructure, communications and other purposes. The World Bank Group is not a bank in a common sense. It consists of two major institutions owned by 184 member countries: The International Bank for Reconstruction and Development (IBRD) and the International Development Association (IDA). Furthermore, it owns several affiliates, among them the Multilateral Investment Guarantee Agency (MIGA) and the International Finance Corporation (IFC).

The IBRD is the founding institution usually referred to as the World Bank. It was established in 1944, initially to assist in Europe's recovery after World War II. Today, it focuses on creditworthy middle-income countries with an annual per capita income of more than $965 in 2004. The IBRD raises most of its funds on the world's financial markets.

The IDA was set up in 1960 as an agency (and member of the IBRD) that could lend to the poorest countries under below-market terms. The IDA lends only to countries with an income of less than $965 per capita in 2004 and that are not eligible to borrow from the IBRD (currently 81 countries).[16] Thus, the IDA eligibility criterion often serves as a rough indicator of being a low-income country. IDA loans are highly concessional, cover

[16] There are some exceptions to this rule, e.g. India and Indonesia, which have a low per capita income but nevertheless are regarded creditworthy enough to be eligible for IBRD loans.

no interest charge (but a "service charge" of 0.75%) and have maturities between 20 and 40 years including a 10-year grace period. IDA assets stem from two sources: Borrowers' repayments and regular replenishments by donor countries on a triennial basis. The 14th round of replenishment (IDA-14) will finance projects over the period ending June 2008. Since IDA-13, the focus of IDA loans is on poverty-reducing projects covering education, health, social safety nets, water supply, sanitation, law, justice and public administration. The IDA also assists in managing the debt-service burden in poor countries. It disbursed US-$17.3 billion (in 2001) and owned an equity capital of $188 billion.

The MIGA offers political risk insurances and guarantees in order to promote FDI into emerging market economies. MIGA was founded in 1988 and has issued more than 650 project guarantees in 85 countries covering $12 billion dollars by June 2003. Its major working principles are focusing on clients, engaging in partnerships, promoting developmental impact and ensuring financial soundness.

The IFC is a member of the World Bank since 1956 and the largest multilateral source of loan and equity financing for projects in the private sector of developing countries. Its main objectives are to promote sustainable private sector investment in developing countries, to assist private companies in developing countries to mobilize financing in international financial markets and to provide advice and technical assistance.

International Monetary Fund

In its history, the International Monetary Fund (IMF) concentrated his activity on assisting developing countries facing current account deficits and macroeconomic instabilities. Since the 1990s, IMF policies and programs shifted more and more towards an impetus on poverty reduction and harmonizing actions with the World Bank.[17] For instance, it was agreed that IMF programs are not allowed to hurt the poor. In November 1999, the Enhanced Structural Adjustment Facility (ESAF), designed to finance triennial adjustment programs, was renamed to Poverty Reduction and Growth Facility (PRGF) and synchronized to the needs of national poverty reduction strategies. The PRGF was aimed to differ from former ESAF programs by placing a stronger emphasis on poverty reduction, national ownership and good governance.[18] PRGF eligibility is based on per capita

[17] In 1986, World Bank and IMF introduced Policy Framework Papers (PFP) to better coordinate their activities. PFPs were designed to solve issues when IMF and World Bank were focusing on different and conflicting policies.

[18] See Paul (2002), p. 10 and IMF (2000a).

income and IDA eligibility. As of March 2004, there are 51 countries with an active PRGF program.[19]

2.2.2 Regional donor agencies

Regional donor agencies include regional development banks (RDBs) and regional supranational entities. While a number of RDBs have developed in different continents, the only regional institution worth mentioning as an ODA donor is the European Union.

Regional development banks

RDBs focus on the economic and social development in countries of a specific region. The four major RDBs are the African Development Bank (AfDB), the Asian Development Bank (ADB), the European Bank for Reconstruction and Development (EBRD) and the Inter-American Development Bank Group (IADB). Additionally, other Multilateral Financial Institutions (MFIs) and sub-regional development banks concentrate their efforts on special sectors or activities.[20] Together with the World Bank, RDBs and MFIs are also grouped as Multilateral Development Banks (MDBs). They are institutions providing financial and analytical assistance for development activities in developing countries. Membership is not necessarily limited to countries from the respective region, but can also be open to other countries. Each bank follows its own independent legal and operational status. RDB provide development finance via long-term loans based on market interest and very long-term loans based on below-market interest rates. To offer market loans, RDBs borrow on international financial markets and re-lend to governments in developing countries. Long-term loans are highly concessional[21] and financed via direct contributions of donor countries, which are replenished on a triennial basis. Additionally, a limited volume of grant financing is offered. The four major RDBs

[19] See IMF (2004), p. 16.

[20] Examples include Caribbean Development Bank (CDB), Corporacion Andina de Fomento (CAF), East African Development Bank (EADB), West African Development Bank (BOAD), Central American Bank for Economic Integration (CABEI), European Investment Bank (EIB), Islamic Development Bank (IDB), International Fund for Agricultural Development (IFAD), Nordic Development Fund (NFD), Nordic Investment Bank (NIB) and the OPEC Fund for International Development (OPEC Fund).

[21] They have terms of up to 50 years, a grace period of ten years and an annual interest rate (administrative charge) of 1.5 percent.

hold an equity capital of $172 billion (end of 2001) and gave loans of $16.3 billion in 2001[22], nearly reaching the volume of the World Bank.

European Union

European Union members provide 55 percent of the world's total ODA (€34.3 billion in 2004). About one fifth of this amount (€6.9 billion in 2004) was managed by the European Commission and allocated to more than 160 countries, territories and organizations. The central coordinating institution to finance development cooperation is EuropeAid, founded in 2001. "Wherever possible, the Commission-funded programmes of development assistance are based on the country's own strategy to reduce poverty, set out in a Poverty Reduction Strategy Paper."[23] The concrete program and project financing depends on political priorities for different regions. For instance, the European Development Fund (EDF) is the main authority for ODA in African, Caribbean and Pacific countries.

2.2.3 Bilateral donors

Each donor country has its own department for ODA disbursements with individual policies, guidelines, frameworks and management staff. In most donor countries, there is even more than one national agency that carries out individual projects. In Germany, for example, there are several executive development institutions (Bundesministerium für wirtschaftliche Zusammenarbeit und Entwicklung (BMZ), Gesellschaft für Technische Zusammenarbeit (GTZ), Kreditanstalt für Wiederaufbau (KfW) and Inwent). Each of them has its own analyzing capacities, strategies, rules and selection criteria so that a complete review is beyond the scope of this study. The largest national donor agency is the United States Agency for International Development (USAID). As a general note, bilateral aid agencies do not concentrate on a few low-income countries but are active in all recipients, although with a more or less strong focus on some of them, as will be pointed out in later chapters. As a total, bilateral donors are responsible for two thirds of worldwide ODA flows.

[22] $3.6 billion of which was granted at below market interest.

[23] European Commission (2005a), p. 8.

2.2.4 Non-governmental organizations

NGOs and private development funds have raised the volume of non-official development assistance significantly in recent years. They are supported by well-known and wealthy individuals and mass media events (e.g., LiveAid concerts). Compared to official creditors, however, the volume of NGO development assistance remains relatively modest. Nevertheless, their organizational structure and "voice" has improved due to the foundation of national and international parent organizations (e.g., VENRO in Germany).

2.3 Present ODA volume

This chapter will present an empirical analysis of the quantity and type of ODA by multilateral and bilateral donors. First, the basic terms will be defined (Sect. 2.3.1). Second, ODA flows will be analyzed on a global and disaggregated level (Sect. 2.3.2). Sect. 2.3.3 concludes.

2.3.1 Definitions

The global forum for defining ODA is the Development Assistance Committee (DAC) of the OECD[24], which gives the following definition: Official Development Assistance is defined as flows to developing countries and multilateral institutions provided by official agencies, including state and local governments, or by their executive agencies, each transaction of which meets the following test:

- it is administered with the promotion of the economic development and welfare of developing countries as its main objective, and
- it is concessional in character and contains a grant element of at least 25% (calculated at a rate of discount of 10%).

Grants are transfers made in cash, goods or services for which no repayment is required. They also include grant-like flows, i.e. loans for which the service payments are to be made into an account in the borrowing country and used in the borrowing country for its own benefit. Furthermore, they include debt forgiveness. The "grant element" reflects the financial terms of a commitment: Interest rate, maturity and grace period (the inter-

[24] The DAC members provided $79.5 billion ODA in 2004, compared to $91.9 billion of all donors' ODA, which represents a share of 86.5%.

val until the first repayment of capital). It measures the concessionality of a loan in the form of the present value of an interest rate below the market rate over the life of a loan. Conventionally the market rate is taken as 10 per cent in DAC statistics. Thus, the grant element is zero for a loan carrying an interest rate of 10 percent; it is 100 per cent for a grant; and it lies somewhere in-between for a soft loan. If the face value of a loan is multiplied by its grant element, the result is referred to as the "grant equivalent" of that loan. Loans, in turn, are transfers for which repayment is required (they are also referred to as credits). Only loans with maturities of more than one year are included in DAC statistics. Data on net loans include deductions for repayments of principal (but not payment of interest) on earlier loans. Thus when a loan has been fully repaid, its effect on total net ODA over the life of the loan is zero.

The terms "(foreign) aid" and "assistance" both refer to flows which qualify either as ODA or as Official Aid (OA). If recipient countries are on Part I of the DAC list of aid Recipients, the term ODA applies. This part includes all least developed countries (LDCs) as well as all low and middle income countries and territories. Grants and loans to more advanced countries and territories (Part II) are referred to as OA. The term "Official Development Finance" (ODF) is used for measuring the inflow of resources to recipient countries, including a) bilateral ODA, b) grants, concessional and non-concenssional lending by multilateral institutions and c) Other Official Flows (including refinancing loans) for development purposes.[25] ODA provided by DAC donors is not necessarily identical to aid flows received by the respective recipients because funding received from donors by multilateral institutions does not necessarily equal those institutions' disbursements in any given year. Furthermore, international statistics differentiate between flows (= actual disbursements) and pledges (planned/future disbursements).

"ODA eligible" are:

- Contributions to listed organizations (including administrative costs),[26]

[25] Other Official Flows (OOF) are defined as transactions by the official sector with countries on the List of Aid Recipients which do not meet the conditions for eligibility as ODA or OA, either because they are not primarily aimed at development, or because they have a grant element of less than 25 per cent. See DAC (2005).

[26] This list includes more than 50 UN agencies and funds, 5 of the European Commission, 2 of the IMF, 5 of the World Bank, 2 of the WTO, 8 of the Regional Development Banks, 103 of other multilateral institutions, 35 main non-governmental and 13 other institutions. Multilateral development banks do not

- Debt forgiveness,
- Technical cooperation,
- Measures of the UN to provide peace (e.g., election monitoring, economic advice, disposal of weaponry and mines),
- Civil police service,
- Social and cultural financial support as long as they promote the capacity of the developing country,
- Aid to refugees,
- Civil use of nuclear energy (including the construction of nuclear plants),
- Promotion of research and development concerned with problems of developing countries (e.g. tropical diseases).

Technical cooperation, debt forgiveness, emergency and disaster relief and administrative costs are subsumed under "special purpose grants". Although they are ODA eligible, special purpose grants do not provide any additional financial resources for development programs and projects. Grants, loans and credits for military purposes, export credits as well as transfer payments to private individuals (e.g., pensions, reparations, insurance payouts) are excluded from ODA.[27]

2.3.2 Empirical analysis of ODA flows

Data

Data on ODA flows is offered by various international institutions. The most complete and updated data is compiled by the DAC. It provides annual data since 1960 for all countries, disaggregated into various subsections according to the type of aid flow, destination (recipient) and source (donor). Until not otherwise specified, the data used in subsequent sections has been obtained by the DAC.

Global trends

Fig. 2.1 shows the aggregate ODA net disbursements of all DAC members since 1960, split into its bilateral and multilateral share.

apply the grant element concept for their market-based lending operations. See DAC (2005).

[27] Export credits are listed under Other Official Flows.

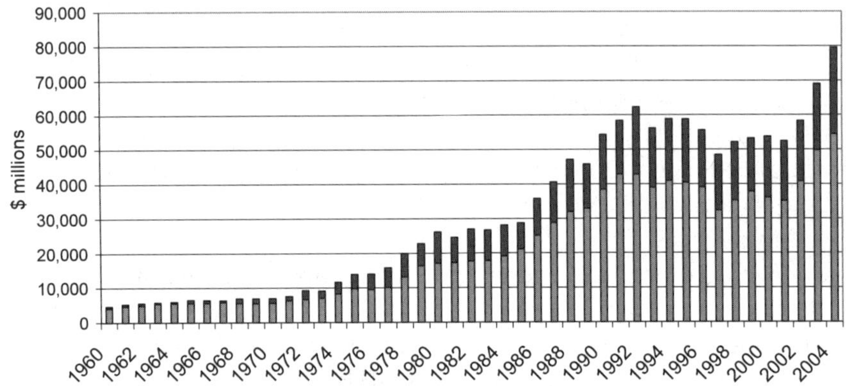

Fig. 2.1. Bilateral and multilateral ODA net disbursements of DAC members, 1960–2004 [in current million dollars]

Source: Author's calculations based on DAC data
Dark color represents multilateral ODA, light color bilateral ODA.

The following characteristics are noteworthy:

- Total net ODA disbursements grew steadily (with only some minor exceptions) from 1960 ($4.7 billion) to a first peak of $62.4 billion in 1992.
- The 1990s saw a downward trend in total ODA net disbursements (the lowest value in the 1990s is $48.5 billion), which is primarily due to a long-term reduction trend of bilateral aid flows since 1992. Strategic aid reductions (e.g., as a result of the end of the Cold War) and a general sense of "aid pessimism" are the main reasons for this development.
- Since 2001, bilateral ODA is on a strong upward trend again.
- Multilateral ODA, reflecting at least partly international development cooperation efforts, has grown in importance (from an average of 12.7% of total ODA during the 1960s to 31% during the 2000s).
- Multilateral ODA decreased between 1992 ($19.6 billion) and 1999 ($15.4 billion) by about 25%, but grew steadily from then and climbed to a new high in 2004 ($25.1 billion).

Expressed as a percentage of Gross National Income (GNI), donor countries comprise different ODA quotas.[28] While some countries have been generous over a long period of time, others have been parsimonious. Fig.

[28] The ODA quota is sometimes also referred to as generosity ratio.

2.2 shows the long-term development of ODA quotas in six major ODA donor countries. France and the United Kingdom provide a higher ODA share of their GNI than the United States. The United States' ODA ratio is among the lowest of all DAC members. Norway's oil revenues and its reputation in international peace and development negotiations are mirrored in its high ODA quota. Some countries (e.g., Japan) show no apparent trend over time.

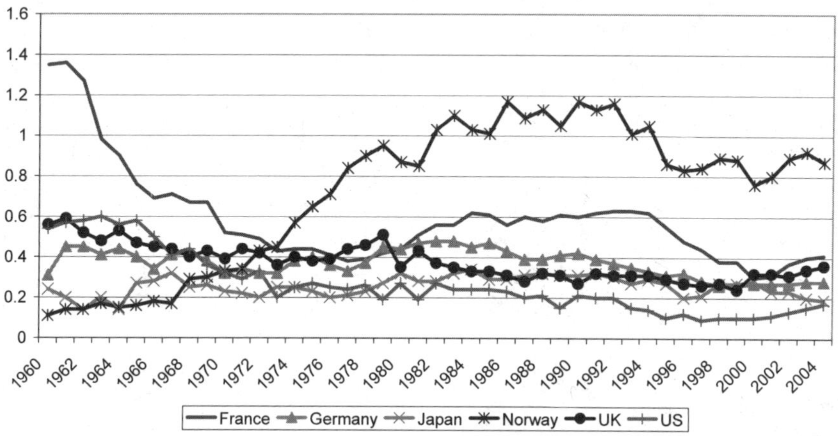

Fig. 2.2. Selected national ODA quotas, 1960–2004 [percentage of GNI]

Source: Author's calculations based on DAC data

Most DAC member countries, however, follow a downward trend during the 1990s in their ODA quota. Despite allocational considerations of donor countries' governments, which will be covered in more detail later, two reasons can be given for this development:

- In some donor countries, the end of the Cold War and thus the collapse of the Soviet Union have led to a decrease of ODA.
- Israel, which has received substantial amounts of ODA from the United States, has graduated from DAC List I and been put into List II of more advanced countries receiving OA instead of ODA.

Table 2.1 shows ODA disbursements by donor country in 2004. Only Denmark, Luxembourg, Norway, Sweden and the Netherlands surpass the 0.7% criteria set by the Pearson Commission in 1968. As a total, $78.6 billions have been disbursed in 2004, which represents 0.25% of GNI of all DAC members (2003: 0.25%). The percentage of multilateral aid varies between 10.2% (United States) and 56.4% (Italy), with an average over all

DAC countries of 27.8%. The largest donors in absolute terms are the United States, Japan, France, the United Kingdom and Germany.

Table 2.1. ODA disbursements by donor country in 2004

	ODA 2004 [mn. US-$]	ODA 2004 [% of GNI]	Multilateral aid [% of ODA in 2003]	ODA to LDC [% of GNI in 2003]
Australia	1,465	0.25	20.0	0.05
Austria	691	0.24	54.7	0.07
Belgium	1,452	0.41	20.8	0.35
Canada	2,537	0.26	33.6	0.07
Denmark	2,025	0.84	41.0	0.32
Finland	655	0.35	44.7	0.11
France	8,475	0.42	28.1	0.17
Germany	7,479	0.28	40.2	0.10
Greece	464	0.23	37.0	0.03
Ireland	586	0.39	30.1	0.21
Italy	2,484	0.15	56.4	0.08
Japan	8,859	0.19	28.7	0.04
Luxembourg	241	0.85	22.8	0.27
Netherlands	4,235	0.74	25.9	0.26
New Zealand	210	0.23	21.9	0.06
Norway	2,200	0.87	28.4	0.36
Portugal	1,028	0.63	42.9	0.14
Spain	2,547	0.26	41.3	0.04
Sweden	2,704	0.77	25.9	0.27
Switzerland	1,379	0.37	27.3	0.12
United Kingdom	7,836	0.36	38.5	0.12
United States	18,999	0.16	10.2	0.04
G7	56,686	0.22	26.9	0.07
EU-15	42,919	0.36	35.3	0.13
DAC Total	78,568	0.25	27.8	0.08

Source: OECD (2005a)

There are several determinants influencing the ODA quota of donor countries, giving an indication for the nature and volume of aid. Round and Odedokun[29] distinguish between non-political (mainly economic) and political factors positively affecting aid efforts of donor countries. Their regression study shows that

- in general, the higher the real income of donor countries, the greater the share of real income given as aid (aid as "luxury good"),

[29] See Round and Odedokun (2004).

- the fraction of income disbursed as aid is inversely correlated to population size of donor countries,
- aid efforts of one donor country are positively influenced by those of other donor countries ("peer pressure"),
- military "adventurism" and interests in individual recipient countries (e.g., providing an air base) positively affect aid efforts.

In contrast, fiscal restraints do not seem to influence the size of aid disbursements. Aid represents a relatively small fraction of donor countries' national budget so that cutting aid would not do much in terms of balancing the budget. Thus, one can conclude that the long-term downward trend in many donor countries' ODA quotas in the 1990s is not attributable to fiscal restraints and neither can the ODA increase since 2001 be grounded on fiscal surpluses.

Type of ODA flows

Table 2.2 presents a schematic overview on the disaggregation of financial flows to low-income countries. The high ODA growth rates since 2001 have not resulted in proportional accumulations of financial resources for projects and programs. Instead, ODA increases contained a high proportion of debt relief, which does not translate directly into an increase in disposable financial resources ($8.3 billion of the $10.7 billion net ODA increase represented debt relief in 2003). Moreover, a significant part came as emergency assistance for individual countries (e.g., Pakistan, Iraq). Deducting the portion of technical assistance paid to consultants from industrial countries and administrative costs of running donor agencies, less than 50 % of ODA was actually available for program and project disbursements in developing countries.

Fig. 2.3 compares the developments of official debt flows (of World Bank, IMF and others) and total foreign aid grants. Since 2001, a shift from loans to grants can be observed. Total foreign aid grants (excluding technical cooperation grants) were between $25 and $30 billion for 1996 to 2001, and then increased to $47.4 billion in 2004.

The high IMF lending (financial crises in Asia, Argentina, Brazil and Turkey) declined after 2002. But also net lending by bilateral creditors ("others") has been reduced, because some emerging market economies (e.g. Russia, Mexico) repaid structural adjustment loans, partly ahead of schedule. The chart reflects the strong cyclical nature of official loans, whereas foreign aid grants represent a more stable source of financial inflow. However, donors also adjust the form of ODA according to the recipients' level of poverty. Official data reveals that LDC receive a considerable higher share of total ODA as grants instead of loans compared to other low-income countries, lower and upper middle income countries (not graphed here, see OECD 2005, p. 41).

Fig. 2.4 subdivides total bilateral grants of DAC members (position I.A.1 in Table 2.2, accounting for 72% of total ODA flows in 2004). The largest position in 2004 is "technical cooperation" (32.8% of all ODA bilateral grants), closely followed by "project and program aid" (25.1%). Disbursements of the categories "emergency/distress relief" and "debt forgiveness" have grown strongly since 2001, accounting for 12.8% and 12.4% respectively, in 2004. Although total bilateral grants nearly doubled from \$32.5 billion in 1990 to \$57.2 billion in 2004, more than half of these additional grants (\$18.3 billion) represent special purpose grants.

Table 2.2. Disaggregation of financial flows to developing countries

I. ODA
I.A. Bilateral ODA
I.A.1. Grants
among them:
I.A.1.1. Project and program aid
I.A.1.2. Technical cooperation
I.A.1.4. Developmental food aid
I.A.1.5. Emergency/distress relief
I.A.1.6. Debt forgiveness
I.A.1.12. Administrative costs
I.A.2. Non-grants
I.B. Multilateral ODA
I.B.1. Grants and capital subscriptions
I.B.2. Concessional lending
II. OOF
II.A. Bilateral OOF
II.B. Multilateral OOF
III. Private flows
III.A. Bilateral
III.B. Multilateral
IV. Grants by NGO's
V. Items not included
VI. Aggregates

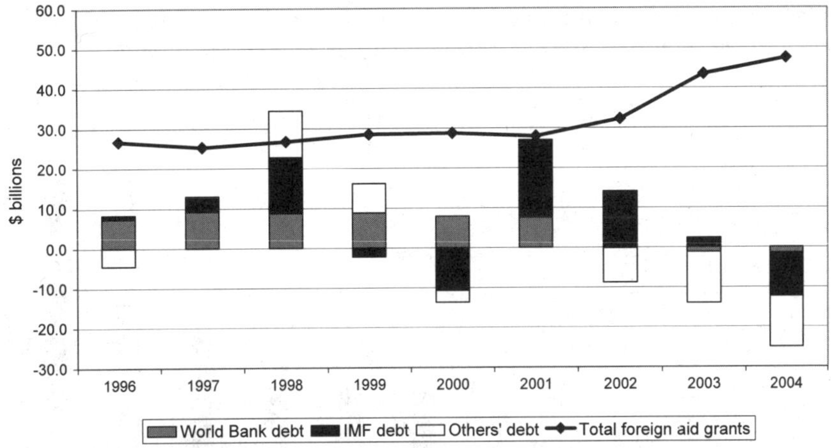

Fig. 2.3. Official debt flows and foreign aid grants to developing countries

Source: Author based on World Bank data (2004c)

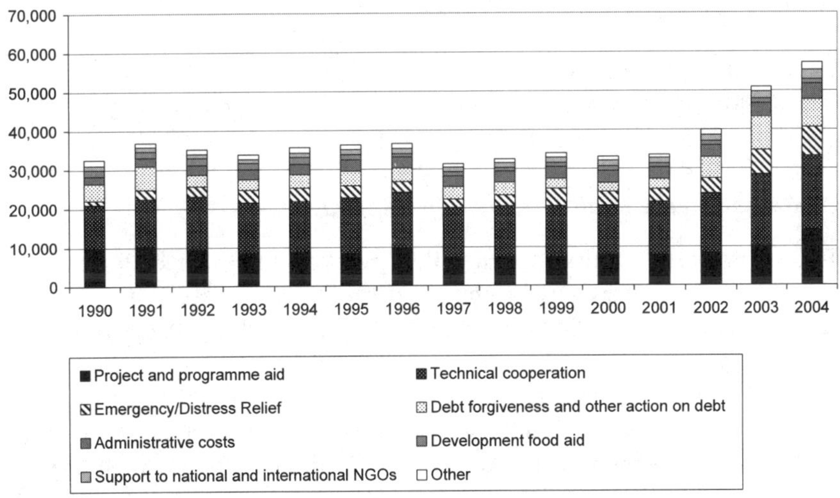

Fig. 2.4. DAC total bilateral grants, 1990–2004 [in $ millions]

Source: Author's calculations based on DAC data

Within the category "project and program aid", a remarkable shift from project to program aid can be detected (Fig. 2.5). Sector program assistance, a subgroup of program aid, dropped from 39% of program aid in 1996 to 21% in 2001, but then increased again to 42% in 2004.[30]

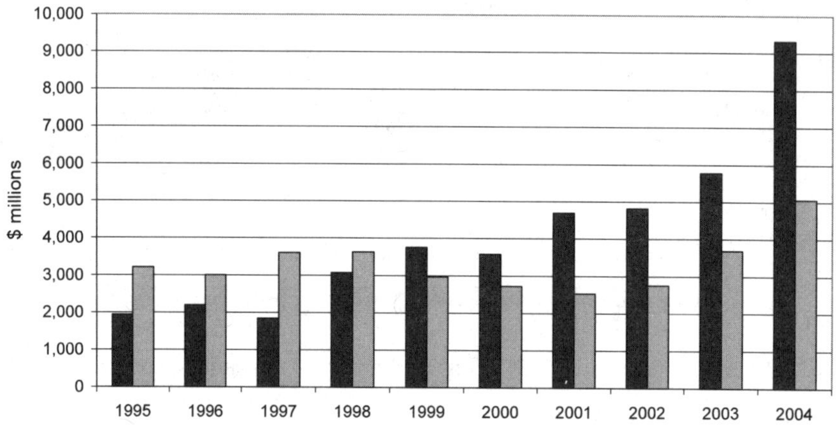

Fig. 2.5. Net disbursements of project and program aid from DAC member countries to developing countries, 1995–2004

Source: Author's calculations based on DAC data
Dark color: program aid, light color: program aid.

ODA and private capital flows in perspective

This section will put the absolute ODA numbers into perspective by giving comparative numbers on different types of private capital flows (equity and debt) as well as NGO assistance and workers' remittances to developing countries. Fig. 2.6 shows the development of net financial flows to developing countries since 1996. Net official flows are defined as total foreign aid (grants ex technical cooperation grants) plus debt by official creditors (World Bank, IMF and others). From 2001, net official flows declined by $32 billion. Although total foreign aid increased by more than $20 billion since 2001, net official lending declined by $52 billion in the same period, reflecting the large repayments to multilateral and bilateral donors. Net private flows (debt and equity) to developing countries, which decreased significantly between 1996 ($281.3 billion) and 2001 ($150.3 billion), have been on a strong upward trend since then to reach an estimated total amount of $301.3 billion in 2004. Total financial flows to de-

[30] More detailed data on the development of project and program aid in different regions or countries is not available from DAC statistics.

veloping countries reached $323.8 billion in 2004, which marks the highest absolute value in history. Offsetting for inflation, dollar depreciation and economic growth by measuring capital flows as percentages of recipient countries' GDP, net capital flows to developing countries were 4.5% of their GDP in 2004. The highest values were reached in the mid 1990s (6% in 1995).

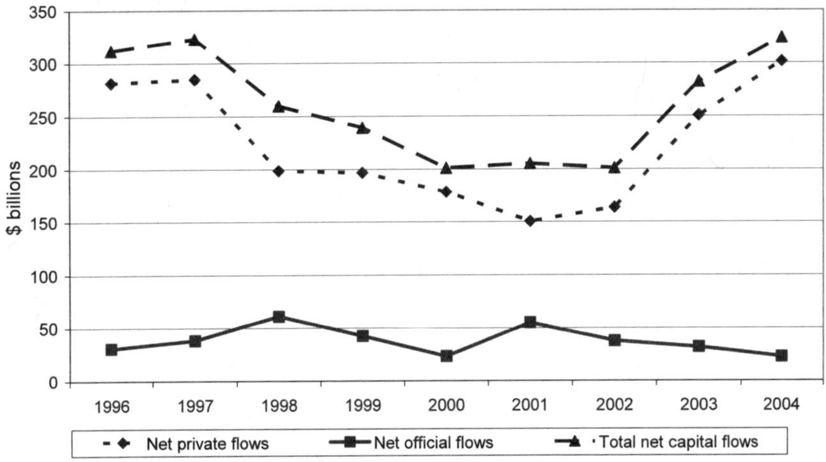

Fig. 2.6. Financial flows to developing countries

Source: World Bank (2004c)

ODA represents the most important source of net capital flows for LDCs (Fig. 2.7).[31] Up to 90% of all net flows are official (ODA and OOF), only a very small percentage is private (and is concentrated on a few countries) due to the lack of business opportunities for foreign investors and the underdevelopment of domestic financial markets.[32]

From a long-term perspective, current account deficits averaged 1.4% of their GDP between 1976 and 1999 in all developing countries and 2.3% in low-income countries. A look at the current account balances of developing countries reveals that they have generally improved since 2000. There are, however, strong regional disparities.[33] Countries with account sur-

[31] Grants disbursed by NGO are excluded in this calculation due to lack of data.

[32] See also Lensink and White (1998) for a formal model of access to international capital markets. The authors confirm that many LDCs are unable to obtain private capital.

[33] The current account balances, as percentage of GDP, were between 2.4 and 4.5% between 1998 and 2004 in East Asia and the Pacific, whereas they were

pluses accumulated foreign reserves, which have increased in recent years.[34] The figures also show that the increase in net equity flows (mostly net FDI inflows) from the private sector to developing countries since the early 1990s has been more stable than net debt flows, which have been more volatile. It has to be noted that a significant proportion of net FDI inflows went to a small number of countries.[35] The share of net FDI inflows to least developed countries has increased steadily from 1% in 1994 to 5% in 2004. FDI outflows from developing countries have risen from $5 billion in 1990 to almost $40 billion in 2004, representing 0.56% of their GNI). As with net FDI inflows, FDI outflows are concentrated on a small number of countries. While net private bank lending to developing countries declined since 1998, net bond lending has returned to an upward trend since 2001, after a rise and fall throughout the 1990s. Most of the rising bond demand is due to emerging economies' bond markets in Asia and Latin America.

NGOs allocate an increasing amount of development assistance to developing countries.[36] Nevertheless, the real value of NGO contributions is difficult to measure due to a number of reasons (measuring the real value of the labor force of volunteers, tracking the flow of NGO incoming resources such as private donations, subsidies and fundraising). In 2001, assistance provided by private voluntary organizations[37] was $7.3 billion (compared to $52 billion of total ODA). Germany and the United States are the countries with the highest level of NGO assistance relative to GNI (both 0.4%). Apart from the fact that those charitable contributions are tax-deductible in these countries, some new well-funded foundations (e.g., Bill and Melinda Gates Foundation with an initial stock of $24 billion 2000) account for the increase of private development assistance.[38]

---

between -3.5% and 9.3% for the Middle East and North Africa, -4.5 and 1.5 for Latin America and the Caribbean and -5 and 1.2 for Sub-Saharan Africa.

[34] More than half of the 2004 increase in foreign reserves can be traced back to China. Its share of total developing country reserves increased to 38%.

[35] Brazil, China, India, Mexico and Russia account for almost 60% of all FDI net inflows to developing countries.

[36] For a detailed description of NGO's development assistance activities, see World Bank (2004c), pp. 119–123.

[37] Only the organizations' own resources.

[38] See Micklewright and Wright (2005) on private donations for economic development.

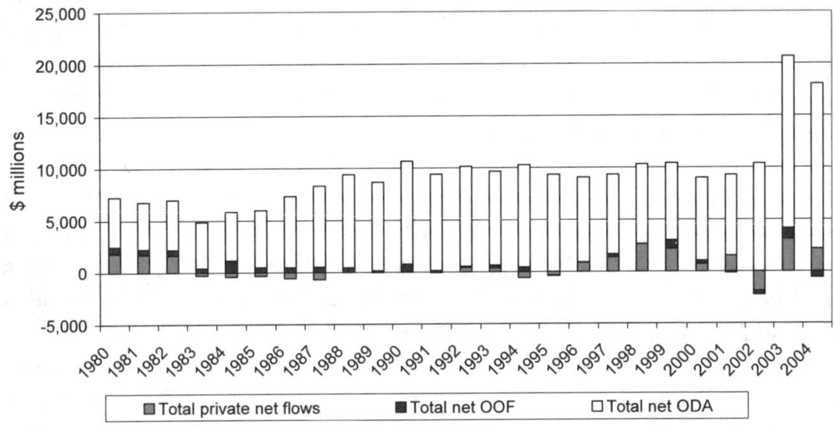

Fig. 2.7. Total net flows to Least Developed Countries, by type, 1980–2004

Source: Author's calculations based on DAC data

Official workers' remittances from overseas residents and non-residents to developing countries have increased steadily to an estimated total of $125.8 billion in 2004, as to $31.3 billion in 1990. China, India, Mexico Pakistan and the Philippines are responsible for the most part of this increase. With respect to regions, Latin America and the Caribbean received $36.9 billion, South Asia $32.7 billion, East Asia and the Pacific $20.3 billion, Middle East and North Africa $17.0 billion, Europe and Central Asia $12.9 billion and Sub-Saharan Africa $6.1 billion in 2004. Low income countries make up an increasing share of remittances inflows, accounting for $43.4 billion in 2004 ($8.1 billion in 1990). The rise of remittances flows can be explained, among other factors, by reduced transaction costs and growing international migration.[39]

Pledges by multilateral and bilateral donors

The UN proposal to spend 0.7% of the national budget on ODA has not been fulfilled on a global scale. Some noteworthy exceptions are Denmark, Norway, Sweden, the Netherlands and Luxembourg. In 2002, at the International Conference on Financing for Development in Monterrey, the participating governments agreed on a specific date (2015) to fulfil the 0.7%

[39] Whether or not remittances are a stable source of capital for development, is discussed in Chami et al. (2003), Solimano (2003), Buch et al. (2002) and Ratha (2003).

criteria. The World Bank members agreed that the World Bank's International Development Association (IDA) increases their disbursement of financial resources by 25% within the next three years, focusing especially on those African countries that fulfil certain pre-defined criteria (transparency, aid effectiveness, accountability).

The European Commission decided in mid 2005 to increase its ODA budget of the EU-25 members stepwise to 0.7% on average until 2015 (0.42% until 2006 and 0.56% until 2010).[40] In absolute terms, this increase would amount to a doubling of European ODA from currently €46 billion to approx. €92 billion. It remains to be seen whether or not this ambitious consensus will hold. Some member countries declared that the pledged ODA increases should not be conducted via national budgets but instead be "innovative sources of development".[41]

The United States have focused their recent commitments in development assistance on two major proposals: The Millennium Challenge Account (MCA) and the US Emergency Plan for AIDS relief. The MCA provides additional funds of $5 billion per year for development assistance in selected countries. The AIDS relief funding began in 2004 with $2 billion and nearly triples the existing US commitment to international AIDS assistance. If accounted for the national ODA quota, United States' ODA would increase from 0.13% of GNI in 2002 to 0.21% of GNI by 2006. The MCA is covered in more detail in Sect. 3.3.6.

2.3.3 Summary

Aggregate numbers on ODA flows to developing countries provide only a limited understanding of current developments in official development financing. On the one hand, it is true that total ODA flows play a minor role compared to private financial flows and workers remittances on an aggregated scale. Furthermore, net official flows[42] to developing countries declined since 2001, a consequence of loan repayments of some emerging market economies struck by financial crises. Finally, due to an increasing proportion of emergency assistance and debt relief, additional ODA only partly translates into additional funds available for projects and programs. Accounting for inflation, depreciation and growth, DAC member countries' ODA quota (as percentage of their GNI) remained at 0.25%.

---

[40] See European Commission (2005b).

[41] See G8 (2005).

[42] Here defined as total foreign aid ex technical cooperation grants plus debt by official creditors.

On the other hand, the disaggregation of ODA flows has revealed that there have been considerable shifts in recent years regarding the type of aid flows. Although pledged commitments are not met by the largest donors, there is a tendency to provide additional ODA in the form of grants instead of loans and in the form of program aid instead of project aid. LDCs and low income countries are among the most favoured recipients in recent years (they receive two-thirds of all recent ODA increases), a trend likely to continue. From the viewpoint of LDCs, ODA still represents by far the highest share of net capital flows and, in almost half of all low-income countries, accounts for more than 50 per cent of total government expenditure.

2.4 Estimates of ODA requirements

The UN High-level Panel on Financing for Development, chaired by Ernesto Zedillo (former president of Mexico), served as an influential study for the Preparatory Committee for the International Conference on Financing for Development (Monterrey, 2002). The final report (also known as Zedillo-Report) concludes that "[t]he inescapable bottom line is that much more funding is needed for official development assistance."[43] Since this study at the latest, a vivid debate has evolved on how much external official development assistance is actually "needed". The bandwidth proposed by economists stretches from "the more, the better" to "no ODA at all" with the majority taking a position somewhere in-between. While some argue that in the long run, ODA will not be a decisive factor for poverty reduction and economic development, others claim that ODA is necessary to reach certain short- to medium-range development objectives and that it may assist in initiating a big push to exit a poverty trap.[44] This section will provide an overview on the cost estimation approaches for assess-

[43] See UN (2001), p. 21.

[44] The Marshall Plan, designed to support Europe's recovery in the aftermath of World War II, is often cited as an example for a successful foreign aid plan. The Marshall Plan provided between $100 and $200 per person for several years, accumulating to almost $1,000 per capita (in 2001 prices). In comparison, ODA to Sub-Saharan African countries amounted to $21 in 2001. However, comparisons with subsequent decades of foreign aid plans are afflicted with several problems. Western Europe had skilled labor, experienced entrepreneurs and managers, and effective financial and judicial systems in place. Another Marshall Plan's objective was depressing the global expansion of communism.

ing the financial needs to reach the Millennium Development Goals (Sect. 2.4.1) and to finance debt relief within the HIPC Initiative (Sect. 2.4.2).

2.4.1 Cost estimates to achieve the Millennium Development Goals

Methodology

The Zedillo-Report estimated an additional $50 billion per year to be necessary in order to reach the Millennium Development Goals (MDG), a figure most often mentioned in the non-academic literature when it comes to "concrete numbers". Yet, the question of how much ODA is needed is afflicted with many predicaments and depends critically on the objectives, the type of estimation technique, unpredictable future shocks and other assumptions (e.g., on the aid-growth-link or poverty reduction elasticities of growth).[45] Although the time horizon is fixed in the case of the MDG (= 2015), formulating estimates for a ten year period poses major difficulties. To start with, a more general implication of the use of MDG cost estimates is pointed out by Reddy and Heuty who note that the international commitment to achieving the MDG is not assured completely. In this case, the costs of achieving a particular objective (the MDG) also depend on "determining whether (or to what extent) the objective should be pursued."[46] According to the authors, the cost estimates sometimes implicitly contain the idea that the MDG are feasible and that the international donor community can afford it. Whether or not the MDG themselves provide an appropriate policy approach will be discussed in Sect. 3.4.

One can distinguish between global ("top-down") and national ("bottom-up") cost estimation approaches. Global approaches attempt to determine how much accumulated financial resources are needed to fulfil the MDG in a global context. The result is then brought down to the years remaining until 2015 to come up with a necessary annual payment stream for the international development community (donors). More recently, national estimates at the country level were conducted. They approximate the needs for meeting the MDG in each country separately and then aggregate all national results.

The standard procedure to estimate the financial resources necessary to reach the MDG (either using the top-down or bottom-up methodology) is a

[45] A proposal that has not been followed so far is the inclusion of a risk premium into the cost calculations for taking into account future risks such as climatic catastrophes.

[46] See Reddy and Heuty (2004), p. 6.

two-step approach. First, the additional GDP growth rate required to reach the MDG is estimated.[47] In a second step, the additional aid to reach that growth is approximated. This technique faces several considerable uncertainties and involves a number of critical estimates on the relationship between growth and foreign aid, a nexus that has been found to be ambiguous at least. All too often, the assumptions are set overly ambitious and prove to be too optimistic, suggesting, for instance, that African countries can repeat in ten years what rich countries took more than five decades to complete (e.g. universal primary school completion).[48] The second step (estimating the additional ODA needed) is often based on two-gap models (see Chapter 4), which assume that economic growth depends on the level of investment (being a function of domestic savings, official aid and other flows) and production efficiency.[49] With respect to the other MDG (28), further links have to be considered as well, such as the relationship between public spending and health/education. Furthermore, the distinct MDG are intercorrelated, meaning that the improvement in one goal influences several other ones.[50] This raises the task of attributing the limited financial resources to the individual goals. Missing sectoral data is often filled with existing cost estimates, which use different calculation concepts, posing further constraints.[51] Finally, the level of aid effectiveness critically affects its outcome and thus the volume of future aid necessary.

Estimates based on the top-down approach

With all these above-mentioned caveats in mind, the following studies provide empirical cost estimates for meeting internationally agreed targets:

---

47 For estimates of growth rates required for the MDG, see Hanmer et al. (1999) and Hanmer and Naschold (2001).

48 For Sub-Saharan African countries, Hanmer and Naschold (2001), p. 16 forecasts an average annual real growth in GDP per capita of 5.9 percent needed to reach the MDG, assuming that no policies will be put in place that additionally favour the poor. Only very few Asian countries were able to accomplish such a growth rate for a longer period of time.

49 See also Gottschalk (2000) for such an approach. This method is widely applied because of its relative simplicity, data availability and feasibility, but has been heavily criticized, most notably by Easterly (1997).

50 See also Brownbridge (2004) on this thought.

51 See Reddy and Heuty (2004), pp. 10–12 for a detailed review on the main methodological problems associated with cost estimates. The authors instead suggest a more comprehensive approach to goal-oriented learning and decision-making, called MDG Institutionalized Financing and Learning Mechanism (IFLM).

- UNDP et al. (1998)
  A forerunner of the Zedillo Report, the UNDP in coordination with the UNESCO, UNICEF, World Bank, WHO and UNFPA has forecasted the financial resources necessary to finance the provision of basic services such as primary education, health and nutrition, clean water and sanitation to all developing countries. The computed financing gap accumulated to $70–80 billion per year.
- UN (2001) / "Zedillo Report"
  The recommendations of the UN High-level Panel on Financing for Development, chaired by Ernesto Zedillo (former president of Mexico), served as an influential study for the Preparatory Committee for the International Conference on Financing for Development (Monterrey, 2002). Although the study admits that "[i]t was beyond the scope of this Panel to make precise calculations of the international resources required […]"[52], it is one of the most cited studies to find out how much ODA is needed globally. Without providing many details on the estimation technique,[53] the Panel speaks of "rough, albeit conservative" estimates and concludes that "meeting the International Development Goals alone would require an extra $50 billion per year of official development assistance […]". These results were obtained by estimating the costs of each goal under the assumptions that the policy orientation of the recipient countries does not alter and that there are no additional gains from trade. Particularly, the amount of humanitarian aid and global public goods needs to be assessed more profoundly. The Panel highlights that is imperative to separate financing for development and humanitarian assistance from finance for global public goods. Although not very precise (Reisen characterizes it as "back-of-the-envelope nature"[54]), the Zedillo-Report indicates the order of magnitude and triggered a number of additional studies.
- Devarajan et al. (2002)
  This study differentiates between the cost of achieving Goal 1 (eradicate extreme poverty and hunger) and Goals 2–8 in order to reduce the problem of double-counting. The costs to achieve the first goal are estimated to be an additional $54–$62 billion annually, those to achieve goals 2–8 at an additional $35–$76 billion per year. The results for the latter are reached by applying country-specific unit costs and then multiplying them by the respective population.
- Pettifor and Greenhill (2003)

[52] See UN (2001), p. 20.
[53] See for some details Poston et al. (2003), p. 5.
[54] Reisen (2004), p. 3.

In a similar approach, the authors conclude that a total of $76 billion annually is needed for reaching the MDG.

- United Nations Millennium Project (2005)
  The UN Millennium Project report agrees that the question of how much financial resources are needed to fulfil the MDG can only be answered via detailed needs assessments at the country level. The estimated numbers include only resources to be spent for projects and programs, not special purpose grants (technical cooperation, emergency assistance, debt relief, and administrative costs). The results suggest that a typical low income country (per capita income of $300 in 2005) needs external financing of about 10–20 percent of GNP. The total costs of supporting the MDG financing gap for every low-income country amount to $73 billion in 2006 and will rise to $135 billion in 2015. Taking into consideration special purpose grants, the costs of meeting the MDG in all poor countries are estimated to $121 billion in 2006, rising to $189 billion in 2015. Accounting for other forms of ODA to be warranted, readjusting existing aid instead of additional aid and recognizing that some countries will no qualify for aid due to a lack in governance, required aid amounts to $135 billion in 2006, rising to $195 billion in 2015.[55]

Although the numbers vary significantly, the results more or less point to a similar direction. Most studies suggest that at least a doubling of ODA, compared to current disbursements, is necessary to reach the MDG.

Estimates based on the bottom-up approach

Global estimates are of limited use for national policy-makers, because they do not reveal the needs of and the necessary resource allocation to individual recipient countries. Thus, a number of estimates at the country level (country case studies) have been carried out. Broadly in unison with global estimates, a study performed by the African Development Bank in 2002 points to an additional $20–25 billion annually in ODA needed for all African countries to reach the MDG. A UN report[56] entails some country studies, e.g. for Ghana and Uganda.[57] There is, by now, no complete but a well progressed coverage of most low-income countries.

---

[55] The authors suggest a doubling of current ODA-to-GNP ratios of donor countries to 0.5% and above.

[56] See United Nations Millennium Project (2005).

[57] Ghana needs annual public investment of $80 per capita in 2006, scaling up to $124 in 2015 (with current levels of approx. $38 per capita). For Uganda,

Comparison and limitations

In general, most studies more or less agree that the MDG are feasible, with their range differing between $40 and $70 billion of additional resources per year in order to meet the MDG in all countries worldwide. In some cases, the results are not directly comparable because of different methodologies (e.g., different base years) and can only serve as a broad indicator. Most methodological shortcomings that have been outlined above for global estimates more or less also apply for country estimates.

The cost estimate results are often misinterpreted as being sufficient to meet the MDG. This is by no means the case. Many more factors play a vital role for development successes than mere additional financing, as has been pointed out in many studies on economic development. Even with the knowledge, the commitment of the international donor community and the necessary resources, aid can only play a limited role in economic development. Moss, for example, claims that even if unlimited ODA funds were available, the MDG would not be met.[58] In the cost estimate studies, however, these additional factors are covered only very generally, e.g. by assuming improvements of the policy environment or noting that capacity constraints will have to be lifted. The cost estimates all more or less fail in putting general and accompanying policies in concrete numbers, a task that is admittedly very difficult if not impossible. Consequently, even if additional resources somewhere in the range suggested above can be mobilized, there should be much caution in interpreting this as an automatic success. Unfortunately, many decision-makers inappropriately concentrate on the number "$50 billion per year", neglecting the shortcomings of cost estimation techniques discussed above. The application of the suggested numbers in recent policy proposals (e.g., the International Finance Facility) is rather obvious. Such a reduction on ODA quantity may undermine future constituencies for aid in donor countries and for political reform in recipient countries.[59]

2.4.2 Cost estimates to finance the HIPC Initiative

Despite financing the MDG, the recent debt relief promised by multilateral creditors has also raised the question of financing. It has been agreed that the debt relief granted will be additional to current ODA disbursements in

Brownbridge (2004), p. 42 estimates that the funding gap to reach the MDG range between 6.4 and 13.6 per cent of Uganda's GDP.

[58] See Moss (2005), p. 5.

[59] See Clemens et al. (2004).

order to maintain the function of World Bank, IMF and RDBs as multilateral creditors of grants and loans. Under the HIPC initiative (see in more detail Sect. 3.4.3), 38 countries are eligible to receive substantial debt relief. IMF and World Bank have provided an estimate on how many financial resources are needed to finance the debt relief based on the following assumptions:[60]

- The total costs include costs under the original initiative (HIPC I) and the enhanced initiative (HIPC II), as well as assistance that has already been delivered.
- Cost estimates are based on debt data after full use of traditional debt-relief mechanisms.
- All countries considered are assumed to request assistance under the enhanced HIPC initiative.
- The total cost of assistance to the Democratic Republic Congo includes relief provided by bilateral and commercial creditors on short-term debt in arrears.
- Each country-specific Debt Sustainability Analysis (DSA) is based on macroeconomic assumptions about exports and fiscal revenues developed by Bank and Fund staffs in consultation with country authorities.

Table 2.3 lists the estimated costs for multilateral, bilateral and commercial creditors. The total estimated cost is $38.2 billion in 2004 at present value terms (= $56.4 billion in nominal terms), from which 68.4 percent belong to the 18 completion point countries and the remaining to the ten decision point countries. Multilateral creditors account for $19.9 billion (= 52.1%) of the total costs. This debt relief represents nearly 100% of the total exposure to these creditors.[61] The IDA share of debt relief ($9.0 billion) has been met within the triennial replenishment rounds (IDA–13 and IDA–14). The potential costs for the IMF ($3.0 billion) will be covered fully by special IMF reserves (PRGF-HIPC Trust and Special Disbursement Account).

Debt relief of other official bilateral creditors amounts to $18.3 billion in total. From these, Paris Club creditors have agreed to grant additional debt relief beyond the amount of relief committed under the HIPC initiative (for details on the agreement see Sect. 3.5.4). At completion point,

---

[60] See IMF and IDA (2005), pp. 40–41. See there for further assumptions on interest and discount rates.

[61] See ibid., p. 60.

most bilateral creditors have cancelled 100% of ODA-eligible and non-ODA eligible debt.[62]

Table 2.3. Distribution of estimated costs by main creditors and country groups [in billion dollars and %]

	Completion Point Cases	Decision Point Cases	Total
Total costs	26.1	12.1	38.2
Bilateral and commercial creditors	12.0	6.4	18.3
Paris Club	8.3	5.5	13.8
Other official bilateral	3.1	0.5	3.6
Commercial	0.6	0.3	0.9
Multilateral creditors	14.2	5.7	19.9
World Bank	6.8	2.5	9.2
IDA	6.8	2.2	9.0
IBRD	0.1	0.2	0.3
IMF	2.2	0.8	3.0
AfDB/AfDF	1.8	1.6	3.3
IDB	1.3	0.0	1.3
Other	2.1	0.9	3.0
Percent of total cost	68.4	31.6	100.0

Source: IMF and IDA (2005), p. 12
Figures may not add up because of rounding.

2.5 Innovative sources of development finance

2.5.1 Overview

"Necessity is the mother of invention." Following this idiom, the last several years have witnessed a variety of new financial instruments proposed to complement and increase ODA. The new approaches have been put under the headline "innovative sources of development finance". However, the word "innovative" does not fit to all the proposals, as some of them

[62] In contrast, the number of non-Paris Club creditors taking part under the HIPC initiative debt relief has declined. An IMF Survey revealed that lack of understanding of the HIPC Methodology is the main reason for this caution.

draw on ideas developed in the 1970s. The proposals made recently can be classified into the following four categories:[63]

- International taxation,
- Lottery systems,
- International Finance Facility,
- IMF financing operations.

The proposals comprise different aspects in development finance. Some of these innovative instruments are said to carry a "double dividend", i.e. performing two tasks simultaneously, e.g. such as reducing global warming and raising funds for development finance (environmental tax).[64] Others include crowding out effects, for example if they lead to reduced ODA pledges of donor countries. Some instruments are better suited for additional grants, while others could provide loans. The subsequent chapters will assess the functioning and prospects of implementation of the various innovative financing instruments. In order to compare and evaluate them, the following criteria are used wherever applicable:

- Revenue potential
- How much revenue can the instrument in question generate? Whenever possible and applicable, empirical estimates are given.
- Technical feasibility
- What technical obstacles have to be overcome in order to assure a transparent and fair organization and management?
- Political feasibility
- What are the chances of political support to introduce the instrument on a global scale? What are the challenges of implementation against political groupings (lobbies)?
- Steering function
  What positive and negative side effects (e.g. price distortions, externalities, crowding out) does the instrument entail?

2.5.2 International taxation

Many products and transactions can be determined for taxation. There is an inaccuracy in the literature on the right use of the word "tax". Normally,

---

[63] Although on the rise, the role of private donations will not be analyzed here. See Micklewright and Wright (2005) for more details on private donations for international development.

[64] See Sandmo (2003), p. 5.

measures restricting international transactions are subsumed under the term "tariff". Moreover, the principle of non-affectation states that tax revenues are not to be allocated to specific expenditures. Nevertheless, the word tax is used in development finance because such a contribution is regarded as an equivalent to a tax for national producers.[65] In sync with the existing literature, this term will also be used here.

Taxation of international currency transactions has long been proposed as an instrument to reduce the volatility of international capital flows. After James Tobin introduced the idea of taxing international capital flows in the 1970s[66], it has been in the academic dispute for decades without ever being put into practice. In the field of development finance, the idea of taxation came up again in the early 2000s by some researchers arguing that a tax could not only reduce speculative capital flows but also generate financial resources for economic and social development purposes. Some authors even see a necessity of international taxation, "because globalisation leads to an erosion of national tax systems."[67]

A number of taxation proposals have been developed, some of which are made it on the agenda of G8, World Bank, IMF and European Commission. The next subsections deal with currency transaction taxes, the taxation of arms, environmental taxes and the taxation of internet services.

Currency transactions tax

A currency transactions tax (CTT) has originally been proposed by James Tobin[68] in the 1970s in order to decrease the volatility of international capital flows and to limit the opportunity of investors to speculate against currencies. The CTT was to throw "sand in the wheels" and to reduce so-called noise trading (speculation). While the CTT attracted new attention in the 1990s because of several large financial crises, the idea of using the tax revenue for development purposes came up in the beginning of the new millennium.[69]

Bottom line for the introduction of a CTT is the differentiation between price stabilizing and price destabilizing speculations in the foreign exchange market.[70] While stabilizing speculations (arbitrage) fulfil an impor-

---

[65] In fact, most taxes act as a value-added tax (VAT).

[66] Proposed already in 1972 and referring to Keynes, the first published forms appear in Tobin (1974, 1978). His real intention, however, was to increase the leeway for national policy, not to put a restraint on exchange rate volatility.

[67] Wahl (2005), p. 5.

[68] See Tobin (1974, 1978).

[69] See for example, Sen (2001).

[70] See Wehrheim and Schmitz (2003), p. 650.

tant function in the price-building process on the international currency market, destabilizing speculations (often short-term) result in functional and allocative deficits. Yet, a lucid distinction between speculative and non-speculative transactions seems rather difficult, given the multitude of traders' activities. One of the reasons for the destabilizing role can be detected in the role of analysts' expectations. If expectations (e.g. about rising demand) are not met, a shock might occur, in which the price might even fall below the original price.[71] Since there are many expectations on the market, prices will fluctuate, thereby creating high volatility. To flatten this effect, a CTT could reduce international capital mobility and undermine short-term speculation flows. Domestic and foreign interest rates then can still show up a difference and thus a potential for speculation, but the tax holds back this speculation.[72]

Many pro and contra arguments of a CTT have been exchanged since Tobin's original idea. Because the focus here lies more on the revenue generating aspects, the arguments will be presented in brief. Proponents of the CTT claim that markets do not function efficiently (e.g., existence of speculative bubbles and noise trading) and that a Tobin tax could act as a shield against speculation by reducing noise trading.[73] Critics argue that market participants base their decision to trade and their expectations on fundamentals, so exchange rate volatility will not be increased, making a Tobin tax unnecessary. Moreover, the information used by speculators is necessary to retrieve equilibrium and market efficiency. Introducing a Tobin tax would reduce market efficiency because it would add to liquidity shortages for everyday operations such as arbitrage and hedging.[74]

In order to solve the trade-off between the two objectives of generating significant resources for development finance and avoiding allocative distortions, Spahn[75] has proposed a two-tier tax with special emphasis on a politically feasible solution. His feasibility study, written on behalf of the German Ministry of Economic Co-Operation and Development, is the most detailed study and suggests a two-fold approach. Besides the original "steering" objective (stabilization of exchange rates), the second objective is of a fiscal nature (generating tax income). In order to achieve both goals,

---

[71] Dornbusch's overshooting model can serve as one explanation for such fluctuations. See Dornbusch (1976).

[72] See Aschinger (1998).

[73] See also Menkhoff and Michaelis (1995), Haq et al. (1996), Reinhart (2000) and Grahl and Lysandrou (2003) for reviews.

[74] See Davidson (1997).

[75] See Spahn (2002). Spahn's conceptions go back to works of Tornell (1990) and Kenen (1996).

two taxes would be introduced: A "Politically Feasible Tobin Tax" (PFTT) with a very low rate (0.01%) as well as an "Exchange Rate Normalization Duty" (ERND) with a very high percentage rate (50–100%). Although the name suggests a proximity to the classical Tobin tax, the objective of the PFTT is not to reduce volatility on the international financial markets, but to generate financial resources. The ERND aims at reducing exchange rate fluctuation caused by speculators. The idea is to insert a very high percentage if an exchange rate falls outside a certain corridor (e.g., demarcation from a monthly average). As long as the exchange rate lies within the band, there will be no "penalty". Although no explicit design is formulated, a close connection to the European Exchange Rate Mechanism is obvious. Proponents of this methodology emphasize that, especially in emerging market economies, exchange rates will be more stabilized and the risks of financial crises due to speculation will be reduced.

The tax base would include spot and forward operations with a maturity of less than one month. Options, futures, and other derivatives would not be directly included but could be indirectly affected by the aforementioned spot and forward operations. According to Spahn, the introduction of a two-tier tax system (Tobin-Cum Circuit-Breaker Tax) has significant allocative and distributive advantages.[76] The levying could come in two ways: Either at the trading desk or when invoiced (i.e. during the settlement/payment stage). Both methods are technically feasible. While the first option is lavish but allows for more detailed information, the second is almost automatically run but does not include all information (e.g., only spot market transactions are visible).[77] Another advantage of taxation at invoice is that it could be connected with the access to the official payment system of the central banks, which would receive the tax income and pool it.

Still, there is uncertainty of who finally bears the cost of the CTT. If hedging transactions (trade of liquidity[78]) are taxed, which Spahn assumes to make up a very substantial part of the tax revenue, increased consumer end prices for households and higher input prices for producing firms could be the result. The reason is that traders (especially in the retailer business) will pass over the CTT on the consumer prices of their products. Passing over the CTT will be the more difficult, the larger the customer (= investing entity) because of his higher negotiation power. In contrast, in-

[76] See Spahn (2002), p. ii.

[77] For both methods and a detailed analysis of the advantages and disadvantages, see Spahn (2002), p. 48ff. While the first approach is also favored by Kenen (1996), Schmidt (1999) and also Landau (2004) opt for the second approach.

[78] See Spahn (2002), p. 12.

vestment funds could pass over the CTT relatively easily to their customers in the form of higher and often invisible administrative costs. However, since there are a variety of actors engaged in exchange rate trading (funds, insurances, central banks, government, private investors, exporters, importers, investment banks), the exact outcome will be difficult to estimate. In general, the margin of currency transactions in developing market economies is higher than in developed economies because of the higher risk involved. A CTT could thus affect the trade volume in the latter more seriously than in the former.

Mende and Menkhoff expand on these points by arguing on a microstructure level.[79] They state that in the light of new findings from the literature on market microstructure, a Tobin tax does not seem viable. Their idea stems from the finding that the traditional exchange rate literature is not well suited for explaining very short-termed exchange rate volatility. They classify three different groups (banks, asset managers and commercial firms) with their own behavioural characteristics and argue that a low CTT does not influence decisions by asset managers (who are regarded as the driving force in the foreign exchange market and are more long-term oriented), and that a high tax rate would result in substantial liquidity shortages.[80] "The available evidence thus suggests that the Tobin tax concept was designed for a scenario of speculating banks and higher transaction costs that simply does not exist at present."[81]

There are several effects that have not been discovered in the Spahn study: First, central banks, in order to defend against appreciation or depreciation of a fixed exchange rate, might have an incentive not to do so and stop intervening in the currency market. The reason is that floating could result in increased tax income once the ERND band is left.[82] However, as the statues of central banks do not include gathering resources for development finance, such behaviour seems rather unlikely. Second, there might be cases of "wrong alert": First, if new information is received by all market participants and priced accurately, but has led to the exchange rate leaving the band, there is speculation without the speculation motive. And if there are upward and downward speculative tendencies that keep the ex-

[79] See Mende and Menkhoff (2003).

[80] See ibid., p. 229. Their analysis on the spread of interbank dealings indicates that 94% of this trade still takes place with a spread lower than 0.05%. Assuming a stock market elasticity of -1, a CTT of 0.1% would reduce the trade by more than 80%; a CTT of 0.01 would still reduce trade by one third. See ibid., p. 241.

[81] Ibid., p. 244.

[82] See Fendel and Stadtmann (2003), p. 280.

change rate in balance, there is speculation, but the alarm will not be activated.[83] Third, if not all currencies are included in the CTT, currencies not taking part can be used as a vehicle to surpass the tax (cross rate effects). Finally, the tax might impact the movement of the exchange rate within the ERND band. The market participants will not only have expectations on the exchange rate itself, but also on the tax and the band. If there is an expectation that the band will be left, this might result in additional transactions (e.g., to escape the tax).

Zee[84] proposed a Cross-Border Capital Tax (CBCT) whose major difference to the Tobin tax is its reduced claim to be a solution to the global capital flows volatility. Very much like the original Keynesian thought, the idea is to merely moderate the impact of volatile world capital flows on a country's domestic economy. Capital imports of destabilizing short-term character will be taxed, while capital exports will be not. Such a Pigouvian tax to internalize negative externalities caused by private speculators could be imposed irrespectively of the international (political) support, as it would be nationally levied and disposed. The CBCT would then not be the right instrument to gain resources for international development finance. It could, however, be used to increase the national development budget (but also for everything else). Because Zee's tax proposal has no fiscal (resource generating) purpose at all, it will not be presented here in detail.[85]

Answering the question of how much potential revenue a CTT can establish critically depends on

- the tax base (i.e. the financial instruments included)
- the tax rate,
- the daily turnover,[86]
- the number of countries (trading places) involved,
- the bid-ask spreads,
- the price and cost elasticities,
- the place and method of levying,
- the method of calculation,
- the likelihood of evasive actions.

[83] See the two scenarios in Fendel and Stadtmann (2003), p. 281–282.

[84] See Zee (2000). See also Dornbusch (1997).

[85] For further details, see Zee (2000) and Spahn (2002), pp. 18–21.

[86] Data on the development of the transaction volume in the exchange rate markets is made available by the Bank of International Settlements in their quarterly or annual reviews.

Table 2.4. Compilation of CTT revenue estimates

Study	Tax rate	Estimated annual revenue	Specific features and assumptions
Felix and Sau (1996)	0.10	$148 billion	Assuming pre-transaction costs of 0.5 per cent and an elasticity of 0.32
Frankel (1996)	0.10	$176 billion	Assuming a reduced transaction volume by 45%, 20% exempted official trading and tax evasion and an elasticity of 0.32
Tobin (1996)	0.10	$50–94 billion, depending on elasticity	30% of the gross volume of transactions serve as tax base
Kenen (1996)	0.05	$90 billion	–
Nissanke (2005)	0.01	$16.8 billion	10% exempted official trading and tax evasion, an elasticity of 0.05
Spahn (2002)	0.02	€20.8 billion	Without transactions in British Pound and Swiss franc

Compiled by author

According to Spahn's own calculations, a PFTT could amount to €20.8 billion annually in the EU.[87] This excludes the financial centres London and Zurich, which in 2004 together made up 34.6 per cent of all foreign exchange market turnover (daily averages).[88] There have been a number of other revenue estimates, whose results are compiled in Table 2.4. The proposals' tax rate assumptions vary between 0.01 and 1 percent, where lower rate are usually advocated by market optimists and higher tax rates by market pessimists. Nissanke notes that "an effective tax rate resulting from the 0.01 to 0.02 per cent tax imposed on wholesale transactions could be translated into additional spreads of 0.04–0.10 per cent or more in retail market segments."[89] He underscores this with subsequent interbank trans-

[87] See Spahn (2002), p. 69. See also p. 5 for a critical note on the different modes of calculation.

[88] See Bank for International Settlement (2005). London is the largest center for currency transactions, accounting for more transactions than New York and Tokyo.

[89] Nissanke (2005), p. 81.

actions until an open position is finally closed and therefore opts for very small tax rates (0.01 to 0.02 per cent).

Nevertheless, a CTT is afflicted with various other challenges, which are mostly of political nature. Without the universal agreement of the international financial community, evasive action into tax havens in offshore countries and allocative distortions will most probably occur.[90] The regional introduction of a CTT (e.g., in the EU)[91] may lead to diversion effects to other countries, with the additional effect of the tax being inefficient. Currently, the political will (especially within the financial community) not only in the United States, but also in Germany and Japan to impose global taxes seems limited, whereas France has repeatedly made clear to support a proposal. This is why Kenen[92] opts for installing the CTT at least in the G7 countries to have a chance of success. However, some authors note the high (prohibitive) additional costs for investors to change trading places[93] and conclude that diversion effects are rather unlikely. Apart from this regional diversion effect, there might be a domino effect in the sense that investors will first flee into treasury bonds, then into other assets if exchange rate transactions are taxed. This could happen if transaction costs will be higher with a CTT and if this would restrict hedging opportunities. However, Spahn and also Tobin note that the impact of a CTT on transaction cost is by far exaggerated.[94] Although depending on the product to be taxed, the additional administrative costs are estimated to be negligible.[95] Patomäki and Sehm-Patomäki propose to introduce a higher tax rate for non-members of the CTT region in order to avoid tax evasion. Patomäki and Denys have written a first draft for a "Treaty on Global Currency Transactions Tax".[96] Intended as a consultative document for discus-

[90] See Eichengreen et al. (1995).

[91] For such a proposal, see Cecil (2001).

[92] See Kenen (1996).

[93] Spahn cites the case of London, which inhabits a natural monopoly in the trade with foreign exchanges and provides market actors with positive network effects. Differentiating between different time zones reveals that a change of the market place within the same time zone lacks alternatives (if the EU plus Switzerland decides to impose a CTT, there is no professional trading place available where investors could flee); a move to another time zone is feasible, but will lead to a loss of the "time zone specific" advantages. See Spahn (2002), pp. 52–53.

[94] See Spahn (2002), p. 65 and Tobin (1996).

[95] The European Commission estimates the administrative costs of a tax introduction to be less than 1 percent. See European Commission (2002).

[96] See Patomäki and Denys (2002).

sion, it might serve as a base for future political negotiations. The following list demonstrates the various political ventures to push forward a CTT:

- 1972: James Tobin's original proposal
- 2001: French Parliament initiative
- February 2002: Great Britain's Parliament initiative
- June 2002: Bericht der Enquête-Kommission des Deutschen Bundestages zu den Herausforderungen der Globalisierung (Germany)
- 2002: Spahn's Feasibility study (Germany)
- July 2004: Belgium passes a law on the taxation of international currency transactions, based on Spahn's two-tier CTT. It requires the support of other EU members.
- September 2004: France: Landau's Report of the Technical Group on Innovative Financing Mechanisms. The Lula Group (Brazilian president Lula, France's president Jacques Chirac, Chile's president Lagos, Spain's president Zapatero) actively supports binding mechanisms to finance development, including a CTT, an arms trade tax, the IFF and additional Special Drawing rights.
- 2005: IMF and World Bank put a CTT on their agenda.

To sum up, the analytical focus concerning a CTT has shifted in four major ways:

1. From the volatility avoidance motive to the generating revenue motive,
2. from concerns about technical implementation to negative diversion effects and political support functions,
3. from the original Tobin tax concept to more differentiated tax concepts,
4. from high tax rates (one per cent) to very low rates (0.01 per cent).

The development of professional tools and computerization in international financial markets has been very progressive throughout the recent years. While older arguments state that a CTT cannot be implemented for technical reasons, this does no longer seem to be the case. Instead, the point can be made that there have been some remarkable improvements in the tax design so that technical feasibility is given. The numbers of most estimates show that the revenue can be quite substantial. However, a high level of uncertainty about its exact size and about possible evasive strategies by market players remains. Although the two-tier CTT made my Spahn and others present an improvement, the major pitfall is the missing political support of some major donor countries.

Arms trade tax

The proposal of taxing the trade in international arms goes back to the Brandt Commission[97], the UNDP and some NGOs, but gained in prominence recently with the publication of the "Report of the Technical Group on Financing Mechanisms" by Jean-Pierre Landau.[98] This report was initiated by the government of France and is supported, among other nations, by Brazil.

An analysis of the effects of an international arms tax begins with the specific characteristics of the arms industry as geo-strategically important sector. Especially in times of political crisis, the demand elasticities in this industry are low. In his study on the supply and demand elasticities of arms, Brzoska[99] concludes that a tax would not have significant effects on the trade volume. The tax revenues could instead accumulate to a very significant amount. Worldwide military spending has approached one trillion dollar in 2003 according to the Stockholm International Peace Research Institute (SIPRI) 2004 report.[100] Even if not the the entire trade volume would be taxed, estimates on potential tax revenue circle around several billion dollars annually. However, the tax costs would probably not be carried by the major exporting countries (United States, United Kingdom, Germany), but by importing countries in Asia and the Middle East (Saudi-Arabia, Taiwan, China, Egypt). Additionally, countries without a sizable arms industry would have to bear the tax because they need to import arms. One possible effect of this price distortion would be an incentive to substitute imports via home production. Especially in the high-tech sector of weapon systems, this could be very expensive and ineffective for poor countries. Higher import prices of small hand fire weapons could also lead to a rise of the shadow economy. Finally, the arms industry could be tempted to pass on the tax to other (supplying and demanding) industries with the result of a growing overall degree of protection. As the practice of international trade has often shown, exporters indeed tend to pass through higher prices to their customers who (in this case) mainly comprise national governments. Thus, the same result could be achieved if governments would directly increase their ODA budget (moreover, the problem of tax collection would disappear).

Major problems are the appropriate tax rate and the selection of weapons to be taxed. In order to cover at least all administrative costs and to generate sufficient resources for development purposes, a minimum tax is

[97] See Brandt Commission (1981).

[98] See Landau (2004).

[99] See Brzoska (2004).

[100] See SIPRI (2004).

necessary. In contrast to the CTT, this rate had to be significantly higher, because the trade volume of arms significantly smaller than the volume of international capital flows. With respect to the types of weapon to be included, the Landau report suggests imposing a tax on all newly produced arms, all used arms as well as all donations. This selection could be based on the UN arms register that differentiates between seven weapon categories and provides the opportunity to exclude certain arms categories (e.g. to allow for self defence of poor countries). In association with a proper selection of goods, a differentiation between input/intermediary and final goods proves to be difficult. On the one hand, double taxation should be avoided; on the other hand, issues such as trade of additional service components and the transfer of technology have to be addressed.

Thus, one can conclude that the taxation of the international arms trade is tainted with numerous problems. Nevertheless, a tax on the international arms trade also receives support, mainly from politicians. Apart from a symbolic and political signal, the concept of letting national industries come up for development finance is more appealing than raising the budget of development assistance. But even if a tax accounted for a significant amount of resources for official development assistance, there would be redistribution effects difficult to estimate. Its implementation must be supported not only by national governments but also by their (often strong) national lobby. More concerns stem from the fact that the arms industry is a strategic industry with a tendency to avoid full transparency. Another argument is that an expansion of the international trade in arms would lead to more tax revenues for development finance, contradicting the intention of peaceful and sustainable development.

Environmental taxes

Environmental taxes have first been suggested at the Environment Conference in 1972 and in a survey of the UN Environment Programme in 1978. This form of tax allows the internalization of negative environmental externalities. Examples of such externalities are global warming and river pollution. The most promising approach is to levy a tax on the use of certain forms of energy. The use of energy harming the environment shall be made more expensive by applying the "polluter should pay" principle. This may include taxing international airline travel as well as the cargo and shipping industry (e.g., via a kerosene tax and carbon dioxide emissions). Apart from generating revenue, an important argument is the reduction of the greenhouse effect, of which carbon dioxide in the main cause. Furthermore, technical as well as organizational innovations (to avoid paying taxes) in energy-intensive industries could be promoted.

An aviation tax could be imposed in four different forms:

1. An aviation fuel tax (= kerosene tax)
2. A charge that could be added to the ticket price
3. A fee for the use of airport corridors
4. A user charge based on emissions.[101]

The first form could generate very remarkable revenues. Clunies-Ross estimates that a carbon tax of $21 per metric ton (which is roughly equivalent to €0.01 per litre or $0.048 per gallon could yield $61 billion dollar if levied on high income countries.[102] In the Landau report, a global kerosene tax of 20% is estimated to generate $10 billion, which is the equivalent to a 2.5% price raise.[103] The very unstable airline market und the high price sensibility of airline passengers pose a challenge to the airline industry even for the levying of a small tax. The recent years have witnessed a very intensive competition and substantial financial difficulties of the air travel industry. Combined with the global price raises of various energy forms and commodities, this suggests that the political support to raise fuel (and ticket) prices will be limited.

The second form of a charge added to the ticket price could also create high amounts of finance. Taking price elasticities into consideration[104], annual revenues of €8–10 billion could be generated.[105] A tax collection of this kind would be rather easy, as there is already a tax on each airline ticket. Political support depends on the importance of the national tourism industry, which could suffer from less airline traffic and on the power of various lobbying groups. Travel agencies could offer tax-free tickets through other countries and bypass the tax.

The third proposal, a fee for the usage of air corridors ("air streets") should be calculated on the basis of how much environmental damage dif-

---

[101] See Jha (2002), p. 12. In mid 2005, France and Germany have committed themselves to introduce an air travel tax. At the international conference on innovative sources of development finance in February 2006 in Paris. The proposal has been put into action by 12 countries and was launched in July 2006.

[102] Here, high income countries are referred to as countries with a per capita income higher than $9,361 in 1996. See Clunies-Ross (2003). Sandmo corrects this figure slightly downward by estimating the quantitative effect of the tax, assuming a long-run price elasticity of -1. See Sandmo (2003), p. 15.

[103] See Landau (2004).

[104] See Bleijenberg and Wit (1998), for example, estimate the price elasticity of holiday travels to be -1.1 per cent.

[105] A 5% tax rate on First and Second Class tickets could result in $8 billion revenue. See Landau (2004).

ferent types of aircrafts produce.[106] Such a fee already exists, i.e. it could be further increased. The forth form is the proposal to have a global auction for kerosene emission rights.

"In spite of the uncertainty that is attached to the magnitude of the relevant elasticities, there can be no doubt that the revenue potential of a global carbon tax is very high."[107] Desai, however, points out that "[l]ocal agreement on new 'green' taxes (like carbon taxes) has often been won with a promise that such a move will be revenue neutral"[108], i.e. that other taxes had to be reduced. Additionally, there is no guarantee that such a national tax income would be used for a global purpose. Opponents of a tax on the use of carbon claim that such a tax is regressive (households with lower income spend relatively more on energy). A more positive light on the issue is shed by Schöb and also Bovenberg[109] who argue that three versions of a secondary ("double") dividend are feasible but not guaranteed: A more efficient tax system, lower cost of public expenditures and a reduction in unemployment. The outcome depends on a variety of factors, among them the tax rate and the elasticities of supply and demand.

Placing a tax on the use of international public goods is another proposal that has been mentioned. It is associated with some problems, depending on the type of global common. International public goods can be defined as "types of activities or products whose benefits spill over, wholly or partly, across two or more countries."[110] Amongst others, deep sea mining, taxing the usage of the High Sea, orbit space and fishing on international oceans deserve more attention here. Putting a fee on deep sea mining has been proposed since the 1970s, but technical difficulties limit the activities within this industry and therefore the revenue potential. However, with the recent price surge of mineral resources, this situation might change in the future. The revenue potential of taxing the use of the geostationary orbit is about to rise with more and more satellites being installed, but nevertheless is very small.[111] Moreover, the strong political competition of the international space industry (US, EU, Russia, China) and the contra-productive steering function limit the success of such as tax. The fishing industry is heavily protected by national subsidies of industrialized countries. A tax could not only generate income, but would also provide a social and ecological steering function towards sustainable fishing. National port authori-

---

[106] For a calculation, see Brockhagen and Lienemeyer (1999).
[107] Sandmo (2003), p. 16.
[108] See Desai (2003).
[109] See Schöb (2003) and Bovenberg (1999).
[110] Kanbur and Sandler (1999), p. 5.
[111] Jakobeit (2001) estimates this tax to generate roughly $20 million annually.

ties could collect this tax rather easily, but political resistance of large fishing countries (Spain, Japan, Russia) remains very high.

Taxation of internet services

Proposals of a "bit tax" go from taxing emails to taxing internet services and sales in general. While the early focus has been put on the equal treatment of online and offline trade in goods, the focus of later works is more on financing development / closing the digital divide with revenues stemming from a bit tax. The original proposal draws back on several authors in the late 1990s.[112] Taxes on emails were estimated to reach very high amounts of resources. In fact, UN estimates result in $70 billion of annual potential revenue with a one cent tax per 100 emails sent. [113]

Just as with the currency transactions tax, a bit tax faces difficulties of global implementation and accounting. A tax account for each email account would have to be set up by all internet service providers, whose number is quite substantial. Internet providers would pass through these costs to the end user. Political support in industrialized countries for such a tax could be limited as it would set an organizational (and financial) hurdle to a key industry.[114] But nevertheless, the taxation of online trade and e-commerce activities will probably be on future agendas. Additional questions center around a volume-based tax (e.g. tax on downloads). Although internet traffic increases strongly (e.g., due to video on demand services and peer to peer networks), such a tax could lack social and therefore political acceptance.

Concluding remarks

The analysis of international taxation alternatives reveals that in most cases, political and technical support is lacking in order to introduce a tax globally. There is no international tax organization to collect and redistribute international taxes. Surely, such an organization would be faced with substantial administrative costs. Regulations covering international trade are controlled by the WTO. But since the WTO speaks up for a general reduction of trade barriers, a raise of trade barriers together with an explicit

---

[112] In some online documents, various authors spoke for the introduction of such a bit tax.

[113] See UN (1999), p. 66. Part of the intensive political protest is due to the economic boom time in which this proposal occurred (the "E-conomy"). For further interest, see Soete (1999).

[114] The bit tax was first opposed by the United States and later also by the European Commission, putting its implementation to a halt.

allocation mechanism (financing for development) would challenge its credibility.[115] The institutions most capable of collecting an international arms tax would be the UN or the World Bank. In Europe, the European Commission could add tax revenues to its EU development budget. Another proposal is to equip the Global Environment Facility, a joint organization of UNDP, UNEP and the World Bank. However, as Jha notes, there are also ideas coming up of founding an international development organization.[116] Whether such an additional large bureaucratic organization would do more good than harm, remains an issue for further discussion.

The problem of legitimacy remains unsolved. As Peter Wahl[117] notes: If the slogan "No taxation without representation" is taken in an absolute form, international taxes were an inappropriate instrument of development finance, as the international community of sovereign states has a very limited decision power. A global governance approach, i.e. the inclusion of political cooperation, democratic multilateralism and institutional arrangements, could be a working base for international taxes. The international community has to cope with a system of decentralized governmental agents, and it will take a long breath to put international taxation into concrete terms.[118]

A critical issue that has not been detected so far is how to communicate the tax burden. If there is a consensus to generate financial resources for development finance, the industry in question will most probably not support it. A tax focusing on another aspect of economic development (e.g., securing local fisheries, stopping environmental deforestation) would have advantages when it comes to implementation. In this respect, some forms of taxes (e.g. a carbon tax) are more feasible in terms of implementation and political support than others, if their revenue is used to reduce negative externalities. The research above indicates that a "green tax" in fact seems more suitable and might achieve more political support than a CTT. Such a tax might also be easier to communicate to the public and to companies. Therefore, the following propositions can be derived: Political support is eased if international taxes are introduced voluntarily and collected on a national basis. Forerunners could then start immediately and no large international tax organization has to be founded. Political support is also higher with low tax rates and a broad tax base. Instead, political support is lower if the revenues are used to finance positions far away from the reve-

[115] Despite this fact, most of all weapon/arms trade is excluded from WTO regulations.

[116] See Jha (2002), p. 17.

[117] See Wahl (2005), p. 17.

[118] See also Jakobeit (2001), p. 67.

nue-bringing sector or if the expenditure purpose is pre-determined and cannot be voluntarily chosen by the national governments.

One proposal to implement global taxes that also has not been discussed yet is to come up with package deals involving several taxes at once. In the Landau report, no priority is given to any form of taxation. Imposing just one tax might be politically feasible, at least for certain countries and or groups, but could also involve significant additional cost such as administrative staff. Instead, by including several taxes into a "development finance package of global taxation", a branch of the World Bank to minimize additional administrative costs could be set up. If each tax only generates a fraction of development finance, political support would be higher as lobby groups could show limited protest. It would also spread the impression that not one country industry is to blame but that all have to donate their share.

Finally, there have always been proposals to put a duty on luxury goods and redistribute the gains. Indeed, wherever luxury prevails, a tax is possible, be it in the Formula One Circuit or in the consumption of caviar and champagne. Yet, much doubt remains on whether these calls can be regarded as forms of development finance. Taxation for development finance critically hinges on whether they will be socially acceptable, generate significant financial resources and comprise comprehensible externality effects.

2.5.3 Lottery systems

Global lottery

The idea of a global lottery assisting development finance has been introduced by Childers and Urquhart[119], but goes back to an unofficial proposal by a Ghana delegation at the UN V Meeting in 1972. Since 2002, this approach has gained additional support from Finland. Lotteries, betting and gambling facilities serve as significant revenue sources of state and local governments. In 2001, the global gaming and betting industry had a gross turnover of $900 billion with net profits after tax of $115 billion.

Two proposals of such a lottery exist: In the first, national lottery agencies could set up additional lotteries. In the second, a new global (worldwide) lottery is operated by a multilateral organization.[120] Ahde et al.[121] fa-

[119] Childers and Urquhart (1994), p. 155.

[120] Currently, about one third of all lotteries are public enterprises, while two thirds are private.

vour the first approach. Otherwise, the authors argue, a competition would take place between local and global lotteries, diminishing the international support of a global lottery.[122] In this case, the main beneficiaries are the national lotteries who then transfer part of the profits to a global institution. Alternatively, one could think of lotteries operated by developing countries (or regions) themselves.[123]

Offering a worldwide lottery service could take place via internet. Such online lotteries do already exist (e.g., El Gordo), although not with an altruistic motive. The advantage to traditional (over-the counter) lotteries is its cost effectiveness[124] and global availability. Although some participants might take part for altruistic reasons, most participants would expect a similar risk-return profile compared to that of a regular state lottery. Some have argued that the global lottery must have a lower expected return (lower prizes) in order not to intensify the competition with national lotteries. This, however, would reduce the incentives to take part in this lottery as well as the revenue potential.

A challenge with lotteries is the fact that low-income groups tend to gamble more than high-income groups.[125] Studies show that the average amount of dollar spent for gambling seems to decrease with higher incomes.[126] While some refer to gambling as voluntary taxation, others criticize it as a regressive tax.[127] Special lottery designs could adjust for the income effect, e.g. by sharing the burden between different income groups. However, Fekjoer states several examples of how the introduction of a lottery with a specific financing objective has actually led to a reduction of the budget.[128] An idea that has not been assessed so far is to design gambling tickets so that players can decide that a certain amount (e.g., one per cent) of his/her profit is deducted automatically to a "development agency account". First, donating parts of the profit is not regarded as a cost and

[121] See Ahde et al. (2002). Their proposal is also known under the "Crisis Management Initiative".

[122] See Addison and Chowdhury (2003), p. 5.

[123] This, however, raises the concern of corruption which is a critical issue in many developing countries.

[124] Internet security has increased in importance, but also in effectiveness so that the cost would be bearable. Even online elections are now being proposed.

[125] In fact, millionaires rarely play lotto. However, they prefer other gambling games such as horse betting.

[126] See Federal Reserve Bank of Minneapolis (2003).

[127] See, for example, Reno (1997).

[128] See Fekjoer (2002). Fekjoer cites the example of a Florida state lottery introduced to assist in the financing of schools. After five years, the proportion of the budget allocated to schools was lower than before.

sharing is more accepted. Second, it might address the bad consciousness and increase charitable spending. Additionally, the lottery would not bear any cost, and the lottery market would not be distorted. Such revenues would add to private donations.

Yet, the overall perception of a global lottery ("gambling for development finance") remains ambiguous. Ethical, cultural, medical and educational issues such as gambling in Muslim countries, gambling addiction or the role of the media in development education must be addressed in this respect.[129] To sum up, the revenue-raising potential of a global lottery is speculative, but can be quite substantial under certain conditions. Whether or not global lotteries will play a significant part in adding resources for development finance remains to be seen.

Global Premium Bond

The premium bond has its origin in the UK where such bonds contain a number used in a monthly lottery.[130] The aggregated expected return on the bond remains unchanged, but individual bondholders can win more or less depending on their luck. In contrast to a lottery where the initial stake is lost, the investment in a premium bond is not. Premium bond sales make up a significant portion of UK's bond market, primarily because prize money is tax free. Thus, a premium bond can be regarded as a combination of investment and gambling. The amount of money invested in the bond is savings; the interest rate on the bond is gambling capital. There are, however, some differences to a pure lottery system: the top prize is lower, the distribution cannot be changed, and the numbers are fixed[131], all resulting in less "entertainment". On the other hand, the gambling transaction costs are lower, because the issuer bears most costs of the drawing. Similar bond concepts exist in Bangladesh and Ireland.

If the premium bond scheme is applied to development finance, a global premium bond would have to be set up. In comparison to a global lottery that could be used to finance grants, a global premium bond would be suited for loan financing. Addison and Chowdhury[132] suggest combining global lottery and global bond. The global lottery can be used to subsidize the loans financed by the global premium bond. For example, developing

---

[129] See Addison and Chowdhury (2003), p. 47 for such characteristics of national lottery markets.

[130] The prizes range from £50 to £1 million. The random number generator ERNIE picks the winners. Each person is allowed to possess £30,000 in premium bonds.

[131] See Addison and Chowdhury (2003), p. 16.

[132] See ibid., p. 17.

economies could receive loan terms that usually only developed countries are provided with. A global premium bond could also satisfy the demand of ethical investments, which is a rising market. If it is comprised by a set of different currencies (basket), exchange rate risks could also be reduced. Moreover, in contrast to the global lottery, a global premium bond better addresses richer investors that buy such bond for tax (reduction) reasons.

2.5.4 International Finance Facility

Setup and revenue potential

The idea of an International Finance Facility (IFF) goes back to the proposal of Gordon Brown, UK Chancellor of the Treasury, in late 2002.[133] In order to achieve the Millennium Development Goals, this "twenty-first century equivalent of the Marshall plan"[134] aims at "doubling official development assistance to half poverty". The first official proposal was introduced in January 2003. The basic idea is a legally binding guarantee of developed countries to bring up additional ODA funds of approximately $50 billion annually. The "primary source of IFF's income is annual payments from donors".[135] Consequently, the donors are the IFF shareholders. The funds would be guaranteed until 2015, giving developing countries improved predictability of aid flows and thus the opportunity to plan on a long-term basis. The proposal suggests that donor countries make a series of long-term and legally-binding pledges, each of them lasting 15 years. On the back of these pledges, the IFF would issue bonds in its own name, i.e. its own liabilities would be securitized on the international bond market. The bonds would be backed by pooled commitments from donor countries. Rating agencies are to ensure that the bonds are treated seriously by the governments. The UK Treasury assumes that the bonds will receive a triple-A rating. Nevertheless, there is still the risk of non-payment. To reduce this uncertainty, the Treasury would only issue a certain percentage (80–85 percent) of the net present value of commitments. Thus, more aid than actually intended would be securitized (over-collateralization). With an expected bond's maturity of 15 years and ten years of annual (or tri-annual) payments to the IFF, the last face value would be due by approximately 2030 (payback period of 2016 to 2030).

The capital raised would be transferred to the recipient countries in the form of grants because loans bear the risk of an increasing debt stock of

[133] See HM Treasury (2005).
[134] HM Treasury (2003a), p. 7.
[135] HM Treasury (2003b), slide 11.

the recipient countries. Within ten years, the facility could bring up to $500 billion. It is important to note that the IFF is not run as a new multilateral institution but as a new financing vehicle. Instead, existing bilateral and multilateral channels will be utilized and each donor country may use its chosen (favourite) mechanism of disbursement (see Fig. 2.8).

Figs. 2.9 and 2.10 show hypothetical income and disbursement patterns, in constant nominal streams and phased streams respectively. The fact that IFF disbursements in the form of grants exceed the IFF income from the donors' pledges during the first years is called "front-loading of aid". The IFF income during the bond repayment phase (2015–2030) is paid by donors' government of a later generation. Thus, the IFF will be relying on the donor commitments to meet its future obligations.

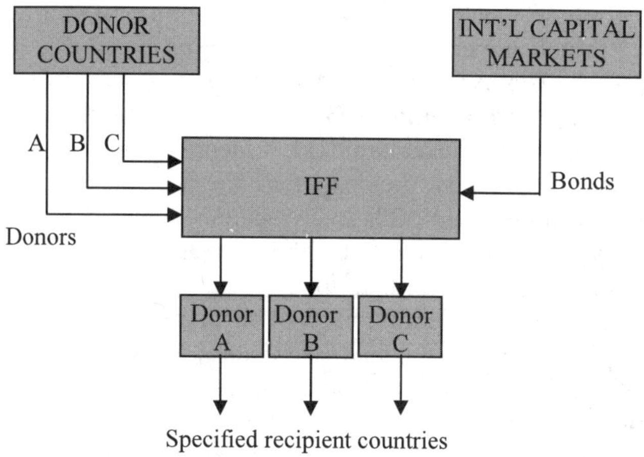

Fig. 2.8. Overview of the International Finance Facility

Source: Adapted from HM Treasury (2003b), slide 12

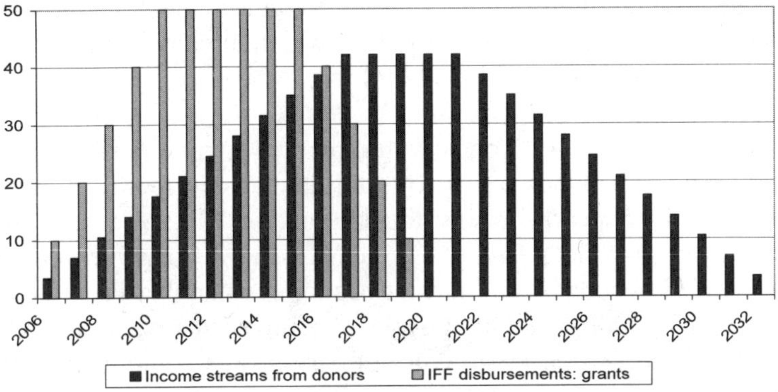

Fig. 2.9. Income streams of the International Finance Facility

Source: HM Treasury (2003b), slide 15

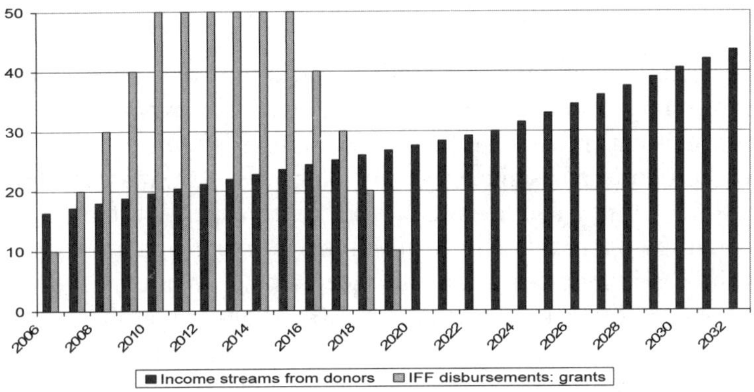

Fig. 2.10. International Finance Facility with phased income streams

Source: HM Treasury (2003b), Slide show, slide 16

Technical feasibility

Regarding the technical feasibility, three aspects have to be considered:

1. Deepness of the international bond market
   In 2002, approximately $360 billion of AAA-bonds has been issued by international agencies. Thus, for the IFF initiative this market seems to be deep enough to digest $50 billion of annual AAA-bonds additionally and the fear of lacking demand is rather low. For instance, the massive liquidity in Asian markets is just

waiting to be invested. The new bonds, however, stand in competition to the bonds issued by the IBRD, which already issues bonds with an annual volume of $15–25 billion.

2. Triple-A rating
   Whether or not the IFF bonds would receive a triple-A rating (the same rating that bonds issued by multilateral development banks receive), will depend on how the international financial markets regard the donor pledges. Since the designated donor governments belong to the strongest and largest economies that can generate enough legal liability capital, a triple-A rating seems realistic.[136] On the other hand, the exact structure of participants is more than uncertain to date, a factor playing a crucial role for rating the IFF bonds. Moss adds to the discussion that IFF debt, because of its off-budget character, requires a premium over regular treasury-issued debt.[137] The official British IFF proposal requests a deposit of 15–30% of all donors' income streams to guarantee the AAA rating.
3. Cost
   Costs occur for setting up the organizational facilities, initial public offering, transaction and negotiation, as well as for paying a coupon, which depends on the market conditions (interest rate). The official proposal's baseline scenario takes 5 per cent interest rate as a reasonable rate. This makes the IFF more expensive than traditional aid by approximately $220 billion in interest payments plus $100 billion in temporary deposits (see point 2). While most donor countries run budget deficits and one could argue that the current ODA budget is also run on credit, the "real value" of the IFF approach ("innovativeness") can only be calculated if the additional costs of borrowing are confronted with the merits of the specific IFF approach. A calculation reveals that $24 billion in extra interest costs over the IFF maturity must be justified if the IFF approach is approved.[138]

---

[136] See Thien (2003), p. 636. However, some supporting countries such as Italy have been downgraded to AA- recently.

[137] See Moss (2005), p. 5.

[138] This calculation assumes a premium of 50 basis points over traditional treasury-issued debt and a total sum of $500 billion over 15 years with a 30-year repayment schedule.

Political feasibility

In terms of political feasibility, the following points deserve special attention:

1. Political coordination and support
   Political coordination is pivotal for success. Especially the fact that pledges for 30 years (including the payback period) will be given, is a substantial political challenge. Only the British government was in favour of the IFF shortly after the initial UK proposal. At the end of 2005, Brazil, France, Chile and Spain (known as the "Lula group") plus Germany declared that they "strongly support pursuing the establishment of such a facility.[139] The United States show a high degree of scepticism. Nevertheless, US participation is not necessary for a successful securitization strategy of ODA, because the IFF also works with smaller resources, although a certain minimum seems to be necessary to cover fix costs. Of course, US support would signal the willingness of global cooperation in financing development.
   Moss[140] argues that a European accounting rule could make the IFF an attractive idea. Debt issued by supranational facilities is not counted as official debt as long as no single EU nation holds the majority. Thus, with at least three nations participating in the IFF (reducing each countries obligation to below 50 per cent), it might be an attractive option for IFF members to "outsource" ODA and manoeuvre around Maastricht criteria. Instead, if allowance is given only for the repayment phase, the political support might be more limited.[141]
2. Idea of front-loading foreign aid
   The concept of paying afterwards, meaning that foreign aid now is paid for by later generations is called dubious by some.[142] In fact, ODA could be raised immediately without any additional cost. Additional financial commitments for future governments would not touch on the current government. Instead, future governments would face a lock-in effect, as they have no choice but to repay. The political self-commitment to expend a certain percentage of GDP for ODA thus transfers into a legally binding commitment of payment on the international financial markets. These, in turn,

---

139 See Brazilian Ministry of External Relations (2005).
140 See Moss (2005), p. 6.
141 See Albin (2005), p. 4.
142 See Deen (2004).

could regard a non-payment as national insolvency. This could undermine the sovereignty of the national parliament to decide on the ODA budget.

3. Despite the organizational setting up, the IFF's success is also subject to several conditions of the developing countries. These would encompass:
   - "pursuing anti-corruption, pro-stability policies and agreeing the necessary transparency in economic and corporate policies to achieve this;
   - committing to the Doha development agenda – a sequenced opening up of markets to global trade;
   - improving the environment for investment and private sector-led growth; and
   - as part of country-owned poverty reduction strategies, agreeing clear and costed plans for building education, health and economic stability."[143]
4. Finally, a condition is that recipient countries must not have any arrears with the IMF, and there must be no UN sanctions for the respective country.

The International Finance Facility for Immunization

A frontrunner of securitization has been introduced with the International Finance Facility for Immunization (IFFIm), starting in 2005 as a test case. The United Kingdom and France plan to expand the fund of the Global Alliance for Vaccines and Immunization (GAVI), whose resources to date consists of $1.3 billion, by approx. $8 billion. The ten year stream of funding is set to begin in 2006. Frontloading immunization and other preventive health care might represent a justifiable case for aid frontloading not only for economic (chance of earlier self-sustained economic growth), but also for moral reasons ("moral imperative"), although this position is not undisputed.[144]

Nevertheless, where ODA disbursements go along with additional service costs (for instance, maintenance of infrastructure such as hospitals or roads), such a frontloading must ensure that these capabilities exist.

---

[143] See HM Treasury (2003c).

[144] HM Treasury (2005), p. 18. On the one side, it is argued that people living in extreme poverty deserve help as soon as possible. On the other hand, frontloading puts a burden on future generations of donor countries.

Prospects

Although there are yet some organizational, technical and political hurdles to overcome, Mavrotas evaluates the IFF as "a promising, forward-looking and creative proposal".[145] Specifically, he sees the advantages of high revenue-raising potential, predictable and stable aid flows and a solid methodological foundation (securitization as an established method in international financial markets). The predictability of aid flows allows long-term development strategies to be planned and implemented, resulting in an increased quality of aid. Forcing donors to repay their ODA pledges to actors on the international financial market who, taken as a whole, possess the power to penalty any non-payment, can indeed be regarded as a major step forward.

2.5.5 IMF financing operations

Gold sale

The large gold reserves of many national central banks go back to the period of the gold standard, where the dollar was backed with gold. At the HIPC conference in Cologne in 1999, the G7/8 members discussed whether the IMF, together with national central banks, could revaluate existing gold reserves in order to finance debt forgiveness for highly indebted poor countries. Gold reserves amount to approximately 30,000 tons. About ten percent belong to the IMF. The current market value of about $40 billion strongly exceeds the balance sheet book value of $8.1 billion.[146] Proponents of a revaluation, among them the British government, that the difference could be utilized to finance debt forgiveness for highly indebted poor countries. A revaluation is only possible if the gold is sold, and it requires 85 per cent of all membership votes.[147] Some members have articulated their support to sell or revaluate gold, if the respective amount is allowed for the national ODA quota. However, a sudden and extensive gold sale could have a negative impact on gold producing countries and diminish the gold reserves of other central banks. Sanford[148] proposes that a

[145] Mavrotas (2003), p. 23.

[146] See IMF (2003) and Kersting and Riedel (2005).

[147] Using some off-market/buyback transactions, the IMF in 1999 and 2000 nevertheless managed to sell gold to Mexico and Brazil at the prevailing market price, and immediately accepted the gold back at the same price to settle repayments due from them. In this process, the value increased from $38 to $285 per ounce. Fur further details, see Sanford (2004), p. 37.

[148] See Sanford (2004), p. 31.

small portion of IMF gold could be sold annually; just enough to offset the World Bank's unfunded HIPC deficit and to cover the loss in reflows, over the next 20 years. The German central bank holds the position that the IMF is not a responsible institution for financing debt relief, but should concentrate on stabilizing international financial markets.[149]

Special Drawing Rights

Special Drawing Rights (SDR) are financing instruments created by the IMF in 1969 to supplement existing official reserves of member countries and support the Bretton Woods system.[150] As an addition to gold and US dollar, each IMF member country can use SDR to maintain the value of their currency by exchanging them with other countries for hard currency. SDR are potential claims on the freely usable currencies of IMF members. With the end of the Bretton Woods system, the role of SDR has declined. The last SDR replenishment (creating new SDR) took place in 1981. SDR represent only slightly more than one percent of the non-gold reserves of all IMF members. Although there have been frequent calls for new replenishment rounds (most notably in 1997), especially by low-income countries, the political support from IMF members has been missing. This is due to the SDR architecture and approval system that relates the borrowing limits to the member countries' SDR quotas. Any changes require an 85 percent majority. Clark and Polak[151] assert that SDR are no longer needed for industrialized countries, because there is enough international liquidity (foreign currencies and gold). Although SDR still count as international reserve assets, they merely serve as IMF unit of account. The share of SDR held by low-income countries is very small, giving them only limited access to borrow. They are, however, allowed to use SDR to repay outstanding IMF and Paris Club debt. The IMF also allows SDR to be transferred voluntarily from industrialized to least developed countries, a transaction that does not require a change in the IMF Articles of Agreement.

Two proposals have been made to reactivate the role of SDR for development finance.[152] First, developing countries could use SDR to build up additional foreign reserve assets. The traditional way of receiving foreign reserves is by buying US Treasury Bonds, which some aid practitioners have called an "aid reversal". Second, it has been suggested to create so-

[149] The German central bank holds this position.
[150] See IMF (2005a).
[151] See Clark and Polak (2002).
[152] See Aryeetey (2005) for an overview.

called "development SDR". The role of the SDR of providing emergency funds in times of financial crises would thus be expanded to include assistance for poor countries to finance their development.[153] George Soros has proposed that developed countries use their SDR to finance global public goods.[154] He calls for intervallic SDR replenishments that will be pooled in an account and estimates that $18 billion could be raised by reallocating existing SDR if the proposed replenishment of 1997 were included. The technical feasibility is one of the advantages of this proposal, as the complete infrastructure of collecting and managing the funds already exists and lies in the hands of a multilateral institution. However, it is intended by Soros that the decision over the choice of public goods relies with a group of individuals, not the IMF or the World Bank. The political support of such a proposal can assumed to be limited at best. Alternatively, each IMF member could decide whether and how to donate its SDR. This reform requires a change of the current Articles of Agreement. Still, the main critique of this approach is the missing advantage over the existing ODA provision.

2.5.6 Comparison and conclusion

The previous sections have analyzed "innovative sources of development finance". The individual proposals depend very much on the instrumental design so that a ranking with respect to revenue potential, technical and political feasibility and level of externalities does not provide valuable insights. Instead, the following catalogue of criteria has been developed and can be used to set apart and evaluate the new financing instruments:

- Additionality
  Whether the new instruments provide *additional* resources depends on a variety of economic and political considerations. IMF gold sales would be for the most part additional. All other proposals may entail crowding out effects whose size and impact should not be neglected. The IFF does not provide any additional resources at all in the long-run.
- Regularity and predictability of future ODA flows
  Proposals leading to *regular* payment streams include international taxation, the IFF, the Premium Bond, the global lottery and development

[153] There is a general tendency of the IMF to extend its role beyond its original role as a lender of last resort. For instance, the IMF has developed a credit line for poverty reduction (PRGF) and increasingly engages in poverty reduction and development issues.

[154] See Soros (2002). See also Stiglitz (2003) for a more radical approach that involves reforms of the entire global financial system.

SDR. In contrast, IMF gold sales could provide a *one-off* financing, although there is some evidence to assume that a stream of smaller sales has less market distortions. However, even with regular resource flows stemming from new sources, it is not assured that they will be stable or predictable over time. In fact, it is more reasonable to assume that avoidance strategies will be developed by those who bear the costs. This holds especially true in the case of a currency transaction tax and the innovative financial service industry, but also for other forms of taxation.

- Level of transaction costs
  Transaction costs to initiate the new financial instrument (e.g., for establishing a new institution) or to keep it running (collecting funds, staff) can reduce the revenue potential. In particular, taxation proposals can have significant transaction costs, depending on the global scope of the instrument.
- Social balance
  It has to be noted that individual tax payers from bilateral donor countries are finally footing the bill. Governments of donor countries should also pay attention to a social balance so that not the relatively poor in industrialized countries finance ODA over-proportionally.

As a general conclusion, it is doubtful whether lottery systems have the ability to assist in extensive financing for poverty-reduction. Similarly, additional SDR do entail no major advantages over the existing ODA provision and allocation scheme. If the ODA "requirements" discussed in Sect. 2.4 are taken as a guideline and technical feasibility is assumed to play no major constraint, only the IFF and the international taxation of currency transactions or the environment can be named as serious proposals with the ability to generate a sizable amount of resources. From these two, the IFF does not lead to additional resources, but is an, albeit innovative, frontloading mechanism. This leaves only international taxation, where political support is limited and varying strongly across donor countries and item to be taxed. Whereas environmental taxes are clearly an idea to follow (also because of their steering function), a currency transaction tax poses strong political resentment. The fact that the original CTT proposal is decade-old and that there are almost no bilateral, leave alone regional or global plans of introducing it (despite some innovative reforms concerning the tax design) underscores the limited support. Consequently, a *rapid* scaling-up providing *additional* resources to finance poverty reduction does not seem very likely in the near future, at least not with the present international governance structures and political motives. The highest degree of "innovation" can be assigned to the International Finance Facility. If indeed a binding mechanism is agreed to stabilize aid flows making them more predictable, this seems to be a higher gain for low-income countries than endless discussions (and no actions) on how to raise additional ODA sources.

2.6 Donor coordination

The question how to raise additional ODA has to be accompanied by a debate on the collaboration among donors. This section will examine in how far multilateral and bilateral donors coordinate their provision of ODA. First, some general aspects of donor coordination will be discussed (Sect. 2.6.1). Next, the chapter examines coordination among multilateral and regional (Sect. 2.6.2) and among European donors (Sect. 2.6.3). Sect. 2.6.4 points to limits of donor coordination and Sect. 2.6.5 assesses whether there is a potential for improvement of coordination by setting up global funds.

2.6.1 Gains and forms of donor cooperation

The importance of donor cooperation is often highlighted in the discussion on aid effectiveness. Before forms and types of cooperation among multilateral and bilateral donors will be analyzed more deeply, some general thoughts on cooperation among aid agencies are worth mentioning. Torsvik[155] confirms that foreign aid does not only have effects in recipient countries but also impacts on the welfare in donor countries: If donors are assumed to act altruistically, poverty alleviation can be regarded as a public good. If one donor provides aid to alleviate poverty, this has a positive effect on all donors. In such a situation, it has been shown that there is a risk of under-provision of the public good because of individual, non-cooperative strategies. On the other hand, too much donor cooperation might result in adverse effects in the recipient country because "the more united and responsible donors act towards the poor in the receiving country the less responsible does the receiving government act."[156] Thus, the question arises whether donors should cooperate and synchronize their aid efforts or rather act independently. For a number of settings, Torsvik confirms that donors are better off with a joint aid policy if they can employ conditional aid contracts to influence domestic policy in the recipient

[155] See Torsvik (2005), p. 504.
[156] Ibid, p. 514.

country.[157] However, without enforceable contracts, he shows that although the net effect on the income of the poor is positive, donors may not have incentives to cooperate.

To date, there are 30 multilateral donor institutions and 37 bilateral donors worldwide.[158] The exact number of NGO engaged in international development cooperation remains unknown but largely outweighs the number of official donors. It is estimated that several hundred NGO are active in each low-income country. According to Ashoff, "[t]his multiplicity of donors, many with projects, programmes, interests, concepts, structures and procedures of their own, increases the transaction costs of development cooperation for donors and partner countries and diminishes the possible impact of development cooperation."[159] These transaction costs include cost for preparation, implementation, monitoring and evaluation of aid.[160] Some countries have even put into practice a "quiet time" during which no donor missions are allowed. A lack of coordination efforts among multilateral, bilateral and non-governmental donor institutions can result in serious inefficiencies such as duplication of efforts or mutual obstruction. In the case of budgetary assistance, missing coordination (e.g., no pooling of resources) may hinder vital structural reforms. Knack and Rahman[161] provide empirical evidence that donor fragmentation (e.g., many small donors and no dominant donors with competitive donor practices) erode administrative capacity in recipient country governments.

Donor coordination was for a long time regarded as the recipient country's duty. Finally, at the UN Millennium Declaration in 2000, the International Conference on Financing for Development in 2002, international donors agreed to closer cooperation and coordination among themselves. These efforts have received a major impulse recently from the Paris Declaration on Aid Effectiveness, held by a High-Level Forum in February/March 2005, also known as Paris Agenda. International donors have

---

157 If no contracts are agreed, the outcome depends on whether or not the government in the receiving country can strategically exploit the altruism of donors.

158 Among the multilateral donors are the EU, 9 international financial institutions (World Bank, IMF and regional development banks), approx. 15 UN agencies and several global funds. The bilateral donors include 22 OECD/DAC members, 6 OECD members not part of the DAC and 9 non-OECD members. See Ashoff (2004), p. 1.

159 Ashoff (2004), p. 1.

160 See Acharya et al. (2006) for the role of transaction costs in aid cooperation. In fact, thousands of quarterly project reports are submitted to multiple oversight agencies „[and] [h]undreds of missions monitor and evaluate these projects and programs annually in many recipients." Acharya et al. (2006), p. 1–2.

161 See Knack and Rahman (2004).

committed themselves to i) systematic support for recipient-owned plans, for the attainment of development results, ii) increased use of national administration systems, and iii) more co-ordinated and predictable actions among multiple aid actors. To achieve this, among other actions, "a set of monitorable targets for changes in donor, recipient and joint behaviour"[162] has been agreed. According to Ashoff, the following types of donor coordination can be distinguished:[163]

- Policy coordination:
  Agreement on principles, guidelines and best practices. The most important forum is the DAC, whose members establish common guidelines (examples being guidelines on evaluation, technical cooperation, the environment, gender issues, good governance, conflict prevention, poverty reduction). Implementation is examined by the DAC in its Peer Reviews. The EU Council of Ministers has also adopted numerous guidelines on the EU's and its Member States' development cooperation.
- Operational coordination:
  Alignment during the implementation of projects and programmes (e.g., co-financing, joint reviews, and evaluations).
- Harmonization of procedures.

Regarding the forms, forums and levels of donor coordination, Ashoff sets apart formal coordination from semi-formal and informal:[164]

- Formal coordination (as an institutionalized forum or binding joint action):
  - General development cooperation issues: UN, annual meetings of the IMF and World Bank, G7, DAC, EU Council of Ministers
  - Development cooperation with certain developing regions, e.g. Strategic Partnership with Africa, Club du Sahel
  - Development cooperation with individual countries, e.g. Consultative Group Meetings, Round Tables, Paris Club for the settlement of debts to official creditors
  - Thematic forums, e.g. Consultative Group to Assist the Poorest (CGAP, theme: microfinancing), Committee of Donor Agencies for Small Entreprise Development
  - Sectoral Forums relating to support for sectoral programmes
- Semi-formal coordination (semi-institutionalized), e.g. regular donor meetings in partner countries chaired by a lead donor or under alterna-

[162] Rogerson (2005), p. 531.
[163] Following Ashow (2004), p. 3.
[164] See Ashoff (2004), p. 3.

ting chairmanship, donor meetings at ministerial level, as in the case of the Utstein group (development cooperation ministers of Germany, Canada, the Netherlands, Norway, Sweden and the UK).
- Informal coordination (often ad hoc, but not necessarily less important because of that): contacts, exchange of information and agreements at working level among the donor ministries responsible for development cooperation, the donors' implementing organizations and their external offices in the partner countries.

In order to diminish such institutional overload and complexity, four general reform proposals exist:

1. Reducing/concentrating the number of donors
2. Reducing the number of recipient countries
3. Concentrating on fewer sectors per recipient country
4. Increasing joint implementation of programs.

In sum, these suggestions mean stronger consolidation and cooperation of aid agencies. Indeed, most development institutions cope with a high number of "clients": They are running operations in nearly every low-income country worldwide. This has also led to considerable "institutional confusion" with a lack of responsibilities or work shares. The complex institutional web also gives all actors an opportunity to blame somebody else in the system for unsuccessful aid projects or programs. Although one should bear in mind that global poverty reduction is not the sole duty of international donors but also naturally relies in the competence of the recipient countries' governments, there is a propensity that donor institutions tend to deny their accountability for failures but claim successes as their own.

A factor that has been assessed to a lesser extent is the role of comparative advantages of institutions to improve donor coordination and increase donor responsibility. The literature on the reform of international development organizations concentrates on the shifting roles of IMF and WTO, whereas the institutional work share of global, regional and bilateral aid agencies remains largely an untouched topic. The basic economic truth concerning the benefits of division of labor and concentration on comparative advantages has not yet arrived in the field of aid agencies' cooperation. Admittedly, such an institutional reform of international development cooperation requires the willingness of all participants to cooperate, to make sacrifices and to convince the public about the need for reform. However, within the current framework, bilateral and multilateral donors seem relatively unwilling to subordinate their individual interests to a greater goal of reforming the global ODA system.

2.6.2 Coordination among multilateral and regional donors

"Good governance begins at home."[165] Some observers have criticised that it is incoherent to demand good governance from clients, but to make an exemption for donor institutions. Indeed, there is a lack of coordination between UN, World Bank and IMF and even within these institutions. For instance, the UN alone consists of more than 30 individual subunits dealing with development policy. While UN and World Bank are internationally accepted as development institutions, the role of the IMF and its scope of operations in poverty reduction and development finance,[166] especially regarding the division of labor to World Bank statutes, are not clearly specified. It has been argued by some that the IMF surpasses its original duties of short-term current account financing and hurts cooperation among donors. "There are indeed no compelling reasons why the IMF should deal with structural problems in developing countries."[167] The experiences of various developing countries provide evidence that their governments align poverty reduction policies according to the needs of the IMF's Poverty Reduction Growth Facility (PRGF); in fact it should be opposite.[168] Birdsall and Williamson[169] argue that the PRGF should be transferred back to the World Bank because poverty reduction remains the World Bank's main field of competence. Conversely, the World Bank is not solely acting as financier for development projects in low-income countries, but also gives structural adjustment loans conditional to macroeconomic reforms, similar to the IMF. Consequently, more radical reforms have been proposed by former US Secretary of State George P. Shultz, James Burnham and others who called for merging IMF and World Bank.[170] They argue that setting up two institutions with different agendas is the outcome of a specific historic setting, but should not be upheld any longer. The major arguments for a fusion are the reduction of the twofold bureaucracy (e.g., two statistical units, publications with similar contents, foreign branches) and the clarification of inconsistent policy suggestions and loan conditions for low-income countries. Burnham has estimated that a quarter of all administrative could be saved by merging the institutions. Additionally, the "clients" as well as the members and shareholders are

---

165 Fischer (2004).

166 See Akyüz (2005), p. 5–7.

167 Ibid., p. 6.

168 See Eberlei and Siebold (2002), p. 44, providing case study evidence for Ghana and Burkina Faso.

169 See Birdsall and Williamson (2002).

170 See Shultz (1998) and Burnham (1999).

nearly identical. Akyüz[171] proposes to establish a single board reducing personnel and other costs in administrative budget. This would not only enhance policy advice to low-income countries, but also improve the chance for recipient countries' staff to carry out negotiations and consultations confronting one voice. The IMF should return activities and facilities related to development finance and poverty reduction back to the IMF. It remains ambiguous whether a complete fusion of IMF and World Bank would be feasible and necessary. As long as the activities and fields of competences do not conflict, IMF and World Bank could remain two independent institutions.

A second aspect is the division of labor between multilateral and regional actors. Most RDBs cooperate closely with the IMF and the World Bank (e.g. joint funding of programs and projects). This cooperation is formally laid out in an official Memorandum of Understanding. RDBs also follow similar guidelines, rules and instruments with respect to project selection, management and monitoring[172], which has induced critical observers to regard RDBs as mere World Bank replicas.[173] But "[a]s regional institutions, they are well positioned to take advantage of their closeness to their clients and their expertise in the region."[174] Examples include regional health programs, coordination of transport infrastructure among neighbour countries, regional energy cooperation and financial regulations. Furthermore, the "lending conditions set by them are perceived differently from the conditions imposed by the classic donor countries (industrial and emerging countries), especially as most of the staff usually come from the region concerned."[175] In some areas, competition is also part of the relationship among MDBs,[176] leading to higher effectiveness of scarce official resources. However, it remains ambiguous whether or not RDBs, in their current state, in fact have strong regional comparative advantages. At the African Development Bank, a substantial percentage of the top level staff consists of non-locals, often former IMF or World Bank staff. Furthermore, Mascarenhas and Sandler studied RDBs with respect to the type of aid (grants vs. loans) that they channel to developing countries and find that RDBs "did little to tailor their grant-loan mix to public good consid-

---

[171] See Akyüz (2005), p. 7.

[172] See Federal Ministry for Economic Cooperation and Development (2003), p. 6.

[173] See Nnedu (2005) who points to the assessment of country performance, which is nearly identical to that of the World Bank.

[174] Kuroda (2000). See also Rojas-Suarez (2002), p. 25 and Culpeper (1994).

[175] Federal Ministry for Economic Cooperation and Development (2003), p. 7 [emphasis left out].

[176] See Bull and Boas (2003), p. 245.

erations, thereby failing to satisfy recipient interests."[177] The role of RDBs in providing assistance for economic development and poverty reduction has been analyzed surprisingly little.[178] More recently, the Meltzer Commission proposed to replace the World Bank and transfer its callable capital assets to RDBs.[179] At the Monterrey Conference, a new joint framework to include RDBs more closely into the international development cooperation was established that will be further convoluted. Yet, recent reforms of the African Development Bank provide mixed evidence: In fact, the share ceiling for non-regional members increased (from 34% to 40%), giving non-regional members a stronger veto option at the Board of Governors that decides with 66.66% majority. Although the majority of shares in every RDB are held by the regional members, the funding arm of the AfDB (the African Development Fund), which controls the country policy assessment test and analyzes how much money "is needed", is almost entirely owned by non-regional donor countries.

2.6.3 Coordination among European donors

Bilateral aid policies of European donor countries are harmonized within the European Union. Still, there are major differences in ODA volume, disbursement patterns and motives across European countries. The Commission itself notes that the EU acts much more harmonious in many other sensible policy fields (such as immigration) than in development cooperation, especially taking into account the fact that clearly specified rules on development policy are laid out in the Nice Treaty as well as in the constitutional draft.[180] There are several reasons for this lack of coordination:

- Within the EU, there are 26 different aid bureaucracies (25 national and one European), each of which is split into a heterogeneous structure of separate departments and actors. Some partner countries are covered by the European department of development cooperation; others are included into the European Neighborhood Policy (ENP) since May 2004 as a result of European enlargement.
- The new member states have adopted the acquis communautaire that also entails complex policy and operational coordinating mechanisms regarding development policy. As "new" actors in development coopera-

[177] See Mascarenhas and Sandler (2005).

[178] One can assume limited interest of global institutions (World Bank, IMF) to assess the role of RDB, although this hypothesis has not been tested yet.

[179] See Meltzer (2000).

[180] See European Commission (2005b), p. 9.

tion, they are building up their own individual agencies. This makes a coherent strategy among European donor countries more challenging.[181]

- The reorganization of the European Commission in 1999 broke with the clear distinction between a commissioner for foreign affairs, one for development and one for trade:

> "Instead, the development portfolio was effectively split between the external affairs commissioner and the development commissioner, with the former being the *primus inter pares* among external commissioners and retaining responsibility for Asia and Latin America. The creation of EuropeAid as the implementing body went only a small way to remedying the inevitable problems of coherence and communication which resulted from this compromise. Despite the relative success of EuropeAid, the reorganisation has left DG Development weakened, and has undermined the overall impact of reform."[182]

In an attempt to overcome these predicaments, the EU Council of Ministers has adopted various principles and guidelines for development cooperation among working parties of the member states and the European Commission. There are also recommendations of an Ad Hoc Working Party on Harmonisation that have been adopted by the EU General Affairs and External Relations Council in November 2004:

1. Establish a roadmap for coordination and harmonization indicating steps to be taken by the Member States and the Commission to enhance the implementation of the Rome Declaration.
2. Member States and the Commission are encouraged to join donor initiatives in accordance with the principle of non-exclusivity.
3. Member States and the Commission are encouraged to decentralize competencies, responsibilities and decision-making to the delegations in order to strengthen flexibility and responsiveness to the local context.
4. Develop a strategy and a timeframe to apply sector and thematic guidelines agreed at EU level to bilateral and Community assistance and use them as a common platform for dialogue with partner countries and the donor community.
5. Develop an EU strategy for multi-annual programming and the harmonization of key analytical and diagnostic input to EU programming cycles around each pilot country's national policy framework and budget cycle.

---

[181] See also a report on the implications of enlargement for European development policy by the European Commission (2003).

[182] Maxwell and Engel (2003), p. 13.

6. Develop an operational strategy for complementarity in the EU.
7. Develop a common framework for implementation procedures.[183]

With the considerations made above in mind, several settings for the future development cooperation in Europe are possible. Maxwell and Engel identify "coherence, coordination and complementarity (CCC)" and the "degree of commitment to the Millennium Development Goals" as the two key drivers of European development cooperation and derive four scenarios, which are shown and explained in Fig. 2.11.

Estimates indicate that 25 percent of all European development aid could be disbursed better if coordination between national and EU donors improved. Still, the basic dilemma remains that there are 26 European actors which would like to keep the opportunity to choose their favourite volume and financial instruments for ODA provision (e.g., France favors taxation, UK supports the IFF), not to speak of keeping the final authority on ODA allocation (see next chapter). Currently, EuropeAid disburses 20 percent of all European ODA. A consequent way forward in sync with European integration efforts would be to transform EuropeAid into a coordinating and allocating institution for ODA of all European member states. Under this proposal, bilateral donors would be reduced to mere financial backers and loose the power over ODA allocation. Concerning the current state of affair of Europe, however, there seem to be rather strong antipathies for such a strategy and only a small consensus to give up this much control.

2.6.4 Limits of donor coordination

Donor coordination has its natural limits in an international aid system with numerous principals and agents, each having their agendas, reports and instruments. Later, Chap. 3 will point out that the number of goals and reports has substantially increased within the last decade, making donor coordination even more complicated. Each aid agency has not only one specific, but many general goals to meet. In the absence of accountabilities, such a collective ownership of goals entails a severe free-rider problem.[184] It should also not be forgotten that donor countries have set up an entire aid industry[185] with tens of thousands of people working in agencies, development ministries and schools of development studies. Consultants,

[183] See Ashoff (2004), p. 4.
[184] See Martens et al. (2002) for more details on institutional economic and principal-agent relations of foreign aid.
[185] See Hanlon (2004), p. 187 and Shikwati (2006) pp. 8–9.

government officials and local administrative staff in recipient countries earn their living from ODA. These groups have a vested interest not to change the status quo and to uphold the existing system, making substantial revisions of strategies and reforms increasingly difficult.

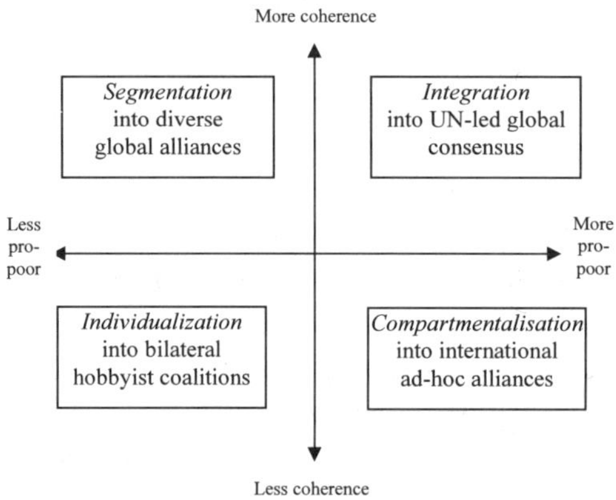

Segmentation scenario: - The Convention produces a consensus around greater Europeanization of development cooperation, including a stronger commitment to CFSP. - National and foreign policy interests remain powerful and aid money flows in large part to 'near-by' and middle-income countries. - Regional agreements are maintained and strengthened, mostly based on foreign and security concerns. - The aid programme remains diversified in focus, with several Member States disagreeing about allocation. - Trade negotiations falter. There is little support for radical opening up of markets.	**Integration scenario:** - Europe develops a more coherent voice on both foreign and development policy - Institutional capacity is created and strengthened to support this. - A greater share of aid budgets is channelled through the EC. - Greater complementarity is actively sought between EC and the EU Member States' international development programmes. - Foreign relations and external actions are differentiated among different regions. - Aid is focused more explicitly on poorer countries and regions; historical groupings such as ACP restructure themselves. - Trade concessions to the poorest countries, such as the EBA, are accelerated.
Individualization scenario: - Lip service is paid to European development cooperation and to principles of CFSP, but in practice, no progress is made with respect to EU institutions. - The Financial Perspectives fail to secure an increase in aid flowing through the EC. - Member States increasingly challenge the decisions and orientations of the Commission; there are no new agreements on Joint Actions. - Member States discuss re-nationalizing EU aid. - Trade talks falter, while bilateral agreements begin to acquire more prominence. - The EU development aid delivery system reaches crisis point by the end of the decade.	**Compartmentalization scenario:** - Movement towards a common foreign and security policy remains slow. - There is little enthusiasm for increasing the share of aid budgets channeled through Europe. - But what aid there is becomes more strongly-poverty focused and better-administered; the EU provides a forum for better coordination among European bilateral donors. - This has implications for the ACP and for other regional groupings, some of whom win and some of whom lose. - Meanwhile, trade negotiations continue, with a pro-poor focus. However, Member States become more reluctant to make concessions which have costs within their borders: policy coherence remains far away. EBA is unlikely to continue.

Fig. 2.11. EU Development cooperation to 2010: four scenarios

Source: Maxwell and Engel (2003), p. 15
Abbreviations: *CFSP* = Common Foreign and Security Policy, *EBA* = Everything But Arms initiative, *ACP* = Africa, Caribbean and Pacific.

Finally, it has been shown in theoretical works and detailed case studies that there are perverse incentives inside development agencies and for contractors in aid-supported activities.[186] Information asymmetries between agency staffs, different incentives structures and distinct institutional rules within agencies aggravate these problems.

2.6.5 Pooling of official development resources

Common pool and global funds

The common pool approach envisions financing development by setting up a global fund filled by donor countries' financial resources.[187] In consultation with developed countries, developing countries would first devise their economic policies and propose projects, which would then be co-financed with resources from the pool. It has to be noted that the focus is not to link special projects to a special way of financing, but to have a general source of funding for all development projects a recipient country aim to undertake.

The ideal common pool can be compared with solutions financing the college tuition of private universities: First, the assessment of the student takes place; the entire financing is postponed. In the same way, donor and recipient countries would first agree on a strategy and then negotiate the financing. In practice, this splitting is afflicted with problems, as the strategies often depend on the way of finance and vice versa. Additionally, aspects such as debt relief involve many parties and might restrict the vector of accessible and feasible strategies. Kanbur and Sandler propose an optimistic scenario by giving the recipient government free hand to use the resources of the pool on their own and also to monitor the expenses.[188] Although their proposal allows for some degree of conditionality, it prohibits the tying of aid to specific projects.

An advantage of the common pool approach is that it addresses the importance of country ownership (see also Sect. 3.6.3). There is growing support for the thesis that developing countries need to divert more and more human resources (e.g., analytical capacity) from own domestic policies to deal with donor countries' concerns (e.g., for planning development programs, undertaking negotiations). The common pool ensures country ownership and at the same time reduces these coordination costs. In a common pool, the recipient country's plan determines several (all) development

186 See Gibson et al. (2005) for an analysis of the political economy of foreign aid.
187 This idea was first introduced by Kanbur and Sandler (1999).
188 See Kanbur and Sandler (1999), p. 38.

opment projects. Overlapping (conflicting) bilateral development arrangements could be reduced, resulting in higher aid efficiency. Another advantage that has so far not been mentioned in the literature is learning effects occurring when the recipient country is developing the strategy, organizing financing events and carrying out own evaluation tasks.

Setting up a global fund also entails several risks. First, it could mean a temporary decrease in aid assistance (e.g., because some donors could disagree with the national strategy and stop providing funds). Second, part of the pool's resources might be misused for non-development purposes. And third, a common pool demands professional management by an international, independent organization and entails cost for staff and infrastructure. Most existing common pools use the expertise and staff of multilateral organizations such as UNEP, UNDP or the World Bank, which act as implementing and executing agencies.

The next section presents some examples of global funds most of which have been assigned to specific purposes. They might serve as a basis for the establishment of a larger common pool. Private foundations will not be discussed here.

Examples of global funds

The *Global Fund to Fight HIV/AIDS, Tuberculosis and Malaria* was created in 2002 as an independent public-private partnership between governments, civil society and the private sector including communities to assist in financing the health sector in developing countries.[189] Currently, more than $5 billion dollars have been committed, most of which take the form of grants. Its focus is on providing financial means (also in cooperation with multilateral organizations), not implementing health projects. The priority is on fighting AIDS, Tuberculosis and Malaria. Also, programs reflecting national (local) ownership are especially encouraged. Another guiding principle of the fund is that programs are only financed if it can be assured that the assistance will not replace or reduce other sources of funding. One of the special features of the Fund is the high degree of transparency and accountability. All documents are fully accessable online in six languages.

The *Global Fund Against Hunger and Poverty* is a proposal from several countries and the UN.[190] It includes a political commitment to make the fight against poverty one of the top priorities in their foreign policies.

[189] See The Global Fund (2004).

[190] Spain, Brazil, France, Chile and the United Nations Secretary General.

Thus, one of the goals beyond financing is to raise political credibility of donor countries (e.g., in the G8).

The *Vaccine Fund* is to support the goals from the GAVI Alliance (Global Alliance for Vaccines and Immunization), which brings together six major stakeholders from the public and private sector (among them UNICEF, WHO and World Bank). The Vaccine Fund was launched in 1999 to ensure equal access to vaccines. It addresses countries with a per capita income of $1,000 or lower.[191] Financing immunization services and purchasing new and underutilized vaccines against diseases such as Hepatitis B or Yellow Fever belong to the main services. It has received a major initiating donation from the Gates Foundation ($750 million). Combined with other donors, the fund has received approx. $1.2 billion that have been disbursed to 71 developing country government immunization programs, as well as additional pledges of $1.3 billion.

In January 2003, the US government has pledged $15 billion over five years to 14 Sub-Saharan and Caribbean countries to prevent new HIV infections and provide antiretroviral treatment to infected individuals. This *US Emergency Plan for AIDS relief* would triple the existing US commitment to international AIDS assistance. The funding began in 2004 with $2 billion. $1 billion is directed to the Global Fund (see above).

At the International Conference on Innovative Sources of Development Finance (February 2006 in Paris), a joint French-Brazilian-Chilean concept paper on an *International Drug Purchase Facility (IDPF)* has been presented. Its main objectives are a secured access to drugs and a more diversified and competitive market for drugs. It is planned that the IDPF includes a binding commitment for beneficiary countries (such as an uninterrupted supply of products at reduced prices and assistance in procurement and supply management) and the invitation of tenders to minimize costs.

The *Global Environment Facility (GEF)*, established in 1991, assists developing countries fund projects and programs that protect the global environment. In particular, projects that are related to biodiversity, climate change, land degradation and the ozone layers are supported. Since its founding, $4.5 billion in grants and $14.5 billion in co-financing have been raised. In 2002, 32 donor countries pledged $3 billion to fund operations for the period 2002–2006. GEF projects are managed by implementing agencies, which involve the UN Development Program (UNDP), the UN Environment Program (UNEP) and the World Bank, and executing agencies.

---

[191] Exceptions are China, India and Indonesia which are also served.

The *Multilateral Fund for the Implementation of the Montreal Protocol (MPF)*, founded in 1991, is dedicated to assist developing countries meet their Montreal Protocol commitments (London, June 1990). To date, the MPF has disbursed approx. $1.6 billion dollars to more than 4,600 projects in 134 countries via the UNDP, UNEP and World Bank. The management consists of an executive committee with equal membership from developed and developing countries.

2.7 Summary and conclusions

Following nearly a decade of reserve in bringing up ODA, the recent years have witnessed a rigorous debate on intensifying foreign aid efforts to assist in global poverty reduction. Chap. 2 has examined the entire "supply side" of development finance by analyzing i) the main multilateral and bilateral actors, ii) their present aid volume and type, iii) estimates on ODA requirements to meet international development objectives, iv) innovative mechanisms of scaling up ODA flows and v) the role of coordination among donors. Although aggregate data suggests a limited role of ODA with respect to other (private) capital flows to developing countries, a disaggregated analysis reveals that there have been considerable shifts in the type of aid flows recently: LDCs are among the most favoured recipients, receiving increasingly more grants instead of loans. These countries obtain a majority of capital from abroad as official development assistance: ODA accounts for more than half of total government expenditure in almost half of all low-income countries.

Nearly all cost estimates assessing the financial needs to achieve the Millennium Goals and to finance the HIPC debt relief conclude that significantly more official financial resources are necessary. There is a growing literature assessing potential mechanisms for scaling-up international aid flows. These encompass the international taxation of transactions and goods, the securitization of aid on international capital markets (International Finance Facility), global lotteries and IMF operations (gold sale, special drawing rights). It has been shown in the previous sections that all of these "innovative sources of development finance" vary strongly in their potential revenue, their technical and political feasibility and their externality effects. Consequently, it is difficult to provide a ranking for the proposals.

It seems not unrealistic to assume that additional sources to finance development could indeed be raised in considerable amounts if political support for the various instruments is growing further. The most recent political discussions in multilateral talks (G8, UN) indicate that scaling up ODA is high on the international agenda of financing development. However, a failure of scaling up aid flows could have serious repercussions on the worldwide system of international development cooperation, which has already experienced an era of "aid fatigue" in the late 1980s and early/mid 1990s. In this respect, large aid inflows "raise the stakes"[192]: They may assist in poverty alleviation under certain conditions, but they are also associated with substantial risks. Furthermore, "[b]y putting a price tag on certain outcomes, calculations from the costing studies reported without attendant caveats create an illusion that any goal can be met, if only the right amount of resources can be mobilized."[193]

While proponents of ODA increases welcome the various innovative approaches and point out that coordination among donors could increase aid effectiveness, others remain much more sceptical. Nuscheler, for example, is very pessimistic that doubling or even tripling official aid flows (to 0.7 percent of donors' GDP) is likely and points, among other factors, to the severe budget constraints of European governments. Rapid scaling up under these constraints is illusionary and makes development policy loosing credibility. Apart from the issue how to gather funds to finance international poverty reduction, critics of the volume-based discussion of ODA point to major allocation and utilization shortcomings. In brief, their reasoning goes that more funds will be rather ineffective and might even be harmful if they are misallocated or utilized inefficiently. These concerns will be the centerpieces of the next chapters, which expand on these thoughts by including the allocation and utilization (= "demand side") of ODA.

[192] Aiyar et al. (2005).
[193] Clemens et al. (2004), p. 4.

3 The allocation of ODA

> We are giving fifty billion of overseas aid. There are a billion poor people in the world. Why don't we just find the poor and give them one dollar a week and do nothing else. No questions asked. What they do with the money is not our concern. That would probably do more to relief poverty than anything else.
>
> Lord Meghnad Desai (2003)

3.1 Introduction

The allocation of ODA does not take place by market forces as in the case of private capital flows. Rather it is the outcome of complex transactions and negotiations between donor and recipient as well as among donors. Both positive and normative questions frame the allocation decision and a variety of issues are of particular importance:

- What is the *actual* aid allocation of bilateral and multilateral donors in recipient countries?
- What are the *motives* behind the allocation decision (altruistic, (geo)political, historical ties, geographical and/or cultural proximity?)
- Should aid be allocated according to the *quality of impact* it has in the recipient region or according to the *needs* of the recipient?
- Should some countries be preferred or *selected* over others?
- Is there an *optimal allocation rule*?
- What are the policy lending/granting *principles* behind the allocation decision?

Consequently, the question how to allocate (very limited) public funds to developing countries has been discussed broadly and controversially in development economics. The existing studies can be categorized into three groups: First, there is a string of literature that attempts to give explanatory factors for observed allocations of aid. The second group of studies evaluates aid allocation against normative criteria. Finally, there are studies that calculate the amounts recipient countries should receive (by normative criteria) and then prescribe the allocation among these recipients.[194] More recently, two ideas have been added to the discussion on positive and normative aid allocation: To select countries based on some index or measurement of success ("aid selectivity") and the search for an "optimal allocation rule" serving as a (poverty minimization) guideline for allocation. Regarding the former, the discussion is circling around the question whether the existence of "good policies" can serve as an effective allocation criterion. Finally, the aid allocation process is embedded into a complex system of donor policies and strategies, which have passed through a number of developments since the mid 1990s that altered the focus of aid allocation policies. In general, they can be described as:

- A shift towards goal-oriented development cooperation (Millennium Development Goals)
- A shift from debt restructuring to debt relief
- A shift from structural adjustment policies to country-owned poverty reduction strategies.

In the present chapter, the starting point for deriving the major explanatory variables for ODA allocation is an analysis of present ODA allocation patterns (Sect. 3.2). Approaches taking into account normative criteria, optimal allocation rules and selectivity will be examined in Sect. 3.3. The shift in donors' allocation policies and their implications will be examined in the subsequent Sects. 3.4 to 3.6. Sect. 3.7 recapitulates.

3.2 Present allocation of ODA

3.2.1 Data sources and limitations

The data on ODA allocation is taken from the DAC database. It provides annual data since 1960 for all sources (donors) and destinations (recipients). Until not otherwise specified, the data used in this section has been obtained by the DAC. Since the potential three-dimensional matrix of bilateral and multilateral donors, recipients and number of years examined is considerably large, the main attention in this section is on the group of LDCs and the derivation of explanatory factors of aid allocation.

---

194 See McGillivray (2004) for a review of these approaches.

3.2.2 ODA recipient regions and countries

Figs. 3.1 to 3.3 provide time-series data on the regional and income level allocation of ODA. Africa, especially the sub-Saharan region, has been under the spotlight of recent allocating decisions, after a declining share of total aid during the 1990s. More than one third of all net official flows (aid plus debt, excluding technical cooperation grants) are allocated to sub-Saharan African countries, accumulating to $25.6 billion in 2004. This represents a surge from relative constant figures between 1998 ($10.2 billion) and 2001 ($10.6 billion) and can be traced back almost exclusively to increases in bilateral aid grants. This tendency is likely to continue: At least half of all pledged European ODA is planned to be assigned to Africa. In 2003 and 2004, the major ODA share goes to LDCs with a GNI per capita of less than $825. Some lower middle-income countries (LMICs, e.g. Algeria, Brazil, China and Thailand), which have a per capita GNI of less than $3,255, also receive a substantial part, while a relatively small fraction is assigned to other low-income countries (OLICs) and upper middle-income countries (UMICs, e.g. Argentina, Chile). Fig. 3.3 depicts the developments of total grants and total net loans from DAC members to LDCs between 1960 and 2004. Loans played almost no role except in the 1970s and 1980s, whereas grants make up the major part. The sum of total grants and net loans to LDCs increased sharply since 2002 to about $16 billion annually in 2003 and 2004.

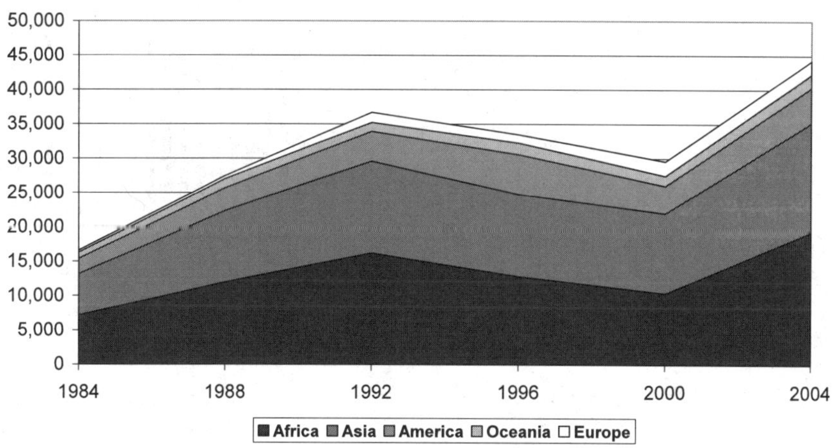

Fig. 3.1. Allocation of total net ODA to regions, 1984–2004 [in $ millions]

Source: Author's calculations based on DAC data

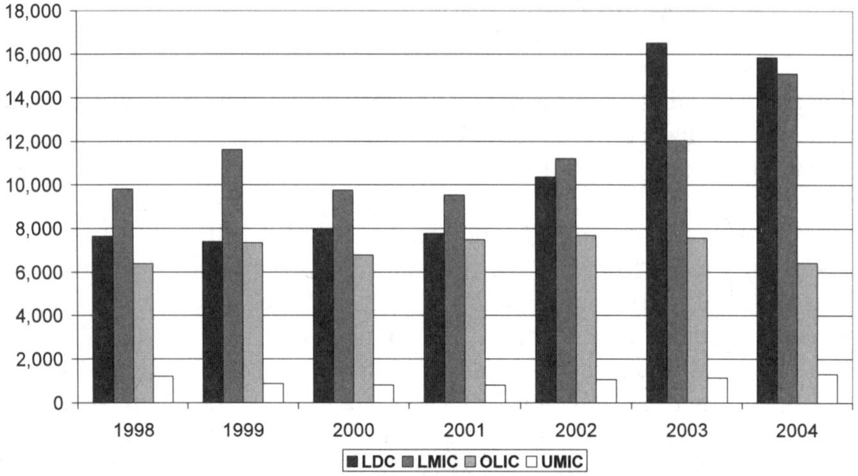

Fig. 3.2. Allocation of DAC's total net ODA to selected country groups, 1998–2004 [in $ millions]

Source: Author's calculations based on DAC data

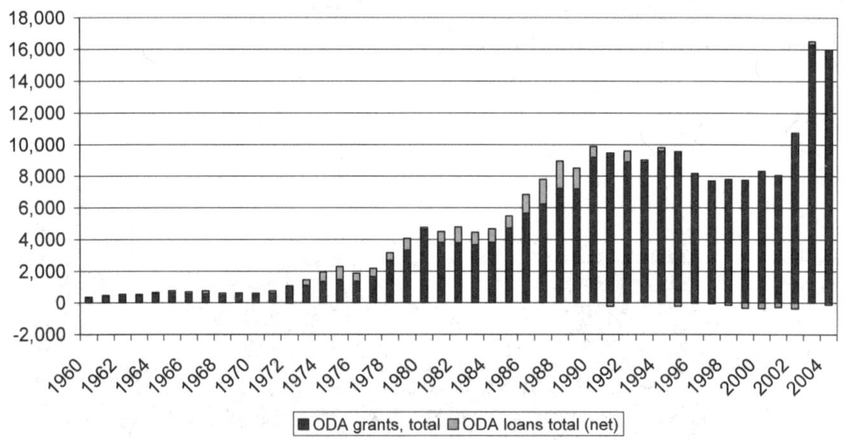

Fig. 3.3. DAC ODA total grants and total net loans to LDCs, 1960–2004 [in $ millions)

Source: Author's calculations based on DAC data

The additional ODA funds to the group of LDCs are allocated among all countries, but with different emphasis. The growth rates of total net ODA disbursements to LDCs have averaged at least 90% for the years 2000–2004 in each LDC.[195] The highest 5-year-averaged annual growth rates have Sudan (175%), Angola (164%), Solomon Islands (169%), Madagascar (169%), Liberia (182%) and the Democratic Republic of Congo (Zaire, 459%). The main LDC recipients in 2004 (in current dollars) were Afghanistan ($1.70 billion), Angola ($1.00 billion), the Democratic Republic of Congo ($1.16 billion), Ethiopia ($1.03 billion) and Tanzania ($1.03 billion).

3.2.3 Factors explaining bilateral and multilateral aid allocation

According to Maizel and Nissanke[196], factors explaining the allocation of aid among recipients can be divided into two groups: Recipients' needs and donors' interest. The leading viewpoint in the late 1970s and 1980s for the allocation decision of foreign aid, as analyzed by McKinley and Little[197] and others, was that donor interest is responsible for the allocation of bilateral aid, while recipients' needs are the main cause for the allocation of multilateral aid. This rather unilateral viewpoint, however, is challenged when applying modern research techniques. It has been shown that bilateral aid in the 1970s and 80s has been more concentrated to poor countries than previously thought.[198] Nevertheless, Berthélemy and Tichit[199] have shown that the importance of donors' interest for aid allocation declined after the end of the Cold War, but that there are still remarkable differences in the degree of donor countries' altruism,[200] with the general exemption of food aid.[201]

[195] Own calculations based on DAC data.

[196] See Maizel and Nissanke (1984).

[197] See McKinley and Little (1977) and following research. The authors concluded that there are "no grounds for asserting that humanitarian criteria have any significant direct influence" (p. 243) on allocation.

[198] See McGillivray (2003) who ran econometric tests of aid allocation suggesting that developmental criteria were important variables influencing bilateral aid allocation during the Cold War.

[199] See Berthélemy and Tichit (2004).

[200] In a three-dimensional panel dataset, Berthélemy (2006) shows substantial heterogeneity in donor behavior. Switzerland, Austria, Ireland and the Scandinavian donors are the most altruistic. Australia, France, Italy and, to a lesser extent, Japan and the United States are among the most egoistic.

[201] Neumayer (2005) finds donor interest to play a role only in the form of preferential treatment of geographically close countries. Neither military-strategic nor export-interests or colonial past seem to matter in the allocation of food aid. Instead, the needs motive matters most.

A large number of factors influence the allocation of ODA, among which the following are noteworthy:

- Bilateral donors give a sizable amount of aid to their geographical neighbours and to their region of origin. One example is Australia that allocates a sizable share of ODA to Indonesia and other countries in Oceania. A similar pattern can be detected for Japan (to Asia) and Europe (to Africa). Table 3.1 provides some details on the geographical pattern of bilateral aid allocation, based on 1980–2000 averages.
- Colonial and historical ties still seem to affect the allocation of bilateral aid positively. More than 70% of British and French bilateral aid goes to their former colonies, and the highest percentage of Spanish bilateral aid is directed towards South America. Similar disbursement patterns can be found for Portugal, the Netherlands and their respective colonies (see also Table 3.1).
- Linguistic and ethnic ties play a factor in explaining bilateral aid flows. France, Belgium Switzerland, Luxembourg and Canada, for example, give high percentage shares of their sub-Saharan African bilateral aid to Francophone countries (Table 3.1).
- Political and strategic alliances between donor and recipient countries serve as a decision factor for bilateral aid. This concerns predominantly the United States and its strategic allies Israel, Egypt and Jordan, who received 31% of all US bilateral aid (Table 3.1).
- Various case study evidence signifies that political changes in donor countries (US), organizational capacity of the recipient organization (Brazil), membership in the Commonwealth and La Francophonie (Canada) and commercial interests (Canada, UK) all matter for bilateral aid allocation.[202]
- Another factor in donor countries affecting aid allocation has been discovered by Lahiri and Raimondos-Møller who developed a model of fo-

[202] Fleck and Kilby (2006) assess the role of political changes in the United States and conclude that with a liberal president and Congress, development concerns receive more weight than under a more conservative Congress. Reinhardt (2006) finds micro-level determinants such as signals of whether recipients will implement aid most effectively to be influential variables and presents evidence for Brazil. MacDonald and Hoddinott (2004) find that human rights and membership in the Commonwealth and La Francophonie affect aid flows and that Canadian aid flows became less altruistic over time (1984–2000), whereas commercial motives gained in importance. The results of McGillivray and Oczkowski (1992) indicate that UK aid allocation is influenced by commercial, humanitarian and political interests and that there is a UK bias favoring Commonwealth members.

reign aid allocation in which they assess domestic political factors and the role of lobbying in donor countries. "Lobbying is done by ethnic groups who are asymmetrically altruistic to specific recipient governments."[203] By differentiating between rich and poor ethnic group lobbies in a donor country, they show that the degree of corruption in the donor country and the degree of aid fatigue in the donor country are explanatory variables for aid allocation.

- Alesina and Weder as well as Svensson find no evidence that corrupt regimes receive less ODA or debt relief.[204] However, there are differences across donor countries: While Scandinavian donors and Australia reward less corrupt recipients, the United States favour democracies, but seem to pay no attention to the quality of governments in recipient countries.
- Neumayer[205] identifies an interesting inconsistency among donor countries: Some allocations are influenced significantly by respect for civil/political rights and personal integrity rights, but most others remain insignificant. Only two countries, Japan and the UK, give more aid to countries with greater respect to both aspects simultaneously. As a sum, the authors conclude from their analysis that "[r]espect for human rights does not exert a consistent influence on aid allocation by most donors. [...] There is not a single donor that would consistently screen out countries with low respect for civil/political and personal integrity rights and would give more aid to countries with higher respect for both aspects of human rights."[206]

[203] Lahiri and Raimondos-Møller (2000), p. 76.
[204] See Alesina and Weder (2002) as well as Svensson (2000).
[205] See Neumayer (2003a).
[206] See ibid., p. 664.

Table 3.1. Geographical pattern of bilateral aid allocation, based on 1980–2000 average

Donor	% of total bilateral aid received by						% of bilateral aid to Africa received by:				% of bilateral aid to Asia received by:		
	U.S. strategic allies	Africa	America	Asia	Europe	Oceania	Former British colonies	Former French colonies	Former Portu-guese colonies	Frm. US colony of Libe-ria	Former British colonies	Former Dutch col-ony of In-donesia	Former US and Spanish "colony" of Philippines
Australia	1.05	8.00	0.14	39.05	0.51	45.43	49.55	2.71	15.42	0.00	21.44	25.59	10.70
Austria	3.09	21.55	4.28	25.38	16.91	0.11	48.29	27.14	8.45	0.15	4.98	42.47	2.17
Belgium	0.49	55.77	9.46	10.10	0.91	0.04	13.26	74.76	1.63	0.12	11.55	17.10	9.67
Canada	2.47	27.77	10.55	21.92	0.84	0.22	37.86	40.72	5.95	0.23	54.86	9.95	5.06
Denmark	2.92	45.01	5.01	21.48	0.37	0.01	68.01	13.01	9.87	0.26	59.06	1.63	1.85
Finland	3.52	44.81	5.96	22.31	3.23	0.07	60.06	2.79	12.28	0.37	37.46	2.48	1.52
France	4.32	56.72	4.23	9.83	1.17	13.58	6.03	72.05	2.19	0.05	22.26	14.54	3.01
Germany	6.52	28.90	10.14	24.97	6.44	0.25	38.91	40.19	5.20	0.94	28.70	9.69	4.05
Greece	1.67	5.66	0.46	14.72	66.96	0.03	22.78	19.53	0.23	0.00	1.47	0.20	0.12
Ireland	0.56	57.50	2.35	5.93	3.69	0.06	64.75	6.51	7.44	0.37	27.88	0.98	2.15
Italy	6.65	56.55	13.30	11.08	7.05	0.00	22.05	24.14	17.21	0.02	18.97	8.02	6.42
Japan	3.60	14.88	8.75	62.57	1.50	1.53	54.21	31.55	3.71	0.52	25.29	18.76	10.10
Luxembg.	0.19	50.29	18.32	16.07	6.72	0.03	21.39	48.05	1.78	0.00	26.45	0.64	5.72
Netherlds.	1.60	32.03	19.00	22.90	3.58	0.14	45.29	23.56	10.36	0.58	47.96	15.91	3.98
New Zeal.	0.01	2.73	0.97	16.19	0.13	67.82	66.34	10.88	4.71	0.35	10.96	25.48	12.30
Norway	0.30	47.14	6.64	22.80	5.44	0.08	57.44	10.02	17.60	0.27	53.53	3.11	2.50
Portugal	0.13	86.85	0.32	5.96	0.45	0.00	0.29	0.14	58.09	0.00	0.26	0.00	0.00
Spain	0.43	23.83	39.01	16.77	2.06	0.00	12.96	41.06	26.82	0.11	6.12	20.62	7.50
Sweden	0.40	40.33	8.75	22.24	3.61	0.03	53.77	2.88	21.93	0.35	44.04	0.25	1.95
Swiss	1.90	33.43	11.55	22.77	4.61	0.07	23.98	48.22	11.70	0.46	47.88	10.09	2.54
UK	1.34	36.86	7.79	26.51	2.80	1.73	71.43	5.49	7.00	0.38	72.31	6.77	1.48
USA	31.15	28.93	14.53	27.71	2.38	2.14	29.93	28.96	7.02	3.38	14.07	2.11	6.51
All DAC	9.79	32.66	10.46	29.64	2.97	3.74	34.51	37.26	8.14	0.67	27.88	12.37	6.95

Source: Round and Odedokun (2004), p. 296, based on the OECD DAC database and World Development Indicators.
Note: The background colors mirror the percentage of aid received and was added by the author.

Larger countries tend to receive more aid in absolute (dollar) terms, but receive less aid per capita. India, China and Indonesia belonged to the top 5 aid recipients in (2000–2003 average) in absolute terms, but are at the bottom in terms of per capita aid disbursements. As for multilateral foreign aid, the European Commission is characterized by a bias in favour of small countries and countries covered under the Lomé Convention.[207] The combined aid receipts of countries with a population less than 10 million account for 30 percent of all total ODA allocation, although these countries account for only 6 percent of the population in all aid recipient countries.[208] The small country bias (also known as population bias) effect can be attributed to several causes. The greater openness of many small economies results in a greater need of financing imports. Moreover, small countries might be favoured by donors because of their benign vote in the UN (allocating ODA to many small countries then is more favourable than ODA to one large country). Finally, aid monitoring costs are lower in small countries, resulting in higher aid effectiveness and more attractiveness for multilateral donors.

3.3 Optimal allocation, aid targeting and selectivity

Over the past years, research on aid allocation has moved from the analysis of actual allocation patterns and the factors explaining their causes to the question how aid should be allocated. The dominant paradigm that has evolved from the existing studies is that aid is more effective in countries with better policies and better institutional quality. The role of good policies will be examined in Sect. 3.3.1. Under the umbrella of maximizing poverty reduction, this paradigm has led to the development of poverty-efficient ("optimal") allocation rules (Sect. 3.3.2) and studying the poverty focus of ODA (Sect. 3.3.3), and, as a result, increased selectivity of ODA recipients (Sect. 3.3.4). One direct policy strategy outcome is the United States' Millennium Challenge Account (Sect. 3.3.5).

[207] See Arvin et al. (2001). The Lomé Convention gives favourable trade conditions to African, Caribbean and Pacific (ACP) countries. See also Powell (2003) for the population bias.

[208] See OECD (2005b), p. 32.

3.3.1 The role of "good policies"

In 1997, Craig Burnside and David Dollar published their study "Aid, Policies and Growth", in which they assessed the relationship among foreign aid, economic policies, and growth per capita using a new database.[209] Their results spurred immense interest among researchers and practitioners and can be regarded as a very influential paper. Burnside and Dollar use a neoclassical growth model and a panel regression technique for 1970–1993 data, including other country characteristic variables. They find "that aid has a positive impact on growth in developing countries with good fiscal, monetary, and trade policies."[210] Put briefly: Aid is more effective when "good policies" are in place. The model covers 56 countries (272 observations altogether, 189 excluding middle-income countries) and controls for institutional and political variables as well as budget surplus, inflation, openness, population, and donor countries' strategic interest. The policy and the aid variable are both endogenously explained, i.e. "aid may be a function of policy and/or […] policy may be a function of aid"[211]. The authors use an interaction term ("aid*policy interaction term") to capture the effect that aid efficiency is dependent on the quality of the economic policies of the recipient country.[212] Their findings were as follows:

- *On average*, aid has almost no impact on growth.
- More bilateral aid is allocated to countries with good policies.
- Aid has not systematically affected the policies pursued in recipient countries.
- Bilateral aid increases government spending (which in turn does not promote growth).
- In general, good policies are "rewarded" by higher aid.
- If more aid were allocated to countries with good policies, the mean growth rate of poor countries in the sample would rise from 1.1% to 1.44%.

Their suggestion was to allocate more aid on the basis of a good policy environment. As Easterly et al. (2003) remark, "international aid agencies, public policymakers, and the press quickly recognized the importance of

[209] The 1997 version is a World Bank working paper. The study was published in 2000 in The American Economic Review. The results also show up in the World Bank Report "Assessing Aid" (1998).

[210] Burnside and Dollar (1997), p. 2.

[211] Ibid., p. 11.

[212] See Hansen and Tarp (1999), p. 12. A substantial share of criticism is devoted to this aid*policy interaction term.

the BD [Burnside and Dollar] findings".[213] It was a theoretical justification for policy makers in various countries to implement a new selective aid policy.[214] "This intriguing result – which is broadly in line with the 'Washington consensus' view of development – is appealing to many."[215]

However, there has also been widespread criticism of the Burnside/Dollar findings. While some address methodological issues, other authors use the exact same dataset and come to different conclusions. Among the methodological issues, the following are noteworthy:

- Grouping the countries may explain the largest share of variation of the aid*policy term.
- Variations in the variables used and defined as well as the indicators used to model good policies alter the results.
- In a remodelling and expansion (of missing data) of the Burnside and Dollar findings, Hansen and Tarp (1999) show that the aid*policy interaction term is insignificant, suggesting that aid is positively correlated also with countries that have a poor policy environment.[216]
- Hansen and Tarp (2001) as well as Dalgaard and Hansen (2001) point to the fact that the Burnside and Dollar results miss the correct inclusion of diminishing returns, i.e. they neglect the existence of a non-linear aid-growth relationship.
- If the outliers in the Burnside and Dollar study are included, the aid*policy interaction term becomes insignificant.
- In contrast to Burnside and Dollar's findings, aid may indeed affect policy.[217]
- "The importance of country-specific circumstances probably accounts for the limited robustness of many cross-section regression findings on the links between policies and growth."[218]
- Dayton-Johnson and Hoddinott, using the Burnside-Dollar dataset, detect regional differences in the sense that outside sub-Saharan countries aid does promote growth despite of policies, whereas in sub-Saharan countries it does only when there are good policies in place.

---

213 Easterly et al. (2003), p. 1.

214 According to Dayton-Johnson and Hoddinott, the governments of the Netherlands, the UK, Canada and Germany were refocusing their ODA policies. See Dayton-Johnson and Hoddinott (2003), p. 2.

215 See Hansen and Tarp (1999), p. 17.

216 See Hansen and Tarp (2000).

217 See Chauvet and Guillaumont (2002). The authors suggest to give more aid to countries with poor policies, because they find that the poorer the previous policy level the more effective aid.

218 IMF (2004), p. 18. See also Lucas (2002).

Easterly et al. (2003) show that the Burnside and Dollar result has to be interpreted very cautiously. They expand the Burnside and Dollar model by collecting additional data (to include 356 observations) covering the period 1970 to 1997 and 62 countries. Using the exact same methodology, their result is that the decisive aid*policy term (that lead Burnside and Dollar to their result) is now insignificant. Due to the analysis of Easterly et al., the proposition that aid creates growth in a good policy environment cannot be sustained. The extension of observations that turns the result upside down shows how the same approach can lead to different results and that the selected data points (especially the selected time period) have a great impact on the result. Thus, the value of these studies is diminished when there are some single, but decisive data points (outliers) involved as is often the case in aid allocation. Usually, extreme outliers are omitted in regression approaches, leading to a more general result which often is intended. In other words: Regression-based studies are a selectivity task as well. In a response, Burnside and Dollar remark that it is the extension of new countries, not filling in missing data points that is responsible for the different results.[219]

3.3.2 Optimal allocation rules

On the basis of the Burnside and Dollar findings, Collier and Dollar (1999) use a larger dataset and the CPIA score developed by the World Bank as alternative index for the policy variable.[220] They confirm the proposition that policy is important, noting that an increase of 1% in aid (measured as a percentage of GDP in Purchasing Power Parity terms), increases growth by 0.6 percent in countries with good policies, by 0.4 percent in countries with average policies, and 0.2 percent in countries with poor policies. This is in line with some earlier findings, which do not make use of an aid policy interaction term, that good policies are important for aid to be effective.[221]

Much more important, however, the authors develop an allocation rule that allows aid agencies faced with limited information about the recipient country to allocate limited aid efficiently and to maximize the number of people lifted out of poverty.[222] The underlying assumptions are: i) policies

[219] Burnside and Dollar (2004).

[220] CPIA stands for Country Policy and Institutional Assessment and describes the World Bank's approach to measure the policy and institutional quality of countries.

[221] See, for example, Hadjimichael et al. (1995) and Durbarry et al. (1998).

[222] See Collier and Dollar (1999).

matter for aid to be effective and ii) the aid-growth relationship is characterized by positive, but diminishing marginal returns. Taking into account political processes and interest groups, the allocation rule ("poverty-efficient allocation") is designed to allocate aid to countries with the most poverty and the best policies, as measured by their CPIA score.[223] It is important to note that the optimal allocation rule of Collier and Dollar minimizes global poverty, not necessarily the poverty in each low-income country. "[A]n extra dollar of aid in any given country decreases the number of people living below the income poverty line by an identical amount as in any other country."[224] Thus, in a poverty-efficient allocation, the marginal cost of poverty reduction is equalized across all recipient countries.

Collier and Dollar show that the present allocation is "radically"[225] different from an optimal allocation. The average cost of poverty reduction (i.e. the average cost of lifting a person permanently out of poverty) is $2,516, compared to $1,333 in an optimal aid allocation as defined above. Reallocating aid to countries with high CPIA scores could, according to Collier and Dollar, double the number of people lifted out of extreme poverty worldwide.[226] Similar results are reached by Baulch[227] who discovered that at least some donors do not allocate their ODA in a way that is consistent with the Millennium Development Goals. In this context, Akram[228] finds no evidence that the level of per capita income has any effect on the volume of aid provided or the level of per capita aid received.

Selecting countries based on their performance in policy and institutional indicators would have serious implications for the pre-existing aid allocation. In a test of their optimal allocation rule, Collier and Dollar find that the lowest marginal cost of poverty reduction (approx. $600) exists in Ethiopia, Bangladesh, India and Uganda. Consequently, in an unconstrained optimum, India would receive the bulk of ODA, whereas countries with higher marginal cost of poverty reduction such as Chile would receive zero allocation. Mosley et al. applied the Collier/Dollar rule for se-

[223] Beynon also confirms the Collier/Dollar findings using an extensive set of sensitivity tests with 25 different scenarios. See Beynon (2003).

[224] McGillivray (2006), p. 6.

[225] Collier and Dollar (1999), p. 1.

[226] For a critical review of the Collier and Dollar model as well as modifications, see Beynon (2003), p. 710.

[227] See Baulch (2004), p. 22. However, there are differences concerning the progressivity of different donor's aid allocations, depending on the MDG indicator chosen. Yet all donors (bilateral and multilateral) "distribute less aid to the most populous and deprived countries that their shares of global poverty, child malnutrition and under-five mortality suggest is needed." (p. 23).

[228] See Akram (2003), p. 1356.

lected African countries. The results listed in Table 3.2 indicate the potential reallocation of aid flows.

Table 3.2. The Collier-Dollar optimal allocation rule applied for African countries

Recipient country	Poverty efficient aid [percent of GDP]	1996 aid [percent of GDP]
Ethiopia	7.52	2.90
Ghana	5.23	2.04
Senegal	7.07	4.03
Uganda	8.51	3.34
Angola	1.20	2.45
Rep. of Congo	4.60	8.86
Sierra Leone	5.64	8.11
Cape Verde	5.95	15.49
Guinea-Bissau	5.86	15.85
Gabon	0.36	1.51
Namibia	1.27	2.27

Source: Mosley et al. (2004), cited in Thiele (2005), p. 41

There are a number of concerns regarding the usefulness of the CPIA score for deriving optimal allocation rules.[229] First, the CPIA score assesses the quality of a country's institutional and policy framework in 20 dimensions, grouped into four categories[230] and there could be trade-offs (conflicts) between the various constituents of the index (e.g., budget balance vs. health care expenditures). Second, there are endogeneity concerns because policies, institutions and growth are interdependent variables (it has been shown by Dalgaard et al. in a causality analysis that changes in the CPIA score are Granger-caused by economic growth). Third, there is an identification problem with other significant variables explaining the impact of aid. More specifically, "the positive interaction between aid and CPIA [...] may well be caused by the low impact of aid in the tropical region."[231] Fourth, growth elasticities of poverty are not uniform as assumed by Collier and Dollar, but can vary substantially as Ravallion (2001) has verified. Fifth, selectivity is subject to recipient countries' conditions: The use of CPIA scores suggests that "in all the countries, whatever their specificities

[229] See Dalgaard et al. (2004), p. 209f.

[230] The categories are Economic Management, Structural Policies, Policies for Social Inclusion/Equity and Public Sector Management and Institutions.

[231] Dalgaard et al. (2004), p. 211.

and preferences, it is the same kind of economic policy (defined as good) which promotes growth and increases aid efficiency."[232]

But other factors play an important role in aid effectiveness, as shown in previous sections. Sixth and finally, there is a controversial debate whether low CPIA scores indicate a poor policy and institutional environment per se, or whether unfavourable initial conditions in recipient countries are causing the low score. As already mentioned, the Collier-Dollar rule grounds its results on the Burnside-Dollar results. But accounting for climatic circumstances, Dalgaard et al. show that the aid policy interaction term becomes insignificant, whereas the term "fraction of land in the tropics and aid" becomes significant. The Collier-Dollar results must therefore be cautioned. At least, the criteria "level of poverty" and "level of policy/institutional quality" must be judged against and carefully evaluated in countries with unfavourable conditions (Chap. 5 will provide more details on such conditions). The Collier/Dollar rule should therefore not be applied in a mechanistic way.

Despite the use of CPIA scores, a number of other factors deserve attention, which will be addressed in the following list:

- The analysis of optimal allocation refers to the total amount of aid from all sources, not to the individual allocation patterns of each donor. Without an "optimal coordination" among donors, achieving optimal allocation becomes a difficult task.
- Vásquez criticizes that the selective approach to foreign aid is "based entirely on World Bank research, most of which is difficult or impossible to reproduce by outside researchers."[233] He also notes that "countries with reasonably sound policies will encounter economic growth without foreign aid."[234] In contrast, Gunning rejects the latter assertion arguing that this would lead to higher taxation as a substitution for aid.[235]
- An important question is how to deal with poor countries that have low scores in policy and institutions but high need of financial assistance (e.g., fragile states, countries in the tropics). Depending on the allocation rule, these countries may be penalized in a pure selectivity regime.[236]

---

232 Amprou et al. (2005), p. 7.

233 Vásquez (2003), p. 1. At least the Burnside and Dollar as well as the Easterly et al. datasets are available at http://www.cgdev.org.

234 Vásquez (2003), p. 2.

235 See Gunning (2000), p. 45.

236 See McGillivray (2006), p. 4.

- Factors such as colonial ties between donor and recipients may facilitate better understanding between the partners and result in improved aid effectiveness. Grounding aid solely on optimal allocation would undermine these links.
- If all donors were to follow a strict poverty-efficient allocation rule, there is a risk of underfunding or overfunding recipients if donor allocation is not closely harmonized. Donor coordination, however, has been shown to have serious lacks in the present institutional framework (Sect. 2.6). At last, if aid flows are based on rules, a different interpretation of the rules (e.g., by donor and recipient) can lead to unpredictable aid flows.

3.3.3 Aid targeting and poverty focus of ODA

The preceding sections provide two major reasons to question the poverty focus of ODA:

- The empirical analysis of ODA allocation and the studies examining donors' motives have indicated that it is not predominantly an altruistic intention inducing donors to give ODA, but a vector of other reasons.
- The present allocation scheme of donors is remarkable different from optimal allocation rules, however defined.

A recent technique developed to measure the poverty focus of ODA allocation is calculating and mapping "aid concentration curves". In his contributions, Baulch[237] compares cumulative shares of ODA disbursements with cumulative shares of population living with less than $1 a day (absolute poverty). In addition to the conventional Lorenz curve, a ranking variable (per capita income) is used, so that an aid concentration on the diagonal would indicate an aid allocation in proportion to the number of poor in each country. Concentration patterns left (above) to the diagonal indicate that more aid is allocated to the poorest countries ("progressive" aid allocation), and vice versa. Fig. 3.4 plots the aid concentration curves for selected donors.

By computing the aid allocation of various donor countries and multilateral donors, Baulch's results corroborate that the way donor countries distribute their aid differs markedly. Some of the largest bilateral donors (United States, Japan) tend to give most of their ODA to richer, middle-income countries, whereas the Netherlands and the UK spend most of their

---

[237] See Baulch (2003, 2004). See there for a detailed description of the methodology.

ODA in poor (least developed) countries. The aid concentration schemes of France and Germany are neither very pro-poor nor anti-poor.

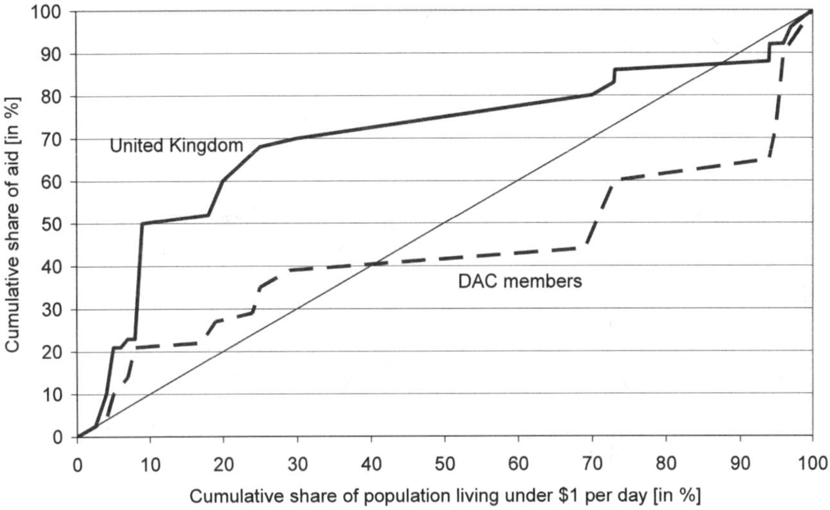

Fig. 3.4. Aid concentration curves for selected donors

Source: Author, based on the methodology of Baulch (2003), p. 10

As for multilateral organizations, the World Bank gives most of its aid to large developing countries with (absolutely) many poor people (e.g., China and India) and to some smaller LDCs. The European Commission, in contrast, gives a substantial amount of aid to middle-income countries (Brazil, South Africa, Tunisia, Turkey), with the UN having aid concentration curves somewhere between these two. Neumayer's study[238] on the determinants of aid allocation by regional multilateral development banks and United Nations agencies reveals that the former focus exclusively on economic need (as measured by per capita income), whereas the latter take into account a number of factors such as human development need, political freedom and distance from the centers of the Western world.

According to the OECD, there is some evidence for the proposition that the share of aid flows to the poorest countries increased since 1990.[239] To show this, the average per capita income in developing countries has been compared with the per capita income of the median ODA recipient, which

[238] See Neumayer (2003b).

[239] See OECD (2005b), p. 39. See there for a more detailed description of the methodology.

can also be regarded as the income level at which the middle dollar of aid was received. The average per capita income of potential aid recipients has risen by approx. 15 percent between 1990 and 2002. The median dollar of aid is now allocated to poorer countries than in 1990.

Nevertheless, the answer to the question if aid is targeted to the neediest depends critically on the choice of measure. In most studies, per capita income, the Human Development Index or poverty lines (people living below a certain income threshold) are applied. If an index of absolute poverty is used, as in a recent sample of Nunnenkamp, "the evidence does not support claims that aid has become more focused on countries with low per-capita income and high incidence of absolute poverty. To the contrary, low-income recipients received a lower share of multilateral aid in the most recent sub-period (1999–2002) than in the more distant past; essentially the same is true when absolute poverty is taken as an indicator of need […]."[240] The data show that the share of ODA going to the poorest countries (in which absolute poverty is above the median) is below 50 percent. For some bilateral donors (e.g., Germany), this percentage has even decreased (from 44.5% in the period 1993–1998 to 43.2% in 1999–2003).[241] According to the progressive pledges made on international conferences, this development seems rather surprising. It seems that multilateral and bilateral donors are hesitant in correcting their allocation for a change of income status of recipients (e.g., China and India still receive substantial absolute amounts of aid despite their high growth rate). On the other hand, more recent allocation patterns, based on aid commitments rather than disbursements, indicate that most ODA is allocated to LDCs, especially in Sub-Saharan Africa (see Sect. 3.1). Finally, it should be added that a comparison within a relatively short time frame (e.g., several years) is subject to the constraint that some share of ODA is disbursed in multi-annual packages, for instance to finance medium- to long-term projects. Clearly, a quick shift in allocation is not advisable in this case and could do more harm to aid effectiveness than good.

3.3.4 Selectivity policies of bilateral and multilateral donors

The empirical findings of Collier, Dollar and others have had wide-reaching implications for the formulation of allocation policies of bilateral and multilateral donors. The idea of rules-based allocation has been adopted by the governments of the United States (Millennium Challenge

[240] Nunnenkamp (2005a), p. 12.
[241] See Nunnenkamp (2005b), p. 18f.

Account, see next section), the UK (DFID), the Netherlands, Canada and Germany[242] as well as World Bank and IMF (2005) in their annual Global Monitoring Reports. The World Bank has concluded that "financial assistance is being increasingly allocated to countries that have reasonably good policies and institutions – that is, countries that can best use aid for poverty alleviation."[243] Dalgaard et al. find that "in a very short time the Collier-Dollar model has moved from an academic idea (with a strong policy message) to something very concrete in the donor community."[244] The proposition that selectivity has increased, is also confirmed by Dollar and Levin (2004). Using a new data set focusing on the 1990s, Dollar and Levin propose a policy selectivity index "measuring the extent to which a donor's assistance is targeted to countries with sound institutions and policies, controlling for per capita income and population."[245] They confirm their previous proposition that the impact of aid depends on the quality of state institutions and policies. They also provide non-regression-based evidence (e.g., polls[246]) that the effectiveness of aid is dependent on good institutions and policies. In their analysis, they account for the fact that the allocation of aid has changed over time.[247] Moreover, their study indicates that selectivity is a phenomenon that increased since the mid 1990s. Other studies confirming this new selectivity trend have been conducted by McGillivray[248] (based on time series data between 1968 and 1999) and Jones et al. (survey data).[249] It is consistent with the fact that after the end of the Cold War, donors pay more attention to developmental criteria.

---

[242] See Dayton-Johnson and Hoddinott (2003), p. 2.

[243] World Bank (2002b), p. 29.

[244] Dalgaard et al. (2004), p. 209.

[245] Dollar and Levin (2004).

[246] Burnside and Dollar quote a recent poll conducted by the World Bank among "opinion makers" showing that 84% somewhat or strongly agree that because of corruption, foreign assistance to developing countries is mostly wasted. See PRSA (2003).

[247] One (valid) purpose of Burnside and Dollar's updated study is that they do not claim that their results do hold in every possible case. Of course, one can construct situations in which the general finding does not hold (a natural problem of cross-country regression analyses).

[248] See McGillivray (2005).

[249] See Jones et al. (2004).

3.3.5 Extensions of the selectivity approach

Besides good policies and sound institutions, additional criteria of selectivity could be used as well. Among other variables, the per capita income elasticity of aid, the vulnerability to exogenous shocks and the level of human capital have been considered.[250] In an attempt to illustrate the predicaments associated with aid selectivity, Amprou et al.[251] provide several extensions, which will be briefly sketched here.

- Selectivity based on one criterion (dichotomic approach):
  Selectivity in the World Bank's and IMF's Global Monitoring Report is carried out by dividing countries into two groups, those with good and those with bad policies/institutions, according to their respective CPIA score. Donors are categorized following the amount of ODA they allocate to each group and thus classified and ranked as donors with low, medium or high aid selectivity. Amprou et al. show that the choice of another distinguishing criterion (here: being an LDC or not) can also be justified. Comparing the two criteria, it is shown that donors' classification is significantly different depending on the criteria applied.
- Selectivity measured by aid elasticities from a model of geographical allocation:
  Amprou et al. develop a number of alternative functions of aid allocation and compare them to the selectivity index originated by Dollar and Levin (see previous section). It is shown that there are major changes in the selectivity ranking if more than one criterion is applied. The four criteria used are the level of income, the quality of governance, economic vulnerability and human capital. In fact, for some of the allocation functions, the ranking is nearly reversed. Especially human capital, which some donors consider much more intensively than others, explains much of this reversal.
- Selectivity measured from an average profile of recipient countries:
  An average profile of the aid recipients of each donor is calculated, weighted by the proportion of its aid allocated to each country. Using the same four criteria as above, donors' preferred criteria can be derived. A rather straightforward result is the low-income focus of the World Bank (due to its mandate). The criterion "good governance" is preferred by the World Bank, but less by the IMF, and even less by the UN. Among the bilateral donors, Japan, Denmark, Spain and Luxembourg place most attention on good governance, whereas France con-

[250] See Amprou et al. (2005), p. 5f.
[251] See ibid., p. 9f.

centrates its allocation according to the level of income per capita (level of poverty) and the level of human capital. The European Commission, the United Kingdom and the United States do not have any specific inclination. Alternative rankings are computed taking into consideration donor preferences resulting from colonial and historical ties. The authors highlight the fact that even minor adjustments may change the ranking significantly.

3.3.6 Millennium Challenge Account

The Millennium Challenge Account is a bilateral aid program that pledges aid grounded on countries' track records in certain indicators. It has been argued by some as being the most straight policy outcome resulting from the Burnside and Dollar findings.

Description and eligibility criteria

The Millennium Challenge Account (MCA) is a US initiative providing additional financial assistance to selected countries.[252] The eligibility hinges on recipient countries' per capita income (see Table 3.3). The intention of the MCA is to give more resources to a small number of countries (15 to 20), a shift from former approaches (e.g., the HIPC initiative) where the number of actual recipients was significantly higher. The financial resources will be provided predominantly in the form of grants and are limited to countries that have shown "a commitment to ruling justly, investing in people, and encouraging economic freedom"[253]. They can thus be regarded as a performance-based "reward" (tied aid). Although funding will be coordinated with other multilateral ODA organizations, it will not be channeled through these agencies. Instead, a governmental corporation called the Millennium Challenge Corporation (MCC) was founded in January 2004 with the US Secretary of State serving as the Chairman of the Board.[254] It is intended that countries who qualified will submit a plan how to utilize MCA funds. Project responsibility and ownership remain with the recipient country.

---

[252] See Brainard et al. (2003) for a detailed overview of the MCA.

[253] See Bush (2002), Millennium Challenge Account – A Presidential Initiative.

[254] Comparing the assistance-to-staff ratios for a number of bilateral aid agencies, Brainard (2003), p. 163 comes to the conclusion that the intended staff of 100 is calculated too low. With a $50 million per member staff annually, he argues the MCA needs more human resources to deal with project proposals worth $5 billion in FY 2006.

Table 3.3. MCA eligibility criteria

Fiscal Year 2004	In order to be eligible, countries must have a per capita income of $1,435 or less and must be eligible for assistance from the IDA (74 countries).[255]
Fiscal Year 2005	In order to be eligible, countries must have a per capita income of $1,435 or less (87 countries).[256]
Fiscal Year 2006	Also countries that have a per capita income between $1,435 and $2,975 are eligible (28 countries in addition to the 87 countries of FY 2005).[257]

Source: Millennium Challenge Corporation (2004)

Eligibility indicators

Countries may qualify based on sixteen criteria in three categories[258]:

- Ruling justly (civil liberties, political rights, voice and accountability, government effectiveness, rule of law, control of corruption),
- Investing in people (public expenditures on health as percent of GDP, immunization rates: DPT3 and measles, public primary education spending as percent of GDP, primary education completion rate),
- Encouraging economic freedom (country credit rating, 1-year consumer price inflation, fiscal policy, trade policy, regulatory quality, days to start a business).

In order to be selected, a country needs to perform above the median in relation to its peers on at least half of the indicators in each of the three pol-

[255] Twelve countries are subject to legal provisions that prohibit them from taking part.

[256] This number refers to the historical cut-off date for IDA assistance.

[257] This group of countries will be judged separately from the countries with per capita incomes less than $1,435. However, Radelet proposes that "[…] this group should be dropped from the MCA […] because these 28 have access to other financing and because their inclusion in the pool raises the risk of politicizing allocation decisions." See Radelet (2003a), p. 179.

[258] In the first category, two indicators are taken from Freedom House, the other four from the World Bank Institute. The indicators of the second category stem from a mix of different sources: Institutional Investor Magazine, national governments, World Bank, The Heritage Foundation's Index of Economic Freedom, World Bank Institute, and others. The third category's indicators are from national governments, WHO, World Bank and UNESCO.

icy categories and above the median on the corruption indicator.[259] However, official documents allow for some exceptions and a significant degree of subjectivity.[260] Consequently, the use of such indicators is controversially discussed in the literature.[261] The following arguments are noteworthy:

- While the public availability of the indicators' data supports transparency, the World Bank Institute Corruption Index is a pass/fail indicator.[262] Based on this index, two countries failed to qualify due to a lower than median corruption index in 2004, four countries in 2005.[263]
- Brainard and Driscoll (2003)[264] have proposed a regional measurement of the recipient countries' performance, e.g. grouping all African countries together and grade them against their peers in the region. This approach would take into consideration regional disparities and characteristics.
- Measuring each country against the median of all countries leaves no ample space for individual country characteristics, individual development strategies or outlier values even in a single category.
- Radelet et al. (2004)[265] criticize the design of some of the indicators (e.g., very narrow and discrete scales that make above the median scores harder to achieve). Hence, they suggest changing the passing criteria to "equal or above".

---

259 The criteria "inflation" is an exemption. A country has to have an inflation of less than 20%, regardless of other countries' values.

260 "The indicators methodology will be the predominant basis for determining which countries will be eligible for MCA assistance. In addition, the Board may exercise discretion in evaluating and translating the indicators into a final list of eligible countries. In this respect, the Board may also consider whether any adjustments should be made for data gaps, lags, trends, or other weaknesses in particular indicators. Likewise, the Board may deem a country ineligible if it performs substantially below average on any indicator and has not taken appropriate measures to address this shortcoming. Where necessary, the Board may also take into account other data and quantitative information as well as qualitative information to determine whether a country performed satisfactorily in relation to its peers in a given category." Millennium Challenge Corporation (2004), p. 2.

261 See Caliari (2003), Radelet (2003a, 2003b, 2003c, 2004) and Kaufman and Kraay (2002).

262 See Caliari (2003), p. 2.

263 See Radelet (2003a), p. 177.

264 See Brainard and Driscoll (2003), p. 1.

265 See Radelet et al. (2004), p. 4.

- Brainard and Driscoll note that "as country data are updated, the qualifying level for each indicator will be a constantly shifting target."[266] On the other hand, the introduction of more competition for financial resources is explicitly intended by the MCA.
- Brainard[267] makes a case in point when it comes to the interrelatedness of indicators. For example, the indicators regarding governance and corruption might be correlated.
- Clemens and Radelet[268] identified a trade-off between the number of MCA countries and aid effectiveness, based on quantitative estimates by Collier and Dollar (2002)[269] and point to the complex task of finding the optimal number of countries for MCA aid. According to their results, the optimum number of countries could lie between 30 and 40, assuming the objective is to reach maximum growth for a maximum number of people.
- The exit problem: Countries qualifying in the first year do not necessarily qualify in subsequent years, either because of poor results in their project activities, a decline of their indicator ratings and a loss of qualification status or because their income rises above the threshold level ("graduation"). Due to possible imperfections in the MCA methodology (e.g., data shortcomings), the authors suggest not to abandon running projects when a country only closely fails to qualify in one indicator, but to send a clear signal by partially reduce funding. In extreme cases of political conflicts, funding could be stopped completely. In the case of graduation, funding could gradually phase out.

Applegarth (2003) proposes to leverage MCA financial resources with private resources[270], to promote profitable investments (profits from MCA projects could be directed towards new MCA projects) and to locate the MCC outside of Washington DC (to set a sign that the MCA is not a Washington-run agency).

---

[266] See Brainard and Driscoll (2003), p. 3.

[267] See Brainard (2003), p. 159.

[268] See Clemens and Radelet (2003), p. 11.

[269] See Collier and Dollar (2002).

[270] Similar approaches include the UK Department for International Development DFID, the Canadian Investment Fund for Africa CIFA or private public partnerships (PPPs).

3.3.7 Summary and conclusions

Recent shifts in the allocation of ODA suggest that substantially more aid is given to low-income countries, predominantly to LDCs in sub-Saharan Africa. Studies have discovered a variety of factors influencing the allocation decision of donors. Among them are donors' (geopolitical and commercial) interest, recipients' needs as well as geographic, cultural and linguistic proximity, quality of governance, civil/political rights and the size of the recipient country (small country bias). These factors are weighted differently across bilateral and multilateral donors, with the tendency of the latter to pay more attention to recipient countries' needs and level of poverty. But there are also significant dissimilarities among bilateral donors in the poverty focus of aid. Aid allocation tends to be oriented towards the goal of lifting as much people out of poverty as possible. However, this does not necessarily assure that it is the poorest people receiving the assistance. There is more evidence for the fact that ODA is targeted towards medium poor countries with at least moderate (not poor) policies and institutional capacities. The question whether or not ODA is more poverty-focused now than in the past is not answered conformingly in the literature.

Optimal allocation rules have gained much in prominence recently. More and more bilateral (and, to a lesser extent, multilateral) donors seem to found their allocation decision on such rules, which could, according to some authors, lift up to twice as much people permanently out of poverty and thus have a greater impact than scaling-up ODA flows. "With the current allocation, a three-fold increase in the total volume of aid would be required to achieve [the] same reduction in poverty."[271] There is evidence to assume that neither a complete shift towards optimal allocation nor a tripling of current aid levels is likely. However, with a more efficient allocation of aid and thus higher aid effectiveness, an increase in the provision of ODA could also gain political support.

Nevertheless, such poverty minimization calculations are also afflicted with a number of problems. Apart from methodological challenges, there is an intensive debate on the adequate choice of indicators best suited to select recipients. It has been shown that the degree of selectivity of donors depends on the preference and design of these criteria and that there is a *confirmation bias* in the sense that aid practitioners and politicians tend to select the study that underscores its intensions best. A radical selective reallocation of aid based on strict rules does not necessarily imply an improvement. This is even more the case as some low-income countries

[271] Collier and Dollar (1999), p. 4.

could be penalized because of policy and institutional deficiencies that may have resulted from poor location (e.g., in the tropics) or other initial disadvantages. Furthermore, the tendency to select recipients according to good governance criteria dilutes the fact that good governance can not only be regarded as a precondition for giving aid, but also as a development objective itself.[272]

3.4 Goal-oriented development cooperation

3.4.1 Description of the MDG

The Millennium Development Goals (MDG) comprise a set of mostly quantitative objectives and performance indicators that describe the global success in development progress. They were adopted by all UN members at the Millennium Declaration in September 2000 and formulated by a working group consisting of members from the UNDP, other UN organizations, the World Bank, the IMF and the OECD. They are based on a catalogue of International Development Goals published in 1996 by the OECD's Development Assistance Committee (DAC).[273] The MDG are frequently applied as a yardstick for measuring the progress in international development efforts. Although there have been many conferences and international commitments throughout the last decades seeking to improve the quality of life of people living in poor countries,[274] the MDG differ from previous initiatives because they have been negotiated at the level of head of states and gathered worldwide support. By 2015, all UN countries agreed to meet a set of quantitative and qualitative targets listed in Table 3.4. The formulation of the MDG can be regarded as applying results-based and outcome-oriented management at the global level.[275] They facilitate a common understanding among donor and recipient countries on goals of development.

---

[272] See Pronk (2001), p. 626.

[273] See OECD (1996).

[274] Alma Ata Declaration (Alma Ata/Russia, 1977), World Summit for Children (New York, 1990), World Summit on Education for All: Meeting Basic Learning Needs (Jomtien/Thailand, 1990), International Conference on Nutrition (Rome, 1992), International Conference on Population and Development (Cairo, 1994), World Summit for Social Development (Copenhagen, 1995), World Food Summit (Rome, 1996).

[275] See Poston et al. (2003), p. v.

Table 3.4. Millennium Development Goals

Goals		Targets for 2015
I.	Eradicate extreme poverty and hunger	1. Halve the proportion of people who live on less than $1 per day 2. Halve the proportion of people who suffer from hunger
II.	Achieve universal primary education	3. Ensure that all boys and girls complete primary school
III.	Promote gender equality and empower women	4. Eliminate gender disparities in primary and secondary education preferably by 2005, and at all levels by 2015
IV.	Reduce child mortality	5. Reduce by two-thirds the mortality rate among children under five
V.	Improve maternal health	6. Reduce by three-quarters the ratio of women dying in childbirth
VI.	Combat HIV/AIDS, malaria and other diseases	7. Halt and begin to reverse the spread of HIV/AIDS 8. Halt and begin to reverse the incidence of malaria and other major diseases
VII.	Ensure environmental sustainability	9. Integrate the principles of sustainable development into country policies and programs and reverse the loss of environmental resources 10. Reduce by half the proportion of people without access to safe drinking water 11. By 2020 achieve significant improvement in the lives of at least 100 million slum dwellers
VIII.	Develop a global partnership for development	12. Develop further an open trading and financial system that includes a commitment to good governance, development and poverty reduction – nationally and internationally 13. Address the special needs of the least developed countries, including tariff- and quota-free access for exports enhanced program of debt relief for HIPC and cancellation of official bilateral debt, and more generous ODA for countries committed to poverty reduction 14. Address the special needs of landlocked countries and small island developing states 15. Deal comprehensively with developing countries' debt problems 16. Develop decent and productive work for youth 17. In cooperation with pharmaceutical companies, provide access to affordable essential drugs in developing countries 18. In cooperation with the private sector, make available the benefits of new technologies – especially information and communications technologies

Source: United Nations website

Goals I to VI are set in quantifiable terms, whereas goal VII and VIII involve the formulation of strategies and frameworks improving environmental sustainability and international development cooperation and are neither time bound nor quantifiable. The base year for goals I–VI is 1990.[276] The 18 specified targets are monitored using 48 indicators. Monitoring and evaluation is controlled by the UN, IMF and World Bank, which collect and disseminate internationally comparable data on the respective indicators and publish regular evaluation reports.[277] While most indicators specify *outcomes*, e.g. in terms of a decrease in income poverty or improvements to health, the targets associated with the goals on education and gender equality are expressed as *inputs* (children completing primary education; gender equality in school enrolment).

The leaders of the Millennium Summit have committed to halving global extreme poverty by 2015. This does not infer, however, that each and every country or region would halve poverty, although the first goal is often interpreted in that way. Some annual reports (e.g., Human Development Report, World Development Report) nevertheless publish data on individual countries' progress towards halving national poverty. The next section will examine the progress of meeting the MDG.

3.4.2 Progress towards reaching the MDG

Most empirical studies estimate that the first Millennium Goal is feasible on a *global* scale. "If the objective is to reduce the poverty rate by about half in the developing world, then based on current trends there is a pretty good chance that this goal will be met."[278] The main reason is the rapid progress in populous India and China.

If the focus is shifted towards the *number of countries*, the results differ. Demery and Walton have estimated that more than half of all countries in

[276] For some countries, especially in Eastern Europe, Africa and Asia, reliable baseline statistics for this benchmark year is not available. Moreover, some countries do not collect data on certain indicators. See Maligalig (2003) for a detailed assessment of measurement issues of the MDG. He suggests that integrated statistical development plans should be formulated.

[277] Nevertheless, there are natural limitations on collecting comparable data. Especially cross-sectional data may not be comparable across countries due to differences in national methodologies and concepts. "By establishing a 'data-hungry' global monitoring system they [the MDG] exert pressure for much-needed improvements in national and international systems for the collection and analysis of data." Poston et al (2003), p. v.

[278] See Collier and Dollar (2000), p. 12.

their sample will not achieve the first MDG.[279] Just as little, the Goals 2–7 will not be reached on a global scale at existing rates of progress. With respect to education, Bruns et al. simulate that more than half of all countries (86 out of 155) might not achieve the goal of universal primary education.[280] The proportion of undernourished people is only falling very slowly in most regions. Furthermore, gender equality is far from being realized; child mortality rates decline slowly in many regions and remain extremely high in Sub-Saharan Africa; maternal mortality rates are high in nearly every region. A general success can be diagnosed for the share of population with access to safe drinking water, which has been reduced considerably.

Regional prospects for the MDG as well as country case studies reveal that progress is distributed very unequally across countries, but also within countries[281] and serious doubts remain whether the MDG will be reached in every region and country (see Fig. 3.5).[282] In Asia, some East Asian countries (most notably the newly industrialized economies) have experienced high growth rates over a long period, which led to significant poverty reduction, higher school enrolment ratios and lower under-five mortality rates over the recent decades. In East and South Asia, extreme poverty was reduced by five percentage points to 24% between 1990 and 1999. Although there are still wide disparities among Asian countries, "Asia is well positioned to achieve many of the targets for the Millennium Development Goals [because of] strong economic fundamentals, declining population rates, an emerging middle class, and high savings rates [...]"[283].

In Latin American and Caribbean countries, relative poverty declined (from 17% to 15% between 1990 and 1999), but absolute poverty rose. The region witnessed low growth rates (GDP per capita of 1.6% on average during the 1990s), low savings rates and rising income inequality. Although most countries are likely to achieve universal primary education and gender equality, some countries (especially from the Caribbean) fall behind.

---

[279] See Demery and Walton (1999).

[280] See Bruns et al. (2003). This number even excludes 16 countries for which data is not available.

[281] For instance, most indicators suggest that rural poverty is greater than urban poverty.

[282] See, for example, Demery and Walton (1999), Collier and Dollar (2000). See also the Global Monitoring Report 2004 of World Bank and IMF (2005).

[283] See African Development Bank (2002), p. 9. See also UNESCAP (2002) for a feasibility study of achieving the MDG in Asia and the Pacific.

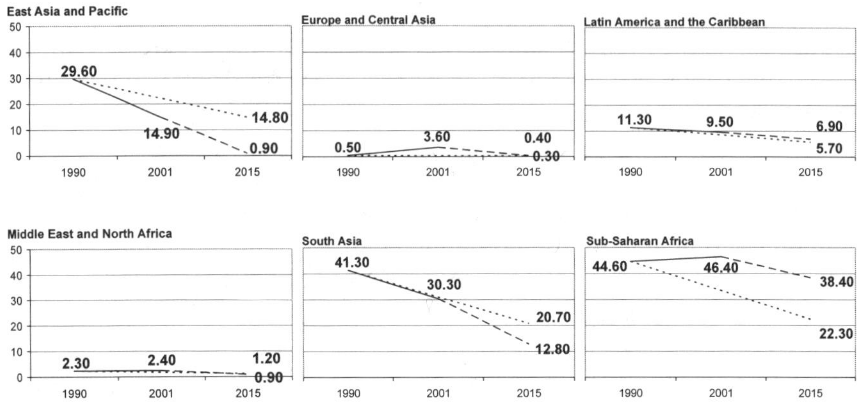

Fig. 3.5. MDG goal I (halving extreme poverty), progress for selected regions

Source: Author, based on World Bank data (2005a)
Note: Values indicate the share of people living on less than $1 a day in %. Actual progress = regular line, projected progress = dashed line, path to goal = dotted line

Eastern European and former Soviet Union countries face the burden of an economic deterioration in the first half of the 1990s. While the Eastern European countries (especially EU accession countries) will achieve most MDG, some Caucasian countries, Central Asia and Moldova will probably not meet the goal of halving poverty.

The most disappointing results are observed in Africa. Some North African countries will be able to halve extreme poverty, while the majority of sub-Saharan countries will not, even with an average economic per capita growth rate of 3.3%.[284] Recent estimates of Clemens et al. suggest that 42 out of 47 African countries are currently "off-track" for all targets.[285] Sahn and Stifel predict that Kenya will be the only African country likely to reach universal primary enrolment by 2015.[286] Estimates of the UNDP indicate that sub-Saharan African countries will not meet the goals concerning hunger, primary education and child mortality within the entire 21st century. Consequently, the Human Development Report 2003 has identified top and high priority countries[287] for each Millennium Goal. 25 out of 31 top priority countries fall under the sub-Saharan region.

[284] African Development Bank (2002), p. 10.
[285] See Clemens et al. (2004), p. 2.
[286] See Sahn and Stifel (2003).
[287] Top priority refers to countries where progress is reversed and urgent action is necessary; high priority countries have moderate, but too little progress.

3.4.3 Millennium Project and MDG+5

Two years after introducing the MDG, a UN commission chaired by Jeffrey Sachs began to evaluate the goals in 2002 and presented its final report in 2005 ("Investing in Development: A Practical Plan to Achieve the Millennium Development Goals", also known as "Sachs report").[288] The report should provide plans how to reach the MDG until 2015. Although it concludes that the international development community is currently "off track" to reach the goals, they still can be met in 2015. Despite the fact that there are region and country specific explanations for why the Goals are failing, the report marks five principal, overarching reasons for being off-track:

1. Poor governance
   Poor governance with respect to macroeconomic policies, functioning institutions, political participation and obeying the rule of law is one main reason for stagnating economic development.
2. Poverty traps
   Many even well-governed LDCs are stuck in poverty traps. Countries in such a situation are facing severe constraints for their economic development which they cannot escape without external assistance. Such constraints include, for instance, countries in geographic isolation (landlockedness), regions with high probability of diseases (Malaria, AIDS) and rapid population growth, but also unsustainable debt burden, where ODA flows are largely offset by debt service payments. Poverty traps are also associated with low saving rates, low tax revenues, low foreign investment, violent conflicts, brain drain and environmental degradation. "The key to escaping the poverty trap is to raise the economy's capital stock to the point where the downward spiral ends and self-sustaining economic growth takes over."[289] The report favours much more development assistance (big push) and debt forgiveness in these cases to invest in basic infrastructure, education and governance.
3. Pockets of poverty
   Some middle-income countries with high regional, cultural and ethnic diversity also face high income inequality and poverty. Some regional parts or groups within the economy lag significantly behind in terms

[288] See Sachs (2005). Including the 13 thematically-oriented Task Force Reports, the total number of pages amounts to 3,000 pages. See also Martens (2005) and Hermle and Gad (2005) for a critique of the MDG+5.

[289] United Nations Millennium Project (2005), p. 19.

of economic development, building so-called pockets of poverty. This does not only concern rural, but also urban areas (slum dwellers).

4. Area of specific policy neglect
   Some policy fields such as environmental policy and gender policy have only weak ministries and weak law enforcement mechanisms and are neglected by domestic and international policy-makers.
5. The present international aid system is not efficient and focused enough. Although the MDG have been agreed by all UN members, multinational institutions (e.g., the IMF) have not encouraged the donor countries to take the MDG as operational objectives. Furthermore, coordination among multilateral and bilateral donors and with the multilateral development banks is still insufficient.

3.4.4 MDG needs assessment

The report suggests a list of quick-win instruments (such as mosquito nets to fight Malaria or free school meals) and large investment programs in the recipient countries including long-term budget planning and harmonization with existing poverty reduction strategy papers. Table 3.5 lists all recommendations. The donor community should, among other measures, at least double their ODA budget and impose new debt sustainability criteria which take the MDG into consideration. The report concludes that the quality of bilateral aid is very low in many cases: Only a small fraction of present bilateral ODA is directed towards MDG enhancing programs or projects; aid is often highly unpredictable, misallocated and not evaluated. At the Millennium+5 meeting (September 2005 in New York), UN members met to discuss the progress of the MDG, with the Sachs report serving as a basis for the analysis. The final document, however, disassociates itself from the 48 indicators the UN secretary has set in 2000 and does not entail any time frame or numbers. There has been strong opposition by some influential countries concerning the version of the final report.[290]

[290] The United States, for example, introduced hundreds of amendments attempting to declare the MDG irrelevant/invalid and not approved by UN members, but only the UN secretary. Moreover, the US attempted to carry through that the MDG are not explicitly mentioned in the final report.

Table 3.5. Ten recommendations of the Sachs report

1. Developing country governments should adopt MDG-based poverty reduction strategies by 2006 bold enough to meet the MDG targets for 2015. If PRSP already exist, they should be aligned with the MDG.
2. The MDG-based poverty reduction strategies should anchor the scaling up of public investments, capacity building, domestic resource mobilization, and official development assistance. They should also provide a framework for strengthening governance, promoting human rights, engaging civil society, and promoting the private sector.
3. Developing country governments should craft and implement the MDG-based poverty reduction strategies in transparent and inclusive processes, working closely with civil society organizations, the domestic private sector, and international partners.
4. International donors should identify at least a dozen MDG "fast-track" countries for a rapid scale-up of official development assistance in 2005, recognizing that many countries are already in a position for a massive scale-up on the basis of their good governance and absorptive capacity.
5. Developed and developing countries should jointly launch, in 2005, a group of Quick Win Actions to save and improve millions of lives and to promote economic growth. They should also launch a massive effort to build expertise at the community level.
6. Developing country governments should align national strategies with such regional initiatives as the New Partnership for Africa's Development and the Caribbean Community (and Common Market), and regional groups should receive increased direct donor support for regional projects.
7. High-income countries should increase official development assistance from 025 percent of donor GNP in 2003 to around 0.44 percent in 2006 and 0.54 percent in 2015 to support the MDG, particularly in low-income countries, with improved ODA quality (including aid that is harmonized, predictable, and largely in the form of grants-based budget support). Each donor should reach 0.7 percent no later than 2015 to support the Goals and other development assistance priorities. Debt relief should be more extensive and generous.
8. High-income countries should open their markets to developing country exports through the Doha trade round and help LDC raise export competitiveness through investments in critical trade-related infrastructure, including electricity, roads, and ports. The Doha Development Agenda should be fulfilled and the Doha Round completed no later than 2006.
9. International donors should mobilize support for global scientific research and development to address special needs of the poor in areas of health, agriculture, natural resource and environmental management, energy, and climate.
10. The UN Secretary-General and the UN Development Group should strengthen the coordination of UN agencies, funds, and programs to support the MDG, at headquarters and country level. The UN country Teams should be strengthened and should work closely with the international financial institutions to support the Goals.

Source: United Nations Millennium Project (2005), pp. xiv–xv

The brief stance on the MDG progress in different regions has shown that there are large discrepancies among individual countries. In order to assess "what is needed" to reach the MDG, a substantial number of analyses have been conduced, covering a variety of different aspects. It is beyond this chapter to give a detailed overview on all these aspects currently discussed, but they all more or less touch on three points: International (external) commitment, domestic (internal) policies and the appropriate framework design:

1. Commitment from donor countries and international institutions:
   When estimates forecasted that the MDG would not be met by most African countries, it was suggested by many that substantially more commitment of the international development community is necessary. Most studies focused primarily on the provision of additional official development assistance and demanded much more external official funds. Estimates of how much external official financing "is needed" vary widely and depend, among other factors, on how effectively the additional aid will be used (see cost estimates in Sect. 2.4.1). Some authors are sceptical on this scaling-up policy. Moss[291] notes that even if unnecessary ODA funds were available, the MDG would not be met. Another bulk of studies concentrated on how international institutions can assist in the process of capacity building[292] and granting market access to developing countries' products. In this regard, a fairer trade regime within the WTO framework is regarded by many as very important for developing countries.
   Some, but relatively little emphasis was placed on the question which type of assistance (project or program aid, technical assistance, training measures) and aid allocation is in fact suited for individual countries.[293]
2. Improvement of domestic policies:
   Many studies underline the importance of domestic policies enhancing poverty reduction via economic growth. According to this understanding, only sustained economic growth will enable poor countries to "grow out of their poverty". There is a large, but nevertheless inconclusive literature on the causes of poverty and the adequate policies to alleviate it. Recently, much attention has been paid to the role of institutions, the rule of law, openness and the quality of go-

[291] See Moss (2005).
[292] See Hakura and Nsouli (2003) on the role of the IMF in capacity building and Leipziger et al. (2003) on the role of infrastructure for achieving the MDG.
[293] Clements et al. (2004) provide an overview on the grants vs. loans issue.

vernance.[294] However, the primacy of institutions attributing to economic growth is not uncontested.[295] Most authors agree that an amalgam of many factors contributes to economic growth in poor countries.

3. Design, specification and appropriateness of the MDG:
Establishing the MDG has undoubtedly resuscitated the discussion on foreign aid and promoted the awareness of pervasive deprivation in LDCs. As the UNDP points out in its Human Development Report 2003, "the setting of [...] global goals drew attention to [the] needs"[296], even if the numerical targets are not met. It has been shown that setting goals has sped up the development towards these goals.[297] However, overly ambitious goals may not motivate but discourage and create an aura of development failure, especially when entire regions are likely to fail. The appropriateness of setting global goals of development and a similar deadline for all countries can be called into question.[298] The MDG, for example, do not differentiate between persistently and transiently poor. They also do not disaggregate between urban and rural poverty. There is the risk that strategies which are suited to alleviate overall (global) poverty are favoured over strategies benefiting the persistently poor and/or the rural poor.[299] The MDG are not directed towards the poorest countries, but concentrate to reduce an overall index of poverty (the head-count index). Consequently, the donor community might be tempted to do what is necessary to reach the global goals, regardless of regional developments. This could even end up in "doing nothing", because East Asia, North Africa and Latin America are likely to reach Goal I without any additional external assistance.

3.4.5 A global plan to combat poverty?

The goal-oriented MDG approach has altered development cooperation by providing a set of universally accepted long-term goals of development.

---

[294] See, for example, Rodrik et al. (2002) and Acemoglu et al. (2002).

[295] See Sachs (2003a).

[296] UNDP (2003), p. 31.

[297] See Herfkens (2005), p. 97.

[298] See Gaiha (2003). The author analyzes the role of international poverty lines, the head-count index and household surveys, which prove to be very sensitive to the data sets used and methodologies applied.

[299] See Gwatkin (2002) for an inquiry into the possibility of progress that fails to reach the poor.

Although the aim of halving extreme poverty globally by 2015 will be achieved based on current trends, there are large regional and country-specific disparities. Foremost, African countries and low-income countries under stress will fall short on the MDG. They "have failed largely for domestic reasons, but international actions often have not helped from a developmental perspective, and sometimes have heightened the problems."[300] An intensive debate has evolved on how to reach the MDG in countries and regions that are currently considered off track. One body of literature focuses on the role of external assistance in the form of additional (financial) resources and (non-financial) international commitment, improved ODA disbursement channels and formulating frameworks addressing and evaluating poverty reduction efforts. Another body of literature addresses the role of domestically-led policies pivotal to poverty reduction. There are considerable efforts of the international community dealing with both of these developments, most notably the debt relief initiative and poverty reduction strategy papers, which will be analyzed in the succeeding two chapters.

Undoubtedly, the idea of goal orientation has improved the way of dealing with long-term economic development. A substantial number of MDG progress reports have been written in the last five years, proving those critics wrong that there are not enough evaluation proceedings in international development cooperation. But the current design of the MDG, understood as a global plumb-line for economic development progress, has brought up the problem that they are hardly operational at a "sub-global" (= national) level. Working backwards from desired outcomes to necessary inputs (needs assessment) at the global level is much more complex than at the project level. The MDG should not be mixed with a business-oriented "Management by Objectives"-approach. Equally less, they should not be understood as ends in themselves but as benchmarks of progress. "Though the Goals reflect consensus on key global development objectives, they are not a new model for development."[301] Thus, the international development community should be careful not to cling to the MDG. Ambitious goals are not to condemn per se, on the contrary. But a broad, global framework neglecting country-specific circumstances is hardly operational from an international perspective and hardly accepted by recipient countries.

Although wide disparities among countries and regions are observed, the scope of objectives and the overly ambitious MDG deadline (year 2015) remain largely untouched. There is still an official rhetoric that the goals can be met. The MDG are regarded as long-term economic goals,

---

300 Wolfensohn and Bourguignon (2004), p. 20.

301 UNDP (2003), p. 30.

and it is reasonable to assume that elected national governments face challenges in aligning their domestic policies (in the case of recipient countries) and their external assistance (donors) to such a time period. However, with respect to economic development in general, fifteen years (2000–2015) provide only very limited time to solve problems of such a huge magnitude as "promised" in the MDG. It also remains debatable whether the year 2015 constitutes a reasonable cutting date. "[S]uccess should not be judged simply by achieving the Goals on time. Halving poverty is not the end of the road [...]"[302]

Defining global goals entails the danger of applying global (in the sense of standardized) development strategies dominating over country- and regional specific strategies taking into account a country's initial economic base as well as historical, cultural, political and geographical factors. But the challenges, circumstances and needs of developing countries are very dissimilar. Even observations at a rather general level may serve as an illustration: In some Central Asian countries, gender issues are much more of a concern than elsewhere. While some East Asian countries face higher environmental problems, the Latin American region is characterized by high income and land inequality and thus a different kind of poverty. A large share of the entire African continent is subject to severe political crisis, geographic constraints and ethnic diversity. Given this miscellany, the World Banks vision of globally defined goals, which shall all be reached until 2015, appears too optimistic.

3.5 From debt restructuring to debt relief

3.5.1 A brief history of early debt restructuring efforts

During the 1970s, many developing countries had to cope with increasing debt: Between 1970 and 1985, the accumulated debt of developing countries more than ten-folded. In 1982, Mexico's government announced that it was no longer able to fulfil its external commitments. Other Latin American and sub-Saharan African developing countries were soon to follow. Most economists agree that the debt crisis cannot be attributed to a single cause, but is the outcome of a multitude of external (e.g., global economic conditions) and internal (i.e., domestic) factors. Among the external are:

- the oil price shocks of the 1970s,

[302] Ibid, p. 30.

- the restrictive monetary policy of the Reagan era, leading to a dollar appreciation,
- the worldwide recession of the early 1980s, reducing the demand for basic commodities from developing countries,
- "new protectionism" of industrialized countries,
- weak debt management by creditor countries.

Internal factors include:

- Weak macroeconomic management (large state budget deficits, high inflation, low savings, overvalued currencies),
- Underdeveloped financial and banking sector, incapable of providing financial resources,
- Missing structural adjustment policies after the oil price shocks,
- Inefficient attraction and allocation of foreign capital,
- Strong focus on import substitution policies in most developing countries (except Asia) and low diversified export structure,
- Weak debt management by debtor countries (e.g., unrealistic underlying growth forecasts),
- Political instabilities (e.g., civil wars, conflicts).

With the lack of access to capital on the international capital markets and the pressure to repay current loans, most developing countries asked the IMF for assistance. However, IMF loans turned out to be small in size and thus proved rather ineffective. Consequently, a number of attempts aimed at overcoming the unsustainable debt burden of developing countries, which will be described in the following subsections.

Baker Plan (1985)

In 1985, the former US Treasury Secretary James Baker proposed a solution for reducing the outstanding debt in highly indebted poor countries (predominantly in Latin America) by offering more bank loans ("fresh money") and a debt management led by the World Bank. Under the condition of structural reforms (decreasing government expenditures, devaluating the domestic currency, freezing wages, lowering imports), these countries should receive more private capital ($20 billion over three years from private banks) and official assistance ($9 billion from multilateral institutions). The plan was that the indebted countries grow out of their debt by increased production and exports. The Baker Plan did not address the reduction of the existing debt stock. International banks remained cautious and feared the "possibility of collective repudiation"[303] and demanded governmental guarantees. The Baker Plan remained ineffective, in part because additional loans were short-termed but financed long term investments (an effect known as maturity mismatch). Critics spoke of a taxpayer bailout.

Bradley Plan (1986)

This "counter-plan" included a discount on public and private debt and was named the "3-3-3" initiative: Three percent of the principal on the outstanding debt was to be written off in each of the next three years. Furthermore, interest rates should be reduced by three percent in the indebted countries which in turn were expected to lift trade restrictions. The World Bank was to offer $9 billion. Although lacking US support, the Bradley Plan was welcomed in the indebted countries and had an impact on how creditors and debtors perceived the debt crisis.

Schumer Watkins Plan

Schumer and Watkins noted that a substantial amount of debt (70–80 percent) was not loans itself but accrued interests. They proposed a change in banking law "so that interest paid by money that had been borrowed from the same bank should not be classified as part of the profit. […] The aim was to undermine profitability of the process of refinancing overdue interest and also to incentivize banks to reduce levels of interest rates so that debtor countries can pay without taking out new loans."[304]

Lawson Plan (1987)

The British Chancellor of the Exchequer, Nigel Lawson, proposed converting all bilateral loans to grants, longer repayment periods and discounted interest rates by three percent below market. Furthermore, new instruments such as debt equity swaps, exit bonds, buy backs, debt for nature swaps and debt for debt swaps were introduced in the debate.[305]

---

[303] Stambuli (1999), p. 17.

[304] Ibid., p. 17.

[305] Debt equity swaps comprised instruments in which private creditors sell their debt (denominated in US-dollars) to buyers (often investors in developing countries) in the secondary market at a discount. These in turn often sold this debt to the domestic government in local currency to finance the purchase. Debt for nature swaps were used to create conservation zones in the country. In exit bonds, debt was cashed for bonds with immediate payment. Buy backs described the

Brady Plan (1989)

The ineffectiveness of former initiatives and the unwillingness of different actors (governments, private stakeholders) demanded new solutions. The Brady Plan recognized that the high level of debt considerably reduced the chances of sustained economic growth in the affected countries. In order to step against the debt crisis in Latin America, former U.S. Minister of Finance Nicholas F. Brady made the proposal to roll over existing debt obligations to bank loans by transforming them into governmental bonds ("Brady Bonds") with long maturity. Existing liabilities were, diminished by a discount, swapped into bonds. The discount was determined taking into account the associated credit risk and maturity. The discount was achieved by either lowering the face value of the bond or by below market interest rates and can be regarded as partial debt relief: It was financed by international banks renouncing part of the outstanding debt and guarantees by international institutions. This was bound to the condition of structural reforms of the developing countries. Only countries that showed the willingness of structural reforms were considered as eligible from the IMF.

The idea behind the Brady Bonds was to create a secondary market, since most claims were held by a very limited number of commercial banks. Brady Bonds were tradable on international markets more easily than debt obligations. "Brady agreements have aimed at, and actually led to, a securitization of the external debt, to a relaxation of credit constraints, and to a restored access to the international financial market."[306]

Altogether, Brady Bonds valuing $46 billion were issued[307] and the results significantly varied by country. Countries with medium income and relatively low indebtedness were successful in restructuring their debt in this way. In 2000, Mexico started with the repayment of its outstanding Brady Bonds. The total amount of Brady Bonds in Mexico was $34.25 billion. In July 2003, the country announced that it paid off all its outstanding Brady Bonds long before maturity date (2019). Apart from the symbolic meaning (signalling that it has overcome the stigmata of indebtedness), Mexico is likely to receive an improved country rating enabling it to have better access to international credits than under Brady conditions.[308] In 2004, Brazil also started to pay back its Brady Bonds with maturity

fact that debtor nations bought their own debt on the secondary market. Debt for debt swap meant switching debt into long-term bonds held by the creditor bank.

[306] Barbone and Forni (2001), p. 116.

[307] See Handelsblatt (2004).

[308] See Ehringfeld (2003).

2014.[309] Other countries were less successful. Ecuador not only defaulted on its Eurobonds, but also on Brady Bonds in 1999. Other, e.g. African, countries' debt was mainly official (non-tradable) and not commercial, which limited the effectiveness of the Brady initiative for these countries.

3.5.2 Club solutions of restructuring debt

Paris Club principles and lending terms

"The Paris Club is an informal group of official creditors whose role is to find co-ordinated and sustainable solutions to the payment difficulties experienced by debtor nations."[310] It was established in 1956 in order to come to an agreement for Argentina's then financial crisis.[311] It consists of 19 permanent member countries who meet on a regular basis (10–11 times a year) in Paris.[312] Since the Paris Club has neither legal basis nor status, it calls itself a "non-institution".[313] It is financed by the French Ministry of Finance. Rieffel highlights that "the Paris Club was not the product of an 'architecture' exercise by the G-7 countries, the IMF, or any other official body [but] a pragmatic solution to a specific problem.[314] The formalization and "institutionalization" took a major step in the 1970s when the principles and procedures were adopted in a UN resolution.[315] However, the Paris Club terms and definitions remain highly specific.[316] Paris Club agreements with debtor countries are based on five rules:

---

[309] The official name is "Capitalization Bonds" (C-Bonds). These high-volume bonds were issued in 1994.

[310] Paris Club (2003).

[311] See Bitterman (1973) for this case.

[312] The members are Austria, Australia, Belgium, Canada, Denmark, Finland, France, Germany, Ireland, Italy, Japan, Netherlands, Norway, Russian Federation, Spain, Sweden, Switzerland, United Kingdom, and USA. Some other countries have been invited to join negotiations in case they had a substantial exposure.

[313] See Paris Club (2003).

[314] Rieffel (2003), p. 59.

[315] The Group of Seventy-Seven (G-77) proposed to replace the Paris Club and the London Club with an "International Debt Commission", the G-7, however, denied. Rieffel speaks of "a remarkable irony if the International Debt Commission comes to life now in the form of the SDRM [Sovereign Debt Restructuring Mechanism]." See Rieffel (2002).

[316] See Rieffel (2003), p. 82–91 for an extensive description of the Paris Club policy constraints, restructuring terms, and special features.

1. Decisions are made on a *case by case basis*. With this principle, the Paris Club members rule out debt restructurings on demand and a generalization of debt relief.
2. Decisions require *conditionality*, i.e. the existence of an appropriate IMF adjustment program. This principle serves as an extension to the case-by-case principle.
3. Decisions require *consensus* among all creditor countries, based on ad hoc negotiations in Paris rather than strict written rules or treaties.
4. Decisions require *solidarity* among all creditor countries in the sense that individual agreements between each creditor country and the debtor country reflect the terms and results achieved in the Paris Club.
5. Decisions require *comparability of treatment*, i.e. after negotiating a deal, the debtor seeks comparable conditions from other (non-official) creditors. Although not mentioned explicitly, the history of Paris Club negotiations shows that the comparability of treatment refers to non-official (= private) creditors and not to other official creditors.[317] An implicit assumption is that multilateral creditors are preferred creditors, which is the case for the World Bank, the IMF, and multilateral development banks: In a default, loans to these agencies are not restructured and they do not provide more financial support if there are any arrears with them.[318] The application of this principle has avalanched a controversial discussion as well as substantial "linguistic confusion"[319].

"From the beginning of the debt crisis in the early Eighties until the end of that decade the prevailing dogma that no southern country was insolvent, but only, at worst, had liquidity difficulties – a temporary cash flow problem – was the basis of the Paris Club's position. Accordingly, the phrase

[317] See ibid., p. 73.

[318] The preferred creditor system has been consistently criticized by politicians and NGOs.

[319] Rieffel (2003), p. 75: „There has been a puzzling evolution over the past fifteen years in this clause. Until 1996 Paris Club agreements differentiated between 'nondiscrimination' applied to nonparticipating official creditors and 'comparable treatment' applied to private creditors. These two aspects of burden sharing were addressed in two separate clauses. In 1996, however, these familiar clauses were dropped in favor of two clauses that encompass nonparticipating official creditors and private creditors. The earlier distinction added a valuable element of flexibility to Paris Club agreements. The principle as currently stated appears to reduce the flexibility that debtor countries used to have in negotiating restructuring arrangements with their private creditors."

'debt cancellation' was taboo during this period."[320] Over time, the Paris Club has modified its lending terms step by step during G7 meetings, resulting in the Toronto Terms (1988/1989), the Houston Terms (1990), the Trinidad Terms (1991), the Naples Terms (1994), the Lyon Terms (1996) and the Cologne Terms (1999).[321] The three major debt restructuring conditions (repayment period, grace period, level of concessionality) were slowly eased.[322] Although the Paris Club commits itself to never include new money in the debt restructuring process, all Terms successively extended the level of partial debt reduction by offering the debtor below-market interest rates on rescheduled loans, which reduces the net present value of the debt and "forc[es] governments to formally acknowledge and finance losses on the past activities of their export credit agencies."[323]

The Paris Club only provides a platform for rescheduling; each member country will negotiate the details bilaterally with the debtor(s) in question. "Paris Club creditors as such generally do not provide exceptional financing through the disbursements of new money that can be used for balance of payments support, including meeting existing obligations. [...] In these respects, Paris Club creditors have a narrower range of instruments than the private sector."[324] Usually, only loans prior to a specific "cut-off date" (normally set to 18 month before a country approached the Club) are subject to restructuring. The underlying reason is that creditors shall be encouraged to lend, knowing that their new loans will not be subject to immediate restructuring.

Lack of bureaucracy and transparency

Critics note that although the lack of bureaucracy in the Paris Club may lead to the rapid completion of negotiations (usually within several days), the lack of transparency and the high degree of power rests with a few officials.[325] Data and descriptions of the more than 330 agreements in the history of the Paris Club are available since the Club established a website in

---

[320] Kaiser (2001).

[321] For a detailed description of the individual Terms, see Stambuli (1999), p. 22f.

[322] Moreover, Rieffel (2003) has analyzed the number of restructuring cases and found that the number of Paris Club restructurings with highly indebted countries has significantly increased between 1988 and 2002.

[323] Powell (2000). Nevertheless, the Paris Club has rarely offered a write-down of the principal (i.e. the stock of debt) but instead rescheduled interest payments. Exemptions include Poland (1991), Egypt (1994), Russia and Peru (1996), mainly due to political considerations.

[324] IMF (2001a), p. 5.

[325] See Caplen (2000).

April 2001. Highly different perceptions regarding the volume of outstanding debt and numeric discrepancies between the data of developed and developing countries aggravate negotiations. Official sector's debt also includes non-market transactions, which are difficult to quantify because they are not marked to market. Moreover, political motivations play a pivotal role in negotiations.[326]

Reverse comparability of treatment

The *comparability of treatment* principle has caused some academic dispute circling around two questions: First, should the principle be extended to include the private bond sector, and second, what about reverse comparability demanded by private investors? When private sector financing was of relatively minor importance (and private banks meet in the London Club anyway), the comparability of treatment clause worked quite efficiently. With the surge of private capital into developing countries, however, the principle came under scrutiny.[327] Originally, comparability was designed to work in one direction only, meaning that debtors are obliged to seek comparable (but not better) conditions from other non-Paris Club creditors. But, in turn, debtors cannot demand a comparable treatment in Paris Club negotiations of conditions they negotiated with private investors.[328] Private investors as well as indebted countries[329] have called for such reverse comparability, arguing that an uneven burden-sharing of debt restructuring will cause "adverse systemic effects on the willingness of the private sector to extend new financing to emerging market sovereigns."[330] The Paris Club members resist implementing reverse comparability, claiming that doing so would have repercussions on the market value of outstanding

[326] See EMTA (2001), p. 3.

[327] Rieffel mentions four problems associated with the principle: The exact definition of multilateral creditors, different treatment in the bilateral agreements following the Paris Club agreement, different treatment because some countries provide additional financial resources, and the increasing importance of private capital flows such as bonds. See Rieffel (2003), p. 74–75.

[328] At least Paris Club countries have no obligation to do so. And in fact, official creditors are rather unwilling to make financial sacrifices when they see that private loans are served instead.

[329] When Russia successfully negotiated to restructure the majority of its outstanding London Club debt (bank debt) in early 2000, it announced to seek a similar solution with the Paris Club (= reverse comparability). A denial of such approach could lead private investors to the conclusion that in this case, the private sector bailed out the official creditors, having a negative effect on future debt relief for emerging market economies.

[330] IMF (2001a), p. 20.

so would have repercussions on the market value of outstanding debt of private investors and therefore reduce financial stability.

The Evian proposal

Until recently, the Paris Club policy did not entail to write-down outstanding debt. Only countries taking part in the HIPC initiative (see next section) were eligible for debt reduction. The "Evian approach" (proposed at the G8 summit in Evian, 2003) is a reform proposal for the Paris Club to handle unsustainable debt levels of HIPCs. The IMF will be asked by the Paris Club to conduct a "Debt Sustainability Analysis" (DSA) for each potential candidate for debt relief. If the respective debt level is viewed as unsustainable, creditor countries expect to agree with debtor countries a tailored and phased debt treatment to bring debt down to sustainable levels. Under the Evian conception, the Paris Club would extend its options to write down debt of non-HIPCs.[331] However, member countries have very different national legislations and attitudes towards writing down debt within the Paris Club framework.[332]

The London Club (Bank Advisory Committee)

The London Club can be regarded as the private banks' equivalent of the Paris Club and is even less formalized. It has emerged as an "ad hoc forum for restructuring negotiations."[333] One bank (usually the one with the largest outstanding loans) will act as a coordinator between the banks and the debtor country. Usually, the meetings take place at the headquarters of the coordinating bank, and not in London. Basis for the analysis of the financial standing of the country is the IMF. The bulk share of London Club debt restructuring concerns middle income countries and not low-income countries, which owe most of their debt to official institutions and not to the private sector. Negotiations in the London Club often take place between unequal partners (banks, debtor and creditor governments).[334] Also, external political factors heavily influence the outcome of the negotia-

---

[331] There has been substantial political pressure from some G7 members and NGO groups such as Jubilee 2000 on this aspect.

[332] The United States, for example, face considerable Congress reservations for granting debt relief.

[333] IIF (2004).

[334] See Uppal and Van Hulle (1997) for a formal model of negotiations in the London Club.

tions.[335] Since the focus here is on official debt and development assistance, London Club operations will not be covered in more detail.

3.5.3 Highly Indebted Poor Country Initiative (HIPC)

Eligibility and debt sustainability

HIPC stands for Highly Indebted Poor Countries and describes an initiative started by World Bank, IMF and various bilateral donors in 1996 to reduce outstanding multilateral debt of developing countries to "sustainable levels". The initiative for the first time puts multilateral debt from preferred creditors on the agenda, which remained untouched until then. While debt relief under Paris Club Agreements was negotiated separately, the HIPC initiative offered a platform for a multitude of debtors and creditors. The original initiative from 1996 became known as HIPC I. Its extension HIPC II enhanced the original initiative by granting greater and faster debt relief.[336] In September 2004, the HIPC initiative has been extended again to end 2006 and takes into consideration eight additional countries[337] that may become eligible based on their end 2004 debt burden indicators.

In order to be eligible for the HIPC initiative, countries must i) face an unsustainable debt burden beyond available debt relief mechanisms,[338] ii) establish a track record of reforms and sound policies through IMF and World Bank supported programs and iii) have developed a poverty reduction strategy paper (PRSP).[339] In order to analyze a country's debt burden, a Debt Sustainability Analysis (DSA) is carried out. The HIPC I debt sustainability threshold is set at a maximum of 200–250 percent of annual export earnings, measured in net present value terms. This limit has been reduced to 150 percent in 1999 with the HIPC II extension. A second

---

[335] In a political economy analysis of Poland's London Club debt restructuring, Mesjasz examines the time period from 1981 to 1994. Between 1981 and 1988, short-run interests of the creditor and the Polish government were dominating the negotiation process. After 1989, when Western governments and Poland had more corresponding interests (e.g., achieving a market economy in Poland), short-term and long-term interests became more balanced. See Mesjasz (2000).

[336] See Michaelowa (2002) who presents an interesting political economy explanation of the enhanced HIPC initiative suggesting that the overall rise of HIPC default risk and the symbolic value of the year 2000 are major explanatory factors. This policy has also been referred to as defensive lending.

[337] Eritrea, Haiti, Kyrgyz Republic, Nepal, Bangladesh, Bhutan, Sri Lanka, Tonga.

[338] Available debt relief mechanisms refer to Paris Club Terms.

[339] A so-called Interim PRSP is sufficient at first. In a later stage, a full PRSP is obliged.

constraint is the debt payments-to-export earnings-ratio, which is limited to 15%. In some very open countries with an export-to-GDP ration exceeding 30 percent (down from 40 percent in HIPC I) and a large debt-to-fiscal revenue ratio exceeding 15 percent (down from 20 percent), the debt sustainability threshold is set at 250 percent net present value debt of fiscal revenues at decision point (down from 280 percent). If a country's debt surpasses these threshold levels even after traditional debt relief mechanisms (Paris Club Terms) have been applied, it qualifies for HIPC assistance. If a country meets the criteria for debt relief, IMF and World Bank commit to reduce the outstanding debt to a level of debt sustainability (Decision Point). However, the final verdict whether a country has reached the Decision Point relies with these institutions and is not automatically guaranteed with eligibility. On reaching the Decision Point, a country may receive interim relief on its debt services.[340] Once the agreed key policy reforms have been executed and a PRSP has been developed and implemented for at least one year, a country reaches the Completion Point. At this point, donors will provide the debt relief committed at the decision point.

The reduction of principal and interest payments is inherently connected to the question of how much debt should be forgiven. The economic literature has created the term "debt sustainability" to describe the frontier characterizing a healthy level of indebtedness. Early propositions of Wold Bank and IMF consider debt sustainable as long as there are regular debt payments of any size. Similarly, most donor countries have interpreted sustainable debt as the ability to serve debt. However, critics have argued that these payments can be made on the cost of social and basic investments, which would negatively affect development. Moreover, incremental small changes in the ability to repay (e.g., due to natural disasters or misallocations) can lead to insolvency. This explains why even a theoretically sustainable "on the edge concept" often results in unsustainable debt situations. Consequently, Kampffmeyer and Taake[341] plead for a risk buffer that takes into account such malfunctions. Most official classifications such as the World Bank's into low, medium, and high indebtedness and the relative size of debt with respect to export proceedings and GDP do not satisfy this requirement. Their definition of sustainable debt should obey the following four rules simultaneously:

[340] In fact, most countries have initially received interim debt relief. However, in some cases, interim debt relief has been suspended by the IMF.

[341] See Kampffmeyer and Taake (1999).

- The debt service to export ratio should not exceed 10–20 percent, depending on the level of openness.
- The exchange rate reserves should not fall below short-term (e.g. one-year) debt liabilities.
- The domestic savings available for investments less its proportion for debt service should not fall below 15–20 percent of GDP.
- The regular public expenditures, which are financed by domestic revenue, should not fall below 12–15 percent of GDP; public investment should not fall below 3–8 percent.

The operational criteria above are especially formulated for HIPCs, but should be subject to country-specific or region-specific circumstances, e.g. to account for the effects of private capital flows. Birdsall and Williamson favor the debt-service-to-GDP-ratio instead of the export-to-debt-ratio and assume a two percent threshold as sustainable.[342] However, as Berensmann[343] point out correctly, the indicator debt-service payments does only mirror the current mortgage, but not the future burden, because many loans entail a grace period. In a more general form, Rieffel's definition points to the same direction: "A country's stock of debt is said to be sustainable if the burden of servicing it is not producing any strains and if current policies and trends indicate that the debt-service burden will not increase in the future relative to the borrowers' capacity to pay."[344] Sachs[345] has expressed the view that all sustainability criteria of the types cited above do not at all represent debt sustainability despite their frequent use. For example, most indicators do not address the government's ability to repay its external public debt and most HIPCs in Africa rely heavily on imports. Moreover, there is hardly any strong empirical evidence for preferring certain debt sustainability indicators over others.[346]

The *Debt Sustainability Framework in low income countries* is a recent proposal[347] that includes a country-specific approach to evaluate debt sustainability, which, contrary to the HIPC criteria, differentiates the debt ratios depending on the quality of institutions and national policies. The latter are measured applying the World Bank's Country Policy and Institutional Assessment-Index. The higher this index, the higher is the ceiling for debt sustainability. This instrument is planned to be used as a

[342] See Birdsall and Williamson (2002).
[343] See Berensmann (2004), p. 12.
[344] See Rieffel (2003), p. 48
[345] See Sachs (2000).
[346] See Hjertholm (1999) and Gunter (2001).
[347] See IMF and World Bank (2004).

plumb-line for future decisions on multilateral grant and loan disbursement. It can be regarded as a major advancement of the HIPC I and II sustainability criteria. Extensions to this framework have been presented by Bunte et al. who suggest setting up a Board of Trustees on Sustainability (BOTOS), which would negotiate a business plan providing a framework for creditor and debtor.[348] Table 3.6 compares regions and country income groups with respect to various debt service ratios in 1990 and 2004 that were obtained in Debt Sustainability analyses of the World Bank.

Table 3.6. Debt ratios in selected country groups and regions for 1990 and 2004

	Total debt service				Multilateral debt service		Short-term debt			
	[% of GNI]		[% of exports and goods, services and income]		[% of public and publicly guaranteed debt]		[% of total debt]		[% of exports and goods, services and income]	
	1990	2004	1990	2004	1990	2004	1990	2004	1990	2004
LIC	3.9	3.0	22.4	10.1	27.7	24.8	11.0	8.5	39.9	17.7
LMIC	4.1	4.5	24.3	13.1	22.3	26.9	16.1	20.8	30.1	16.5
UMIC	–	8.1	15.6	17.0	13.5	14.9	17.2	18.6	27.5	18.3
LAMIC	4.5	5.6	19.8	14.5	19.4	21.4	15.2	18.0	30.5	17.3
East Asia & Pacific	4.8	3.0	17.5	6.8	17.7	23.0	16.0	29.7	20.5	16.8
Europe & Centr. Asia	–	8.9	–	19.6	10.0	14.3	18.2	20.2	36.0	19.8
Latin Am. & Caribb.	4.2	8.1	23.8	26.4	27.6	24.4	16.6	12.4	39.7	16.2
Mid. East & No. Afr.	6.3	4.4	21.4	10.6	13.1	24.3	14.1	13.1	22.5	12.9
South Asia	2.9	2.9	27.6	12.4	25.3	21.2	9.9	5.3	30.1	6.1
Sub-Sahara	–	2.9	13.5	7.9	30.0	23.0	11.6	13.3	–	18.0

Source: World Bank (2006a)

Notes:
LIC = low-income countries, *LMIC* = lower middle-income countries, *UMIC* = upper middle-income countries, *LAMIC* = lower and middle-income countries

Nevertheless, despite many proposed indicators, setting a fixed (objective) debt sustainability frontier has been subject to criticism.[349] Countries with a high productivity of their financial resources may be solvent even with a

[348] See Bunte et al. (2004).
[349] See Nunnenkamp (2001), p. 6 and Ajayi and Khan (2000).

high index of indebtedness, while countries with a high share of consumption may be heavily in debt despite a relatively low index. Put differently, a country may be highly indebted despite a low debt/export ratio because it uses the loans for consumption, while other countries may exceed the debt-export ratio of 150% but can be solvent because they put the resources into productive (long-run) investments. It is also questionable whether a clearly specified debt frontier might provide adverse incentives. Countries close to the 150% limit could accumulate debt to qualify for the HIPC initiative. This incentive is the larger the higher the promised debt reduction.

HIPC track record[350]

By August 2005, 38 countries potentially qualified for HIPC debt relief. Of these, 18 countries have reached the Completion Point and will receive debt relief. Their debt stocks declined by an average of 64% from $59 billion to $21 billion (see Fig. 3.6). Ten more countries have reached the Decision Point. The total debt stock of the 28 Decision Point countries is estimated to decrease from $84 billion to $33 billion (measured in 2004 NPV dollars). Six of ten countries in the interim period are advancing with the implementation of their macroeconomic programs, while the remaining four do not have an IMF program in place. Seven of ten interim countries have completed a full PRSP.

Measured by the net present value of debt relief, the HIPC initiative has been relatively effective.[351] However, the results vary significantly by country. Some countries have indeed achieved a debt reduction that is likely to stay sustainable (Ghana, Madagascar, Mali, Tanzania); other countries' debt will most likely increase to unsustainable levels soon.[352] One could also account for the duration of the entire HIPC initiative (1996–2006) and put the results into perspective.

[350] See IMF and IDA (2005) for data used in this section.

[351] See Cohen (2001), p. 364 for a critical note on the use of net present value calculations in the HIPC. According to Cohen, there is a lack of understanding of the true market value of debt to be written down. Discounting unpayable debt at market discount rates seriously distorts the real debt burden. Furthermore, the interest rate for computing the net present value is a critical determinant of the real value of debt relief. The higher the interest rate, the lower is the net present value of debt to be cancelled. Changes in market interest rates can significantly change the debt burden of HIPCs and thus provides a hidden adjustment screw.

[352] See Berensmann (2004), p. 1.

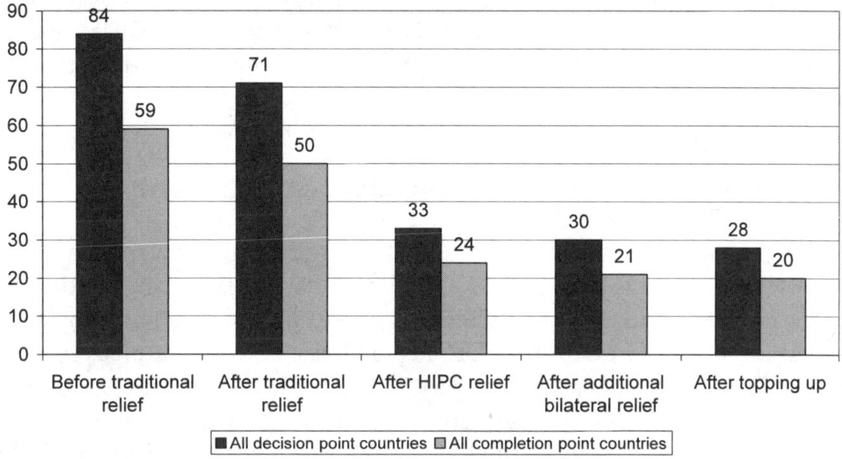

Fig. 3.6. Debt stock reduction in HIPC countries [in $ billions and 2004 NPV]

Source: IMF and IDA (2005), p. 9
Note: A topping up is granted exceptionally to those HIPC countries proving that external developments have significantly worsened their economic prospects and diluted earlier assumptions (e.g., about commodity prices).

It remains contested whether or not the HIPC initiative has led to higher shares of expenditures for poverty reduction on average. IMF and IDA point out that poverty-reducing expenditures (measured as absolute total, as a ratio to government revenue and as a ratio to GDP) have increased steadily from 1999 to 2005.[353] During this period, external debt service payments have declined.[354] But there is mixed evidence that the HIPC initiative (e.g. via its conditional PRSP documents) has triggered this improvement. More precisely, there are so far no solid empirical proofs that the rise in poverty-reducing expenditures is correlated with declining debt service payments, although this is frequently assumed to be the case.[355] Not only is the greatest share of debt-service payments during the HIPC in-

[353] See also World Bank (2002a) for development and estimates of social expenditures in HIPC countries.

[354] Debt service-to-export ratios, as a weighted average in all 28 Decision Point countries, declined from 15.7% (average 1998–1999) to 8.7 % and are expected to fall to 5.8% in 2006. See IMF and IDA (2005), p. 51.

[355] Dijkstra and Hermes (2001) provide supportive evidence for the hypothesis that debt relief has reduced uncertainty about debt service payments which increases the effectiveness of government policies. Whether or not poverty-reducing investments have increased, remains a different issue.

terim period covered by creditor countries and may adulterate the effect. Also, as Sect. 3.2 has pointed out, ODA disbursements to HIPCs have increased significantly, which could have caused the effect of additional poverty-reducing investments.

3.5.4 Multilateral debt relief: 100% debt cancellation?

The experiences of HIPC I and II elicited desire of the American and UK Minister of Finance to call for a 100% multilateral debt cancellation for LDC. Formerly referred to as the G8 Proposal for Debt Relief, the Multilateral Debt Relief Initiative (MDRI) is the latest outcome of pledges made at the G8 Summit in Gleneagles (July 2005).[356] The G8 members agreed to completely cancel multilateral debt of estimated $37 billion owed by 18 eligible countries[357] over the next 40 years. This plan was backed by IMF, World Bank and the African Development Bank in September 2005.[358] Approximately 70 percent of this debt is due the World Bank, the remainder to IMF and African Development Bank. By granting this debt relief, the average net present value debt to export ratio is estimated to fall from 140 percent (after HIPC relief) to 52 percent after implementation of the G8 proposal.[359] Bilateral donors have approved to provide the necessary financing of debt relief as well as preserving their regular financing towards the multilateral institutions, i.e. to finance the foregone principal and inter-

[356] The proposal was initially agreed upon at the G8 Finance Ministers' Meeting in London, June 10–11, 2005.

[357] Most eligible countries have reached the Completion Point of the HIPC initiative and include Benin, Bolivia, Burkina Faso, Zambia, Uganda, Tanzania, Senegal, Rwanda, Mali, Guyana, Honduras, Madagascar, Ethiopia, Ghana, Mauritania, Mozambique, Niger and Nicaragua. 20 more countries (10 interim and 10 pre-Decision Point countries) are potentially eligible for a similar treatment of debt cancellation.

[358] See Development Committee (2005). The Boards of IMF and IDA will decide in February 2006 on which countries will participate in the MDRI. It is expected that MDRI implementation will begin on July 1, 2006 (= Fiscal Year 2007). However, the decision and form to grant debt relief is ultimately under the individual responsibility of each institution. The IMF, for example, has agreed that all countries with a per capita income of $380 per annum or less, regardless of being HIPC or not, will receive MDRI debt relief. Countries with an income above that threshold will receive MDRI debt relief from bilateral contributions administered by the IMF. Consequently, the composition of eligible countries slightly differs from the IDA list and covers 19 countries, among them two non-HIPCs. See IMF (2005b).

[359] See Development Committee (2005), p. 2.

est repayments (= reflows losses) of the IDA.[360] Thus the debt relief would be additional to current bilateral ODA disbursements. However, despite the official commitment to replenish IDA resources, no explicit solution has been agreed to cover the future financing gap. Details on the exact relief dates and cost-drivers are negotiated, but not fixed at present. The choice of the cut-off date, the number of eligible countries and the type of coverage (fully disbursed credits vs. debt disbursed and outstanding) are still uncertain and subject to discussion. The IMF has announced that it will use the profits of 1999–2000 off-market gold transactions and transfer these into a Trust Fund to finance its MDRI share. Furthermore, despite creditors' rhetoric, debt relief may crowd out foreign aid.[361]

The complete cancellation of multilateral debt, although likely to be spread over a number of years, has been welcomed by many, but also criticized by others. First, proponents of a 100% debt cancellation put forward the argument that poor countries that have received complete debt cancellation will make more poverty-reducing and social investments in health and basic infrastructure than countries whose debt is only partially reduced. It remains disputed, as already mentioned above, whether this argument is valid. Second, the complete write-off is not the end of the road. Most economists agree that being able to borrow from external sources (private and official) is a fundamentally important instrument to foster investment and to finance economic growth. Therefore, the argument that the MDRI provides a fresh start for developing countries and thus is sufficient is rather weak. Third, it must not be forgotten that IDA loans are concessional and that they represent approximately 50 percent of income for multilateral donors.[362] Consequently, IMF and World Bank paid utmost attention to the fact that multilateral debt relief is ultimately financed by bilateral donors, who pledged to compensate the institutions for any losses of multilateral assets. Furthermore, IMF and World Bank staffs argued in a 2001 statement[363] that they have to ensure financial support for all developing countries. "Total debt cancellation for those countries alone would

[360] The compensation for repayments is estimated at $42.5 billion over the full 40-year period of the 38 potential countries and would include disbursed and outstanding debt. This figure would rise to $56.5 billion if eight additional countries were covered. If not financed, IDA's assets would be reduced by 27 percent and 36 percent, respectively. IDA's total assets as of June 30, 2005 are $130.4 billion, as in its financial statements.

[361] See Arslanalp and Henry (2004), p. 17 who show that aid inflows have decreased with the HIPC debt relief initiative.

[362] The other half is financed via regular donor replenishments.

[363] See IMF and World Bank (2001a).

come at the expense of other borrowing countries [...]"[364]. It must be assured that there are enough financial assets for multilateral donors to provide in the future. Substantial write-offs could result in a weaker equity capital position of the institutions on the international capital markets and higher borrowing costs. Fourth, a moral hazard problem may occur with a 100% debt cancellation. A general cancellation of multilateral debt for poor HIPC would favor them over poor non-HIPC, which failed to qualify for the initiative due to better debt management and better policy performance. This would not only mean a reallocation towards a specific country group, but also a penalty for countries with strong performance, setting wrong incentives, e.g. to boost up debt in anticipation of similar debt cancellation. Therefore, it seems legitimate to persist on the prevailing procedure that countries calling for a debt cancellation run through the entire HIPC process until Completion Point. Fifth, it remains hard to diagnose what share of debt just reflects a "window cleaning" procedure in the sense that some debt would not have been repaid anyway and cancellation is merely a process of clearing the books. The releasing effect of debt cancellation is then diluted.

3.5.5 Summary and conclusions

The international framework of debt relief has significantly developed over the last decade. The focus has shifted towards providing multilateral debt cancellation for the poorest and most highly indebted countries within a multi-donor framework. Yet, the ultimate decisions to grant debt relief are made following negotiations among individual donor countries (G8 platform). Under remarkable pressure of other bilateral donors, NGO and the public, the G8 members have finally agreed that multilateral debt owed to World Bank, IMF and African Development Bank will be completely written off in the near future, probably starting July 2006. Still, final details still have to be elaborated. The debt relief granted is additional to current ODA disbursements in order to maintain the function of World Bank, IMF and regional development banks as multilateral creditors of grants and loans. Nevertheless, some issues remain unsolved and several others newly arise with this recent decision. Among them, the following are especially noteworthy:

1. Elaborating on objective and operational definitions of debt sustainability criteria

[364] IMF and World Bank (2001a).

2. Estimating the potential net benefits of debt cancellation for the poor (are they systematically overestimated?)
3. Clarifying the comparability of treatment (Do donors treat recipient countries alike? Should they? Once the cancellation of principal actually takes place, non-affected countries may demand similar treatment.)
4. Closing the potential short-term financing gap
5. Securing long-term financing of development
6. Ensuring that indebted countries cure the underlying causes of indebtedness to achieve permanently sustainable debt levels
7. Keeping debt sustainable in the future

Issues 1–4 have been already dealt with. The final three refer to the long-run perspective and to the objective to make debt relief an exemption rather than the rule. Within the entire discussion on debt relief, these matters are somewhat neglected. Including conditional PRSP documents into the HIPC eligibility framework was an important step, because it facilitated the ownership of strategies to alleviate poverty (see in more detail in the next chapter). But the HIPC initiative should also be accompanied by a long-term strategy to give HIPCs a vision to grow out of their debt. Poor countries must have the opportunity to borrow investment capital from official and private lenders. They also must have the opportunity to sell their products on the world markets. From the perspective of creditors, this includes providing additional (official and private) finance and rethinking market openness in some critical sectors (e.g., primary commodities), which are characterized by a relatively high level of protectionist (tariff and non-tariff) trade barriers. From the perspective of debtors, it must be learned that debt relief is not granted automatically in cases of growth failure, but that it represents a "once-in-a-lifetime present" and that addressing the underlying domestic causes of indebtedness, which include structural current account deficits, oversized state budgets, inefficient use of scarce resources, high inflation and overvalued currencies, is essential. Although debt relief may spur economic growth under certain conditions, it has been outlined in earlier chapters that the poverty-debt/aid-growth nexus is very complex and that debt relief is not at all sufficient for future economic growth. It has to be made sure that there will be no new debt accumulation circle once the "old debt" has been forgiven. Unfortunately, some countries experience just this. The dynamics of debt, as they are theorized in intertemporal borrowing models and growth-cum-debt models (see Chap. 4), highlight the critical link to future economic growth. The HIPC and the MDRI frameworks are still lacking this link.

Keeping debt sustainable in the post-HIPC era is a topic that was for a long time relatively deserted within the HIPC literature.[365] Bringing a single debt measure down to a critical threshold at a single point of time provides no guarantee against future debt crises. HIPCs require macroeconomic sustainability (that is, fiscal sustainability as well as current account sustainability[366]) after having received HIPC relief. Fedelino and Kudina[367] find that, on the basis of current fiscal policies, debt levels will remain unsustainable even after the HIPC initiative. Due to the conditionality of HIPCs to invest more in poverty reduction, the fiscal balance may in fact be weakened.[368] Scaling down expenditure programs, generating a higher level of domestic revenue and securing higher non-debt-creating grants are mentioned as potential policy options. These might, however, lead to a short-term policy dilemma: The first option is not really feasible with respect to international agreed development objectives, the second is viable only in the long-run, because reforming taxing systems takes considerable time, and the third option could manoeuvre some HIPCs into even higher aid dependency than presently existing. Burnside and Fanizza[369] also conclude that the debt relief-for- poverty reduction conditionality could result in short-run increases of inflation as a result of increased domestic spending on poverty reduction.

Edwards[370] has developed a model that investigates the connection between debt relief and current account sustainability in a typical HIPC. In particular, he recognizes that economic conditions of HIPCs are likely to change after debt relief was granted. The model shows that whether a country achieves external sustainability will depend on the availability of concessional loans going forward and the future path of grants and donations. Exemplified in the country case of Nicaragua, Edwards argues it is reasonable to assume that "extremely severe external sector adjustment

[365] Ndung'u et al. (2004) have presented an edited volume on these issues recently.

[366] See Cuddington (1995), Edwards (2002) and IMF (2000b).

[367] See Fedelino and Kudina (2003).

[368] The projection is, however, subject to various limitations concerning the assumptions on future growth rate, inflation, exchange rate and interest rate developments. Nissanke and Ferrarini (2001), p. 21 have shown that the projected real growth rates assumed for HIPC countries are often overly optimistic. IMF and World Bank (2001b), Table 5 have compared the real GDP growth rates of 1990–1999 and estimated 2000–2010. Many growth projections seem very unlikely (e.g., Zambia: 1.0 and 5.2 percent, respectively). The estimated average real growth rate for 2000–2010 is 5.5 percent.

[369] See Burnside and Fanizza (2004).

[370] See Edwards (2003).

[and a] massive real exchange rate devaluation" might be necessary, having in turn negative implications for fiscal sustainability.

The careful weighing of arguments made in the last sections is an important precondition for successful debt relief. Debt cancellation is neither good nor bad per se, but must be viewed against the specific circumstances of the country in question. In this respect, there have been some remarkable improvements in the management and commitment of debt relief lately. Still, it is an illusion to believe that debt cancellation is a sufficient condition to economic growth and poverty reduction.

3.6 From structural adjustment programs to poverty reduction strategies

3.6.1 Structural Adjustment Programs and conditionality

Structural Adjustment Programs (sometimes also labelled "Structural Adjustment Policies", SAPs) have been for a long time the dominating policy instruments of World Bank and IMF. The first SAPs were launched in 1980 in order to help countries facing balance-of-payments-deficits and at the same time maintaining economic growth.[371] They included Structural Adjustment Loans (SALs) and Sectoral Adjustment Loans (SECALs), which provided finance in return for specific policy reforms. They were estimated at three to five years. SALs contained conditionality clauses touching areassuch as currency devaluation, fiscal adjustment, privatization, liberalization (e.g., reducing tariff and non-tariff barriers of trade) and restructuring the agricultural planning system.[372]

There has been an early and intensive debate on the effectiveness of SAPs, conditionality and their implications on economic development.[373] Many contributions, however, neglected that it is insufficient to assume that conditionality was successful if a recipient government has changed its policies in the course of a structural adjustment program.[374] Instead, the following four cases that must be set apart:

1. No reforms were implemented, but conditionality occurred.

---

[371] See World Bank (1980), pp. 67–68.

[372] Amsden (1989) has coined the term „getting the prices right"for such a market-driven system. Interestingly, Amsden pointed out that the East Asian countries were so successful because they managed to get the prices "wrong", not right.

[373] See, among others, Kuck (1998) and Dreher (2004) for overviews and Easterly (2005) for a critique.

[374] See Gunning (2000), p. 2.

2. Reforms were implemented, which would have taken place without conditionality.
3. Reforms were implemented due to conditional clauses, but were not sustained.
4. Reforms were implemented due to conditional clauses and were sustained.

Only in case 4, conditionality can be viewed as effective. The ineffectiveness of conditionality in case 1 is straightforward. In case 2, conditionality was redundant, and in case 3, reforms prove to be only temporary. The distinction made above also illustrates the limits of regression analysis in this field: A clear one-way causation of conditionality and reforms is often very difficult to establish. Apart from this methodological consideration, a variety of arguments have been exchanged. The most important reasons why conditionality fails to work in practice is the lack of adequate commitment services, for instance a credible threat to reduce or even cut off aid. Examples for such a deficiency include donors' opposition due to political motivations or banks attempting to protect their loan portfolio from default.[375]

Collier[376] has proposed to reformulate traditional (ex ante-) conditionality to a selectivity approach, based on countries' retrospective performance, also known as ex-post conditionality. Thus, by "creating star performers"[377], countries with successful growth records could serve as a role model for poorly performing countries. The main point of critique addressed the missing consideration of social costs associated with structural adjustment. The strategy to reduce the fiscal deficit resulted in an undersupply of basic services such as clean water or social expenditures (e.g., health services), thereby especially hurting the poor. SAPs did not include social clauses that helped to ensure a smooth transition because social problems were regarded as temporary. Moreover, a trickle-down effect, (i.e. spillover effects running through the sectors of the economy), did not occur as assumed. As a consequence, SAPs were frequently relaunched and lasted substantially longer than initially planned. New proposals (expressed, among others, by UNICEF) aimed at guaranteeing a minimum standard of living throughout the structural adjustment phase. As a result, the World Bank subsequently included social evaluations in their regular reports and focused more on the social impact of structural adjustment.[378] This initial "side issue" became more and more a priority and finally paved

[375] See Rogerson (2005), p. 541.
[376] See Collier (1998).
[377] Nissanke and Ferrarini (2001), p. 23.
[378] See for example World Bank (2000a) and Siebold (1995).

the way for the term "poverty reduction" as a major World Bank objective. Still, as Führmann summarizes, despite the inclusion of social clauses, the basic economic strategy of growth and trickle-down effects remains rather untouched.[379]

Similar to the World Bank, nevertheless with a focus towards macroeconomic stabilization (such as low inflation), the IMF also set up a variety of loan programs, starting as early as 1963 with standby loans, the Compensatory Finance Facility (CFF) and the Extended Fund Facility (EFF). Structural loans were first introduced in 1986 with the Structural Adjustment Facility (SAF) and with the Enhanced Structural Adjustment Facility (ESAF) in 1987. SAF and ESAF were lending facilities that granted poor countries concessional development assistance. The condition was to install a policy program with a macroeconomic focus on stability. Further instruments were the System Transformation Facility (1993–1995) and Contingent Credit Lines (1999–2003). While the former were especially designed for transition countries, the latter aimed at helping emerging market economies facing financial crises.

The empirical literature evaluating IMF conditional programs and their effectiveness is considerably large.[380] More recently, some studies have been published measuring the effect of SAPs on growth (and employment) and their compliance with conditionality. The results vary by the statistical methods used as well as by the length, type and number of the IMF programs in the sample. Dreher (2004) provides an extensive review of studies on the effects of IMF programs and distinguishes between Before/After, With/Without, and Regression-based approaches[381]. Before/After studies were undertaken mostly in the 1980s and 1990s, covering periods between the 1970s and 1990s and a relatively small number of countries. They compare the growth rate before and after an IMF Program. The results showed that the effect of IMF programs on growth was either positive or not significant. With/Without studies of the 1980s came to different results, including positive, negative and inconclusive effects. In this approach, a country group with a running IMF program is compared with a group that has no program. Regression-based studies covered a larger number of countries (43–135) and IMF programs

379 See Führmann (2003), p. 19.

380 One of the first studies was undertaken by Beveridge and Kelly (1980). See Dreher (2004) for a detailed overview of the literature.

381 See Dreher (2004). The data availability for the different types of studies changed when the IMF started its database Monitoring Fund Arrangements (MONA) that contains performance criteria and structural benchmarks. On the other hand, this database only contains programs that have been reviewed by the Executive Board.

ger number of countries (43–135) and IMF programs (up to 764) as well as periods (several decades). Although different results (positive, negative, and inconclusive) were achieved, the latest examinations with very large samples predominantly suggest a negative effect of SAPs on growth.[382] However, the huge differences in the methodology, number of programs, countries and side effects allow for no clear consensus. In addition to that, Easterly points toward the difficulties that arise from the frequent repetition of SALs to certain countries and finds that "[t]he probability of a subsequent loan does not decrease with the number of loans already received".[383] Interestingly, 17 out of 18 countries that received high adjustment lending between 1980 and 1999, were included in the Highly Indebted Poor Country Initiative, in contrast to 8 of 17 countries with relatively low adjustment lending.[384] Table 3.7 provides more details on SALs in African and ex-Communist countries.

Although it can be rejected that SALs caused the poor growth rates of SALs receiving countries, "it would be hard to argue that their [IMF and World Bank's] involvement in the country had a *positive* long-run effect."[385] Finally, international institutions themselves often evaluate the results against their ex ante objectives and "expectations they created"[386]. In August 2004, a new operational policy ("Development Policy Lending") has formally superseded the former adjustment lending.[387] This new policy reflects and harmonizes policy updates, additions, clarifications and guidelines issued over the last decade. By this, the World Bank finally acknowledges that there is no blueprint for development policy as postulated in the "Washington Consensus".

---

[382] See, for example, Hutchison (2001), Barro and Lee (2003), Przeworski and Vreeland (2000). Studies that found a positive effect on growth are, among others, Bagci and Perraudin (1997) and Dicks-Mireaux et al. (2000).

[383] Easterly (2005), p. 7. In fact, ibid., p. 3 argues that „countries that received adjustment loans did so because they were having poor macroeconomic and growth outcomes, and so it would not be surprising if we found a negative association between these outcomes and adjustment loans without correcting for selection bias." However, this selection bias problem is affected „if […] not eliminate[d]" (p. 4) by the frequent repetition of adjustment loans signalling that the former therapy has not been effective.

[384] See ibid., p. 10.

[385] Easterly (2006), p. 67.

[386] See Easterly (2005), p. 3.

[387] See World Bank (2004a).

Table 3.7. SALs, growth and inflation in poor countries with most SALs received

	Number of IMF and World Bank adjustment loans, 1980–1999	Annual per capita growth rate from the date of first structural adjustment loan [in %]	Annual inflation rate from first adjustment loan to 1999 [in %]
African countries that were in the world's top twenty of Structural Adjustment Loans received 1980–1999			
Niger	14	-2.30	2
Zambia	18	-2.10	58
Madagascar	17	-1.80	17
Togo	15	-1.60	5
Côte d'Ivoire	26	-1.40	6
Malawi	18	-0.20	23
Mali	15	-0.10	4
Mauritania	16	0.10	7
Senegal	21	0.10	5
Kenya	19	0.10	14
Ghana	26	1.20	32
Uganda	20	2.30	50
Top ten Recipients of Structural Adjustment Loans over 1990–1999 among ex-communist countries (growth and inflation measured from first adjustment loan to 1999)			
Ukraine	10	-8.4	215
Russian Federation	13	-5.7	141
Kyrgyz Republic	10	-4.4	25
Kazakhstan	9	-3.1	117
Bulgaria	13	-2.2	124
Romania	11	-1.2	114
Hungary	14	1.0	16
Poland	9	3.4	52
Albania	8	4.4	40
Georgia	7	6.4	37

Source: Easterly (2006), pp. 66–67

3.6.2 Washington Consensus and Post-Washington Consensus

The term "Washington Consensus", introduced by John Williamson[388], was originally meant to describe "the lowest common denominator of policy advice being addressed by the Washington-based institutions to Latin American countries"[389], but now expresses "an extreme and dogmatic commitment to the belief that markets can handle everything."[390] The Washington Consensus can be regarded as a set of economic principles underlying the SAPs. The original package of policies involved ten propositions:

1. Fiscal discipline
2. A redirection of public expenditure priorities toward fields offering both high economic returns and the potential to improve income distribution, such as primary health care, primary education, and infrastructure
3. Tax reform (to lower marginal rates and broaden the tax base)
4. Interest rate liberalization
5. A competitive exchange rate
6. Trade liberalization
7. Liberalization of inflows of foreign direct investment
8. Privatization
9. Deregulation (to abolish barriers to entry and exit)
10. Secure property rights

Important theoretical work underlying these principles was undertaken by Bhagwati, Krueger and Balassa.[391] However, the economic principles stated above are elements of "an agenda for a specific part of the world at a particular moment of history".[392] Moreover, it is questionable whether a consensus on the above policies really existed. In general, many economists agree that the Washington Consensus list entails imperative elements of economic growth to be addressed, But similarly, they are careful to apply them uniformly to all countries and/or situations (e.g., during or after financial crises). Much more confusion arises when the term is taken as a synonym for "neoliberal politics" or "market fundamentalism", which was not Williamson's initial intent. Williamson himself notes that a lot of definitions in the literature do not embrace his original meaning of the term,

388 Williamson (1990). See also Priewe (2005), p. 22ff.
389 Williamson (2000), p. 251.
390 Ibid., p. 252.
391 See Bhagwati (1978), Krueger (1985) and Balassa (1982).
392 Williamson (2000), p. 256.

which has led to a semantic dilemma. But in his interpretation of the principles, they still more or less provide "a useful summary of the advice the Bank dispenses." While Williamson defends nine of the ten propositions to be "potentially pro-poor"[393] (i.e., having a positive impact on the reduction of poverty), he expands "interest rate liberalization" by the need for a financial supervision.

Many researchers have criticized the IMF's policy recommendations before, during and after the Asian crisis and point out the fact that its blueprint does not function equally well in all countries.[394] Among others, the following facets are noteworthy:

1. The crisis preconditions of various countries and country groups varied substantially from another (e.g., Latin American vs. Asian countries). The Washington Consensus was born in a Latin American context with its high inflation/closed economy/state dominance syndrome.[395] Applying this approach to other countries (e.g., LDCs), is inappropriate, as these countries will be affected differently by external shocks.
2. Markets do not always work perfectly due to asymmetric information or negative externalities. In this case, the price mechanism only works imperfectly and needs to be accompanied by a supporting role of the state.
3. The IMF demanded budgetary discipline as well as a reduction of the current account deficit. However, if the rate of return on investments is higher than the cost of capital (interest rate), then a current account deficit may be sustainable and even lead to growth.
4. The assumed "trickle-down effect", in which long-term sustainable economic growth would benefit the poorest people, did not take place. One result was that poor households suffered most severely from the crisis.
5. To increase capital flows to crisis countries, the IMF proposed higher interest rates, which may hold back domestic investment. Also, higher interest rates could reduce the bank's net worth and in fact worsening the banking crisis.[396] Demirguc-Kunt and Detragiache show that high real interest rates may lead to a higher fragility of the banking sector.[397]

393 Ibid., p. 258.
394 See, among others, Stiglitz (2002).
395 See Stallings (2004).
396 See Stiglitz (1998) for the latter.
397 See Demirguc-Kunt and Detragiache (1997).

6. Structural reforms, not an initial element of IMF policies, were demanded in sync with the World Bank's structural assistance. For example, the IMF demanded the closing of inefficient and bankrupt banks. It has been argued that this led to panic-like bank runs, to a shortage of liquidity and domestic loans and to a contraction of domestic investment.

The literature on the search for a new development agenda, following the Washington Consensus, has splintered into several strands. One branch, initiated by Stiglitz (1998), is to favor a "post-Washington Consensus".[398] Stiglitz's proposition is to significantly broaden the policy objectives by including sustainable development, technology transfer, competition, (in)equality and democracy issues. According to Stiglitz, this wider agenda could only be based in part on the original Washington Consensus. Instead, a broader (universal) understanding would be necessary.[399] In an extension to the ten original "commandments" of the Washington Consensus, Rodrik[400] formulated ten additional goals in his "augmented Washington Consensus": Corporate governance, anti-corruption, flexible labor markets, WTO agreements, financial codes and standards, prudent capital account opening, non-intermediate exchange rate regimes, independent central banks/inflation targeting, social safety nets, and targeted poverty reduction.

The Stiglitz critique does not claim the Washington Consensus policies were generally wrong, but that they led to the wrong focus, neglecting other important factors, such as the efficiency of the financial system or the problem of sequencing financial reforms.[401] This is consistent with Priewe's finding that the principles are not wrong but can lead to a dead-end if combined without country-specific adaptation.[402]

A second branch, led by Burki and Perry (1998), acknowledges the success of the Washington Consensus (in its original meaning) in at least some aspects and proposes a second generation reform agenda that focuses more on institutional reforms with the aim to reduce poverty.[403] A similar agenda has been framed at the United Nations International Conference on

[398] Stiglitz (1998).

[399] He remains silent, though, on the question which institution should receive the power to establish this form of development policy. Such an institution would be likely to apply a standard approach to every country due to scarce research resources. It would also not be politically feasible to create such an institution or to expand the legal status of some of the existing institutions.

[400] See Rodrik (2001), p. 15.

[401] See also Stiglitz (2002).

[402] See Priewe (2005), p. 25.

[403] See Burki and Perry (1998).

Financing for Development (Monterrey, 2002). Latest proposals such as the one by Maxwell[404] who suggests a "meta-narrative approach" go even further and cannot be filed under the "consensus" literature any longer.

In sum, the Washington Consensus proposed a general framework for a set of countries at a certain point in history. It should not be mis- or over-interpreted, but reduced to what it actually aimed to describe: the situation of some Latin American countries during the 1980s under their special initial conditions (high inflation, state dominance, closed economy). Unfortunately, the IMF and, to a lesser extent also the World Bank, have also applied it in many other cases and moved towards a "one size fits all" design for its policy proposals. While this has been successful in some cases, it has been deteriorating in others.

3.6.3 Poverty reduction strategy papers (PRSP)

The missing success of earlier initiatives as well as rising political pressure stemming from individuals (Stiglitz, Sachs), research institutions and NGOs about the ineffectiveness of structural adjustment policies and consensus-based strategies paved the way for the IMF and the World Bank to shift their focus towards more country-specific poverty reduction. "The poverty issue is so red-hot that IMF and World Bank staff began to feel that every action inside these organizations, from reviewing public expenditure to vacuuming the office carpet, should be justified by its effect on poverty reduction."[405] Starting with Comprehensive Development Frameworks (CDF), introduced in 1999, the World Bank formulated guidelines as to how it conducts business with donors and recipient countries. They encompass four guiding principles:

- A long-term, holistic visions of countries' needs (including macroeconomic, social and structural needs),
- A focus on results rather than inputs,
- Country-ownership,
- development partners should foster partnerships as a support to country-owned strategy.

Building on CDF, so-called Poverty Reduction Strategy Papers (PRSPs) were introduced in December 1999 following the G-7 HIPC debt relief summit in Cologne. Initially, PRSPs should serve as a connection between the HIPC initiative and the Millennium Development Goals. Countries can

[404] See Maxwell (2005), p. 67.
[405] Easterly (2001), p. 2.

only participate in HIPC II if they agree on a national strategy to reduce poverty. In a very short time, however, PRSPs have become "the reference document for a large part of international development aid."[406]

Content and Process of a PRSP

According to the World Bank, PRSPs "describe a country's macroeconomic, structural and social policies and programs to promote growth and reduce poverty, as well as associated external financing needs. [They] are prepared by governments through a participatory process involving civil society and development partners, including the World Bank and the International Monetary Fund (IMF)."[407] There are five core principles underlying a PRSP:

1. Country-driven and -owned processes and partnership orientation
   Participation of all kinds of private actors and civil society groups in the formulation of a development strategy is required. It is assumed that social participation will lead to increased ownership and success of the development strategy. The dialogue between donors, recipient governments and social partners should be enforced.
2. Comprehensiveness in scope
   In order for the society to take part in the PRSP process, the documents, analyses and the formulation of policies must be understandable and reasonable.
3. Results-orientation
   Long-term strategies must be disaggregated into smaller processes, which have to be evaluated on a regular basis by making use of qualitative and quantitative indicators.
4. Medium and long-term perspective:[408]
   The focus of PRSPs is on medium and long-term oriented outcomes and underscores the awareness that poverty reduction is a long-term process involving institutional changes, capacity building and strengthening governance.
5. Prioritization
   Recognizing the limited funds available, priorities must be chosen together with feasible policies and funding proposals.

Initially, all 77 countries that qualified for IDA loans were obliged to present a PRSP. Now, 81 countries have signalled to prepare a PRSP. In the

---

[406] Paul (2002), p. 1

[407] World Bank (2006b).

[408] See Klugman (2004), p. 3.

first period, so called interim PRSPs (I-PRSPs) were accepted because a full PRSP may take more than one year. "I-PRSPs were intended to be short documents that described a country's current poverty situation and policies, and presented a plan for preparing a full PRSP."[409] A country's full PRSP is then analyzed by IMF and World Bank in a Joint Staff Assessment (JSA).[410] Until March 2006, 60 countries have prepared an Interim PRSP and 51 have presented their full PRSP to the Board of Executive Directors of the World Bank. The basis for approval is the soundness and credibility of the framework presented by the country, not necessarily an agreement to all actions set forth in the PRSP. Upon acceptance, World Bank and IMF then provide the necessary funding und develop a CDF.[411] Other bilateral and multilateral donors are expected to align their ODA to the PRSP.

The following areas must be covered by a country in its PRSP report:

- Assessing poverty and its key determinants,
- Setting targets for poverty reduction,
- Prioritizing public actions for poverty reduction,
- Establishing systematic monitoring of poverty trends and evaluating the impact of government programs and policies,
- Describing the main aspects of the participatory process,[412]
- A description of macroeconomic and structural policies to support sustainable growth in which the poor participate,
- A documentation of improvements in governance, including public sector financial/fiscal management,
- Formulating appropriate sectoral policies and programs,
- Presenting realistic costing and appropriate levels of funding for the major programs.[413]

---

[409] IMF (2002), p. 7.

[410] Joint staff assessments should also help the governments of poor countries as well as other participants involved to better understand the evaluation process of IMF and World Bank. In practice, however, "JSAs are virtually unknown outside the narrow official circle and consequently have no impact on the broader policy debate." IMF (2004), p. 4.

[411] The concessional loans usually given by the World Bank's branch IDA are now linked to the formulation of a PRSP. Also the IMF announced that future loans will be aligned to the PRSP and PRGF.

[412] See Klugman (2004), p. 4. Note that the staffs have been instructed by the executive boards to describe but not to evaluate the participatory process.

[413] See ibid., p. 4.

Each year, the countries in question publish a Progress Report. The PRSP process runs through several general phases as depicted in Fig. 3.7. The country is asked to provide the JSA with information on the participatory process and how this affects the content of the strategy. Existing programs, processes and running national as well as sectoral projects shall be included into the analysis. Furthermore, PRSPs shall be in sync with existing policies and budgets approved by the government.

There are two financing mechanisms of preparing and aligning PRSPs: The IMF's credit program is the Poverty Reduction and Growth facility (PRGF). The World Bank applies Poverty Reduction Support Credits (PRSC, formerly SALs) in its Country Assistance Strategies (CAS). The latter can be regarded as the World Bank's "business plan" for individual countries and indicate the composition and volume of ODA granted. The PRSC provide financial support from the World Bank for countries implementing their PRSP.

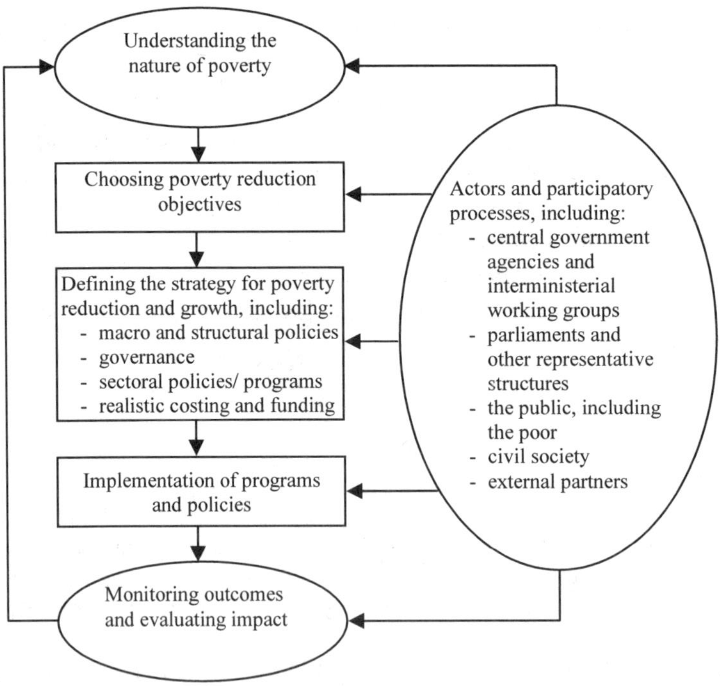

Fig. 3.7. Process of a PRSP

Source: Klugman (2004), p. 5

A critical evaluation of the PRSP framework

Some have evaluated the PRSP framework positively and speak of a paradigm change in development policy.[414] For instance, Paul notes that "PRSP has all the makings of a new development aid paradigm"[415]. However, it also entails the risk of being a "SAP sub-product"[416], thus losing credibility. Craig and Porter are more direct in their critique: "National development plans become PRSPs, expanded structural Adjustment Funds (ESAFs) become poverty reduction and growth funds (PRGFs)."[417] The question arises whether PRSPs are in fact only prolonged SAPs. Führmann[418] assesses whether one of the two conceptions Washington Consensus and Post-Washington Consensus are dominant in the PRSP approach. She concludes that PRSPs contains elements of both conceptions, but recognizes a paradigm shift concerning a more active part of the (recipient) government, a broader set of objectives and a focus on the role of sequencing. Craig and Porter point in the same direction, arguing that PRSP "are best seen as part of a 'Third Way' re-morphing of neoliberal approaches, a new convergence in which governments and agencies of various stripes in both liberal OECD and developing countries are focusing on optimizing economic, juridical and social governance […]."[419]

There has been no official evaluation covering all PRSP countries yet. However, apart from a vast number of country case studies, there have been some preliminary reviews conducted by the IMF in cooperation with the World Bank[420] and by regional development banks.[421] These preliminary assessments draw on different sources (country PRSP teams, external views of development partners and stakeholders, World Bank and IMF reviews and results from an international conference with participants from all relevant fields) and give a general overview on the acceptance and first experiences of countries formulating their PRSP. The major findings are that the whole PRSP approach is promising, but needs to be followed by concrete actions by the recipient countries and fulfilled pledges by all development partners. Some of the key observations are as follows:

---

414 See, for example, Eberlei (2003), p. 412.

415 Paul (2002), p. 28.

416 Ibid., p. 29.

417 Craig and Porter (2003), p. 57.

418 See Führmann (2003), p. 31ff.

419 Craig and Porter (2003), p. 54.

420 See IMF (2002), IMF (2004), World Bank (2004b).

421 See Asian Development Bank (2003).

- Recipient countries started at very different levels of economic and social development, indicating that the PRSP approach is flexible and adaptable to different country circumstances.
- The importance of country ownership as a guiding principle is widely acknowledged.
- The broad acceptance of the donor community is necessary.
- A shift in focus towards better implementation is necessary.
- The need for setting more realistic goals (e.g., with respect to countries' growth potential and the MDG) is widely acknowledged.
- More and better-schooled local capacities are needed to deal with formulating and executing PRSPs.
- The quality of poverty data collection and analysis is lacking in many PRSP countries.
- Policy priorities must be clarified by recognizing political, budgetary and human resource constraints. Existing PRSPs indicate a lack of prioritization, sequencing and specificity of public actions.[422]
- Including other development facets such as gender, HIV, good governance, corruption and rural development deserves crucial attention and must be aligned within the overall PRSP framework.

The two most detailed official PRSP evaluations (dating from July 2004) have been conducted by the IMF's Independent Evaluation Office[423] and the World Bank's Independent Evaluation Group (formerly known as Operation Evaluation Department).[424] These reviews evaluate the relevance of the overall approach, the application of the underlying principles and preliminary results and the effectiveness of World Bank support and alignment. Its main findings indicate that the PRSP in fact assisted in combining sector strategies and poverty reduction. Bank lending has increased for countries with PRSP. However, lending was higher in countries where "government leadership and aid management was already strong"[425], following performance-based lending policies grounded partly on the analytical result of Burnside and Dollar on aid effectiveness (see earlier chapters). In terms of outcomes, GDP per capita growth rates in PRSP participating countries have not been higher than in non-PRSP countries. The quality of policies and institutions did not improve faster than in non-PRSP coun-

---

[422] See IMF (2002), p. 14.

[423] See IMF (2004).

[424] See World Bank (2004b). The evaluation techniques include country case studies, cross-country analyses, surveys, and results from inside and outside the World Bank.

[425] World Bank (2004b), p. vii–viii.

tries. Some social development indicators show improvements (e.g., school enrolment, number of teachers), while others do not (e.g., infant mortality rate). Furthermore, the evaluation indicates that differing country characteristics and initial conditions are not considered. The scope for treating countries according to their individual setting is insufficient. The evaluation fails, however, in delivering a more detailed assessment of the role of country-specific circumstances.

Despite these voluminous official reviews, a number of individual scholars point to additional shortcomings of the preliminary PRSP documents. Luke, for instance, notes that not enough attention is being paid to income generation through the productive and export sectors, given the importance of the export sector for most developing countries.[426] Others criticize that the PRSP focus relies predominantly on the composition of public expenditures (in particular of the social sector). Instead, more emphasis should be put on long-term poverty-reducing measures (e.g., investments in infrastructure and public expenditures management systems). Again, others note the rising gap between the two goals of macroeconomic stability and increased spending to reduce poverty in PRSP countries.[427] Countries might be tempted to propose a PRSP according to the expectations of the World Bank and the IMF, because their approval is necessary.[428] Similarly, Schneider warns that countries might prepare two PRSPs, one long-term oriented (official) "best case"-PRSP aimed at achieving the Millennium Development Goals in 2015 and another (unofficial) realistic one focusing on medium-term economic stability.[429] Finally, a common feature of PRSP documents is the fact that PRSP countries tend to present overly optimistic scenarios concerning their future economic growth rate. Indeed, most PRSP documents assume an average future GDP growth rate between five and seven percent, a value that only a handful of high-performing East Asian economies have reached over a longer period.

Country ownership vs. conditionality

The international experience with structural adjustment under conditional clauses has been disappointing. While the inclusion of conditionality clauses proved successful in some countries, many country cases provide

---

[426] See Luke (2003), p. 68.

[427] See Schneider (2003), p. 414 and Bliss (2003), p. 420.

[428] The World Bank's evaluation report of 2004 reveals that „[c]ountries have focused more on completing documents, which give them access to resources, than on improving domestic processes." World Bank (2004b), p. viii.

[429] See Schneider (2003), p. 414.

evidence for the fact that the conditions were a burden hindering economic development.[430] It is now widely acknowledged (even by IMF and World Bank officials[431]) that a country's development cannot improve unless it is achieved by the respective country itself. A development process solely led (or even forced) by international agencies is regarded as unsustainable and seldom succeeds unless there is broad understanding, support and capacity within the country. Studies confirm empirically the dominance of domestic conditions over outside (external) "effort" (e.g. of multilateral institutions).[432]

According to the World Bank, country ownership is understood as "sufficient political support within a country to implement its developmental strategy, including the projects, programs, and policies for which external partners provide assistance."[433] The local government must gather enough support for its strategy among its stakeholders, which includes ministries, parliaments, civil society organizations, private groups and individuals. A first conception of country ownership has been developed by Johnson and Wasty. The authors introduce a four dimensional variable (locus of initiative, level of intellectual conviction among key policy makers, expression of political will and effort toward consensus-building among constituencies) reflecting the intensity of ownership and note that the relationship between program success and ownership can be characterized as *post hoc ergo procter hoc* circulation, in which ownership is existing when the program has been successful, and non-existing otherwise.[434] Killick et al. as well as Johnson expand on these thoughts.[435] In essence, ownership means to accept the full responsibility for a program's consequences. But apart from domestic (internal) acceptance, country ownership also unfolds an

---

[430] See for a recent overview Sharpe et al. (2005) as well as Johnson (2005).

[431] At the IMF Executive Board Meeting in March 2001, IMF officials agreed that ownership is essential to the successful implantation of a program and that conditionality cannot compensate for a lack of ownership. See IMF (2001b).

[432] See Dollar and Svensson (2000). While the earlier study finds that their variable "government commitment" is positively correlated to the project outcome, Dollar and Svensson confirm that domestic political economy factors matter significantly more for program success than conditionality clauses. See these sources for more empirical studies.

[433] World Bank (2005c).

[434] See Johnson and Wasty (1993). Boorman (2001), p. 8 argues similarly: "[O]ne must avoid the temptation to equate failure to implement reforms with a lack of ownership, which would make ownership a tautological requirement for program success."

[435] See Killick et al. (1998) and Johnson (2005).

external perspective as Entwistle and Cavassini[436] point out correctly. This includes the understanding of multilateral and especially bilateral donors that the needs and priorities of individual countries should be at the heart of international development cooperation and that external assistance should be aligned with the PRSP. However, creditor and debtor countries often take conflicting positions on what ownership means. Taken to one extreme, country ownership "implies that the Fund and other official creditors expect the country to take responsibility for doing what the international financing institutions (IFIs) insist they must do. [...] At the other extreme, advocates for developing countries sometimes have argued that ownership means that IFIs should depend entirely or very largely on borrowers to design their own policies. Ownership, in that view, may be incompatible with policy conditionality."[437] A midway understanding of ownership requires mutual understanding of the positions and a process of dialogue and negotiation between donor and recipient. This does not infer necessarily that all stakeholders must come to a consensus. Whether or not country ownership and conditionality are compatible remains a disputed issue, while it is widely uncontested that conditionality cannot substitute for country ownership. But according to Birdsall,[438] conditions can attribute to ownership, signalling a government's credible commitment to hold up reform efforts. Similarly, Branson and Hanna argue that conditionality can be regarded as a commitment of the donor party, and the local government commits itself via ownership of its programs.[439]

Country ownership will not expand overnight. Instead, vested interests of governments, social groups and other stakeholders are often manifested and subject to slow change, making ownership both fragile and dynamic.[440] An important step to increase country ownership is to integrate the PRSP into the national development plan and to institutionalize the participation of various stakeholders in the decision-making process. Country ownership also implies that the local government has the institutional capacity not only to set up a national development plan, but also to negotiate it with its stakeholders. Consequently, decision-making processes within the PRSP framework must be embedded in an institutionalized system of the stake-

[436] See Entwistle and Cavassini (2005).
[437] Boorman (2001), p. 4.
[438] See Birdsall (2000).
[439] See Branson and Hanna (2000), p. 3.
[440] There is a broad string of public economics literature assessing the role of special interests for government policy choices. See, for example, Grossman and Helpman (1994) for the *protection for sale* argument and more specifically Dixit (2003) for special interests and constrained reforms in less developed countries.

holders. Hanley, in turn, stresses the fact that in order for civil society organizations to participate, they need experience and skills to provide their own analysis and be able to confront officials with new ideas or critique, which may bring forth the need for additional training.[441] It has been argued by some that there should be clear procedures regarding the participation of certain political groups (e.g., Parliament) in the decision process of formulating the PRSP, because this ensures a broad country ownership. On the other hand, countries' political environments vary so widely that clear rules for political influence may be counterproductive. The IMF proposes to establish several good practices such as information sharing and openness of decision-making, building on existing national processes and institutions, involving all significant stakeholder groups and improving feedback for both countries and development partners.

Is there more country ownership with the PRSP than before? Most studies acknowledge that participation of the society in formulation of PRSPs has indeed increased but have difficulties in quantifying the level of increased participation. In particular, NGOs have been integrated more closely in the negotiation (not necessarily in the decision-making) process and in the dialogue with the local government. However, whether or not this participation has resulted in a better outcome (e.g., improved program design, higher aid effectiveness, higher transparency or increased empowerment) is difficult to determine and relies on a careful case by case judgement,[442] in part because ownership is only one of a number of prerequisites to successful program implementation. Indirect proxy variables that assess the level of ownership may include indicators of political openness and unity and administrative capacity.

"One-size-fits-all" vs. country specificity

The PRSP principles are formulated in a very broad and general conception to embed many countries. They address a number of issues pivotal for poverty reduction. But the condensed and very ambitious time constraints to finalize a PRSP (imposed by IMF and World Bank) and the increasing "external" pressure (e.g., MDG framework) and internal pressure (e.g., through national NGO and social groups) have resulted in a rather general and standardized framework and strategy advice, as has also been pointed out in PRSP evaluation reports. Thus the question arises whether the PRSP

---

[441] See Hanley (2002), p. 49.

[442] See Entwistle and Cavassini (2005) for an analysis of various country experiences.

approach is well suited to be a guiding framework for the diverse community of least developed countries.

It has always been tempting by politicians and economists to look at successful economic development strategies and imitate them. "Why isn't the whole world experimenting with the East Asian model to develop?" Can poor countries adapt strategies from more advanced countries such as Middle and Eastern European or East Asian countries; can the latter serve as "shining examples"? Is there a dominating development strategy applicable to all countries, a one-size-fits-all strategy with rather standardized economic policies, concepts and instruments? The experiences with IMF and World Bank economic and political advice suggest that these institutions have created a mindset which contributes strongly to the perception that they give standardized economic policy advice. This is also underlined by the fact that they have written down their policy approaches in operational and strategic manuals.

Following Henke and Boxill, "industrialization and economic development are the results of very complex social, political, and economic processes both at the domestic and international level, rather than the result of abstract economic formulas."[443] Even for the East Asian case, there has been no congruence on the success determinants,[444] and the Asian Newly Industrialized Economies can be characterized by at least three differing models of economic development.[445] An additional factor seriously limiting the transferability of economic development concepts is time.[446] Not only are comparisons of strategies limited because of dynamic economic conditions (e.g., increased capital mobility), but also are long-term effects important in evaluating the success of an individual development strategy. Copying a development strategy without paying attention to such time lags could result in serious flaws. Finally, methodological shortcomings (as for example in cross-country studies) and the lack of robust causation links aggravate the preference of some policies over others. As a result, it re-

[443] Henke and Boxill (2000), p. 200.

[444] According to the influential Miracle study of the World Bank, Asian countries experienced high economic growth rates "by getting the basics right" World Bank (1993), p. 5. These basics included a market-friendly approach as summarized in the Washington Consensus. Amsden (1994), p. 628 criticizes that the success in some East Asian countries has much more complex determinants than just the focus on fundamentals.

[445] See Perkins (1994), p. 655. The laissez-faire policy in Hong Kong and, to a lesser extent, Singapore, shows remarkable differences to state interventionist development concepts in Korea and Taiwan.

[446] See Schabbel (2001), pp. 83–87 for a comparison of strategies and development patterns in Middle and East European and East Asian countries.

mains rather doubtful that there is a standardized procedure or a blueprint to promote economic development in every country of the world.

A similar line of reasoning can be derived for poverty reduction policies. Admittedly, there are a number of policies better suited than others. It is also fruitful to take a look at other countries' experiences. But these policies and experiences should be embedded into a consistent domestic and regional development strategy. While country ownership has received much attention in the debate on PRSP recently, reflecting the question of responsibility for the development strategy, *country specificity* has been to a great extent neglected. The term has been used in a UNDP Peer Review System designed for preparing the Human Development Report[447], but has not been adequately defined in the literature so far.[448] Country specificity addresses the uniqueness of a country's starting point in economic and social development and the vector of individual circumstances influencing its development path. This vector encompasses a list of economic and non-economic aspects such as geographical, historical, cultural, political and social factors. It has been understood early by many scientists that a country's intrinsic circumstances influence its economic and social development. Furthermore, some branches of literature have evolved dealing with the aspects mentioned above (e.g., the role of geography or culture for development and poverty reduction). However, there seems to be a lack of systematically including these factors into development policy frameworks.

3.6.4 Summary

The PRSP approach has manifested in a short period of time as a solid framework for all partners in development finance. Nevertheless, the list of critical issues included (and not included) in the preliminary assessment of the IMF and the World Bank is extensive. Some point towards the risk of overloading the entire PRSP process. However, not acknowledging the complexity of economic and social development by concentrating on rather standardized "recipes" has proven to be suboptimal at least and in some country cases even counterproductive. Despite the many challenges

---

[447] See UNDP (2002), p. 2. The report speaks of the need for a systematic, but flexible peer review system "in order to accommodate differing country contexts."

[448] World Bank Senior Vice President and Chief Economist, Francois Bourguignon, has used the term at a recent presentation rather loosely, speaking of country specificity as "seeking pragmatic solutions".

within the entire PRSP framework that have been addressed already, two will be highlighted here:

1. Alignment
   Although PRSPs are widely accepted among donor and recipient countries, the consistency with i) national development plans in recipient countries and ii) with existing development assistance plans of bilateral creditors remains reserved. It must be assured that each donor active in a recipient country does interpret the PRSP in the same way. While multilateral institutions have incorporated the PRSP, bilateral donors must cooperate closer with multilateral donors and among themselves and align their development assistance to the objectives in the PRSP. In this context, Bliss speaks of "recipient country focused development assistance" instead of "donor country focused development assistance".[449] This also implies that PRSPs are binding to the creditor countries' national development assistance budget, a fact that has not been appreciated in most national ODA departments, because it may require a reorientation and in some cases even an end of existing national development programs and/or projects, which in turn might also lead to a loss of political influence.[450]
   Another challenge is to align short-term projects with the long-term orientation of a PRSP. PRSP countries must receive assistance and expertise in order to translate their strategy into practical, operational plans that can be carried out at the local level.
2. Country-specificity
   As has been pointed out in previous sections, there is a lack of the PRSP framework with respect to country- and region-specific circumstances. One proposal is to synchronize the World Bank's Country Assistance Strategies more closely with the PRSP process or even merge them into one document. This combined document then should focus on existing strengths and starting conditions and identify the necessary additional ingredients in a "Need Assessment". Chap. 5 will deal more closely with regional conditions and their role for poverty reduction and development finance in low-income countries.

[449] See Bliss (2003), p. 419.

[450] For example, German development assistance has a rather strong focus on project financing, whereas PRSPs aim at more sector-wide solutions including basket financing and even contributions to the national budget of recipient countries.

3.7 Summary and conclusions

This has chapter dealt with the allocation of ODA. In the opening section, the present allocation and explanatory factors have been analyzed (Sect. 3.2) and confronted with optimal allocation rules (Sect. 3.3). Although a poverty-minimizing allocation is afflicted with a number of shortcomings, the strategy to choose aid recipients based on their track record in certain indicators, particularly good policies, has gained much support recently. This is partly due to a confirmation bias among aid practitioners/politicians. The drift towards increased selectivity may exclude the neediest from receiving ODA. In fact, the poverty-focus of aid remains relatively low.

Sects. 3.4 to 3.6 of this chapter have outlined three major trends shaping the policies of international development cooperation: i) Goal-orientation, ii) debt relief and iii) country-owned poverty reduction strategies. The goal-oriented approach provides a set of universally accepted long-term objectives of economic development named the Millennium Development Goals. Yet, it has become clear that some countries (especially from sub-Saharan Africa) will fail on these goals within the proposed time horizon and that there are strong disparities between regions and countries. Granting debt relief instead of restructuring may enable poor and highly indebted countries to "start anew". However, it remains to be seen, whether the proposed 100% debt cancellation in the Multilateral Debt Relief Initiative, i.e. providing debt relief regardless of historic or future performance, will be effective and sustainable. It will depend, among other factors, on the ability of recipient countries to eliminate their individual underlying structural causes of indebtedness by generating future economic growth. The PRSP approach especially highlights the role of country ownership, i.e. the broad participation of the entire national community in finding and implementing its development strategy. However, it historically originates from IMF and World Bank conditional clauses and structural adjustment policy, still representing a rather generalized one-size-fits-all approach. It has been shown that the specificity of countries' local conditions plays no important role so far in development policy frameworks.

Country ownership, debt relief eligibility as well as selectivity are founded in countries' past performance, not their attitude towards future reforms. There are, up to now, no indications that the selectivity approach has spurred poverty reduction in low-income countries. Despite various methodological limitations, the allocation strategy of selecting recipient countries only on the base of their past economic and political performance does overlook country- and region-specific circumstances. Unfavourable local conditions may slow down or even prohibit good economic and political performance. In such a case, a country with a "good will" to reduce poverty may face difficulties in obtaining financial assistance, because it cannot prove a sufficient track record. In fact, when selectivity fails to account for country- and region-specific conditions, this may constitute a reward for those countries with such a good performance that enables them to reduce poverty even without any external official assistance. Consequently, it remains doubtful whether ODA should be completely denied in countries with low scores in policies and/or institutions. Similarly, a lack of ownership does not necessarily need to prohibit ODA allocation, if it is employed well and directed towards poverty reducing measures.

What all sections in this chapter have shown is the strong planning mentality of international donors, suggesting that there is a top-down plan ready to subscribe to in order to achieve poverty reduction. Official terminologies pointing towards such a frame of mind include:

- Setting Millennium Development Goals
- The global plan to fight poverty / a Marshall Plan for the world's poor (UK Chancellor of the Exchequer Gordon Brown)
- The "end of poverty" (book by Jeffrey Sachs)
- "Make poverty history" (Live 8 Concerts)
- Aid financing a "Big Push Forward" (UK Prime Minister Tony Blair)
- Structural Adjustment Loans
- Multilateral institutions giving approval to national policy strategies ("signing-off").

Rich donor countries seem to know what's best for low-income countries, which is why they have invented a network of conditional clauses and strategies of assistance:

> "We impose so many conditions on those countries that receive money: they have to be gender sensitive; poor people must participate directly; they must have sustainability; they must have environmental friendliness; and they must have transparency, accountability, and so on [...] If we think of our own historical development process, or that of any developed country, none of the criteria was fulfilled."[451]

It has been written in the first sentence of this chapter: "The allocation of ODA does not take place by market forces as in the case of private capital flows." After the analysis in this chapter, one may add that instead of a market, it is planning forces that to a great extent form the allocation of ODA. This is even more interestingly because aid allocation policies have

[451] Desai (2003), cited in Hanlon (2004), p. 181.

for a long time highlighted their ambition to introduce free markets in low-income countries. In fact, planners should know that planning development processes in foreign countries (with not well understood local conditions) is a highly uncertain adventure. Also astoundingly is the fact that the direct poverty focus of this planned assistance has been found to be moderate at best. Instead, data suggests that aid is predominantly assigned in order to promote long-term economic development, not immediate poverty reduction. Multilateral institutions and bilateral donors were guided by the inherent belief that aid will lead to economic growth and that this growth will benefit the poor. Disentangling the linkages between these macroeconomic aggregate as well as finding out on the utilization of ODA in recipient countries will be the main motivation of the next chapter.

Finally, the planning mentality is accompanied with a strong rhetoric among donors stressing their responsibility to assist in worldwide poverty reduction. However, donors are not held accountable for successes or failures. There are no pay-offs or rewards for successful aid projects, as for example in private markets' investment projects. Similarly, there are no sanctions or consequences in the case of failed projects. The international community has just started to notice that evaluation plays an important part following the execution of aid projects and programmes. One of the greatest challenges for a planned, non-market allocation process of aid in this respect is the lack of feedback loops from the "demand side", i.e. the neediest people in the recipient countries.

4 The utilization of ODA

> [T]he West spent $2.3 trillion on foreign aid over the last five decades and still had not managed to get twelve-cent medicines to children to prevent half of all malaria deaths.
>
> William Easterly (2006)

Having analyzed the supply side of development finance (Chap. 2) as well as the process of allocating official funds (Chap. 3) and the manifold implications associated therewith, Chap. 4 finally addresses the "demand side" of ODA and the potential channels of aid affecting poverty reduction in a recipient country. The enquiries here are fourfold:

- How is ODA actually disbursed and utilized in low-income countries (Sect. 4.1)?
- Does foreign aid lead to poverty reduction via economic growth (Sect. 4.2)?
- What are the interdependencies between ODA, poverty reduction, inequality and economic growth (Sect. 4.3)?
- What are the macroeconomic consequences of ODA in recipient countries, especially in cases of sudden, large increases of ODA (Sect. 4.4)?

4.1 Sectoral decomposition of ODA

4.1.1 Data and definitions

The most detailed data for sectoral ODA distribution is compiled by the OECD. Long-term trends of aid activities are only available for aid commitments rather than actual aid disbursements. Commitments are defined as a firm obligation, expressed in writing and backed by the necessary funds, undertaken by an official donor to provide specified assistance to a recipient country or multilateral organisation. Bilateral commitments are recorded as full amount of expected transfer, irrespective of the time required for the completion of disbursements. Commitments to multilateral disbursements are reported as the sum of i) any disbursements which have not been previously notified as commitments in the year reported on and ii) expected disbursements in the following year.

Table 4.1. Two-digit classification of sectoral distribution of ODA

I. Social infrastructure and services
I.1. Education
I.2. Health
I.3. Population programs
I.4. Water supply and sanitation
I.5. Public administration and civil society
I.6. Other social infrastructure and services
II. Economic infrastructure and services
II.1. Transport and storage
II.2. Communications
II.3. Energy
II.4. Banking and financial services
II.5. Business and other services
III. Production sectors
III.1. Agriculture, forestry, and fisheries
III.2. Industry, mining and construction
III.3. Trade and tourism
IV. Multisector assistance
IV.1. General environmental protection
IV.2. Women in development
IV.3. Other multisector assistance
V. Total sector allocable (I+II+III+IV)
VI. Commodity aid /general program assistance
VI.1. Structural adjustment assistance
VI.2. Food aid designed to promote development
VI.3. Other general program assistance
VII. Actions related to debt
VIII. Emergency assistance and reconstruction
IX. Administrative costs of donors
X. Support to NGO's
XI. Unallocated/unspecified

Source: Taken from OECD DAC statistics
The disaggregation continues until the 5-digit level. Note that subsection V is the sum of the preceding sections I to IV. Consequently, either the sections I to IV or Section V should be used.

Disbursements are defined as the release of funds to, or the purchase of goods or services for a recipient (= the amount spent). Disbursements record the actual international transfer of financial resources, or of goods and services valued at the cost of the donor. Commitment data is therefore afflicted with a higher inaccuracy and need not necessarily mirror actual patterns of utilization.

In order to disaggregate the distribution of ODA, a five-digit-level classification scheme is used by the OECD. Table 4.1 gives an overview of the categories at the two-digit level, which is most frequently used in statistics.

4.1.2 ODA commitments according to sector

Fig. 4.1 presents a general picture on the development of sectoral distribution of ODA in low-income countries. There has been a tendency away from physical infrastructure as well as agriculture towards debt relief, education and health. This development confirms the policies described in Chap. 3, particularly the HIPCs and MDG initiatives. The decrease in ODA spent for agricultural purposes is partly due to the end of Green Revolution[452] assistance in India. However, agricultural assistance to other regions such as Africa and South Asia also declined.

Fig. 4.2 shows the regional variation in different sectors of aid distribution. Most interestingly, the percentage for social infrastructure and services is lowest in Sub-Saharan Africa. Although one may argue that other categories such as debt relief, emergency assistance and program assistance are also directed towards social sectors, this result stands in contrast to donors' recent pledges to expand on social expenditures. The 2004 data is not diluted due to special actions (emergency aid or debt relief). In Africa, whose disaggregated ODA distribution pattern within the last ten years is shown in Fig. 4.3, the share of ODA distributed to the social sector remained relatively constant at around 30% between 1995 and 2004. The share of ODA used for actions relating to debt relief has increased since 2000; the share of emergency aid increased since 1998. In contrast, the shares of economic infrastructure, production sector and multisector aid declined. Since 2000, program assistance has also been descending.

[452] Green revolution refers to the increase in crop yield using improved strains of wheat, rice, maize as well as modern techniques (chemical fertilizers, irrigation, mechanized harvesters, pesticides) with the objective to forestall famines.

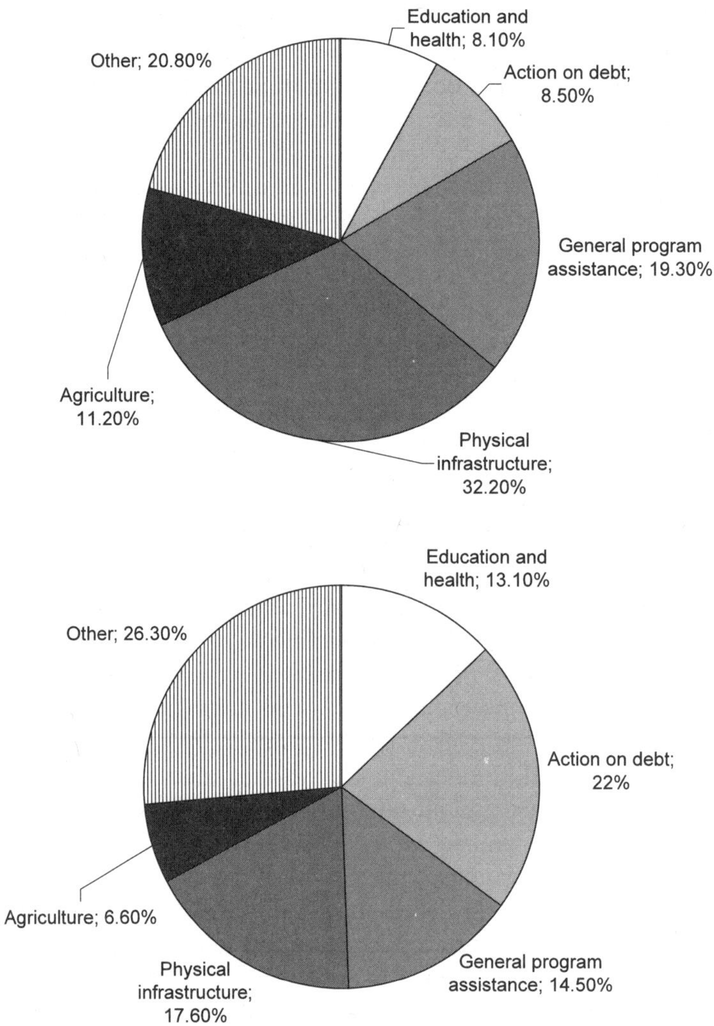

Fig. 4.1. Sectoral distribution of ODA to low-income countries

Source: World Bank (2005b), p. 93

Upper chart: 1990–1992, lower chart: 2000–2002

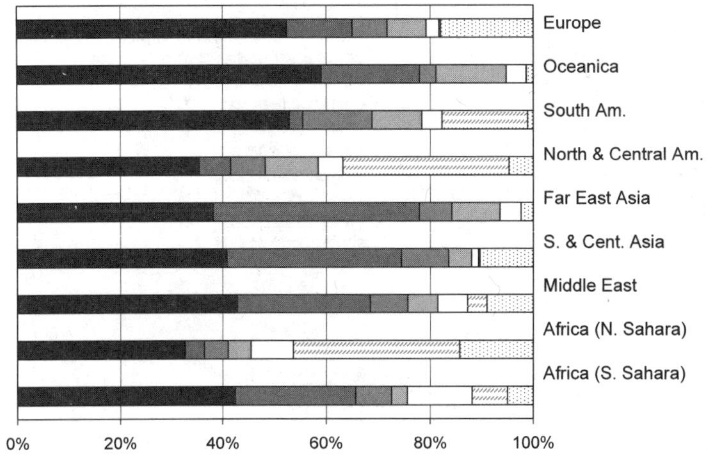

Fig. 4.2. Sectoral distribution of total ODA by all DAC donors to low-income countries in 2004 for various regions [in %]

Source: Author's calculations based on DAC data
Notes: Countries in transition are excluded. Categories from left to right: Social infrastructure and services, economic infrastructure, production sector, multisector, general program assistance, actions relating to debt, emergency assistance.

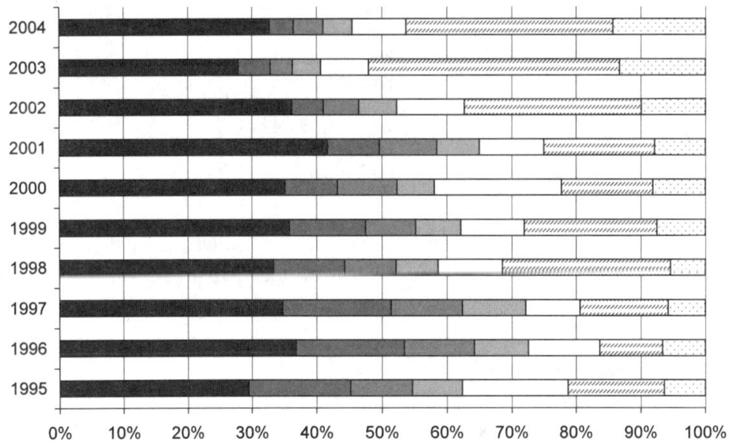

Fig. 4.3. Sectoral distribution of total ODA by all DAC donors to sub-Saharan Africa between 1995 and 2004 [in %]

Source: Author's calculations based on DAC data
Notes: See Fig. 4.2 for categories.

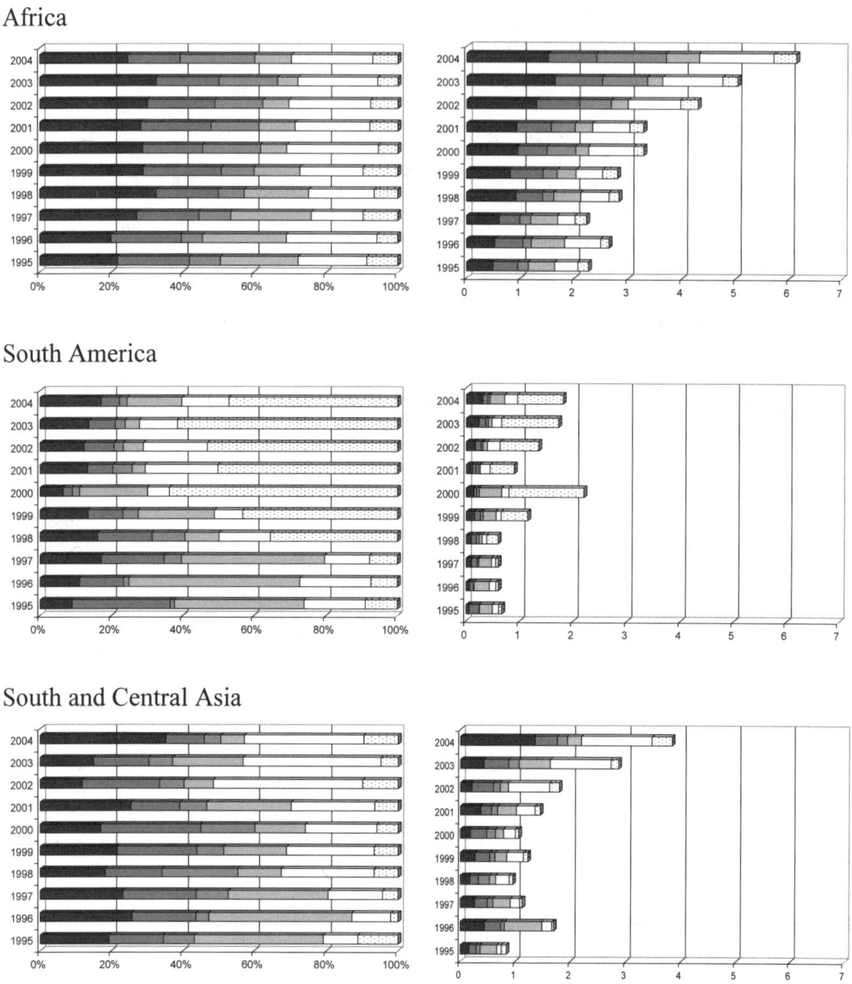

Fig. 4.4. DAC donors' ODA commitments in the sector "Social infrastructure and services" donors to various regions, 1995–2004 [left chart: distribution in %, right chart: total in US-$ billions]

Source: Own calculations based on DAC data
Notes: The categories from left to right are education, health, population programs, water supply and sanitation, public administration and civil society, other social infrastructure and services.

Diasaggregating the section "Social infrastructure and services", some discrepancies across regions can be observed. Fig. 4.4 shows the development of allocation shares as well as the absolute volume utilized in the category social infrastructure and services. As envisioned in the MDGs, commitments in these sectors have improved over time as is visible in the charts on the right. Commitments in education and health have become the most important or one of the most important social categories. However, the development of relative and absolute commitment in water supply and sanitation is very volatile in every region and did not improve much. In relation to other social commitments, its share actually declined substantially between 1995 and 2004 throughout all observed regions. The large portion "Other social infrastructure and services" in South America covers assistance to employment, housing and other social services and cultural management. It also includes research when the sector could not be identified. Public sector and civil society assistance also rose strongly in South and Central Asia (absolute and relative) and Africa (absolute), and remained on a similar level (approx. 20%) in South America.

The data suggests that ODA is predominantly utilized as assistance to promote economic development (program aid, debt relief, infrastructure, production sectors and multisector) in the recipients. Although clearly attributable social commitments rose in absolute terms, they remained relatively constant compared to other forms of utilizations. In Sub-Saharan Africa, only approx. one third of all ODA flows into social sectors, directly affecting the lives of poor people. Instead, it has always been at the heart of ODA utilization to improve the economic conditions in recipient countries, i.e. to spur economic growth. It was not only assumed that this would lead to a self-sustained growth path, but that low-income groups would also benefit over time. The links between macroeconomic aggregates that would support this perspective will be analyzed in the next section.

4.2 ODA and economic growth

4.2.1 Theoretical approaches

Many theoretical contributions have analyzed the impact of foreign capital inflows on domestic economic growth. One string of literature is especially interested in the effect of foreign aid inflows. Many foreign aid models are still based on the classical Harrod-Domar model, which will be described in this subsection. The driving argument brought forth in order to justify foreign aid is that it can fill the gap of missing domestic capital. This idea has resulted in so-called gap models (second subsection). Another string of literature attempts to define the reasons and potential solutions of these gaps. Poverty trap and the big push argument will be covered in the subsections 3 and 4. A special form of aid is loans. Models analyzing the impact of debt on economic growth will be presented in the fifth subsection.

Although none of the theories can claim to adequately address the complexity of the economic growth process, they provide useful insights on how foreign aid can affect economic growth.

Harrod-Domar model

One of the first models on economic development was the aggregate growth model by Harrod (1939) and Domar (1946).[453] Their approach took up earlier work by Keynes who had shown that an increase in investment leads to an over-proportional increase in income via demand (multiplication effect). Apart from the income effect, investment also increases production capacity. This dual character of investments was first modelled by Harrod and Domar (HD). The following assumptions apply:

- The existence of a Leontief (i.e. a linear-limitational) production function (fixed ratio between labor and capital),
- Capital is the only binding constraint, whereas labor is available,
- There is no substitution possible between capital and labor,
- There is a linear relationship (a fixed proportion) between capital and output.

According to Harrod and Domar, economic growth depends on the savings rate, the ratio of capital to output (capital coefficient) and the depreciation rate. The following assumptions hold:

1. Domestic savings (S) are proportional to the national income (Y): $S = s \cdot Y$, with s as the savings rate.
2. Relationship between capital and national income: $K = k \cdot Y$, with k as the capital coefficient (capital/output ratio).[454]
3. Net investments lead to a change in the capital stock and to a change in income: $\Delta K = I = k \cdot \Delta Y$.
4. Ex post, savings equal investment in an equilibrium state: $S = I = \Delta K$.

It follows that

---

[453] See Harrod (1939) and Domar (1946).

[454] The capital-output ratio can be regarded as a measure for capital productivity. For example, if an additional (incremental) investment of $1.000 will raise the output by $500 in the subsequent period, the capital-output ratio is 2. Thus, more capital relative to output ceteris paribus reduces growth, because this reflects a lower efficiency in the use of capital. Often, k is also referred to as the incremental capital output ratio (ICOR). Put simply, the ICOR states how many units of additional capital are needed to achieve one unit of additional output.

$$S = s \cdot Y = \Delta K = k \cdot \Delta Y \,. \tag{4.1}$$

Division results in:

$$\frac{\Delta Y}{Y} = \frac{s}{k} \,. \tag{4.2}$$

Eq. 4.2 is known as the HD equation. The growth rate of a country (left side of the equation) is proportional to its savings rate and inversely proportionate to the capital coefficient (right side of the equation). Accordingly, growth can only be positively affected by more investment (= higher s, since S=I) or a lower capital-output ratio. Since the latter is assumed to be held constant, it follows that the higher the investment rate (i.e. the accumulation of capital investment via domestic savings), the higher the growth rate in the succeeding period.

It can be shown that the model is instable ("knife-edge-growth") and weak in several aspects.[455] The first point of critique concerns the link between savings and investment. Even if sufficient savings are mobilized, it is far from certain these savings will employ new investment capacities. Savings might be invested abroad (foreign assets), crowd out other investment (aid fungibility) or leave the economy illegally (capital flight), which has been shown to seriously affect low-income countries in particular. Second, the assumption of a fixed capital-output ratio has proven to be unrealistic.[456] Third, the model has been criticized for not being a real theory, but merely a tautology. Its explanation power for economic policy and the use of instruments thus remains very limited.[457] Yet, the model was easy-

---

455 For a critical review of the Harrod-Domar model, see Frenkel and Hemmer (1999), pp. 9–25.

456 See Gylfason (1998), p. 42.

457 Easterly (1999), p. 2 expands that Domars intention was to discuss short term recessions and investment in the United States and not to model long-run economic growth. Empirical studies that have examined the link between private investment and growth usually confirm that there is a positive relationship. For public investment, the results vary. On an aggregate level, the evidence on the impact of investment is mixed. At least, the predictions made by Lewis (1954, 1976, 1978), Rostow (1960) and other development economists in the 1950s, 1960s and 1970s that a higher investment ratio will lead to higher growth have not been fulfilled. Moreover, the composition of public investment matters more than the quantity of public investment itself. See Devarajan et al. (2002), p. 11. Their cross-country study on the relationship between public investment, private investment and growth by shows no positive correlation for a sample of African countries.

to-use and computable and served as a planning model for decades. Economic planners could set a target growth rate, and knew the savings and investment rate necessary to achieve it. Alternatively, planners set the desired levels of savings and investment and knew about the growth rate.[458]

Gap models

The HD model has been extended by including the external sector and applied to a variety of developing countries in order to determine the necessary rate of investment given a target growth rate. In fact, it is still used today in World Bank simulations and projections on the necessary aid quantity. The line of reasoning is that there is a gap between the targeted investment and the capital available for it within the country, which could be filled with official financial assistance from abroad. This idea was later brought forth by Chenery and Strout as well as Rostow.[459] Put simply, in such a model aid contributes to savings, which increases investment and therefore growth. Thus, aid was regarded as a plain resource transfer into poor countries where foreign direct investment was not channelled via market forces. It adds to the capital stock of the recipient until the country is able to enact in self-sustained growth without foreign assistance.[460] "Since virtually all of the aid advocates used the Harrod-Domar/Financing Gap model, this was one of the largest policy experiments ever based on a single economic model."[461]

This rather simplistic positive relationship between foreign aid and growth did not remain undisputed. A counter argument was that capital from abroad may lead to lower savings in the domestic country, thereby in fact reducing economic growth.[462] Despite this argument, however, there was an optimistic view concerning the ability of the government to plan and to use aid efficiently with the help of foreign assistance.

A number of models have been developed on the foundations of HD. Two more recent endogenous growth models with special reference to foreign aid have been introduced by Fischer and Easterly[463] and Barro.[464] In

---

[458] See Gillis et al. (1983), p. 122.

[459] See Chenery and Strout (1966) and Rostow (1960). Rostow was also economic advisor under the Presidents Eisenhower, Kennedy and Johnson and pledged for increased foreign aid to developing countries for political reasons.

[460] See also Diwan (1968), p. 529.

[461] Easterly (1997), p. 8.

[462] For support of this argumentation, see for example Rahman (1968) and Weisskopf (1972).

[463] See Fischer (1991), Fischer (1993), Easterly (1993).

[464] See Barro (1991) and Barro and Sala-i-Martin (1995).

the Fischer/Easterly model, variables such as trade openness, macroeconomic stability, budget surplus, inflation, and financial repression are included. The Barro model further contains initial GDP per capita, school enrolment and fertility rates. In an application of these models, Durberry et al.[465] come to the following results:

- The external economic environment plays an important role for growth performance,
- There is evidence that poor countries benefit from greater foreign aid inflows if they inhabit a stable macroeconomic environment,
- There seems to be an optimal aid allocation in terms of aid/GDP (at approx. 40–45%),
- Very low or very large aid inflows are associated with slower growth.

Hjertholm et al.[466] point out that the setting of a specific target growth rate in the HD model is crucial for the idea of gap models that have been developed since the 1960s. The original gap idea stated that if a target growth rate is assumed, the difference between domestic savings and the investment rate needed to achieve this target can be defined as the savings gap. One can differentiate "between the *ex ante* savings gap (the difference between desired investment and domestic savings and the *ex post* savings gap (the difference between actual investment and domestic savings)."[467]

So-called two-gap models extend the afore-mentioned approach by the fact that growth is not only limited due to a constraint in domestic savings/investment, but also to a constraint in foreign exchanges. This second gap (also referred to as "foreign exchange gap" or "trade gap") arises from the notion that a developing country needs to import certain goods and services (e.g., strategically important goods) to increase domestic production, but that export earnings are often not sufficient to finance imports.[468] If private capital is not available, an inflow of foreign (official) aid might close the foreign exchange deficit.[469]

---

[465] See Durberry et al. (1998).

[466] Hjertholm et al. (1998), p. 4.

[467] Ibid., p. 4. Also, a certain capital-output ratio, in analogy to the HD model, is taken as a datum.

[468] Again, a separation can be made between the ex ante trade gap and the ex post trade gap. An empirical examination on the role of foreign exchange for economic development is provided by Manne (1963). He finds that a small increase of foreign exchange would increase Mexico's growth rate by 2.5 percentage points.

[469] See Nissanke and Ferrarini (2001), p. 6.

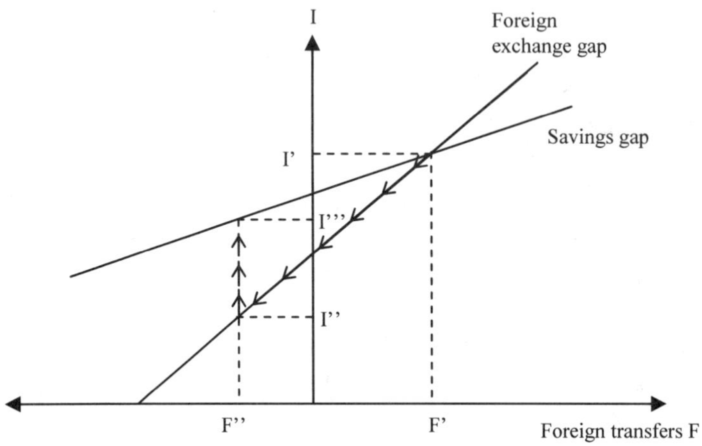

Fig. 4.5. Two-gap model

Source: Bacha (1990), p. 287 (modified)

A formal model was first propounded by Chenery and Strout as well as McKinnon.[470] The authors make use of an extended HD model showing the domestic need for foreign capital goods. The larger gap (either savings or foreign exchange gap) will be the bottleneck and thus limit the target growth rate. In their model, Chenery and Strout assume a "minimum import level […] required sustaining a given level GNP",[471] which seems justified by the inelastic demand for some imported manufactured goods (intermediate goods).[472] An illustration of two-gap models is given in Fig. 4.5. The savings and the foreign exchange gap are represented by the two lines. They represent constraints to investment. If foreign transfers are lower than F', the foreign exchange gap line is binding and limiting investment (and thus growth). If foreign transfers are higher than F', the savings gap is constraining investment. In the point of intersection, both gaps are binding. If foreign transfers are reduced from F' to F'' (e.g., through an external shock), investment is reduced to I'', thereby following the foreign exchange constraint. In the medium run, however, net exports will rise be-

[470] See Chenery and Strout (1966), McKinnon (1964).

[471] Chenery and Strout (1966), p. 689.

[472] For an analysis of the elasticity of substitution between domestic and foreign inputs in two-gap models, with special focus on Argentina, see Michalopoulos (1975). The author concludes that at least for some countries two-gap models provide only a very limited basis for projecting foreign exchange needs.

cause of idle domestic capacities until the savings gap becomes binding. "Underlying microeconomic mechanisms are not made explicit, but a neo-classical story could be told that domestic prices go down as unused capacity emerges: this devaluation of the real exchange rate would then explain the upward movement of exports."[473]

Gap model extensions encompass a three-gap model by Bacha[474] who introduced a fiscal gap that can be binding if there is a connection between public and private investment (e.g., crowding out effects) and the former is limited to a certain ceiling. This third gap can be relevant for highly indebted countries and was discussed against the background of the 1980s debt crisis of Latin American countries. Conditional debt relief from donor countries can then provide an effective measure to provide an incentive for countries to cope with the fiscal gap.

Gap models have served as a major theoretical justification for foreign aid since the 1960s. According to these approaches, foreign aid was welcomed because it filled the gaps described above. An important aspect was and still is its practicability for empirical examinations.[475] A recent study by Gottschalk[476] also uses a theoretical framework based on the HD model. It applies the gap model in order to calculate the external financing needed to achieve the Millennium Development Goals in 2015 (see Chap. 3 for more details on this policy framework). Gottschalk's study provides evidence that halving poverty by 2015 solely with economic growth is highly unrealistic.[477]

---

[473] See Bacha (1984), p. 264 and Bacha (1990), p. 286–288.

[474] See Bacha (1990) for an illustration. See also Taylor (1990, 1991 and 1994) for a discussion of a three-gap model and Iqbal (1995) for an application to Pakistan.

[475] World Bank economists developed a Minimum Standard Model (MSM) when Chenery became chief economic advisor to the World Bank. The model also had two revisions: The Revised Minimum Standard Model (RMSM) and the Revised Minimum Standard Model Extended (RMSM-X). In these models the savings, foreign exchange and fiscal gap is calculated. Easterly (1997), p. 13 cites Jos Verbeek, the World Bank's RMSM-X coordinator, who estimates that 90% of all World Bank economists use some kind of RMSM model to make projections.

[476] See Gottschalk (2000).

[477] Using a savings gap model, the author first calculates the incremental capital-output ratio needed to achieve a certain growth rate. In a second step, the gap between this required investment and national savings needed is determined. In order to achieve the MDG, he estimates that annual average net financial resource flows of \$86.4 billion to sub-Saharan Africa and up to \$281.1 billion to Latin America and the Caribbean are necessary. Even if these external financial

Critical voices argue that foreign aid is, in fact, not gap reducing but gap producing/enhancing, thereby hindering economic development.[478] Furthermore, in many countries, official aid flows could not substitute the missing foreign exchange reserves due to increased import substitution policies.[479] Influential works of Easterly[480] criticize the use of the extended HD gap model for long-run economic growth. He emphasizes that the model's assumption that current foreign aid will go into current investment and into the GDP growth rate of the next year is unrealistic.[481] In his test of the model with cross-country data (covering 1965–1995), he also found that only 6 out of 88 countries showed a positive relationship between aid and investment, all others a negative relationship. Easterly concluded that the HD framework is not suited as a model to estimate aid requirements for domestic economic growth. Easterly's pessimistic view is challenged by Ranaweera[482] who advocates the use of the model despite its known shortcomings. His arguments stem from a practitioner's point of view that relies on rough estimations of a country's economic situation. Thus, the "financing gap" serves as an approximation for politicians and officials of international organizations when preparing for negotiations but is by no means a sufficient basis. Nissanke and Ferrarini's criticism[483] points in the same direction.

Hussain[484] also points out the weaknesses of the dual gap approach. First, there is the inaccuracy of estimating a gap for a predefined growth rate. Second, predicting growth rates in developing countries is extraordinary difficult. Third, savings especially in poor countries are often held in

resources could be realized, the results also reveal that growth rates of 8.2% (sub-Saharan Africa) and 10.2% (Latin America and the Caribbean), respectively, are necessary over more than a decade to halve extreme poverty by 2015.

478 See Bruton (1969), p. 440 and 445. Providing an economy with foreign aid may lead to the situation where original distortion (why foreign aid was used for in the first place) is not eliminated but upheld.

479 See Thorbecke (2000), p. 27.

480 See Easterly (1997). Easterly's article recalls the "history" of the HD and the gap model approach and shows how merely dogmatic, historical and political factors favored its continuous application.

481 See ibid., p. 5.

482 See Ranaweera (2003). See also there for an exact description of the RMSM variables and computing procedure.

483 See Nissanke and Ferrarini (2001), p. 4. The authors note that Easterly's criticism has been widely recognized and that it could be applied to any other theoretical model, "when models are applied mechanically for practical purposes without due calibrations."

484 See Hussain (2001), p. 91.

non-financial form, holding back investment although there are private savings.[485] This may lead to an overestimation of savings and investment and to an underestimation of foreign resources needed. Fourth, there is the (often unspoken) assumption that all foreign capital inflows ("aid") are used to finance investments. As is known from the debate on aid effectiveness, this tends not to be the case, partly because of the design of programs (e.g., food aid), but also because of corruption or other distortions. As alternative, Hussain proposes to use the Balance of Payments Constraint Growth Model of Thirlwall.[486] Thirlwall's Law states that the growth rate of open economies in the long run can be expressed as the growth of export volume divided by the income elasticity of demand for imports.[487]

This Keynesian-type Balance of Payments model argues that the current account balance imposes a constraint to growth if a rising domestic demand cannot be satisfied by domestic production and exports (which are needed to finance the import demand). Therefore, the concentration on accumulating capital via net investment is too narrow. The economic policy advice for developing countries is to reduce the income elasticity of demand for imports or to raise the income elasticity of demand for exports.[488] Foreign aid in the sense of this model can contribute to growth by financing the excess of imports over exports. However, Thirlwall's Law and the Balance of Payment Constraint argument are not undisputed.[489] The model has been applied to a sample of 24 African countries and used to estimate the foreign exchange gap. Again, as in Gottschalk's study, the underlying policy objective is to finance the Millennium Development Goals.[490] The author, however, admits that country characteristics have not been included to fine-tune the model. The model is set up in a way that it calculates the required capital inflow for a year t+1 compared to a base year t. Imbalances in the base year therefore are reproduced in subsequent periods, leading to a "snowball effect" (p. 109) "if nothing is done to improve export performance relative to imports" (p. 121). The result suggests a fi-

[485] See Hussain (1997).

[486] See Thirlwall (1979) and Thirlwall and Hussain (1982).

[487] For an extensive review of Thirlwall's Law, see for example Dutt (2002) and Perraton (2003). A time-series test of Thirlwall's Law for Brazil is provided by Bértola et al. (2002) who confirm the existence of a long-run relationship between Brazilian GDP, terms of trade, and world income. Thirlwall's law acts as a basis of a large body of post-Keynesian growth models.

[488] See Hussain (2001), p. 95. A formal description of the model is also provided there.

[489] See in particular Krugman (1989).

[490] Hussain adopts the projections of the UN Economic Commission for Africa, in which a target growth rate of 7% annually on average is set. See ECA (1999).

nancing gap of $44.8 billion annually (in 1998 dollars) during a five-year period. This compares with 21% of the total sample's GDP.[491]

As Hjertholm et al. (1998) note, instead of merely filling gaps, foreign aid should help *closing* gaps.[492] A developing country should, in the long run, be able to finance all imports with its own export earnings so that financial aid from abroad represents only a temporary relief. This can be achieved via export promotion, while import substitution is regarded as an inferior option today.[493] Export promotion with foreign aid can take place by a) influencing the policies in the developing country, b) improving infrastructure and c) direct export subsidies.[494] The empirical results, however, seem to be mixed. While some studies show a positive impact of foreign aid on export promotion, others imply that foreign aid negatively affects exports.

Finally, it has to be noted that all gap models assume that foreign aid flows are received and utilized by the recipient country completely. This assumption has been shown to be rather unrealistic, as will be pointed out in subsequent chapters (e.g., on aid absorption). Other challenging aspects include i) the effects of foreign aid on fiscal behaviour, ii) unsustainable debt burdens and iii) the relationship between the exchange rate and foreign aid (Dutch Disease effects). Gap models implicitly assume that foreign aid is an autonomous resource transfer that can be isolated and measured.[495] But in fact, foreign aid inflows influence a variety of macroeconomic fundamentals and also touch on the behaviour of decision-makers with the recipient country's government.

Poverty traps

Neoclassical theory can only insufficiently explain why some very poor countries did not experience growth, even with substantial capital inflows from abroad. One observation in these countries is that GDP per capita growth rises with the inflow of capital but decreases again when this inflow is stopped. Growth effects are only temporary at best, which has induced some economists to conclude that very poor countries are caught in

[491] With respect to strategic planning, "all" a government needs to perform such calculations are estimations of income elasticities of demand as well as data on the terms of trade, the export volume and the initial current account (deficit or surplus).

[492] Hjertholm et al. (1998), p. 3.

[493] Import substitution policies have been pursued to a great extent in the 1960s und 1970s in South American economies. Their success remained rather limited.

[494] See Hjertholm (1998), pp. 29–34 for details.

[495] For an extensive overview of these issues see Hjertholm et al. (1998), p. 7–28.

a "poverty-trap". A poverty trap can be characterized "as a stable steady state with low levels of per capita output and capital stock. This outcome is a trap because, if agents attempt to break out of it, then the economy has a tendency to return to the low-level steady state."[496] Nelson (1956) explains a low-level equilibrium trap with the following thoughts:

> "The malady of many underdeveloped economies can be diagnosed as a stable equilibrium level of per capita income at or close to subsistence requirements. Only a small percentage, if any, of the economy's income is directed toward net investment. If the capital stock is accumulating, population is rising at a rate equally fast; thus the amount of capital equipment per worker is not increasing. If economic growth is defined as rising per capita income, these economies are not growing. They are caught in a low-level equilibrium trap."[497]

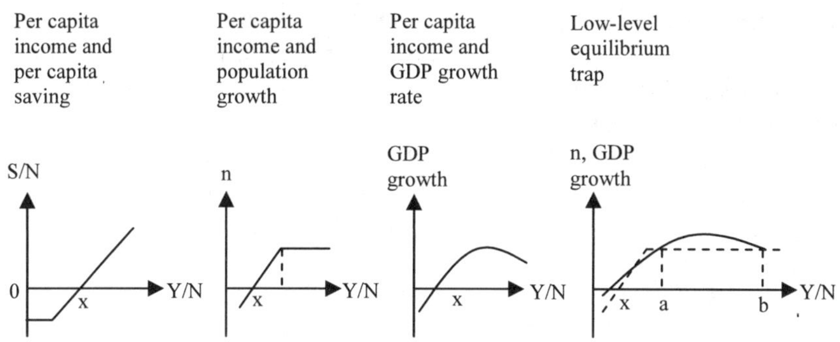

Fig. 4.6. Nelson's low-level equilibrium trap

Source: Wagner et al. (1983), p. 34 (modified)

In his model, the assumption of population growth with rising per capita income is critical.[498] It follows from the idea that population growth can be defined as the birth rate minus the death rate plus the rate of net immigration. With rising per capita income, better medical techniques will lower the death rate and hence increase the population rate.[499] This link between

[496] Barro and Sala-i-Martin (1995), p. 49.
[497] Nelson (1956), p. 894.
[498] For a complete review of the model, see Nelson (1956), pp. 894ff.
[499] See ibid., pp. 897–898.

population growth and per capita income remains highly disputed.[500] Fig. 4.6 explains Nelson's low-level equilibrium trap. The saving function is constructed in a way that saving is only possible beyond a certain minimum per capita income (existence minimum). The second graph shows a neo-Malthusian population growth: With rising per capita income, population growth rises due to a decrease in the death rate. This decrease has its natural limits, so that population growth is constant from a certain point on. The third graph follows from the first and second graph: In point x, saving and population growth is zero, leading to no GDP growth. The forth graph results by overlapping the second and third graph. It shows a low-level equilibrium trap. Between x and a, the population growth n is higher than GDP growth. The per capita income then is reduced to the existence minimum. If the economy manages to achieve a GDP growth higher than n (between a and b), then a new equilibrium point can be reached and the trap be escaped.

Another justification for a poverty trap goes as follows:[501] Countries focusing on agriculture experience diminishing returns to scale, whereas when they develop, they turn to production in sectors with increasing returns. During the phase of increasing returns to scale, investment and capital accumulation is more productive than in the phases of diminishing returns, leading to higher savings and output and making the growth process self-sustaining. If these benefits are exhausted, the country might experience diminishing returns again.

Finally, a poverty trap illustration can be derived from a multi-equilibrium Solow-model allowing for non-linearities in the production function (see Fig. 4.7). k is the capital labor ratio, s is the saving rate, n is the population growth rate, δ is the depreciation rate. The curve symbolizes the average product of capital function in a Solow-Swan model; the horizontal line expresses the effective depreciation line for the capital labor ratio.[502]

Foreign aid inflows by a large country or institution to a country currently at a low-level equilibrium k_{low} have to have a minimum size. If this donation does not promote the recipient country to come across k_{middle}, then the country will fall back to k_{low} and the donation effect was only temporary. In order to achieve long run economic growth, the donation

[500] Although it seems that this "population trap" is valid in most of the poor African countries, it cannot be generalized. For an analysis of the historical evolution of the relationship between population and growth, see Galor and Weil (2000).

[501] See Barro and Sala-i-Martin (1995), p. 49.

[502] For further details, see Barro and Sala-i-Martin (1995), Chap. 1.

must be at least so large that the country can "jump" to the next stable point k_{high}. Alternatively, the country could raise its saving rate s, which would shift the curve upward.

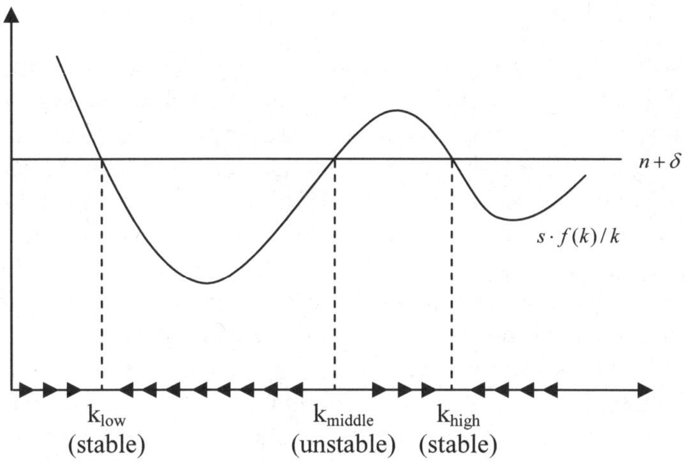

Fig. 4.7. Illustration of a poverty trap

Source: Barro and Sala-i-Martin (1995), p. 50

It can escape the poverty trap if the curve is above the depreciation line. Interestingly, it is sufficient that the saving rate is raised only temporarily.[503] Barro and Sala-i-Martin suggest that the temporary higher saving could also be financed by international loans. However, they also question the existence of shifting returns to scale. Recent works by Bloom et al. and Quah[504] confirm the "poverty trap" argument and suggest the existence of "twin peaks" or "convergence clubs". Countries with similar initial conditions seem to group together, giving rise to multiple equilibria.

Nelson as well as other economists (Myrdal, Singer, Nurkse) offered several solutions to the poverty trap: Apart from various changes in the social structure (reaching from a stronger emphasis on entrepreneurship, government investment programs incentives such as subsidies for education to imposing a limit to the family size), capital inflows from abroad can

[503] If the country manages to surpass k_{middle} with higher savings, then lowering the saving rate would not lead the country into the poverty trap again. Alternatively, if the population growth rate n is lowered, a country can also escape the poverty trap.

[504] See Bloom et al. (2003) and Quah (1997).

assist in escaping a poverty trap. Foreign assistance, if large enough, can be an instrument to achieve the minimum level in order for growth to be self-generative by either increasing temporary savings ("shifting the entire curve upwards") or decreasing the population growth rate.

The "Big Push" argument

Other economists were less optimistic about a gradual escape out of the poverty trap. Furtado, for example, warns "against the illusion that it is feasible to pass from stagnation to development by means of a steady though slight effort."[505] The fight against infectious diseases (e.g., Malaria, AIDS) may illustrate a case in which a very high level of protection by vaccination is necessary to reach as much people as possible, to prohibit the disease from spreading again.[506] In order to be effective and generate more income, "simultaneous investments in infrastructure, communication, and information dissemination are needed to achieve multiplier effects."[507]

Following these thoughts, it has been argued by many that trapped countries need a "big push"[508] or a "critical minimum effort"[509] to escape poverty. A poverty trap show analogies to the vicious circle theories: Because of their low per capita income, developing countries lacked savings and capital formation. Other factors such as missing monetary or social infrastructure also contribute to the shortage of domestic capital formation, lead to a low growth rate of technical progress and have repercussions on the per capita income (see Fig. 4.8).

---

[505] Furtado (1961), p. 67.

[506] The World Health Organization (WHO) confirms that despite a variety of problems connected with the distribution of vaccination (a major one of them being logistics), a shortage of financial means often increases the chances of an infectious disease spreading again. Moreover, the more often new epidemic outbreaks occur, the more intelligent do the viruses grow. Additionally, the governments of poor countries often see no need to continue the vaccination when the disease seems to have vanished, although a prolongation of treatment is often necessary.

[507] Thomas et al. (2002), p. 52.

[508] Rosenstein-Rodan (1943).

[509] Leibenstein (1957).

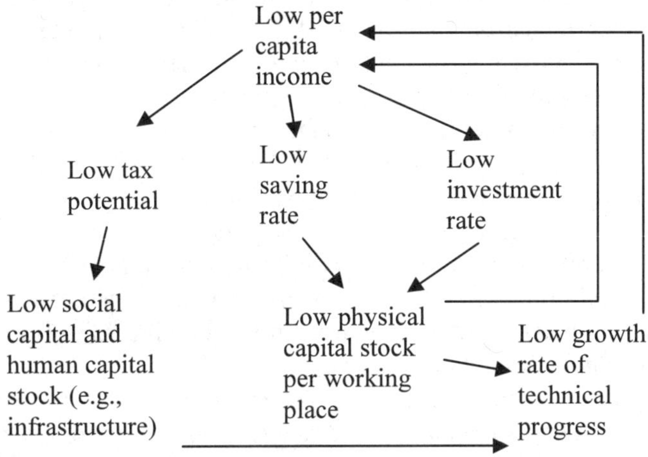

Fig. 4.8. Vicious circle of economic underdevelopment

Source: Bender (1995), p. 519
Translation by author

In analogy to the gap models, a big push could be financed with foreign aid. Rosenstein-Rodan[510] first claimed that a critical "mass" of aid is necessary in order to have an impact at all ("Big Push theory") and that it can help countries escape the poverty trap and make the "move from a bad to a good equilibrium".[511] In a model of the big-push theory, Murphy et al. (1989) note that certain spillovers (e.g., demand spillovers, investments in jointly used infrastructure) can increase the chance of investments across industrial sectors ("coordinated investment"[512]). "[S]imultaneous industrialization of many sectors can be self-sustaining even if *no* sector could break even industrializing alone."[513] The authors conclude that a big push seems to be feasible in economies "where industrialized firms capture in

[510] See Rosenstein-Rodan (1943, 1961, 1984). See also Nelson (1956) and Leibenstein (1957).

[511] See Murphy et al. (1989). Further works examine the big push under the label of "threshold externalities". See Azariadis and Drazen (1990) as well as Ghosh and Wolf (1990). Bowman and Anderson (1963) stress the importance of a minimum literacy rate for rapid economic growth.

[512] See Murphy et al. (1989).

[513] See ibid. A concept arising from this is the theory of balanced growth. See for example Nurkse (1953). A contrasting view is taken by Hirschman (1958) who advocated unbalanced growth, pointing to the forward and backward linkages in production.

their profits only a fraction of the total contribution of their investment to the profits of other industrializing firms."[514] This can be facilitated via market size effects (increasing demand or increased market size).[515] Sauer et al.[516] provide an empirical examination of Murphy et al.'s approach. Using cointegration tests on a country-by-country basis, they support the big push theory in general by indicating that a large number of industries switched from no cointegration in the first period to cointegration in the other. This method is based on the idea that sectors "participating" in the big push show a similar trend in industry indicators such as GDP or real wages. Finally, Vellutini draws the conclusion that a growth "miracle" (e.g., East Asia) can be interpreted as the result of liberalization of private capital flows and a governmental "small push".[517]

Similar to gap models, the Big Push and poverty trap arguments are still widely deployed in today's development strategy thinking, as for example in the UN Millennium Project. However, there is only limited empirical evidence to uphold their theses. In statistical tests, Easterly[518] rejects that there has been no growth in the poorest countries (poorest fifth) as hypothesized by the poverty trap. Dividing these countries into above-average and below-average foreign aid receivers does also not reveal any differences in the economic growth rate. He insists that "the poorest countries *can* grow and develop on their own."[519] Kraay and Raddatz[520] confirm Easterly's results finding that saving rates in poor countries are not as low as a poverty trap situation might predict. Although the authors do not reject that poverty traps can occur theoretically, they call into question that a large scaling-up if aid is a necessary condition for sustained increases in growth. The persistence of low income in many African countries cannot be explained by poverty traps:

> "This does not mean that increasing aid to Africa (or other poor countries) is a bad idea. Rather, it suggests to us that we should not expect any disproportionate growth effects of large-scale aid. [...] While savings rates and productivity do clearly increase with income levels, we find that they do not increase in the right nonlinear way required to generate poverty traps. We also find that a poverty-trap view of aid relying on these

[514] See Murphy et al. (1989).
[515] See also Shams (1999), p. 2. As Rosenstein-Rodan (1961), p. 63 remarks, free international trade reduces the size of the minimum push required.
[516] Sauer et al. (2003).
[517] See Vellutini (2002), p. 453.
[518] See Easterly (2006), p. 37ff.
[519] Ibid., p. 40.
[520] See Kraay and Raddatz (2005).

mechanisms leads to counterfactual predictions for the relationship between aid, investment, and growth."[521]

Finally, it should be noted that each and every country has been "underdeveloped" once in its history. Following the poverty trap or vicious circle theory, there would be no developed country today,[522] as only a minor number of now industrialized countries developed with external assistance.

Debt and economic growth

A special form of foreign aid is loans, which usually entail a grant element (a minimum of 25 percent in order to be eligible as ODA) and a grace period (up to 10 years), but whose principal and interest must be paid back to the creditor. Loans make up a considerable proportion of international aid flows and have been used by debtor countries to varying extents. The following section reviews the relationship between debt finance and domestic investment, particularly the lending/borrowing model and the role of optimal indebtedness.

The classical intertemporal borrowing-lending-model describes an optimization behavior for the utility of a debtor country that has a two-period budget constraint with two given levels of income (y_0 and y_1) and a two-period utility function U (C_0, C_1). The maximization the country's utility is graphed in Fig. 4.9. The production possibility frontier (PPF) represents all combinations of current and future outputs a country can choose. Combinations below the PPF are inefficient; combinations above are not feasible without access to international capital markets. Thus, in a closed economy, point A represents one of many optima in an autarky position, with a domestic interest rate r that is higher than the world interest rate r*. The slope of the budget line at point A is -(1+r).

With access to international capital markets, there are two positive effects for a borrowing country:

1. The lower cost of capital because of the lower world interest rate allows a higher future consumption (point B).
2. The current consumption can be expanded to point C (higher utility function).

The horizontal distance between points B and C represents, according to Obstfeld and Rogoff[523], the current account deficit of period 0, split into

[521] Kraay and Raddatz (2005), p. 3 and 31.
[522] See Dorn et al. (1998), p. 26.
[523] See Obstfeld and Rogoff (1998).

extra investment (A-B) and extra consumption (A-C). Easterly[524] defines the elasticity of intertemporal substitution as well as the discount rate as the two main variables influencing a country's borrowing behavior. Although a country that borrows from abroad may generate higher welfare in the current period, part of the borrowed capital goes into current consumption. In very poor countries, where borrowed capital finances basic consumption needs, the necessary returns from investment in order to repay outstanding debt in future periods are not readily generated. One possible reason is diminishing returns to capital, which could lead to declining net benefits of additional investments as debt increases.[525]

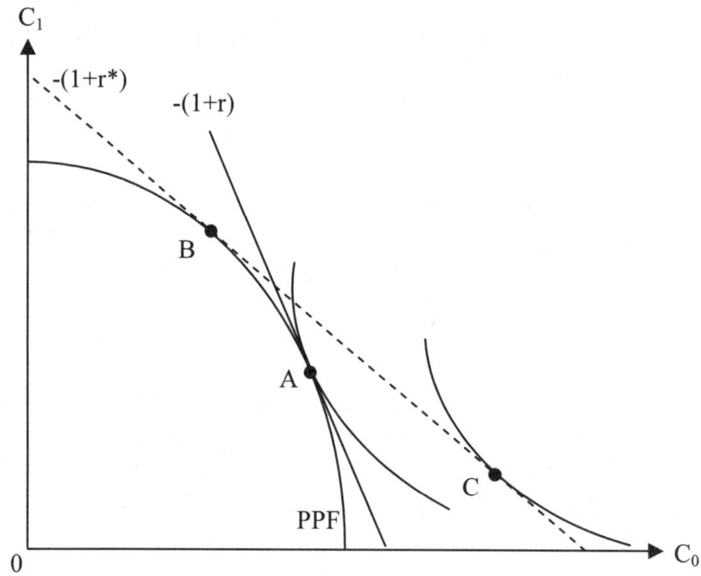

Fig. 4.9. Borrowing from abroad

Source: Nissanke and Ferrarini (2001), p. 2

[524] See Easterly (1999).
[525] See Bhattacharya and Clements (2004), p. 49.

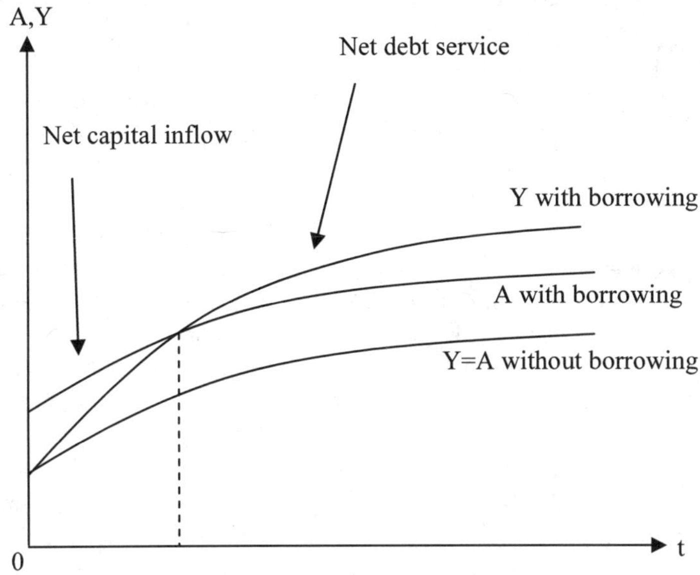

Fig. 4.10. Growth-cum-debt model

Source: Nissanke and Ferrarini (2001), p. 6
Note: *A* = Absorption, *Y* = income

The two-period model of the last section illustrates the basic principle of borrowing and lending. The growth-cum-debt-model depicted in Fig. 4.10 shows income Y and domestic absorption A over time. In an autarky situation, Y equals A (lower curve). If the country accesses international capital markets, national income can be raised with net capital inflows. In this period, absorption exceeds national income. In the future period, debt service payments take place and absorption is lower than income. It is assumed here that the additional capital is used to finance productive investments that yield a return able to overcompensate debt service.[526] Consequently, the "Y with borrowing" curve is higher than the "Y without borrowing" curve.

While debt cycles represent an inherent feature of borrowing, it is also rather straightforward that countries cannot borrow indefinitely. If current account deficits are not followed by surpluses, negative impacts on growth and macroeconomic stability will occur.[527] Thus, borrowing countries need

[526] See Nissanke and Ferrarini (2001), p. 6.

[527] Usually, investors will demand higher interests for the higher insolvency risk. Models of the Ponzi debt games class deal with the idea whether governments

to pay attention not to cross a certain level of debt accumulation. This level is referred to in the literature as debt overhang, debt threshold, debt solvency limit or debt sustainability.[528] Debt overhang, according to Krugman[529], represents a situation in which an existing debt stock is sufficiently large that creditors do not expect it to be fully repaid.[530] With a high outstanding debt level, more and more foreign resources are used to finance existing debt, discouraging domestic and foreign investment[531] and hence reducing economic growth.[532] These fears can arise because of a probability of future tax raises or debt-induced crises. The lack of investment will reduce a country's income, resulting in a higher debt-income ratio leading to a further disincentive effect.[533] Beyond the direct negative economic impact, adverse effects of indebtedness can come in the form of reduced government incentives to bring forth fiscal reforms because an improvement of the budgetary position would raise pressures of creditors to repay outstanding loans.[534] Such a cautionary position can also be assumed for long-term investments. Instead, short-term profit-oriented projects will prevail. Other risks include capital flight of private investors. A situation of debt overhang is also known as the debt Laffer curve.[535] The idea is to regard debt as a tax on debtor's resources.[536] Fig. 4.11 shows how the expected repayment is dependent on the value of outstanding debt.

---

can "play a game" in which they roll over debt indefinitely in order to never increase taxes. Blanchard and Weil (2001) show that this approach of rolling over debt forever is feasible under certain conditions.

[528] The most commonly used indicators are the debt-to-exports- and the debt-to-GDP-ratio. Sect. 3.4.3 has dealt with measurement issues of debt sustainability in more detail.

[529] Krugman (1988), p. 2. One of the first contributions on this topic is Sachs (1984, 1986).

[530] More analytically, "a country has a debt overhang problem when the expected present value of potential future resource transfers is less than its debt." Krugman (1988), p. 5.

[531] See Greene and Villanueva (1991) and Savvides (1992).

[532] See Clements et al. (2003), p. 3–4.

[533] See Chowdhury (2001), p. 4.

[534] Such a concern was already raised by Krugman (1988), p. 14 who pointed out that there is no reason for a country to adjust, because the reward goes solely to its creditors. For the creditors, in turn, this means that they should give less incentives for policy adjustment than necessary in order to receive at least a part of their debt.

[535] Cohen (1993).

[536] Such a viewpoint can be borrowed from the business management literature on corporate finance. A company facing a project with positive net present value will usually undertake the project because it increases the value of the company.

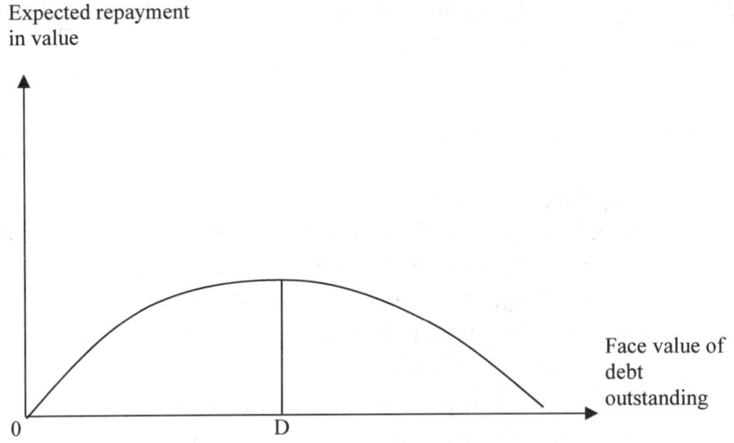

Fig. 4.11. Debt (relief) Laffer curve

Source: Author

Once a certain level of indebtedness has been exceeded, the expected repayment will fall because of the effects explained before. On the "left side" of the debt Laffer curve (up to point D), a further increase in the face value of debt outstanding would lead to a higher expected repayments in the future, while on the "right side", an increase would lead to a reduction of repayments. The empirical support of the debt Laffer curve is, however, inconclusive.[537] A recent study by Clements et al. finds that high levels of debt can depress growth in low-income countries via its effect on the efficiency of resource use rather than via a crowding out on investment.[538] In general, however, they confirm the existence of a debt threshold level.

How long the borrowing periods can be, i.e. how long a growth-cum-debt strategy can be upheld, remains ambiguous. One condition for solvency is that the country has enough export earnings to service its outstanding debt. Since both debtor and creditor are not interested in a total default, two strategies may evolve: If a country faces the risk of insolvency, the creditors could lend additional resources with a certain prob-

Instead, if the firm is highly indebted, it might not undertake this project, because all of the return would go to its creditors, even if the value of the firm would be increased.

[537] See Clements et al. (2003) for a review of empirical studies. Estimations on the threshold level (with respect to GDP) vary widely.

[538] See Clements et al. (2003), p. 18.

ability that a payback will occur in a future period.[539] Alternatively, they might accept a reduction in their loans.

4.2.2 Empirical observations

The empirical literature on the relationship between aid and growth can look back on several decades of research. Some of the earliest empirical studies to examine the relationship between aid and growth were Griffin, Griffin and Enos, and Papanek.[540] The latter disaggregated capital inflows into private capital and foreign aid and found a positive aid term. Other early studies such as the one from Voivodas, however, report a negative relationship.[541] Despite countless econometric studies that have been undertaken since then to clarify the aid-growth relationship, no consensus has emerged. The large size of economic and non-economic variables complicates this relationship, and the task has developed more and more to an econometrician's exercise, attempting to reduce econometrical limitations (e.g., with respect to robustness or non-linearities). The impact of aid has been assessed at the macro- and microeconomic level, using cross-country and single-country case studies. This field of literature is so vast that some researchers have constructed meta-studies on the existing evidence and categorized it according to the results and methodologies.[542] As the authors themselves notice, this "survey approach is subject to pitfalls."[543] The most important caveats are the different quality of studies and the probability that different authors made similar mistakes.

Early empirical work applied HD and Solow-type regression equations (first-generation studies) and concentrated on the aid-savings correlation. The most studies come to the conclusion that foreign aid has a positive impact on savings but that the impact is not as large as the aid flow itself.

In second generation studies, the focus shifted towards the aid-investment-growth relationship. The analytical base was still dominated by thinking in terms of capital accumulation, savings and investment. Only

---

[539] See Krugman (1988), p. 10 for this argument. For example, a rise in commodity prices for certain goods might enable resource-rich countries to be able to repay their outstanding debt because of larger export earnings. Another important point to consider is the fact that although the creditors taken as one group have a collective interest in prolonging their loans, each individual creditor's best strategy is to opt out and let the other creditors extend their loans.

[540] See Griffin (1970), Griffin and Enos (1970) and Papanek (1973).

[541] See Voivodas (1973).

[542] See, for example, Hansen and Tarp (1999) who recall 131 regression studies.

[543] See ibid., p. 6.

very few studies show a negative relationship, with a body of studies finding evidence for a positive correlation between aid and investment. The evidence on the aid-growth relationship is nevertheless mixed. Among 71 analyzes, only 1 found a statistically negative relationship between aid and growth, 40 showed a positive impact of aid on growth, whereas 31 report inconclusive (statistically insignificant) results.[544] This can be explained with a lack of a "strong analytical framework that can be used to compare and evaluate the causal relationships in the various studies [since a]id is given for many different purposes and in many different forms."[545] Many case studies provide evidence that foreign economic assistance can in fact yield in positive economic returns. Nevertheless, studies conducted at the macro-level find strong difficulties in proving such a positive relationship, which has led to the formulation of the micro-macro paradox by Mosley.[546] It states that there seems to be a contradiction between microeconomic and macroeconomic studies. While the former show successes of aid projects, the latter cannot sufficiently establish a link between aid and macroeconomic variables. One reason seems to be the difficulty of finding statistical significance in empirical correlations. Another is to capture all influential variables in an operational analytical model. Recent works by Hansen and Tarp as well as Moreira, however, question the existence of a micro-macro paradox and argue that theoretical models do show a positive aid-growth relationship.[547]

Third-generation studies cover large amounts of data (many observations and many countries), use panel data and cross-country regression analysis,[548] take into account non-economic variables and address the problem of non-linearities in the aid-growth nexus. Nevertheless, most studies differ more or less with regard to conceptual and methodological issues.[549] Third-generation studies are particularly interested in finding the necessary conditions for increased aid effectiveness. Hansen and Tarp conclude that the existing literature on the aid growth link supports the proposition that aid improves economic performance.

---

544 See Hansen and Tarp (1999), p. 9.

545 Ibid, p. 1.

546 See Mosley (1987).

547 See Dalgaard et al. (2004), Dalgaard and Hansen (2001) and Moreira (2003).

548 A noteworthy exemption is Ghosh and Wolf (1998) who leave the path of regression studies and present a decision tree model.

549 Ravallion (2003a), p. 1 is right in pointing out that all (even small) differences in the methodology used must be carefully considered: "[D]ramatically differing positions taken in this debate [on poverty] often stem from differences in the concepts and definitions used and differences in data sources and measurement assumptions."

4.2.3 Summary

Early theoretical models (gap model, poverty trap, big push) suggest that foreign aid can promote economic growth via enhanced savings and investment, assist a country in closing a financing gap and initialize an economic development path from which the poor will benefit in the long-run. This sort of thinking is still widely accepted in development economics and serves as a guideline for economic analyses. However, there is rising support for the notion that foreign aid is not gap-reducing, but gap-filling and thus prolongs the existence of the gap. Empirical evidence on the aid-growth nexus is mixed and allows for no general conclusions. Regarding the role of debt, it can be concluded that additional capital from abroad can promote economic growth if it is used to finance productive investment that yields a return able to overcompensate the future debt service. Still, many low-income countries consume the major share of borrowed financial resources and thus experience unsustainable debt overhangs.

The ongoing academic dispute indicates that there is no consensus on the aid-growth nexus. Most empirical studies fail to provide a clear causality. Applying other/additional data, selecting other threshold levels, omitting critical countries, using lagged indicators and a variety of other econometrical operations qualify the meaning of the results. Recent studies question the gap model technique, the Big Push and the poverty trap argument and reject the imperative of a start-up financing with foreign aid that has for a long time dominated development economics. Thus, one can firmly conclude that the aid-growth nexus is too complex for a general answer. Consequently, researchers have shifted their attention towards testing more specific hypotheses. Among them, the following deserve attention:

- Collier and Dehn look primarily at countries experiencing an external shock. In a regression analysis, they find significance that a rise in aid flows to such countries is particularly effective after negative external shocks such as a fall in export prices.[550]
- Collier and Hoeffler analyze the effect of aid in post-conflict countries.[551] Their result is that aid can be helpful for these countries, especially several years and not immediately after a conflict.

---

[550] See Collier and Dehn (2001). More generally, Chauvet and Guillaumont (2001) show that in economically instable countries (e.g., fluctuating terms of trade) aid is more effective, because it gives a country the opportunity to deal with economic shocks without changing policy reforms. In contrast, political instability reduces the effectiveness of aid.

[551] See Collier and Hoeffler (2004).

- In a "climatic model", Dalgaard et al. emphasize geography as an important country characteristic influencing growth. Among other variables, they examine the landlockedness and the tropical land area and note that aid is less effective in countries that have a large share of tropical land.[552]
- Easterly and Levine[553] argue that measures of tropics, germs and crops explain cross-country differences through their impact on institutions.
- Beck et al. find that countries with better-developed financial intermediaries experience faster declines in measures of poverty.[554]
- Engerman and Sokoloff point out that colonial ties are a relevant factor in determining the relationships between donor and recipient countries of foreign aid.[555]
- Aid seems to be more effective in countries where structural characteristics change slowly over time (e.g., due to geographical circumstances).[556]
- Moreover, the extent of democracy,[557] structural vulnerability,[558] and the presence of a totalitarian government[559] are influential and significant variables in the aid growth nexus.

4.3 ODA, inequality, poverty and growth

The following sections present an overview on the interdependencies between ODA, inequality, poverty reduction and economic growth. First some basic definitions will be provided (Sect. 4.3.1), followed by on overview on existing paradigms (Sect. 4.3.2). The subsequent sections analyze trickle-down growth (Sect. 4.3.3), the concept and measurement of propoor growth (Sect. 4.3.4), distribution with growth (Sect. 4.3.5), direct sectoral policies (Sect. 4.3.6) and economic transfers (Sect. 4.3.7). Sect. 4.3.8 presents empirical results, Sect. 4.3.9 summarizes.

---

552 See Dalgaard et al. (2004). Earlier models that analyze the link between economic development and the geography of countries go back to Bloom and Sachs (1998) and Gallup et al. (1999).
553 See Easterly and Levine (2002).
554 See Beck et al. (2004).
555 See Engerman and Sokoloff (2005).
556 See Dalgaard et al. (2004), p. 192.
557 See Svensson (1999).
558 See Guillaumont and Chauvet (2001).
559 See Islam (2003).

4.3.1 Definitions

An individual in a society is considered poor if her actual standard of living does not satisfy a minimum level of social norms. To differentiate between poor and rich individuals or households, a so-called poverty line is marked meaning that a pre-determined consumption level is set assuring the basic nutritional requirements. Very generally, people with an income under the poverty line are considered to be poor. Poverty is thus measured in absolute levels of living, whereas inequality concerns disparities in the relative levels of living. Most data on poverty and inequality rely on household consumption expenditures (or income) gathered in surveys. From it, the World Bank derived its (global) poverty line of $1 per day and person in 1991 (once on a 1985, now on a 1993 base year). Between 1981 and 2001, poverty determined by this $1/day measure has fallen from 40% to 21% of world population.[560] This universal poverty line, valid for all countries, is not undisputed, because it follows the idea of a fixed purchasing power (absolute poverty), of which the real value is kept constant.[561] Other caveats are data availability on consumer prices and the purchasing power parity (PPP) values, troubles arising from differences in the quality of goods and the gravity impact of some countries (e.g., China). In contrast, the concept of relative poverty acknowledges that individuals have different social preferences and that poverty depends on the social environment: It is subject to the income levels and the poverty status of other individuals.[562]

One way of measuring relative poverty is to set the poverty line as a certain constant fraction of mean income (e.g., the lowest quintile of the population).[563] This can result in constant or even higher poverty when the income of the poor has risen, depending on the development of the mean. Moreover, with this definition, there will always be poverty. A number of other indices measuring poverty have been developed in the literature. The

---

[560] Also the absolute number of the poor has declined by 350 million between 1981 and 2001. However, this number must be interpreted carefully, as the number of the poor remained nearly constant during that period when excluding just one country, China.

[561] The procedure to derive the $1 poverty line consists of several steps. First, the $1 is converted into the 1993 value of local currency, using the World Bank's Purchasing Power Parity Table. With a local consumption deflator, this value is updated to the target year and then combined with household data to obtain the headcount-index andother indices.

[562] See Ravallion (2003a), p. 4.

[563] Eurostat uses this method.

following list of indicators is not complete but covers the main approaches:[564]

- The *poverty headcount* measures the number of people living under the poverty line; the *headcount index* calculates its proportion of the whole population. Inequality among the poor (in terms of severity of poverty) cannot be measured with this index, as persons some cents below the poverty line count the same as those further below the line.
- In order to obtain information on the severity of poverty, the *poverty gap index* is derived, measuring the deficit below the poverty line. It is defined as the mean over the population of the proportionate poverty gap, which is given by the distance of the poor below the poverty line, as a proportion of the line. The non-poor are counted as having a zero poverty gap; the higher the value, the more severe is the level of poverty.[565]
- The *Watts index*[566] is useful to measure inequality among the poor. It is the population mean of the log of the ratio between poverty line and censored income. Using the maxims of an ideal poverty index of Zheng,[567] the Watts index is referred to by many development researchers as being the best poverty indicator currently available.
- The *total growth elasticity of poverty (GEP)* is defined as the relative change in the poverty headcount between two periods for a one percent growth of mean income with a constant poverty line in real terms. However, some point to the difficult task of interpreting this index.[568]

---

[564] A lot of studies stress the notion that poverty is a multidimensional problem. Despite of measuring poverty solely in economic terms, other measurements can be used involving the current state of health (e.g., birth rate), the human capital (schooling rate), the exposure of the poor to external risks (criminal rate), the participation of the poor in social and political decision-making („voices of the poor", also referred to as participatory equity).

[565] This index does also exist in a squared form.

[566] See Watts (1968).

[567] See Zheng (1993). Originally, Sen (1976) presented three axioms to be central for poverty measurement. These are the focus axiom, the monotonicity axiom and the transfer axiom. The focus axiom states that the measure is invariant to changes of income of the poor. Monotonicity entails that every reduction of income of the poor must be associated with an increase in poverty. The transfer axiom holds that any transfers reducing the inequality among the poor reduce poverty. Later, the axiom of additive decomposability has been added. It means that aggregate poverty can be written as a population weighted mean of the poverty measures across different groups. Zheng (1993) and other authors have further enhanced this set of axioms.

[568] See Agence Francaise de Développement et al. (2005), p. 81f.

$$GEP = \frac{\partial P}{\partial Y} \cdot \frac{Y}{P} \quad (4.3)$$

- The *partial growth elasticity of income* is the relative change in the poverty headcount for a one percent growth of mean income holding inequality constant.
- The *growth incidence curve* has been developed by Ravallion and Chen.[569] It is obtained by graphing the growth rate at every percentile of the distribution and can be interpreted as a distribution-corrected growth rate. It is an instrument to verify whether changes in the distribution of income were poverty reducing.
- The Human Poverty Index, used by the United Nations, builds on Sen (1997).[570] It is a composite index comprising the three measures longevity,[571] knowledge,[572] and standard of living[573] also captured in the Human Development Index.

Taking into account disparities in the levels of living, absolute inequality has to be set apart from relative inequality. If two incomes, A and B, both double (e.g., from 4,000 and 8,000 to 8,000 and 16,000 respectively), absolute inequality has risen (from 4,000 to 8,000), while relative inequality has remained constant. Thus, if all incomes rise by the same rate, relative inequality stays the same. Voices criticizing that inequality is rising typically point towards absolute inequality numbers; those who argue inequality is falling often refer to the concept of relative inequality. Neither approach is wrong or right per se.

Besides relative and absolute inequality, inequality between countries and within countries has to be differentiated. Inequality between countries is weighted by the size of populations. Although a lot of poor countries did not grow in the last decades, some large countries (such as China and India) grew with a high rate, reducing total inequality between rich (industrialized) and poor (developing) countries. In contrast, inequality within countries, also in industrialized countries, tends to rise. Ravallion refers to these developments as the falling between-country component of global inequality.[574]

---

[569] See Ravallion and Chen (2003). See there for an application of this index to China.
[570] See Sen (1997).
[571] The probability at birth of not surviving the age of 40.
[572] Proportion of adults who are illiterate.
[573] Measured by the proportion of persons without access to safe water and health services and malnourished children under the age of five.
[574] Ravallion (2003a), p. 7.

4.3.2 Conflicting paradigms

Since the 1990s, the World Bank and other international development organizations increasingly focus on poverty reduction in developing countries. The dominating paradigm of the 1990s stated that economic growth can spur poverty alleviation. In the last few years, the term "pro-poor growth" has been formulated, reflecting a shift in the center of attention on poverty-oriented growth policies.[575] However, there is an ongoing debate on the question whether growth alone is sufficient to benefit the poor. While proponents underline this by empirical studies showing the positive relationship between growth and poverty reduction, opponents argue that economic growth alone may be insufficient to alleviate poverty. Empirical studies examining the relationship between poverty and economic growth come to ambiguous conclusions. A variety of statistical examinations shows that despite some growth success of poor countries during the last decades, poverty remained high, especially in least developed countries. It has also been shown that distributional policies can at least complement economic growth, and under certain conditions even foster growth. This depends on initial country circumstances, country characteristics and the objective function chosen by the planner.

The high number of studies exploring the poverty-inequality-growth nexus makes it impossible to present a homogenous picture with lucid theoretical links. "The mainstream literature has not so much evolved as fluctuated over the past 50 years."[576] It is important to highlight several aspects in advance before reviewing the main causal relationships. First, the methodology of econometric studies varies considerably and brings about various results. The differences in testing hypotheses, controlling for other variables and interpreting data pose major shortcomings.[577] Second, as has been shown above, there are also a lot of different indices and measurement techniques. Third, the two populous countries India and China influence the measurement of worldwide poverty significantly. Consequently, there are arguments for leaving these countries out when calculating poverty and inequality issues in other poor regions such as Africa.

There are several channels for growth affecting the poor. Depending on the definition, they can be said to be pro-poor or not. The academic literature has defined the term "trickle-down" to describe how the poor may benefit from macroeconomic growth. An alternative is Chenery and Ahluwalia's

[575] Note that *pro-poor* growth means *anti-poverty* growth.

[576] Dagdeviren et al. (2004), p. 126.

[577] This is a more general point worth mentioning and applicable to a wide range of econometric analyses. It is not a critique per se.

model of growth with redistribution. Moreover, direct and indirect transmission channels exist: In one way, growth raises the income of the poor if directed to economic sectors and regions in which most poor people work, as well as impacts on the factors of production they use excessively.[578] An indirect way is redistributing the merits of "any" growth (not necessarily pro-poor growth) using special taxing systems favoring the poor or direct transfer payments. While the trickle-down mechanism is based on market-optimism (in a well-functioning economy, the poor will benefit automatically from any growth), proponents of direct and indirect policies targeting the poor are market-pessimists, in which the state must proactively care for the poor and restore market failures and distortions. These contrasting views will be described in the subsequent sections.

There is also a controversial debate on the relationship between growth and inequality. The traditional argument by Kuznets[579] is that inequality seems to increase during early stages of economic growth because of transformations from rural to urban and from agricultural to industrialized economies. After some time, inequality tends to fall again (inverted U-shaped function). One modern position, however, claims that there is an inherent trade-off between inequality (also: equity/distribution) and growth (also: efficiency) in the sense that policies specifically directed at the poor will result in distortions in an economy and henceforth a reduction of growth. This loss can more than compensate the gains of the poor and result in a net loss to an economy. Some recent studies challenge the existence of such a negative equity-efficiency trade-off. One example often cited in this context is the development success of some East Asian countries that combined rapid per capita growth with relatively stable inequality and a significant alleviation of poverty.

4.3.3 Trickle-down growth

There is a longstanding debate whether economic growth in general does improve the lives of the poor or not. One particular question is whether and when economic growth generated by rich households will also favor poor households. While some scholars claim that such economic growth will be vertically percolated down to the poor, at least in the long-run, others doubt this mechanism. Some economists even assert that there is in fact a trickle-up not only to the middle income class but also to the very rich

[578] See Klasen (2003).
[579] See Kuznets (1955).

people.[580] The trickle-down idea was developed in the 1950s and 1960s. Trickle-down suggests that rich households get richer first. In a second period, the poor benefit when the rich begin to expend the gains of growth, although the exact "trickle-down mechanisms [were] not always clearly specified."[581]

An early study by Thornton et al.[582] has examined the relationship between poverty and growth in the period 1947–1974 and concluded that trickle-down effects existed before 1963, but petered out after 1963. They found no statistically significant trickle-down effect for any demographic group after 1963 and proposed "expanded programs directed specifically at poor families".[583] This result is, however, not undisputed.[584] Following Norton (2002), the subsequent equations can be set up to describe the relationship connecting the growth of the poor and the rich:[585]

$$Y_p = \alpha + \beta_r \cdot Y_r \tag{4.4}$$

$$Y_r = \alpha + \beta_p \cdot Y_p \tag{4.5}$$

with Y = per capita income of the rich (r) and the poor (p) and the β's acting as class income transfer coefficients. The β's represent the change in poor (rich) income caused by a change in rich (poor) income. Trickle-down growth then means that β_r must be positive. Empirical estimations are difficult, because a multitude of other variables has a significant influence on the growth rate. Norton presents the results of a simple regression analysis correcting for geographic variables such as landlockedness and tropical environment, indicating that both trickle-up and trickle-down effects can be observed, with the net effect tending towards the latter. Using the disaggregated Human Poverty Index and data from the United Nations, he reveals that increasing the income of the rich reduces poverty more than

580 See Todaro (1997), p. 163.

581 Shorrocks and van der Hoeven (2004), p. 1.

582 See Thornton et al. (1978). See also Anderson (1964).

583 Thornton et al. (1978), p. 394. In their study, the authors use a definition of poverty with an increasing threshold for the period between 1963 and 1974.

584 Hirsch (1980) showed that the results of the Thornton et al. model are sensitive to various specifications and that the original specification used by the authors may be inappropriate. See Hirsch (1980), p. 151. Most of the significant results vanish if a relative instead of an absolute poverty measure is used (Hirsch takes a "percentage change in poverty" variable).

585 See Norton (2002), p. 264.

directly increasing the income of the poor, thereby strongly confirming the existence of trickle-down effects.[586]

One important channel that has been highlighted in the literature with respect to the question how growth of the rich affects the poor is increased investment via borrowing and lending. In a seminal contribution, Aghion and Bolton[587] examine the role of credit market imperfections and credit rationing. They formalize the relationship that an accumulation of wealth of the rich frees more funds to the poor for investment purposes. Wealth does trickle down from rich to poor individuals and results in a new, but not necessarily efficient distribution outcome. This outcome can be improved by wealth redistribution policies which reduce distortions of the poor to maximize profits and thus increase the long-run efficiency of the economy.

The existence of trickle-down effects has important implications for the formulation of policy instruments such as taxation, government expenditures and an economy's trade-off between efficiency and inequality. The trickle-down theory still haunts development theory and policy, but has been criticized more often in recent past. One of the main arguments against trickle-down is that it does alleviate poverty only to a limited extent, because the poor (which are often self-employed) have fewer links to the rest of the economy than middle or upper income groups. "If the poor are malnourished, are uneducated, live in remote areas, or are discriminated against, the gains of economic growth are likely to escape them."[588]

4.3.4 Pro-poor growth

The quest for a concept to design economic growth policies specifically for poor countries has dominated the literature on growth and poverty in the last years. This approach is known as "pro-poor growth" and although widely used in the recent literature, there is no consensus on what it really means. The UN and the World Bank are among the main proponents of this approach[589] and have also labelled it "broad-based growth". Early concepts can be traced back to Ahluwalia and Chenery who combined distributional and poverty elements to the growth rate by differentiating be-

[586] See Norton (2002), p. 269. He acknowledges, however, that this result can be partly attributed to the difficulties of measuring the true incomes of the poor. Additionally, the simulations are based on a ceteris paribus clause, which is problematic because the incomes of the poor and the rich both grow, as the mere existence of trickle-up and trickle-down effects shows.

[587] See Aghion and Bolton (1997).

[588] Loayza and Raddatz (2005), p. 18.

[589] See UN (2000), World Bank (2000b).

tween population-weighted and poverty-weighted growth rates.[590] Its contrasting thought is known as "immiserizing growth", which occurs when an increase in economic activity leads to a fall in real living standards of the poor.[591]

There are different strings of definitions used in the current literature. In the simplest (weakest) sense, growth is pro-poor when it reduces poverty regardless of any distributional shifts. In other words, if economic growth reduces poverty by 1%, this growth is pro-poor, regardless of the growth rate and poverty reduction of other households. Stronger definitions include distributional aspects. So while the first definition addresses poverty, the second focuses on inequality. The latter requires for growth to be pro-poor that it benefits the poor more than people with an average or high income. This designation of pro-poor growth can be depicted by an ordinary growth rate times a distributional correction factor.[592] Thus, poverty alleviation can be decomposed into two parts: Economic growth and changes in the distribution of income.

Several other ways of measurement have been proposed:

- Growth is pro-poor when the growth rate of income of the poor is higher than the average growth rate.[593] This case implies that relative inequality decreases.
- The share of the poor in the rise of income is equal or higher as their population share.[594] This involves a decline in absolute inequality.
- Kakwani and Pernia built a *pro-poor growth index* showing the ratio of two elasticities: the growth elasticity of total poverty reduction (α) and the elasticity of poverty reduction in the case of distribution-neutral growth (β), i.e., holding inequality constant.[595]

$$PPGI = \frac{\alpha}{\beta} \tag{4.6}$$

[590] See Ahluwalia and Chenery (1974). Their work on redistributive mechanisms for poverty reduction remained rather ephemeral with the upcoming neoliberalism in the 1980s.

[591] A theoretical explanation of immiserizing growth was introduced by Bhagwati (1958) and Bhagwati (1988). It goes back to works of Edgeworth (1894) who called it indemnifying growth.

[592] See Ravallion (2004a), p. 6.

[593] See White and Anderson (2001), Kakwani and Pernia (2000).

[594] See White and Anderson (2001).

[595] See Kakwani and Pernia (2000).

An index greater 1 is then considered to illustrate pro-poor growth.[596] Index values between 0 and 1 can be judged as being moderately pro-poor, whereas values lower than 0 indicate that growth is anti-poor. In addition to this index, Kakwani and Son developed the *poverty equivalent growth rate*, capturing also the level of the actual growth rate.[597] It is defined as the rate of growth giving the same reduction of poverty as the current rate of growth if there were no inequality. Formally, it is the pro-poor growth index times the growth rate of mean income.

- Derived from the concept of the growth incidence curve, the *rate of pro-poor growth*, as presented by Ravallion and Chen, is the mean growth rate of the poor.[598] It is calculated by multiplying the ordinary rate of growth with the ratio of the actual change in poverty over time to the hypothetical change in poverty that would have occurred if growth were neutrally distributed. It is also the area under the growth incidence curve up to the headcount index, divided by the headcount index. If distributional shifts are poverty reducing, the rate of pro-poor growth will be higher than the ordinary growth rate, and vice versa.
- The *poverty growth curve*, introduced by Son,[599] is based on Atkinson's theorem and links the generalized Lorenz curve with changes in poverty.[600] The generalized Lorenz curve is the ordinary Lorenz curve (describing the percentage share of income of the bottom p percent of population) multiplied by the mean income of society. Based on the definition that growth is pro-poor when the poor benefit more than the average, an upward shift of the entire generalized Lorenz curve implies decreasing inequality and therefore a reduction of poverty. Its advantage comes with the easy calculation and data availability, as the index can be obtained by using (national) income data.

---

[596] Note that this index, applied to the simplest definition of pro-poor growth (growth is pro-poor if it reduces poverty) implies a value of greater 0 to represent pro-poor growth. See Kakwani and Pernia (2000) and also Baulch and McCulloch (2000).

[597] See Kakwani and Son (2002).

[598] See Ravallion (2004a), p. 4. Because the growth incidence curve focuses on percentiles, it is not the same as the mean growth rate in the income of all poor. Son (2004) shows the difference in an example.

[599] See Son (2004).

[600] See Atkinson (1987). Atkinson provided a link between second-order dominance and poverty reduction. Son (2004) shows that under Atkinson's theorem, an upward shift of the generalized Lorenz curve results in poverty reduction using a distributional definition of pro-poor growth. This holds for all poverty lines and all poverty measurements.

There is no winning concept in this definitional debate. In fact, the multitude of indicators has resulted in a large number of publications, but complicated the comparability of results. Some examples with simple numbers may illustrate this. Let the average overall growth rate be 5 percent and the growth rate of the poor 1 percent (this scenario will be abbreviated with "5–1"). Following the weakest definition, the growth rate of the poor, 1 percent, is pro-poor. Ordinary growth is thus renamed pro-poor growth, as poor people benefit in absolute terms. Lopez points out that, although one can follow this definition, one has to take into account political economy implications arising from such an uneven growth scenario.[601] Taking into account distributional effects (i.e. applying the various other definitions), the growth rate in the example above would not be considered pro-poor. However, using a distributional definition, a "2–3" scenario would be favored over a "6–4" situation, despite the fact that in the latter, both average and poor households would be better off. Put the other way around, contracting economies (with a negative growth rate) can show "pro-poor growth" and in fact represent no absolute gain to the poor. This shows that "pro-poor growth" is not equal to "reducing poverty" and that policies considered to be good for growth do not necessarily have to be beneficial to the poor.

In a strong absolute sense, pro-poor growth means that the absolute income gains of the poor must be higher than those of the rich, which in reality seems difficult to achieve.[602] Klasen, however, notes that this strong definition can be suitable for assessing pro-poor growth in a non-income dimension (e.g., enhancing health care, reducing child mortality).[603] Finally, a non-technical definition Kakwani and Pernia focusing on the strategic aspect of pro-poor growth states: "A pro-poor growth strategy entails the removal of institutional and policy-induced biases against the poor, as well as the adoption of direct pro-poor policies."[604] This includes macroeconomic (e.g., infrastructural biases against rural areas, improved access to credit, progressive tax system) and microeconomic (e.g., monopoly pricing) policies.

---

601 See Lopez (2004a), pp. 4–5.

602 If the rich ($20,000 per capita income) exhibit a growth rate of 1% (equaling $200), pro-poor growth in a strong absolute sense requires that the poor ($2,000 per capita income) must achieve a growth rate more than 10% (i.e., more than $200).

603 See Klasen (2005), pp. 5–6. He cites the example of schooling. A 20% increase in years of schooling of the poor might be equivalent to ¼ year of additional schooling, whereas for the rich, a moderate 10% increase might mean one more year. This can hardly be regarded as pro-poor.

604 See Kakwani and Pernia (2000), p. 4.

To sum up, the decision whether growth is pro-poor or not depends critically on the social welfare function of the observer.[605] This also partly explains the discrepancies in the results on the links between growth, inequality and poverty and the policy conclusions drawn.

4.3.5 Distribution with growth

Chenery and Ahluwalia's central motif is that distributional objectives should be regarded as an integral part of development strategies and should not be delinked.[606] For example, tax-financed transfers from rich to poor households can affect not only the income of the poor (positively), but also the savings and capital accumulation of the rich (negatively), thereby having an ambiguous overall effect on the income of the poor. In their contribution, Chenery and Ahluwalia argue that distributional objectives should be expressed in terms of desired income growth rates for poor households. According to the authors, there is no conflict between the objectives of economic growth and distribution, if one assumes that transfers of income between different groups of households are allowed. This changes, however, if political considerations are included into the analysis. Especially in least developed countries, large income transfers between different socio-economic groups are unlikely. Another special feature of the poor in such countries is that many of them are self-employed and do not enter the wage economy. Their model lists the following principal assumptions:

- Dualistic structure of production in developing economies (use of hired labor as well as self-employment),
- Concentration in the ownership of capital,
- Different access of certain socio-economic groups to employment opportunities resulting from geographical, social or educational barriers,
- Differences in the savings behavior of different socio-economic groups,
- Differences in the population growth rates of different socio-economic groups.

The focus is on three socio-economic groups (rich: top 20 percent of population ranked by income levels, middle: 40, poor: 40), between which wages serve as the linkages. These income linkages are the core of this in-

[605] In theory, assuming a social welfare function has some major advantages, because it can be used for economic planning on a micro and macro basis and also for comparing alternative settings. In practice, however, such a function is difficult to obtain.

[606] See Ahluwalia and Chenery (1974), p. 209.

tegrated theory of growth and distribution. The model builds on Harrod-Domar assumptions.[607] The growth rate of each group hinges on

- the savings of this group (determining the capital accumulation),
- the productivity of capital,
- the nature of the wage linkages,
- the population growth rate.

Two types of capital used to produce goods and services are distinguished: K^l denotes capital that is linked to other groups. It stands for capital owned by the rich and the middle group, using hired labor and thus generates wage flows to the poor. K^n is capital owned solely by the rich and is not linked to incomes of lower income groups. The output of each capital stock is distributed between wages and non-wages (equaling profits in the case of non-linked capital).

Ahluwalia and Chenery show that the distribution of income among the three groups is determined by the distribution of the capital stocks as well as the wage and productivity parameters. The model allows for different savings rates of the poor, the middle and the rich, which will rise with per capita income, as well as different population growth rates, which are held constant among the groups for simplicity reasons. The different population growth rates have an impact on the per capita growth rate as well as on the distribution of income, because a higher growth rate of population results in a lower growth of per capita income. This again reduces the savings of the respective group.

The model can be scaled to reflect certain typical country conditions, e.g. high population growth rates, extremely low savings rates of the poor or different productivity growth rates (modeled by changing the capital

---

[607] Harrod and Domar showed that investment has a dual character. Not only does demand increase via multiplication effects, but also does supply expand, because investment increases the production capacity. According to Harrod and Domar, economic growth depends on the savings rate, the ratio of capital to output (capital coefficient) and the depreciation rate. The Harrod-Domar equation $\frac{\Delta Y}{Y} = \frac{s}{k}$ explains that the growth rate of a country (left side of the equation) is proportional to its savings rate and inversely proportionate to the capital coefficient (right side of the equation). Thus, growth can only be positively affected by more investment (= higher s due to the ex post identity of savings and investment) or a lower capital-output ratio. Since the latter is assumed to be held constant, it follows: The higher the investment rate (i.e. the accumulation of physical investment via domestic savings), the higher the growth rate of the succeeding period. See Harrod (1939) and Domar (1946).

output ratio). It then can be used to simulate several distributional strategies:

- Consumption redistribution strategy:
- A fraction of total income is transferred from overall income to the income of the poor in the form of additional consumption. This implies a reduction of the income of the rich and, consequently, also of the poor and the middle because of the wage linkages.
- Investment redistribution strategy:
- This strategy aims at directing public resources to help the poor building up a capital stock. It includes, among others, investments in human capital and access to physical infrastructure, features that improve the productivity of the poor. In comparison to the consumption strategy, the resulting increases are initially smaller but self-sustaining over a longer time period.
- Wage restraint:
- Keeping the wages of the rich low and thereby increasing the profit share redistributes income towards the rich and shall also raise the incomes of the poor (trickle-down argument). Alternative policy instruments are lower taxes for the rich or other fiscal measures.

The model calculates the growth impact on the three socio-economic groups. Its specific feature is its repercussions, as policies designed to benefit one target group may have adverse effects on other groups. The results show that

- the consumption transfer strategy is effective and dominates in the short-run, but lacks in the long-run. This is derived under the assumption that the poor will not increase their saving when receiving consumption transfers. However, some poor target groups can only be reached via such consumption transfers (e.g. through nutrition or basic health care programs), eventually leading to much higher productivity gains than assumed in the model.
- the investment transfer strategy can be effective in improving the patterns of asset concentration over time. In contrast to the consumption strategy, the poor benefit from a permanent additional capital stock increase.
- the wage restraint strategy results in a decline in initial per capita consumption, a slower growth in consumption and lower productivity of the poor, which is not compensated by higher savings and consumption of the rich.
- the strategies are not mutually exclusive. In fact, a mix of strategies (e.g., in sequencing or group targeting) can be very effective.

4.3.6 Direct sectoral policies

One major aspect of pro-poor growth concerns the sectoral and/or regional distribution of growth as well as an economy's structural adjustment. Following this line of reasoning, Loayza and Raddatz[608] show in a multi-sector theoretical model that not only the size of economic growth matters for poverty alleviation, but also its composition. Growth raises the income of the poor if it is directed to those economic sectors and regions in which most poor people work, as well as impacts on the factors of production they use excessively. In the case of the poor, the main factor of production is unskilled labor (and land), and the sector to focus on is the rural/agricultural sector. Although the tertiary sector can at least be partly considered as labor-intensive, it must be differentiated according to the level of human capital needed to carry out services. Sectoral policy fields include:

- Policies promoting productivity gains,
- Policies expanding the human capital among the poor (especially among women),
- Policies addressing the structural adjustment of an economy,
- To a certain extent: Policies promoting the migration from rural to urban areas (the neoclassical growth model suggests that this increases the wage for the migrants as well as for the poor staying in the rural areas).

Among these policies, structural adjustment policies (SAPs) have been promoted extensively in the last decades, with often disappointing results, which can be traced back to the SAPs design itself as well as the poor implementation. Easterly even argues that growth elasticity of poverty has been reduced by SAPs. The risk associated with a concentration of policies on specific sectors and regions is that the poor may also suffer disproportionately high from economic downturns.
Ravallion and Datt showed in their study on India's rural areas that rural growth reduced rural poverty[609] and that the sectoral composition is of high importance to the poverty reduction in rural areas. Kappel et al. also find support for Uganda: "[...] good agricultural performance is the key determinant of direct pro-poor growth in the 1990s, while lower agricultural growth is the root cause of the recent increase in poverty."[610]

[608] See Loayza and Raddatz (2005).
[609] See Datt and Ravallion (2002) and Ravallion and Datt (1996).
[610] Kappel et al. (2005), p. 27. For specific literature on the agricultural sector, see Timmer (1988) and Ravallion (1995).

4.3.7 Indirect growth impact on poverty via transfers

Classical development theories place only limited value on the use of targeted resource transfers to poor countries and have for a long time highlighted the macroeconomics of savings generating growth. There are, however, not only costs but also benefits associated with targeted transfers, which vary according to the target group, the socio-political as well as socio-cultural environment. The main benefit, in general, comprises a reduction in poverty levels. More specifically:

- Transfers encourage more risk-taking (via the establishment of safety nets) and can provide insurance against uninsured risks. It has been shown that at least some degree of social security is essential for poverty reduction.
- Transfers increase the asset base of the poor which in turn enables them to take an active part in the growth process.
- Targeted transfers can be effective when market imperfections exist and when redistributions improve efficiency.
- Transfers may help to achieve the non-income oriented goals of development policy.[611] Support is given by Klasen who states that "[r]elying on income growth to solve the non-income poverty problem is unlikely to be the most effective approach to addressing non-income poverty."[612]

The disadvantages of transfer policies identified in the literature include adverse incentive effects (e.g., for labor supply[613] or for the ability to generate domestic savings), high administrative costs, leakage effects (e.g. due to corruption), marginal welfare costs and insufficient resource availability. Transfers can also lead to dependencies and poverty traps once the transfers are reduced or completely removed.

Among the costs, the following can be distinguished:[614]

- Administrative costs: For collecting information and conducting household surveys to reduce errors of inclusion and exclusion.[615] These costs will be the higher the more detailed the targeting and the larger the size

---

611 While the first goal is to halve poverty by 2015, the other goals (MDG II to VI) represent the non-income dimension of poverty.

612 Klasen (2005), p. 19.

613 Rector and Lauder (1995) argue for such a welfare dependency hypothesis claiming that transfers diminish the incentives of poor people to search for jobs.

614 See Coady et al. (2002), p. 5ff.

615 Including the non-poor and excluding the poor from programs.

of the program is.[616] Identifying the poor and the non-poor also raises the question of crossing the poverty line, i.e. the poor just below the poverty line will receive resources and could be better off than the non-poor just above the poverty line, thereby creating incentive costs (see below).

- Private costs: Opportunity costs in the form of foregone income opportunities (e.g., queuing, obtaining certifications, and so on).
- Incentive costs: Households may change their behavior in order to take part in the program, and for example reduce their labor supply, their income and their propensity to generate savings. The higher the prospective transfer volume, the higher the incentive costs. The costs also depend on the transparency of eligibility criteria.
- Social costs: Such costs may arise because recipients could regard their own poverty status as humiliating and could refuse the transfers, lowering the effectiveness of the program.
- Political costs: Depending on the support functions of the recipients and non-recipients, e.g. whether the recipients are (important) voters and determine the budget, they feel socially included or excluded etc.
- Trade-off costs: Policy interventions may (negatively) impact other factors important for growth. "Reducing inequality by adding further distortions to external trade or the domestic economy will have ambiguous effects."[617]

The higher the costs outlined above, the less resources will be available for distribution. Additionally, post-program costs, e.g. for evaluating the success of programs, or costs of leakage must be included that further reduce the available resources. Regarding the types of transfer policies, the following can be distinguished:

- Indicator targeting
  Resources are transferred according to poverty indices and observable indicators. This method is subject to shortcomings in data collecting, measurement and adverse incentives.
- Conditional transfers
  Resource transfers are directed to poor people, provided that they meet certain conditions/requirements, e.g. regular school attendance.
- Community-based transfers

---

[616] Nevertheless, a higher level of detail in the targeting process can go along with a lower total administrative costs as a share of the total costs, if a finer targeting means a reduced number of recipients.

[617] Ravallion (2003b), p. 15.

Communities have an informational advantage over governmental organizations when it comes to the needs of the local population. If they take over the design of the transfer programs and the distribution of resources, the central government only has to provide them. This brings forth an increase of bureaucratic workload and the danger of corruption at the local level.

- Self-targeting/self-selection
  Self-targeting works if the participation in a program entails higher costs for the non-poor than for the poor, so that the poor have incentives to join the program while the non-poor have not. One example is that recipients of transfers are required to work for the public for a low wage (workfare programs).
- Geographical targeting
  Also referred to as poverty mapping, geographical targeting relates to indicator targeting and is widely used to allocate resources to the poor. Depending on the information available, there are several approaches reaching from one-dimensional approaches (allocating according to one variable, e.g. nutritional status) to multidimensional approaches (the index is calculated as the sum of variables such as illiteracy rate, access to electricity and running water and occupants per room).

A general conclusion on the success of these types of transfers cannot be drawn, as most studies evaluating their impact vary according to their geographical, cultural, and socio-dynamical background. In clarifying the outcome of direct transfers, it is important to recognize the different socio-economic groups, i.e. who transfers how much to whom? For instance, inequality is also reduced when the very rich transfer resources to the (only) rich. However, poverty is not affected in this case. Empirical studies indicate that there are examples of success and failures. The important question arises whether such transfers, under certain conditions, dominate other policies (e.g., reducing distortions that are the cause of inequality and poverty). In this case, transfers represent a necessary instrument to accompany growth-promoting policies. At least, there is a growing supportive literature that transfer policies have a positive effect on the poor in the short-run. Thus, they cannot be rejected as a waste of resources but should be implemented in a consistent pro-poor growth strategy. Dagdeviren et al. present a framework in which a comparison shows that redistributional policies can under certain conditions outpace a distribution-neutral increase in economic growth.[618] Direct transfers will be taken up again as a potential instrument to alleviate poverty directly in Chap. 5.

[618] See Dagdeviren et al. (2004), p. 126.

4.3.8 Empirical observations

The number of academic contributions related to growth, poverty reduction and inequality is large. This section presents major findings and identifies the main strings of literature that have been developed. It has to be noted that earlier studies sometimes equalize inequality with poverty.[619]

Growth and poverty

A substantial number of studies find that a sustained positive growth rate, on average, reduces poverty. This is a finding reaching a relative high standard of consensus among researchers in the field of development economics and stems from cross-country studies,[620] time-series studies[621] as well as microeconomic household analyses for various countries.[622] Additionally, a number of studies come to the conclusion that absolute poverty falls with economic growth.[623] With respect to the weakest definition of pro-poor growth (i.e. ignoring distribution), empirical observations support the view that growth is pro-poor, but the extent to which growth reduces poverty is highly uneven (at a given growth rate, poverty reduction is very uneven across countries).

Among the many studies, Dollar and Kraay's recent contribution[624] deserves particular attention. The authors investigate the link between overall income (measured in per capita GDP) and income of the poor (defined as the bottom 20 percent of the income distribution). Their sample covers 80 countries over four decades and reports an almost one-to-one relationship, i.e. growth in the overall economy is reflected fully in the growth in income of the poor.[625] The authors also test for long-term robustness and reflect the issue whether economic crises impact disproportionately on the poor. They find that

- growth is not less pro-poor now than it was in the past,

---

[619] Inequality must be regarded as an older research issue compared to poverty, although they were sometimes seen as synonyms in the past.

[620] Dollar and Kraay (2002), Lopez (2004b) and Besley and Burgess (2003) provide evidence.

[621] See Ravallion and Chen (2003).

[622] To cite just two studies: Bibi (2005) for Tunisia and Contreras (2001) for Chile.

[623] See several World Development Reports (e.g., 1990) as well as Ravallion (1995) and Fields (2001).

[624] Dollar and Kraay (2002).

[625] The results seem to bee robust even after controlling for a variety of econometrical issues.

- there is no evidence that crises disproportionately affect the income of the poor,
- openness to international trade as well as rule of law do raise the income of the poor and the overall economy proportionately,
- stabilizing inflation is "super-pro-poor" as it reduces poverty as well as inequality.[626]

Thus, Dollar and Kraay conclude that policies favoring macroeconomic growth are good for the poor because they raise the mean income of the poor without having negative effects on the distribution of income. They confirm the trickle-down argument and propose to maximize economic growth with fiscal discipline and low inflation. In another paper with a focus on absolute poverty, Kraay (2006) computes that growth in average incomes accounts for most of the variation in changes in poverty.[627] Also, in contrast to many other papers, he finds that the traditional set of explanatory variables usually operated with in econometrical studies shows almost no significance as determinants of growth in per capita GDP. He thus confirms that a policy package intended to reduce poverty should rely on determinants of growth in average incomes (protection of property rights, sound macroeconomic policies, and openness to international trade). Kraay's results do not, however, infer that pure economic growth is enough for poverty reduction. The manifold econometrical shortcomings rather suggest that cross-country evidence seems to have only limited explanatory value for policies engaged in poverty reduction. There is ample space for more micro-level and case studies on this matter.

A selection of case studies on pro-poor growth has been recently published by the World Bank and some national development departments.[628] They confirm that growth has been poverty reducing in selected countries in the 1990s. On average, a one percent increase in GDP per capita has reduced poverty by 1.7 percent per year on average (annual change in the

---

[626] Their definition of „super-pro-poor" is equivalent to pro-poor growth involving positive distributional shifts.

[627] See Kraay (2006), forthcoming. Average incomes are defined as the average annual growth rate over the spell of household average income. Changes in relative incomes are measured using the average annual proportional change in the Gini index as well as the discrete-time distribution component of the change in the headcount measure of poverty. Kraay's results show that growth in average incomes accounts for 70 percent of the variance in the short run, and 97 percent in the long run. Changes in relative incomes account for only 30 percent of the variance of changes in the headcount measure of poverty.

[628] See Agence Francaise de Développement et al. (2005).

poverty headcount). Within the sample, 11 of the 14 countries were able to reduce poverty and witness economic growth.

Growth and inequality

On the growth-to-inequality relationship, some studies confirm the Kuznets hypothesis, which claims that inequality seems to increase during early stages of economic development because of the transformation from rural to urban and from agricultural to industrialized economies. With more and more workforce working in the urban area and in the industrialized sector and less workers in the rural area and agricultural sector, inequality then tends to fall (inverted U-shaped function).[629] In support of this hypothesis, Barro[630] discovered that a rising Gini index is bound to low GDP values[631] and then descends. Other recent observations doubt the existence of such a Kuznets curve. Dollar and Kraay found no tendency for growth to be biased against poor-income households at early stages of development.[632] Some other empirical studies also rejected the Kuznets hypothesis, for instance Deininger and Squire or Bruno et al.[633] Indeed, most recent empirical observations indicate that there is no significant affiliation between economic growth rates and inequality at the country level.[634] On average, inequality is neither positively nor negatively connected with growth but rises as often as it falls.[635] Ravallion notes that although these results seem quite robust, there are several caveats that have to be kept in mind. Among them are measurement errors in the changes in inequality over time as well as the fact that a constant relative inequality can still mean increases in absolute income disparities.[636] Ravallion shows that absolute disparities between the rich and the poor have actually risen with growth in income.

Regarding the reverse relationship, i.e. the impact of inequality on growth, Myrdal has first shown that income inequality can hinder growth due to its negative effects on productivity and investment[637] (inequality-to-growth relationship). Some researchers[638] also hold up this hypothesis that

---

[629] See Kuznets (1955).
[630] See Barro (2000).
[631] Lower than $1,636 in 1985 dollars.
[632] See Dollar and Kraay (2002).
[633] See Deininger and Squire (1998) and Bruno et al. (1998).
[634] See, for example, Dollar and Kraay (2002) or Ravallion (1997).
[635] See Ravallion (2001).
[636] See Ravallion (2004a), p. 8.
[637] See Myrdal (1984), p. 154.
[638] See Alesina and Rodrik (1994) or Perotti (1996).

income inequality has a negative influence on growth, e.g. via the incidence of undernutrition. Higher inequality increases undernutrition[639] and malnourished farm workers are less productive.[640] Moreover, malnourished children will suffer long-term difficulties in education. Further empirical evidence does support the view that decreasing inequality spurs growth through a variety of mechanisms:

- Political economy:
  Individuals prefer to minimize their tax payments, because the result of public expenditures, e.g. public goods like infrastructure, is available to everyone irrespective of the level of taxation. Progressive redistributive policies are then negatively correlated to economic growth because they reduce capital accumulation.[641]
- Socio-political:
  One side effect of inequality is that it creates incentives for poor individuals to resort to illegal actions (e.g., in the shadow economy, crime), thereby reducing growth.[642]
- Credit constraints:
  As has been explained above, the existence of credit constraints prevent the poor from investments, thereby reducing growth.

There are, however, also arguments supporting the opposite view, claiming that higher inequality will lead to higher growth. Under Kaldor's[643] hypothesis, for example, rich households save more of their income than poor. Assuming positive relationships between investment and savings and investment and growth, economies with higher inequality will experience higher growth. Some recent studies also come to the conclusion that inequality positively affects growth.[644]

Growth, initial inequalities and initial poverty

Some contributions testify that countries with high initial income inequality exhibit lower growth rates.[645] "In a country with high initial inequality, the same rate of pro-poor growth will lead to smaller reductions in poverty

---

639 See Dasgupta and Ray (1986) as well as Ravallion (1992).
640 See Strauss (1986).
641 See Alesina and Rodrik (1994).
642 See Alesina and Perotti (1996), Demombynes and Özler (2002).
643 See Kaldor (1956).
644 See Forbes (2000) or Li and Zou (1998).
645 See, for example, Persson and Tabellini (1994) and Birdsall et al. (1995).

as the poor are starting from a lower base […]."[646] The explanation is straightforward: A higher initial inequality means that the poor share fewer gains from growth and also from future growth. Support for this is presented by Ravallion who argues that the higher inequality, the lower the poverty-reducing impact of growth, because the poor are further away from the poverty line and start from a lower level.[647] For economic policy, this may either mean that countries with high inequality need growth that is more centered on the poor or that initial inequality needs to be reduced before focusing on growth.

The level of inequality within the group of the poor also matters. High inequality within the group of the poor allows for a designated rate of pro-poor growth to result in high poverty reduction in the first period because a lot of the (richer) poor live close to the poverty line and will soon climb up. The same rate of growth can subsequently lead to lower poverty reduction in the second period, followed again by a higher poverty reduction in the third period.

Similar to initial inequality, the level of initial poverty also determines the rate of poverty reduction. As many poor live close to the poverty line, they soon can cross it. Lopez presents empirical support for this argument.[648] Lopez and Serven have set up a matrix showing the elasticity values for different poverty lines and inequality levels (measured by the Gini[649] coefficient). The numbers in Table 4.2 show several features:

- They correspond with a finding in the literature that high initial inequality is harmful to poverty reduction (compare, for example, the 0.6 with the 0.3 columns).
- High initial poverty also serves as a barrier for poverty reduction (see, for example, the upper second column).
- They sustain the argument that poverty and thus poverty policies are affected by the impact of growth on the change in inequality.

Empirical evidence for the diverse impact of relative and absolute inequality on poverty is represented by Ravallion (see Table 4.3). Apart from income inequality, other types of initial inequalities have been identified as

646 Klasen (2003).

647 See Ravallion (1997, 2001) and Son and Kakwani (2004).

648 See Lopez (2004b), p. 17.

649 The Gini coefficient is a number between 0 and 1, where 0 corresponds with perfect equality and 1 with perfect inequality. The Gini index is the Gini coefficient multiplied with 100 to express a percentage. If graphed, the Gini coefficient represents the area between the perfect distribution (45 degree) line and the Lorenz curve.

having a significant influence on economic performance in poor countries, among them gender inequality,[650] inequality in the ownership of capital and human assets, inequality of land distribution as well as sectoral and regional disparities (e.g., urban/rural).[651]

To recapitulate, the empirical evidence provides a heterogeneous picture and statements on the development of poverty and inequality stretch from very pessimistic to very optimistic. All measurements are tainted with a multitude of statistical issues and necessary normative assessments. Aggregated indicators additionally face weighing problems for the individual indices. Apart from the various indices of pro-poor growth explained in the opening section, the empirical assessments of growth and poverty reduction show that there is a significant variation of poverty reduction for a fixed growth rate. Cross-country studies, using averages across initial country conditions conceal certain effects and can therefore be misleading for policy recommendations. This may happen when some initial conditions or policies favor the poor, while others benefit the rich.

Table 4.2. Growth and inequality elasticities of poverty

Growth elasticity				
PL\ Gini	*0.3*	*0.4*	*0.5*	*0.6*
0.16	-6.2	-3.3	-2.0	-1.2
0.33	-4.0	-2.2	-1.3	-0.9
0.50	-2.8	-1.6	-1.0	-0.7
0.66	-2.1	-1.2	-0.8	-0.5
0.90	-1.4	-0.9	-0.6	-0.4
Inequality elasticity				
PL\ Gini	*0.3*	*0.4*	*0.5*	*0.6*
0.16	12.9	7.7	5.3	4.0
0.33	5.2	3.3	2.4	2.0
0.50	2.5	1.7	1.4	1.2
0.66	1.2	0.9	0.8	0.8
0.90	0.4	0.4	0.4	0.4

Source: Lopez and Serven (2004).
Poverty lines (PL) are given as a share of *GDP* per capita. How to read: A value of -6.2 means that at a poverty line of 16% of *GDP* and a Gini coefficient of 0.3, the growth elasticity of poverty is -6.2.

[650] See, for example Klasen (2005).

[651] See Fields (1980), Bourguignon and Morrison (1998) and Ravallion and Datt (1999), p. 9.

Table 4.3. Diverse impacts on poverty according to survey data

Impact on poverty

		What is happening to average household income between the surveys?	
		falling	rising
What is happening to *relative* inequality?	rising	16% of spells: Poverty is rising at a median rate of 14.3% per year	30% of spells: Poverty is falling at a median rate of 1.3% per year
	falling	26% of spells: Poverty is rising at a median rate of 1.7% per year	27% of spells: Poverty is falling at a median rate of 9.6% per year

Impact on poverty

		What is happening to average household income between the surveys?	
		falling	rising
What is happening to *absolute* inequality?	rising	4% of spells: Poverty is rising at a median rate of 7.3% per year	52% of spells: Poverty is falling at a median rate of 6.2% per year
	falling	38% of spells: Poverty is rising at a median rate of 6.0% per year	7% of spells: Poverty is falling at a median rate of 5.9% per year

Source: Ravallion (2004b), slide 34–35

Nevertheless, some findings have emerged on which there is a general consensus:

- Economic growth is important for poverty reduction.
- Growth itself does not seem to have, on average, a positive or negative influence on the distribution of income.
- The impact of growth on poverty is lower in countries with high inequality.
- Initial country inequalities seem to have an important effect on the economic performance of countries and the effectiveness of foreign aid.

4.3.9 Summary

Sect. 4.3 has presented an analysis on the complex links between economic growth, debt, foreign aid, inequality and poverty. Two positions have for a long time dominated the debate on poverty reduction. One argues that growth is a sufficient condition for poverty reduction in the long run. Poverty and/or inequality are understood as the product of a malfunctioning growth process and should be treated with improved growth policies. The other position holds that direct social transfers and structural policies are necessary to help the poor not only in the short to medium-run, but also in the long-run, as poverty does not seem to be a temporary problem in many countries. While the proponents of the first approach criticize that such transfers inhibit additional costs (equity-efficiency and insurance-efficiency trade-off) and are mostly ineffective, the proponents of economic transfers call into question the trickle-down growth argument on which the poor must depend upon. The World Bank has recently attempted to match both positions by highlighting pro-poor growth. However, whether growth is defined as pro-poor or not depends on the social welfare function of the "planner" and thus has raised a number of methodological issues in the scientific community.

The explanations so far have revealed that the theoretical links between growth, poverty and inequality are ambiguous and the outcome of complex transformation processes of societies. Empirical evidence indicates that there are success stories where high economic growth goes alongside a reduction of poverty levels, but also very disappointing country cases.[652] A number of factors can cause growth to be pro-poor. One decisive element seems to be the level of (initial) inequalities. Actual solid policy conclusions, however, are difficult to draw from general theoretical and empirical findings, as they depend on a multitude of factors in the respective economy. If, for example, economic growth is promoted by the government in a country with low inequality and this growth comes with an increase in inequality, the poor will not benefit from it. In this case, growth-promoting policies would not be an effective instrument for poverty reduction. Consequently, relatively standardized economic policy advice, as has been shown in Chap. 3 to still dominate international aid agencies, seems inadequate to address poverty reduction in low-income countries, especially when considering their specific circumstances and conditions. Chap. 5 will address the role of initial inequalities as one country-specific condition in more detail.

[652] The case of Uganda shows that periods of success and failure can follow very rapidly on another. See Kappel et al. (2005).

4.4 Macroeconomic consequences of ODA

This section will address possible difficulties resulting from an expansion of ODA flows to LDCs, a problem that many LDCs are likely to face in the years ahead. Most obviously, increases in ODA will amplify aid dependency, a fact that has been confirmed by several country studies.[653] But apart from increasing dependency, a variety of macroeconomic challenges exist for recipient countries, concerning the monetary and fiscal impacts of a large capital inflow as well as the effects on the exchange rate and export competitiveness. The extent to which LDCs are affected by these problems is strongly shaped by the way they are *able to use, use or misuse* additional aid. The next section will provide some thoughts on aid absorptive capacity and diminishing returns, additionality and crowding out effects, fiscal and monetary policies and potential impacts on corruption.

4.4.1 Diminishing returns, absorptive capacity and dependency

Additional transfers do not come at zero cost. In fact, they can be very costly or even be outweighed completely, a situation also known as "leaky bucket".[654] Indeed, studies have confirmed the existence of diminishing returns to aid,[655] which are put down to administrative costs (e.g. tax collection and running agencies) and crowding out effects (see next section) diminishing the gross payout. The so-called aid saturation point, i.e. the point from where the marginal benefits of one additional dollar of foreign aid become negative, is estimated by most studies to lie between 15% and 45% of GDP and varies strongly across countries. In countries with poor policies and institutions, the saturation point is estimated at only 5–10% of GDP. Doubling current aid flows to LDCs with good policies and institutions (i.e. allocating approx. $40–60 billion ODA to these countries) will result in absorptive problems in almost all recipient countries.[656] Other authors[657] have calculated that, in order to be absorbed effectively, two thirds of all additional ODA needs to be directed towards India and China, the countries with the highest absolute numbers of poor people and highest levels of absorptive capacity.

---

[653] See, for example, Aiyar et al. (2005) on a sample of five African countries and Andrews et al. (2005) for Ethiopia.

[654] See Okun (1975).

[655] Elbadawi (1999) finds that beyond a certain threshold, more ODA negatively affects the volume of exports (sample of 62 countries).

[656] See Devarajan et al. (2002).

[657] See Heller and Gupta (2002).

The ODA absorptive capacity issue has grown in importance over time. When the 0.7 percent target was set by the UN in 1970,[658] the per capita income in industrial countries significant lower and did not pose a macroeconomic absorption problem. Moreover, the number of countries belonging to the "poorest country"-category was much larger. Until today, the share of the world's population in LDCs has fallen, mainly because some individual countries (China, India, Indonesia) have grown in population. At the same time, the per capita income of the poorest countries has stagnated at best. Therefore, the financial resources implied by increasing ODA to 0.7 percent of GNP increased relative to the donors' GDP in LDCs.

ODA absorptive capacity determines whether financial assistance from abroad is well utilized in developing countries. Countries eligible to receive ODA are countries facing substantial weaknesses in the management of financial resources. Public financial management systems in LDCs are found to work poorly. Moreover, most LDCs lack institutional capacities and quality of governance. Tasks for which capacities lack are highlighted by a recent study of the World Bank and the IMF and include "formulating budgets, classification systems, commitment controls, cash management, budget reporting, audit, and regulatory capacity."[659] Under such circumstances, large inflows of aid can exceed the capacities of governments. More specifically, aid flows puts pressure on other additional, but scarce resources such as decision-makers' time, administrative staff, buildings, warehouses, port capacity, and so on. Such bottlenecks are most severe "in countries with fragile institutions, poor infrastructure, and weak human capital."[660] There are, however, some LDCs in which good governance and absorptive capacity are in place. According to the Millennium Project report, these countries should qualify for a "fast-track" status, receiving substantial increases in ODA as soon as possible. Moreover, post-conflict countries have been found capable of absorbing large ODA increases.[661] Nevertheless, as a general directive, it is reasonable to assume that the more additional ODA is allocated to least developed countries (instead of lower-middle-income countries), the greater the macroeconomic absorption problem becomes.[662]

---

658 Following the recommendations of the Pearson Commission in 1968/69. A reasonable explanation or evaluation on the appropriateness of this figure has not been conducted since then.

659 World Bank and IMF (2005).

660 Clemens and Radelet (2003), p. 5.

661 See Collier and Hoeffler (2004).

662 See Collier and Dollar (2002) as well as Heller and Gupta (2002).

The size of ODA with respect to other forms of budgetary revenues (e.g., tax revenues) is important to understand the dependence on ODA in developing countries. In some African countries, for example, total aid amount to more than 10 percent of GDP.[663] Aid dependency ratios indicate how dependent recipient countries are on foreign aid. The following ratios can be set up:

1. Aid as a percentage of GNI (or gross domestic income)[664]
2. Aid as a percentage of total government expenditure
3. Aid as a percentage of gross capital formation
4. Aid as a percentage of international trade/imports.

The second indicator is most widely used to express aid dependency, because it reflects the scale of external aid relative to state activity. Out of 52 low-income countries, 22 countries receive ODA worth more than 50% of government expenditure.[665] Out of these, 11 even receive aid worth 75% of government expenditure. Very high dependency ratios are found in Burundi (88%), Democratic Republic of Congo (592%), Guinea-Bissau (170%), Nicaragua (103%), Mozambique (88%) and Sierra Leone (128%), most of which are (post-) conflict countries. The other aid dependency ratios (some numbers are presented in Table 4.4) must be interpreted carefully, because high ratios are not always a sign of large aid flows, but, as in the case of Africa, can be the outcome of falling incomes, imports and investment. The very high dependency ratios for the African continent are nevertheless staggering. In such situations, it is likely that the local government will not follow the interests of local voters, but those of donors.

Assuming an increase of ODA to developing countries as projected in the Monterrey Conference and the Millennium Project Report, a substantial increase of international financial assistance could reach these countries. Under a set of assumptions, Moss and Subramanian have estimated for 52 low-income countries that aid dependency is likely to increase significantly (see Table 4.5). In the average projection, the number of countries with aid to government expenditure ratios of above 50% (above 75%) would increase from 22 to 35 (11 to 17). Apart from a higher volume, the speed of scaling up ODA flows is an important factor influencing the economic impact in recipient countries. It is reasonable to assume that the lar-

663 See Heller (2005), p. 10.

664 This indicator serves as a proxy for defining the "aid saturation point", i.e. the point from where the marginal benefits of one additional dollar of foreign aid become negative. See more in Chap. 3.5.

665 See Moss and Subramanian (2005), pp. 3–4. Data is from 2003 (and 2004 where available).

ger and faster the increases in aid flows, the sooner diminishing returns will materialize.

Table 4.4. Aid dependency ratios for various regions and country groups

	Net ODA		Aid per capita		Aid dependency ratios					
	[$ billion]		[$]		[aid as % of GNI]		[aid as % of gross capital formation]		[aid as % of imports of goods and services]	
	1998	2003	1998	2003	1998	2003	1998	2003	1998	2003
LICs	21.2	32.1	10	14	2.7	3.0	12.9	13.1	11.1	11.4
LMICs	18.7	21.8	7	8	0.6	0.5	2.1	1.8	2.1	1.6
UMICs	3.6	3.8	11	11	0.2	0.2	1.0	1.0	0.6	0.5
LAMICs	56.2	76.2	11	14	1.0	1.1	4.0	4.2	3.3	3.1
East Asia & Pacific	8.4	7.1	5	4	0.6	0.4	1.9	0.9	1.9	0.9
Europe & Central Asia	8.9	10.5	19	22	0.9	0.8	4.1	3.3	2.2	1.7
Latin Am. & Caribbean	5.6	6.2	11	12	0.3	0.4	1.3	1.9	1.2	1.3
Middle East & N. Africa	5.4	7.6	19	24	0.9	1.0	4.0	4.2	3.3	3.5
South Asia	4.9	6.2	4	4	0.9	0.8	4.2	3.6	5.1	4.2
Sub-Saharan Africa	14.5	24.1	23	34	4.7	6.0	23.9	29.5	12.4	15.9

Source: World Bank (2006a).
Regional aggregates include data for economies not specified elsewhere. Income group totals include aid not allocated by country or region.

Table 4.5. Aid intensity under 'Big Push' scenarios

	Number of countries (out of 52) with an ODA/government expenditure of …	
	> 50%	> 75%
Current	22	11
Projection scenarios:		
a. Double aid to all	34	18
b. Triple aid to top performers	30	13
c. 8% GDP in new ODA	32	11
d. $130 billion total new ODA	38	18
e. $70 per capita new ODA	38	20
f. $143 per capita spending	34	19
Projection average	35	17

Source: Moss and Subramanian (2005), p. 4
Note: Calculations are based on IMF data.

4.4.2 Additionality and crowding out effects

As has been noted earlier, granting debt relief does not necessarily translate in additional free funds available for spending. In fact, the donor countries' original idea of providing relief to (highly) indebted countries was to actually increase the backflow of outstanding debt by setting more realistic debt restructuring schedules, thereby decreasing the amount of resources available for recipient countries. More recently, however, aid allocating decisions have been combined with debt relief decisions. This involves two cases: In the "positive" case, countries receive debt relief (e.g., under the HIPC initiative) and, as a result, receive more (not necessarily official, but private) resources (e.g. due to a better credit rating). In the "negative" case, countries receive debt relief and borrow resources again from donor countries. In this case, highly indebted countries would be "rewarded", while good performers would be penalized for their good policies.

With debt relief being a subcategory of ODA, additionality can be defined in different ways:[666] Debt relief is additional if it does not lead to lower levels of other non-debt relief-related aid flows for the debtor. Put differently, if debt relief is not additional, a crowding out effect occurs, reducing the level of other aid flows. In a broader definition, debt relief can be defined as additional if it leads to greater aggregate resources being

[666] See Powell (2003), p. 4.

made available, either to the debtor country itself or to another (third-party) recipient country. Ndikumana has investigated the relationship between debt alleviation programs (relief and forgiveness) and ODA for the period 1980 to 2000.[667] A positive relation implies additionality of debt relief and debt forgiveness, a negative relation implies ODA crowding out by debt relief and debt forgiveness. The computations include the donor side (asking whether donors disburse less ODA following debt relief) as well as the recipient side (asking whether recipients that received more debt relief and debt forgiveness receive less ODA). For the recipient side, the cross-sectional regression results show a positive relationship between the volume of debt relief received and ODA and concessional loans received. Countries under the HIPC initiative also received more ODA.[668] However, for the donor side, the results do not show statistically significant effects. "Therefore, debt relief seems to have affected the allocation of ODA among recipients but not the supply of ODA by donors."[669]

Clemens and Radelet[670] have examined whether or not additional aid leads to crowding out effects in the sense that other donors reduce their assistance. They find no significant evidence for crowding out effects in countries with a recent conflict (or countries formerly part of the Soviet Union). However, for countries not associated with recent conflict there is a slight (but insignificant) tendency for large increases in US aid to crowd out other donors. This result stands in contrast to the study of Round and Odedokun who find peer pressure effects of aid and Schweinberger and Lahiri who confirm crowding out effects among donor countries occur.[671]

Finally, crowding out can also include evasive actions. Additional income taxes may affect people's working behaviour; a currency transaction tax or a carbon may lead to diversion effects. In general, individuals tend to avoid activities that attract the tax. Firms, on the other hand often pass over additional cost to consumers, resulting in higher consumer end prices, which in turn affect market demand and supply.[672] These effects have already been discussed in the chapters on innovative financing mechanisms.

---

[667] See Ndikumana (2004).

[668] For each extra dollar of debt relief, recipients of debt relief received approx. 9.6 cents of ODA and 23.8 cents of concenssional loans. The results for additionality of debt forgiveness are less significant and depend on the estimation method. See Ndikumana (2004), p. 336.

[669] Ndikumana (2004), p. 337.

[670] See Clemens and Radelet (2003), p. 6.

[671] See Round and Odedokun (2004) and Schweinberger and Lahiri (2006).

[672] See Bhaduri and Skarstein (1996) who assess the impact of foreign aid on domestic demand.

4.4.3 Impact on recipient countries' absorption and spending

Foreign aid can have deleterious effects on the national budget if aid substitutes for tax revenues. Although Collier[673] argues that this may have a positive (short-run) impact on the private sector, it may hamper national accountability in the long-run. When receiving more ODA, a recipient government can decide to absorb it and/ or to spend it.[674] Absorption is defined as the widening of the current account deficit due to incremental aid. In other words, absorption leads to a real resource transfer from donor to recipient country and allows the foreign aid to enter the economy. Spending is defined as widening of the fiscal deficit due to incremental aid. Thus four possible strategies appear: Absorption without spending (case 1), absorption and spending (2), no absorption and no spending (3), and spending without absorption (4).

1. Aid is absorbed but not spent. In this case, aid acts as a substitute for domestic financing of the national budget. The government does not widen its expenditures, but the Central Bank sells foreign exchange and removes domestic currency from the economy. This strategy makes sense in the short-run in order to cut the government deficit or to fight inflation.
2. This is the case in which aid is absorbed and spent. Expenditures can be extended up to the amount of foreign aid received.[675] The government disburses local currency, which is taken up by the central bank for foreign exchange. The government can either spend it on domestic goods (widening the fiscal deficit) or on imports (appreciating of the domestic currency). The latter case will be discussed in more detail later. The balance of payments would remain unchanged if ODA were spent entirely on imports. An example of the latter case is ODA financing imports of antiretrovirals for the treatment of AIDS. If expenditures increase less than the amount of aid received, this might be a sign of aid fungibility, describing a situation in which projects formerly financed by national resources are now financed (at least partly) by foreign aid. Feyzioglu et al.[676] have indeed shown that aid is to a large part fungible. Additional ODA paid out in the form of project assistance could spur aid fungibility.

---

[673] See Collier (1999).

[674] See Aiyar et al. (2005).

[675] To be exact, expenditures can also exceed the amount of foreign aid received, if they are financed by an increase of domestic borrowing.

[676] See Feyzioglu et al. (1996).

3. In this case, aid is neither absorbed nor spent. Instead, the foreign aid remains in the Central Bank. This strategy might be effective in the short-run to smooth high aid volatility or to accumulate foreign reserves.[677]
4. Spending but not absorbing foreign aid mirrors the poor macroeconomic management of recipient governments, which increase their expenditures, but do not allow the central bank to buy domestic currency. Instead, the government attempts to increase spending and accumulating foreign reserves at the same time. The consequence must be either an increased borrowing from the private sector or financing the increasing fiscal deficit by inflation.

According to Aiyar, only strategy 2 is convincing: "Absorbing and spending is, in general, the first-best response to aid. Absorption ensures that there is a real transfer of resources to the recipient country, while government spending draws resources away from the traded goods sector."[678] The other strategies serve different policy objectives and may be tolerated in the short-term, but will not lead to increased spending that benefits the poor. The absorbing and spending case is, however, not regularly observed in LDCs. Instead, the spending but not absorbing case is found to happen too often, although it should be clear that spending aid and at the same time building up reserves with it is a hardly feasible solution. This indicates that macroeconomic management, especially the coordination of fiscal, monetary and exchange rate policies must deserve utmost attention in LDCs' governments. Table 4.6 presents the results for a sample of five countries that have received large amounts of aid.[679] Strategy 2 has been pursued only rarely (Mozambique). Instead, the recipient governments tend to follow a "spend all or nothing" approach, while in four out of five cases only a minor share of the additional ODA was absorbed.

4.4.4 Type of aid and government revenue

Does the type of ODA affect recipient governments' revenues? The most important distinction regarding the type of official flows is between grants and loans. Grants are additionally available resources for recipient countries' governments, substituting for or complementing domestic resources.

[677] Ghana followed this strategy and created a buffer fund after high aid inflows in 2001, a drop in 2002 and another surge in 2003.

[678] See Aiyar et al (2005), p. 29.

[679] These countries have been chosen because they inhabit strong institutions, suggesting relatively high quality of governance.

Table 4.6. Absorption and spending of ODA increases in selected LDCs

	Not spent[2]	Partly spent	Mostly spent	Fully spent
Not absorbed[1]	Ghana (0 / 7)			Tanzania (0 / 91)
Partly absorbed	Ethiopia (20 / 0)		Uganda (27 / 74)	
Mostly absorbed				Mozambique (66 / 100)
Fully absorbed				

Source: Aiyar et al. (2005), p. 29.
Notes: "Absorb"-variable = Non-aid current account deterioration as a percent of the incremental aid inflow (truncated at 0 and 100). This variable is the first entry within brackets for each country."Spent"-variable = Non-aid fiscal balance deterioration as a percentage of the incremental aid inflow (truncated at 0 and 100). This variable is the second entry within brackets for each country.

If they serve as substitute for national revenue, not only could aid dependency from donor countries increase. Recipient governments could also be tempted to delay or even prohibit necessary reforms in order to continue to receive aid. Additionally, they also might be less willing to put efforts into fiscal consolidation. Indeed, a study by Gupta et al.[680] confirms that tax revenue performance of developing countries and especially LDCs stagnated or even declined since the early 1990s. Loans, in turn, entail future repayment. They urge decision-makers to uphold revenue collection (e.g. taxation) to be able to cover interests and loan. In practice, however, many developing countries have not been able to repay their outstanding debt and have accumulated debt, often resulting in debt crises. In part, this goes back to the growth effects which are not realized until many years in the future and thus generate only little income to pay back loans. This development has often been taken as an argument to favour grants over loans, especially in cases of emergency assistance and food aid. The Meltzer Commission[681], for example, has recommended that multilateral donors (World Bank and regional development banks) should provide predominantly grants to developing countries. Following the Commission, US President Bush proposed that up to 50 percent of the funds provided by development banks should be provided as grants.

Sanford[682] has examined the impact of a switch from IDA loans to IDA grants and concludes that phasing out loans by gradually increasing the

680 Gupta et al. (2004).
681 See Meltzer (2000).
682 See Sanford (2002).

share of grants is a feasible option. Multilateral aid organizations such as the World Bank, on the contrary, are concerned that they might run out of funds or that they cannot maintain their lending levels. The IDA's Articles of Agreement (Article V, Sect. 3 and Sect. 1b) spell out that financing should take the form of loans; grants should only be delivered under special circumstances. There are also restraints for some national donors to deliver a large share of grants.[683] The praxis of donor countries to provide loans with a high share of concessions (grant element) as well as the fact that loans are frequently (at least partly) forgiven, provide evidence to assume that grants and loans are increasingly perceived interchangeably by recipient countries.[684] Mascarenhas and Sandler test differences among the mix of grants and loans for three classes of donors (multilateral, regional and bilateral donors) which fund public goods in developing countries. They propose that activities exhibiting a relatively large share of international benefit spillovers should be funded by grants, whereas activities with more recipient-specific benefits should be financed by loans. Otherwise, the possibility for free-riding and a suboptimal provision would occur.[685]

The results of an empirical study by Clements and al.[686] suggest that a doubling in loans (measured in percentage of GDP) causes governments revenues to increase. However, a doubling in grants leads to declining domestic revenues and also to higher foreign aid dependency. Each additional aid dollar in the form of grants is offset by 10–28 cent (depending on the statistical method applied) due to lower domestic revenues. On an aggregated scale, an increase in total foreign aid (net loans plus grants) decreases a recipient country's domestic revenues. The corruption control variable (weak institutions) has been found to play an important factor for the results. In very corrupt countries, almost all of ODA grant doubling is equalized by a fall in domestic revenues.

---

[683] The German government, for example, needs approval of the Parliament to significantly raise the grant share of its ODA disbursement.

[684] Some add that IDA loans have a grace period of ten years and, in that respect, are similar to loans. This view however, is short-sighted as multilateral banks receive in fact a stream of IDA loan repayments from the 11th year onwards, which is used to finance new loans and grants.

[685] See Mascarenhas and Sandler (2005), p. 1096.

[686] See Clements et al. (2004), p. 48. The study included more than 100 countries and covers 30 years. Their results prove robust for lagged values, two-way causality and endogeneity between aid and revenues.

4.4.5 Dutch Disease effects of additional aid

It has been shown that countries in which natural capital makes up a large proportion of total wealth grew at a lower pace (1965–1998) than countries with a small proportion of natural resources. The prominent case of the Netherlands reveals that resources can indeed be a curse for economic development, a phenomenon known as Dutch Disease.[687] It goes back to experiences of the Netherlands in the 1960s, when natural gas fields off the coast were discovered.[688] Another historic example is Spain, importing manufactured goods for gold (gained from its colonies) and neglecting its own manufacturing industry. Put simply, a country experiences a structural shift by concentrating too much on exports of natural resources and importing manufacturing goods. Consequently, the own manufacturing sector will contract. In the long run, the costs associated with this contraction will outweigh the short-run benefits of the resource boom.[689]

The Dutch Disease effect may also be relevant if ODA flows enter an economy. Additional foreign aid inflows enhance demand in the tradables and nontradables sector. While the former could be satisfied by more imports, the latter could lead to higher production and higher wages, pushing up the domestic price level.[690] In relation to the prices of tradables, the prices of nontradables would increase, thereby increasing the real exchange rate, which is argued by many to have negative impacts on the economy's international competitiveness. Since a substantial ODA share is provided to governments whose expenditure pattern is directed towards non-tradables such as public services, there is a likelihood of short-run Dutch Disease effects.[691] Such effects would counteract the effect of additional aid, especially if one takes into consideration that high domestic inflation predominantly affects poor and middle income groups. The net impact of potential Dutch Disease effects of ODA will depend on the

---

[687] This term was first used in 1977 by *The Economist* to describe the gas discoveries on the Netherlands in the 1960s. See also Chowdhury (2004), pp. 5–19 for a detailed survey.

[688] Similar effects were observed for minerals in Australia and oil in the UK and Norway. Also the sub-Saharan country Gabon is a case where oil discoveries in the 1970s have led to the Dutch Disease effect of shrinking industrial and agricultural sectors because of the appreciation of the currency and capital movements to the oil sector. See Zafar (2004).

[689] See Corden and Neary (1982) and Snape (1977) for theoretical models of the Dutch Disease effect.

[690] See Nkusu (2004), pp. 9–13 for an analytical framework.

[691] Mavrotas (2003), p. 17.

production and trade structure of the country under scrutiny,[692] the country's vulnerability to "aid shocks" (sudden increases or reductions of aid flows) and whether or not macroeconomic policies are in place to flatten Dutch Disease effects or even to allow them. The latter case refers to an examination by Aiyar et al.[693] who find that some aid recipients resist absorbing aid (by restricting the sale of foreign exchange by the central bank) because they fear Dutch Disease effects to harm their international competitiveness. Analyses for Nigeria, Ghana and Uganda seem to confirm Dutch Disease effects[694]. Andrews et al., on the other hand, find no evidence that increased aid to Ethiopia has negatively affected its export competitiveness.[695] Similar results are presented by Sackey (2001) for Ghana and Nyoni (1998) for Tanzania.[696] Langhammer concludes that countries cases witnessing a Dutch Disease effect are rare because a massive concentration of aid on few countries has not often occurred.[697] Such cases, however, are often "good policies" cases, i.e. countries that received substantial foreign aid due to a (positive) change in policy orientation. This leads to an endogeneity problem: Recipients expecting an ODA increase because of their good policies may face a decline of their quality of policy due to rising government expenditures or Dutch Disease phenomena. The mixed empirical support of Dutch Disease lends support to the hypothesis that country circumstances matter significantly. In some cases, an appreciation/depreciation of the national currency was the outcome of other macroeconomic policies; in others, reduced export volumes were often the result of declining world prices. In sum, a robust causal link between aid inflows and a deteriorating export performance is hard to establish.

The implementation of effective policies to offset potential Dutch Disease effects needs to anticipate higher aid levels, and promote "investments that will tackle potential bottlenecks to expanded productivity in the nontraded goods sector – in effect 'keeping ahead' of the factors that can create pressures for a real appreciation of the currency."[698] One strategy to

[692] Small countries experiencing a large, temporary inflow of foreign exchange, e.g. foreign aid, are found to be more affected by Dutch Disease effects. See Bhaduri and Skarstein (1996), p. 195.

[693] See Aiyar et al. (2005), p. 31.

[694] See, for example, Younger (1992). See also Adam and Bevan (2003) for Uganda who point to the complex relationship between aid flows, real exchange rates, export volumes and welfare.

[695] See Andrews et al. (2005), p. 35.

[696] See Sackey (2001) and Nyoni (1998). The Ghana case refers to the period 1962-1996, the Tanzania case to 1967–1993.

[697] See Langhammer (2002), p. 13.

[698] Heller (2005), p. 11.

limit potential Dutch Disease effects of ODA is to let the central bank accumulate foreign reserves. However, this also includes well-known risks, one of them being an increase of the domestic interest rate level, thereby also increasing debt service costs. Another approach is to channel the additional ODA precisely in the nontradable sector (e.g., infrastructural investments) in order to increase its productivity and production potential ("capacity building"), which could lower the pressures stemming from the price increase in the nontradable sector.

4.4.6 Additional ODA and corruption

Empirical observations regarding the effect of additional ODA on corruption are mixed. Corruption data is not available for a longer time period, making robust time-series regressions difficult. Alesina and Weder conclude from their analysis (covering 1984–1995) that an increase in foreign aid increases corruption in the recipient country, but also point to several econometrical problems so that these results must be interpreted very cautiously.[699] They are, however, in sync with Svensson[700], using a game-theoretic model in which corruption is used as a proxy for rent-seeking. Under the assumption that economic policy is determined by powerful social groups, he confirms that in countries which suffer more from such groups, aid is associated with higher corruption. More recently, Bräutigam and Knack[701] find for a set of African countries that there is a robust statistical relationship between high aid levels and deteriorations in governance. Knack,[702] instead, notes that only certain forms of aid such as technical assistance may deteriorate bureaucratic quality and the rule of law; aggregated aid flows, however, do not stand in a significantly relationship to corruption. Tavares[703] confirms that less corrupt governments also receive less aid due to a variety of reasons not associated with corruption. Taking into account this bias, he finds that an increase in aid in fact reduces corruption.

---

699 See Alesina and Weder (2002), p. 1135.

700 See Svensson (2000).

701 See Bräutigam and Knack (2004), p. 276.

702 See Knack (2001). The corruption variable is used as part of a set of governance indicators including bureaucratic quality and rule of law.

703 See Tavares (2003).

4.4.7 Additional ODA and aid volatility

Fluctuations in ODA flows can occur either because of external changes (e.g., of ODA pledges) or as a response to domestic changes (e.g., poor governance). It has been shown that unstable budget revenues are a major cause of economic inefficiency. Estimates on aid volatility show that ODA flows are indeed very volatile and that aid volatility is higher in countries depending very much on aid.[704] Furthermore, governments' decisions of how much the public services will be increased depend on whether the potential aid flows are perceived as certain or uncertain. Disaggregating by the type of aid flow, emergency aid is (by nature) more volatile than other capital flows. In comparison to other financial flows, ODA is more volatile (standard deviation of 21.4) than private remittances (16.3), but less volatile than FDI (40.0).[705]

Assuming that at least the dominant part of donors' pledges is fulfilled until 2015, ODA flows to LDCs are likely to increase significantly in the near future. Moreover, donor countries increasingly give program aid (budgetary support and sectoral assistance) instead of project aid. On the one hand, this shift might lead to a reduction of transaction costs, because program aid is managed primarily by the government and does not entail additional staff for managing individual aid projects. On the other hand, project aid, although disbursed annually, is usually funded on a more stable multi-year basis, whereas program aid is disbursed annually on more volatile terms, for example reflecting recipients' performance.[706] If the donor community decides to introduce several innovative sources of development finance simultaneously, instead of concentrating on one approach, aid volatility will be affected, too. ODA already stems from a variety of different sources, including multilateral and bilateral donors, vertical funding initiatives and NGOs. Expanding the number of aid transmission channels is thus likely to increase aid volatility. First, each of these mechanisms is afflicted with individualistic uncertainties as has been discussed in the previous section. Second, most of these innovative approaches will be subject to adjustment in the first running years or harmonized, as they have not yet been put into practice.

The World Bank's policy is to provide program aid predominantly to stronger performing countries able to cope with volatile aid inflows. This "avoidance strategy", however, is less appropriate to address the situation

---

704 See Bulir and Hamann (2003). The authors estimate aid volatility to be 30–60% of the mean.

705 See World Bank (2005b), p. 106.

706 See Eifert and Gelb (2005), p. 24.

of LDCs. In countries with weak financial budget management systems in place, budgetary support could act as additional investment to strengthen these systems. Flexible budgetary commitments such as a combination of fixed and variable tranches could increase aid predictability. The disbursement level of variable tranches could depend on a recipient country's success in meeting certain predefined objectives. Thus, committed flows for a multi-year period provide a stable, predictable source of income that can be adjusted according to a country's performance. In order to prevent countries from facing high budget revenue volatility because of unstable ODA inflows, building up reserves (e.g., by setting up a stabilization fund) can help to cover imports for some months. Similar to the World Bank's HIPC Trust Fund, in which the multilateral share of pledged debt relief is accumulated ahead of time and disbursed gradually, setting up "country trust funds" could help to mobilize enough resources and reduce volatility. Among the innovative financing mechanisms, the International Finance Facility is the instrument providing the most substantial form of predictability. Donors will give legally-binding pledges that the additional funds will be guaranteed until 2015.[707] The International Finance Facility could be effectively integrated in a trust fund system.

4.4.8 Impact on ODA distribution

A strong expansion of ODA flows will affect the existing allocation scheme. As has been shown in the chapter on ODA allocation (3.1), aid is not solely distributed to countries with the most relative or absolute number of poor people. Historical, cultural and (geo-) political ties play an important role. If the international donor community agrees on minimizing global absolute poverty (halving until 2015), a case can be made to distribute additional aid funds to countries inhabiting a large number of absolute poor people (China, India), but that do not belong to the poorest countries. More than now, additional aid would then have to be directed towards Asian and Southeast Asian countries with a large number of absolute poor. This could, however, collide with some recent initiatives focusing on the African and especially sub-Saharan region. The absorptive capacity issue is of utmost importance in this respect. On the one hand, additional aid needs to be directed to the relatively poorest countries in order to push up their absorptive capacity frontier via training, education, investment in

[707] There are some concerns that national ODA quotas will drop with the beginning of the repayment phase. This depends on whether and when IFF disbursements are allowed for the ODA quota.

human capital and public service management and to be consistent with recent pledges made to African countries. On the other hand, such measures will (most likely) yield only limited positive effects in the respective countries in the short and medium-run, thus challenging the success of the MDG. In other words: Too little spending in Asian countries may endanger the success of reaching the global goal of halving the number of absolute poor, too little spending in (relative poor) Africa may result in high political cost.

4.4.9 Summary and conclusions

The recent ODA pledges by multilateral and bilateral donors have commenced some concerns on their macroeconomic impact. Although there is mixed evidence of additional ODA resulting in crowding out effects and increased corruption, there are substantial reservations on

- the degree of absorptive capacity in low-income countries, especially in those countries that already receive large amounts of aid relative to their GDP,
- negative effects on recipient countries' absorption and government spending,
- adverse exchange rate effects (Dutch Disease) and
- higher volatility of future aid flows.

Given these risks, the question arises how the present and pledged funds should be allocated. Previous findings (Chap. 3) have pointed out that existing allocation schemes are biased in favour of small countries, political allies and countries with a colonial and cultural proximity to bilateral donors. If there are indeed limits to the efficient use of additional resources, several options evolve. First, donors could follow an evasive strategy by allocating aid to countries that are not affected by the above mentioned risks. This would favour richer countries with relatively strong skills in their public management systems. However, allocating ODA solely on past performance criteria (e.g., GNP) may result in the promotion of countries with many relative poor, but not many absolute poor people and thus negatively affects international goals to reduce extreme poverty (e.g., MDG). Second, donors could allocate additional ODA preferably to low-income countries to increase their capacities. This seems to be the case according to recent data, although the additional financial resources used to strengthen public sector management, build up fiscal institutions and finance qualifications and training remain relatively modest. This strategy seems to be a necessary step to ensure that additional aid inflows are not only spent but also absorbed efficiently. It could assist in lifting countries on a self-sustained development path. On the other hand, such a long-term development strategy could also lead to present aid flows not reaching the present poor.

5 The role of regional conditions for poverty reduction and ODA

> [T]he future task of development economics lies in recombining existing theories and developing new, complementing theories that will systematically delineate the diversity of developing countries.
>
> Jang-Sup Shin (2004)

5.1 Economic development vs. poverty reduction

The previous three chapters have analyzed in detail the entire "ODA value chain" of aid provision, allocation and utilization. Without reviewing all the evidence and problems, it seems that donors' attitude and motives towards giving aid is of particular importance. Even assuming that donors' interest is solely led by the thought of reducing poverty worldwide, there are two sides confronting each other: The "optimists" and the "pessimists", or as William Easterly points out in his book *The White Man's Burden*, the "Planners" and the "Searchers". The dissimilar viewpoints originate from a different understanding of whether and how aid works. Planners

- argue that foreign aid provides additional financing, technical assistance and policy advice to low-income countries, thereby fostering economic development,
- call for a substantial increase of ODA and favor a big plan in order to eliminate poverty,
- mostly follow general, blue-print-like, top-down strategies suggested and imposed by foreign, outside agencies,
- set up global development objectives to be met within a predefined time frame,
- utilize aid to develop countries and to transform bad governments into good ones.

The Searchers' response is that

- a planning mentality fails to supply the poor with what they need the most,
- a planning mentality lacks motivation to carry out and execute ventures and receive rewards,
- planning developments of other countries neglects the complexity of societies,
- all earlier international development goals and plans have failed,
- planners do not take responsibility and are not held accountable,
- poverty reduction strategies must be adjusted to find out and then take into account local conditions of the poor,
- "[t]he right plan is to have no plan."[708]

> "A Planner thinks he already knows the answers in advance; he thinks of poverty as a technical engineering problem that his answers will solve. A Searcher admits he doesn't know the answers in advance; he believes that poverty is a complicated tangle of political, social, historical, institutional, and technological factors."[709]

It has been shown in Chap. 3 that a planning mentality as described above is still common among aid agencies and that aid is more employed to promote economic development than reducing poverty. However, nearly 50 years of experience with foreign aid have provided sufficient evidence that the power of ODA to promote economic development in foreign countries is very limited and that the traditional arguments and solutions put forward (trickle-down, poverty traps, big push) are not supported by empirics. Even more alarming are the manifold macroeconomic impacts associated with large and sudden ODA increases. As a consequence, if foreign aid has been indeed found not to have a positive long-term impact on economic development, it should be either cancelled or reformed. The question whether ODA so far has actually had an impact on poverty reduction remains disputed as current statistics, theoretical and empirical studies provide a heterogeneous picture. Concluding from the analysis so far, the poverty focus of ODA, albeit official rhetoric (pro-poor growth, optimal allocation), has not improved significantly. One of the greatest challenges remaining is to provide ODA that helps the poor directly and does not sustain deprived governmental structures by working through them.

There are a small but rising number of researchers who opt for a radical reorientation of the contemporary ODA system. Easterly (2006) devotes a

[708] Easterly (2006), p. 5.

[709] Ibid., p. 6.

substantial part of his book on the misconception of ODA and criticizes the planning mentality of donors. Shikwati (2006) even suggests stopping ODA flows completely in order to break up power structures which prohibit economic and democratic reforms and the inclusion of the private sector. The present system feeds an entire aid industry, promotes bureaucracy, aid dependency and corruption, manifests the boundaries of colonial times and buries incentives for entrepreneurs to engage. By focusing on the objective to spur economic development, Shakwati claims, the international natural resource industry, banks, accountant firms and local subsidiaries of multinational companies are among the main beneficiaries of ODA.[710] Furthermore, aid substitutes for local savings, causes Dutch disease and corruption. In Shikwati's opinion, the solutions to the African poverty problem can only stem from the African people themselves, not from foreign directives. Both, Easterly and Shikwati, stress that a lack of markets, political and economic freedom is responsible for the African tragedy, not a lack of foreign aid.

Taking a neutral position in this scientific and dogmatic debate, Chap. 5 examines whether ODA can have a better impact on poverty reduction if its "customer-focus" is improved by tailoring ODA to the local conditions of the poor. It may be the case that the strong emphasis on (good) policies for poverty reduction is systematically overstated[711] because other, more basic inequalities between countries and/or regions affect poverty and its alleviation. Although there are many studies on the impact of ODA in low-income countries, there is only a relatively small strand of literature asking why poverty has been reduced very unevenly across regions. Recent noteworthy examinations include

- Sachs, addressing the role of geographic conditions,
- Ravallion emphasizing the role of initial inequalities as influential variables in the poverty reduction process,
- Dayton-Johnson and Hoddinott detecting regional differences in the effectiveness of aid,[712]

[710] Cooksey provides an overview on studies assessing the role of private accounting companies who are large beneficiaries of ODA. Privatization mandates, financed out of British development aid, amount to 193 for PriceWaterhouse-houseCoopers and 153 for KPMG alone. See Cooksey (2004), p. 9 and the literature cited there.

[711] See Gallup et al. (1999), p. 53.

[712] In outside sub-Saharan countries aid does promote growth despite of policies, whereas in sub-Saharan countries it does only when there are good policies in place. See Dayton-Johnson and Hoddinott (2003).

- Dagdeviren et al. noting that poverty alleviating policies require controlling for specific country circumstances[713], and
- Dalgaard et al. highlighting that countries located in the tropics are disadvantaged. In their study, the variable "share of land located in the tropics" explains a significant part in aid effectiveness:

> "While we find the evidence in favour of a strong interaction between policy and aid weak, our empirical work reveal a disturbing and rather robust pattern: Over the last thirty years, aid seems to have been far less effective in tropical areas. It is very hard to believe that aid, inherently, should be less potent in the tropics. Hence the explanation is likely to be found elsewhere. Perhaps tropical areas have particular needs in ways of foreign assistance; needs which may not so far have been met to a sufficient extent? Accounting for the nature of the interaction between climate and aid seems to be a worthwhile topic for future research. Such investigations would surely have to move beyond the reduced-form aid regressions, which so far has dominated the scene. Disentangling the channels through which aid matters for productivity seems to be a crucial research topic at this stage."[714]

Building on these works, it is the objective of this chapter to assess the role of regional conditions for development processes in low-income countries, the effectiveness of aid and poverty reduction strategies. The proposition is that there are regional differences in the local conditions (initial inequalities) that matter for poverty reduction strategies and the utilization of ODA. This is even more an interesting field of research as the previous chapters have indicated that present poverty reduction strategies and the utilization of ODA take place in a relatively standardized and inefficient way, providing disappointing results in many low-income countries. The general response of international donors was not to reform their strategies but to select those countries in which their incumbent strategies work best (selectivity).

The present chapter proceeds as follows: Sect. 5.2 first clarifies how regional differences have developed historically and which region-specific conditions are addressed here. Sect. 5.3 will tackle the question whether there is leeway for ODA to directly alleviate poverty in a context of region-specific conditions. Sect. 5.4 derives some reform proposals for the present system of international aid flows.

---

[713] See Dagdeviren et al. (2004).

[714] Dalgaard et al. (2004), p. 212.

5.2 Region-specific conditions in economic development

5.2.1 The historical origins of diverse regional conditions[715]

The conquest of Incas and Aztecs by the Spanish in 1532 is often cited as the first example of the "superiority" of Western civilization. Explanatory factors put forward for Europeans subduing native Americans are the advanced military techniques (cannons and other weaponry), earlier horse domestication in Europe, the spread of epidemics and plagues (smallpox, measles, typhus, influenza, bubonic plague), advanced shipbuilding, a politically centralized order (allowing the finance of expeditions) and last but not least writing (allowing faster and more precise delivery of information).

Asking why Eurasia seems to have had a head start over other regions has led to several early stereotype answers such as innate biological advantages of some human beings and the idea that civilizations of the cold North are more innovative than those of the South. Over time, these labels have been rejected by scientists.[716] There is much more evidence that differences in regional conditions can be traced back as early as the Neolithic Revolution, i.e. the gradual transition from a hunting and gathering mode of subsistence to food production, crop cultivation and agriculture. Deeper causes of advantages of some regions over others originate from findings of molecular biology, (bio-)geography, geology, epidemiology, linguistics and the history of technological innovations. A number of factors led to social, political and technological advantages of various regions:

- The roots of regional inequalities stem from the development of agriculture. Some civilizations experienced agriculture earlier than others; some, like the Aborigines, never. Some copied agricultural techniques, whereas others developed it on their own. Better nutrition allowed human beings to become more populous and stronger; systematic crop planting, domesticated mammals and plants favored higher productivity, higher output, higher population densities (due to settledness and stocks) and specializations (professions). Disease-causing agents of domestica-

[715] This section draws on the findings of Jared Diamond (1997) and the writings cited therein. Another recent contribution with historical perspectives on the development of regional differences is Hibbs and Olsson (2003) with special reference to biogeography and geography shaping the prosperity of nations today.

[716] The majority of research indicates that there are no differences in the intelligence or capabilities of some people over other. Instead, intellectual abilities are shaped by the social environment and learned knowledge. Diamond (1997) also proves that northern civilizations were not more innovative than other peoples.

ted mammals first led to similar pathogens and then to resistances among human beings. The combination of all these factors created the prerequisites for politically centralized, socially and economically differentiated and technologically innovative civilizations.

- Eurasia had the largest variety of domesticable wild plants and animals: Most of the founding wild plants were located in the Near East. The Mediterranean climate (mild, humid winter and long, dry summer periods, periodical cycles) yielded one-year plants with large grains/fruits.[717] Topographic diversity brought about a variety of different plants with staggered harvesting periods.
  The successful domestications of animals almost entirely occurred in Eurasia.[718] The reasons were the fact that Eurasia is the continent with the largest joint landmass and distinct biological features of the animals to be domesticated including feeding, growth rate of maturity, reproduction, disposition and social order.
- The east-west axis favored the diffusion of technological inventions and spreading of plants, animals, which was especially important due to the rare number of agricultural origins. Add to that the relatively low geographical and topographical barriers compared to other continents. Places on the same latitude have similar day length, seasonal cycles, temperatures, rainfall and pathogens, allowing for similar biological signals (e.g., for sprouting). In contrast, Africa and America had a north-south axis where the speed of diffusion was significantly lower.[719] Moreover, the one-sidedness of transmission channels from Europe to America due to the scarcity of domesticable animals in the latter was crucial for the impact of plagues and diseases, predominantly in America.
- Evolution and diffusion of technologies:
  The readiness of societies and the environment to foster innovation has been (and still is) characterized by regional differences. Many factors impact on the innovativeness: Life expectancy, evolution of patent laws, training facilities, economic order, the degree of individualism and risk-taking, scientific thinking, attitude towards different opinions, religion

---

[717] There are a number of incidents making Eurasian plants more useful than Americas. Corn, for example, was only half as productive and fertile as European wheat, had stronger husks/shells and lower protein content.

[718] 13 out of 14 domestications originated in Eurasia, just one in South America, none in Australia and Sub-Saharan Africa. In contrast, many African mammals were not domesticated, but tamed (elephants, cheetahs, eagles, giraffes, wildcats, brown bears).

[719] The average speed of east-west diffusion was 1,000 to 5,000 meters per year, north-south only 300 to 1,000 meters.

and technology, form of government, climate, availability of natural resources. Even though some societies are more innovative than others (e.g., Africa's innovativeness was for a long time restricted due to slavery), there are innovative societies on every continent, as technology diffuses via (peaceful) trade, espionage, emigration or war. The receptivity and acceptance of technology depends, among other factors, on the geographic location (core/periphery),[720] the stage of development, the economic advantages, social prestige, the compatibility with the interests of local elites and the degree of visibility of the advantages.[721]
- The evolution of territorial power from bands and tribes over chiefdoms to (national) states proceeded with different speed and intensity.[722]

Jared Diamond shows that Eurasia had many advantages over other continents concerning the above-mentioned factors. The often-cited diversity of the African continent included not so many advantages, but actually provided more obstacles: In its long history, large population movements have resulted in many multi-ethical and different populations and languages.[723] Its much smaller size compared to Eurasia, its topographical and geographical difficult conditions, the limits of north-south diffusion and the lack of domesticable plants (which did not flourish in other regions, e.g. due to winter rain instead of summer rain) and animals (only the guinea fowl) gave Africa a temporal disadvantage, which manifested during colonialization (path-dependent development trajectories).

---

[720] For instance, the Islamic region was located in the center, sub-Saharan Africa at the periphery.

[721] Complex technologies spread to regions with sufficient skills such as writing and computing.

[722] Bands are defined as small nomads (hunters and gatherers), usually within a family kinship. Present (though rare) examples include pygmies, aborigines and Inuit. Tribes have settlements and a leader (non-heritable). Chiefdoms are characterized by social classes, a heritable leader, some bureaucratic layers and specializations (professions). States developed from chiefdoms and have many bureaucratic layers and conflict prevention instruments (e.g., laws). The advancement to states provided some advantages over smaller social groups: Increased population growth and density led to many potential conflict relations, which are better settled in a state. Furthermore, the possibility of finding decisions and the contribution of surpluses/goods to a central entity served as compelling reasons in favor of states.

[723] Without the Aborigines, all major groups of the species human being is present in Africa: Black, White, Pygmies, Khoisan.

5.2.2 The impact of region-specific conditions on economic development

Plain economic theory assumes "point economies", i.e. space, in which transactions actually take place, is not further specified. However, economies are also countries with individual borders, rivers and mountains, located in special regions with differing climate, different types of natural resources and a distinct (historically grown) development path. Various subfields within the literature on development economics have started to analyze such region-specific conditions influencing economic development. Nevertheless, these subfields still remain "academic islands" and have not yet been included into the economic mainstream leave alone transformed into improved policy advice.[724] Economists such as Jeffrey D. Sachs, Andrew D. Mellinger and Wing T. Woo point to spatial inequalities as one cause of economic underdevelopment and insist that geographical and ecological variables directly impact economic activity.[725] They argue that economic development strategies must direct all efforts to overcome these initial spatial disadvantages. To finance the necessary investments, they favor large economic transfers from abroad. However, the recent years have also seen a dominance of research on the role of institutions, led by William Easterly, Ross Levine and Daron Acemoglu. They reject the idea that geography and even policies represent significant variables influencing the income level. "[…] endowments and policies have no independent effect once we control for institutions, contrary to a number of stories, and […] institutional quality seems to be a sufficient statistic for accounting for economic development."[726] According to these authors, geography plays only an indirect role, *caused* by the choice of certain institutions over others. Despite this struggle about the role of institutions and geography, cultural diversity and regional socio-economic factors seem to have a pivotal impact. The next subsections will review the major arguments regarding the role of natural capital, geography, institutional heritage and socio-economic environment.

---

[724] Theories developed in other professions (geography, anthropology, sociology) often do not "match" modern economic modeling and "[t]he different social and human sciences […] have sadly become increasingly separated through narrow specialization – and none more so than economics." Lal (1998), p. x.

[725] See, for example, Sachs (2003a).

[726] Easterly and Levine (2002), p. 33.

Table 5.1. Wealth per capita and components, by region, 1994

	Total wealth	Human resources	Produced assets	Natural capital	Agricul-tural land	Forests and protected areas	Minerals and fossil fuels	Natural capital	Human resources
	[in thousand dollars per capita]				[percentage of natural capital]			[percentage of total wealth]	
North America	325	248	62	15	53	25	22	4.74	76.21
Pacific OECD	302	205	90	7	63	22	15	2.46	67.85
Western Europe	236	176	55	6	68	23	9	2.37	74.34
Middle East	146	56	27	63	11	1	88	43.11	38.22
South America	94	70	16	9	52	23	25	9.21	73.92
Eastern Europe and Central Asia	63	31	22	10	50	12	38	15.54	48.85
North Africa	54	37	14	3	37	2	61	5.17	68.35
Central America	52	41	8	3	77	22	1	6.17	78.72
Caribbean	47	32	10	5	83	5	12	10.66	68.51
East Asia	46	35	7	4	78	9	13	7.92	76.41
East and Southern Africa	30	20	7	3	65	22	13	10.02	65.39
West Africa	22	13	4	5	75	10	15	21.37	60.04
South Asia	22	14	4	4	90	4	6	16.69	64.32

Source: Dixon and Hamilton (1996), rounded by author and own calculations
Note: Members of OECD Pacific comprise Australia, Japan and New Zealand.

Natural capital

The World Bank distinguishes a country's wealth into human resources, produced assets and natural resources. The latter is subdivided into i) agricultural land, ii) forests and protected areas and iii) minerals and fossil fuels. The most valuable natural resource before industrialization was farmland, which gave an incentive to conquer other countries and continents, resulting in large migration flows. Land was a central production factor and land-abundant countries like Argentina or Canada belonged to the richest countries in earlier centuries. Alongside land, energy commodities (e.g. coal, oil, minerals, natural gases) and precious metals (e.g., gold, silver, platinum, copper) count as valuable natural resources. Concrete data on the wealth of countries' natural resources is scarce. According to calculations made for the World Bank, agricultural land is still the most important natural resource, accounting for more than 50% of wealth for all countries except in the Middle East and North Africa, where minerals and fossil fuels make up the largest part (see Table 5.1). For developing countries, the share of agricultural land is even higher (between 65 and 90 percent). The problem with these data is that the calculation is based on the use of the resources (use value)[727] so that implications must be drawn very carefully. As a percentage towards total wealth, natural capital plays a more important role in poorer regions (more than 10% of total wealth in the Caribbean, East and Southern Africa, West Africa, South Asia, Eastern Europe) than in developed countries (e.g., Western Europe: 2.4%).

By failing to account for reductions in the stock of natural resources, GDP figures can be misinterpreted.[728] In cases of resource abundance, countries' GDP growth could stem from natural resource depletion instead of increased production. Calculating GDP deductions for deforestation, soil degradation, pollution effects and depletion of mineral resources, i.e. a complete account of natural wealth, is extremely difficult.[729] One approach is to treat natural capital similar to other forms of capital, that is: to deduct the loss in natural resource value between two periods from GDP. Alternatively, the (given) natural capital stock can be regarded as an endless stream of cash flows (annuity). Given a discount factor, the net present value of the stock of natural resources can be computed. The assumptions made (e.g. what discount rate to use) critically affect the outcome. Moreover, as data for oil-abundant countries show, natural resource endowment

[727] See Dixon and Hamilton (1996), p. 16 for a description of calculation methods and assumptions.

[728] See Winter-Nelson (2005), p. 1507.

[729] There are also complex interdependencies. Forest depletion, for example, may represent additional farmland or uncover ways to exploit additional minerals.

is difficult to identify, because new resource fields such as gas or oil fields are frequently found and change the level of proven reserves.

The supposition that countries endowed with large amounts of natural resources have a natural advantage over resource-poor countries cannot be confirmed in general. Some Arab countries indeed grew rich due to their abundance of oil and gas. Botswana has been one of the fastest-growing countries of the world because of its endowment with diamonds in combination with sound resource management policies. Others, such as Russia, Nigeria or Mexico were not so successful. In fact, mineral-driven resource-abundant countries belong to the weakest growth performers.[730] An analysis of Sachs and Warner (1995) confirms that economies with a high ratio of natural resource exports to GDP tend to have low growth rates, after controlling for the level of initial per capita income, trade policy, government efficiency and investment rates. Official World Bank data seems to confirm these findings (Fig. 5.1).

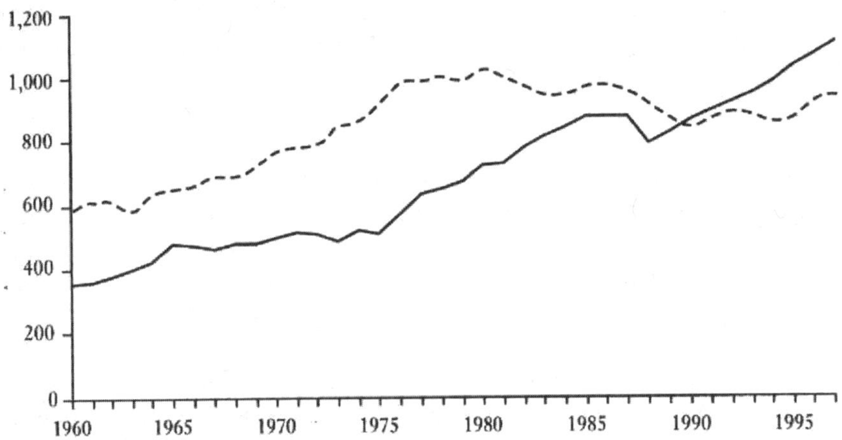

Fig. 5.1. Median GDP per capita of resource-rich and resource-poor countries [in constant 1995 US$]

Source: World Bank (1999)
Regular line: resource-poor countries, dashed line: resource-rich countries

[730] See Auty (1997).

There are several explanations for this result:

- Dutch disease:[731]
  As already explained in Sect. 4.4.5, countries may experience a structural shift by concentrating on exports of natural resources and importing manufacturing goods with the result that the own manufacturing sector will contract. Although a shift away from own production in the domestic manufacturing sector towards cheaper imports is not necessarily negative, the manufacturing sector provides important linkages to other industries (positive externalities). Forward linkages take place if the resources themselves are used up in other industries as inputs. Alternately, backward linkages occur if goods from other sectors are used as inputs by the resource extraction industry. Such linkages (banking industry to finance operations, machinery for exploitation, infrastructure investments for transport) can contribute to the industrialization of the entire country. If linkages do not exist or develop, a resource boom will not add economic growth to a developing country.
  Furthermore, countries that have explored new natural resources may raise their consumption to unsustainable levels. If other countries find substitutes and world market prices for these resources drop, the country consumes too much and saves too little (in order to sustain the former consumption level). Countries may also assume the revenues from the resource boom to rise further in the future. Such overly optimistic anticipations for future earnings might distort public investment (e.g., by funding projects with low or even negative internal rate of return).
  However, a recent model by Eliasson and Turnovsky shows that the intensity of the Dutch Disease effect varies according to the type of natural resource examined. A resource sector with renewable resources can, under certain assumptions, coexist in an economy that experiences ongoing growth in other sectors. The growth rate would be even higher if the renewable resource were absent. As far as intertemporal dynamics are concerned, the authors assume that "[t]he accumulation of a larger equilibrium resource stock (in response to greater resource abundance) requires less harvesting in the short run, more employment in the final output sector and therefore a positive short-run relationship between resource abundance and growth."[732] Depending on the resource sector, some such as high-tech oil drilling industry pay above average wages. This might lead to workers of other industries also claiming higher

[731] This phrase was coined in 1977 by *The Economist*. See also Chowdhury (2004), pp. 519 for a detailed survey on the literature about Dutch Disease.
[732] Eliasson and Turnovsky (2004), p. 26.

wages. Instead, the agricultural sector is a rather low-skilled sector, where workers could become locked in low-skill intensive industries. Point resources (e.g. mining) tend to be more capital-intensive to exploit than crop plantations and there is good reason to assume that ownership is more concentrated in the former, eventually raising inequality.

- Transportation costs and technological progress
  With a fall in transport costs throughout the last century, owning natural resources is not as important any more. Countries without large natural resource endowments (e.g., Japan) were also able to industrialize by importing the resources needed. Resource-deficient countries earlier abandon protectionist policies and more consequently shift their comparative advantages to capital-intensive high-tech sectors.
- Government control
  Governments take an active management part in most countries with a high percentage of natural resources. Instead of undertaking supportive policies (such as establishing linkages, taxation of resource exports to finance infrastructure and education, and generate savings from export earnings to be used in economic downturns), there is evidence that governments fail to come up with effective policies and even produce negative outcomes. One reason is that the state activity itself is pumped up and that market reforms in resource-abundant countries are more difficult to execute. More specifically, it is the resource-abundance itself that may augment the problems of reforms. Reasons include a higher level of corruption, but also a lower endowment with social capital (social cohesion). Moreover, abundance of land resources promotes the competition for land and often results in unequal land distribution. In turn, resource-lacking countries are less prone to policy failure (and consequently, to growth failure) than resource-abundant countries. The political control over natural resources has been an important issue in the transformation of former socialist countries, where resource rents have been wasted or appropriated by ruling elites.[733] The abundance of natural resources limits the incentives to reform, because they reduce the opportunities for direct rent appropriation.

To benefit from natural wealth, transparent and accountable resource management is essential, which is underscored by recent international initiatives such as the IMF's *Guide on Resource Revenue Transparency*. Good

---

[733] See Esanov et al. (2001), p. 1. A model by Dalmazzo and De Blasio (2003), in which an autocratic government maximizing its revenue by extracting resource wealth is assumed, confirms that political reforms lead to reduction of rents by the elites. If this assumption is weakened, e.g. by introducing a social welfare function, the probability of reforms rises.

management practices also induce capital flows to other industries.[734] Long-term strategies, e.g. by setting up a national development plan to encounter possible external shocks, can be coupled with the establishment of special funds for investments in human and social capital.

Geography

Geography was early discovered as playing an important role in economic development and goes back to Adam Smith's notion in *The Wealth of Nations* that industrialization begins at locations with navigable waterways and favorable conditions. Lee was one of the first economists to point out that climate is a major factor for economic development.[735] He outlined geography's impact on crop and animal production and human health. McNeill and Braudel emphasized geographical advantages as pivotal for Europe's development.[736] However, the integration of many economies into the global economy has led some researchers to assume that distance and geographical/spatial factors do not matter any longer. Low transport costs and innovations in information and communication technologies spurred viewpoints such as the "end of geography" or the "death of distance".

More recently, space has again become an interesting topic of research, mainly in international trade theory.[737] The New Economic Geography (NEG) builds on research of Paul Krugman[738] and highlights the importance of space in economics. The NEG provides analytical approaches to include increasing returns to scale, transportation costs, agglomerations, product differentiation and the economics of cities and hubs into economic trade theory; it thus follows the new trade theory. But the NEG does not found its theoretical analysis on *physical* differences of countries, which also have a very significant impact on economic development. "These models illustrate the possibility of *'self-organizing'* [emphasis added] spatial patterns of production based on agglomeration effects, rather than differences in climate, transportation costs, ecology, etc".[739] These self-organized new patterns can develop even with identical physical geogra-

[734] A good case is Botswana, where the good management of diamond production has led to investor's confidence and additional investment.

[735] See Lee (1957). See also Kamarck (1976) for an early study on the tropics and economic development

[736] See McNeill (1963) and Braudel (1972).

[737] The classical economic geography was introduced by von Thünen (1826), Weber (1909), Christaller (1933) and Lösch (1940).

[738] See Krugman (1991).

[739] Gallup et al. (1999), p. 12.

phy by focusing on the propensity of how workers and firms agglomerate in space.[740] The NEG explains the existence and change of clusters and derives patterns in international trade flows.

Regarding geography in economic development, four factors are important here:

- Topography
  Coastal and landlocked economies have different abilities to take part in the international division of labor. Transporting goods over long distances is cheapest on water routes (ocean-navigable waterways). Consequently, transportation costs in landlocked countries tend to be higher than for coastal ones. Estimates based on shipping data from Limao and Venables indicate that a median landlocked country's shipping costs are more than 50% higher than those of median coastal countries.[741] Improvements in infrastructure and transit (so that the median landlocked country becomes a country among the best 25th percentile of all landlocked countries) reduce this penalty to 39%. Estimates with cif/fob data generate lower, but still high numbers (42% and 26% respectively). Redding and Venables[742] determine that internal geography is an important factor creating substantial cross-country variation, e.g. in the access to foreign markets.
  Consequently, landlocked countries must invest a higher share of their investment in infrastructure to achieve the same output. In order to reduce their cost disadvantage, landlocked countries could instead concentrate on export goods with a high value per weight to overcome transport costs. There is empirical evidence that some landlocked countries have been indeed successful by exporting heavy and valuable commodities such as gold, silver and tin.[743]
  If transport passes through one or more neighbor countries to reach a port, sufficient and compatible infrastructure among all affected countries must be assured. This is even more the case in low-income coun-

---

[740] See Ottaviano and Puga (1997), p. 1.

[741] See Limao and Venables (2001), p. 16. The applied definitions include freight and insurance. The real transport costs might entail additional costs such as idle costs.

[742] See Redding and Venables (2003).

[743] Gallup et al. (1999) have included transportation costs into an AK growth model. They show that the economic growth rate of an economy is inversely correlated to the transportation costs because they raise the costs of imported goods. In a model with intermediate products, the authors show that relatively small transaction costs can have large effects on output and growth when the share of intermediate inputs in final demand is large.

tries, where alternatives such as air transport might not be available or too expensive. Large landlocked cities in developed countries are sometimes cited as an example that geography is irrelevant and as an argument that disadvantaged locations can even serve as major tourist attractions (Las Vegas) or service hubs (Denver). But these cities are close to a huge domestic market, and the high level of human capital allows even regions in disadvantaged climate or location to produce economic surpluses. Physical capital is drawn to these cities by the existing human capital, in contrast to cities in poor regions.

- Climate
  Three types of tropical climate can be differentiated: Wet equatorial (characterized by constant heat, rainfall and humidity), dry equatorial (hot arid climates and desert areas with rainfed agriculture being practically impossible), and alternately wet and dry equatorial (regions between the wet and the dry equatorial climate, monsoon regions).[744] The determining factor in these climates is the amount of rainfall, not the temperature alone. More specifically, it is not the average amount of rainfall, but the extreme variation (sometimes no rain over a complete season) that is important and that critically affects entire crops. In tropical climates, frost and winter are absent, giving rise to the rapid growth of viruses, pests, and parasites. The biological endowment has also determined the domestication of working animals, most of which are native to Europe and North America, not Africa.
  Soil and farming conditions vary substantially across climates and require distinct knowledge and farming methods. "Agriculture is the dominant economic sector in developing countries, yet these countries cannot follow the path trod by today's rich nations when they in turn were poor because the basic agricultural conditions in the less developed countries are different."[745] The soil in the tropics must be protected against the sun, but also against the (rare) hard rain. The extreme variation in climate throughout the year worsens the disintegration of the soil. In most tropical regions, the soil also lacks fertility. Rare exemptions comprise some sorts of alluvial and volcanic soils that proved to be quite fertile (e.g. alluvial soil areas south of Lake Albert in Uganda and

[744] Except for South Africa, Lesotho, Swaziland and some very Northern regions, a large part of the African continent is characterized by tropical climate (more than 75%). In South America, tropical climate occurs everywhere except Argentine, Chile and Uruguay. Brazil's tropical climate is, however, more favorable due to the moderate conditions in the highlands. Most of South and Southeast Asia is also affected by tropical climate.

[745] Kamarck (1976), p. 22.

volcanic soil areas in Rwanda and Burundi). The economic implications of a severe climate are manifold:

- Hot humid climate reduces the efficiency of workers, cattle and land. This is first via the sun's plain physiological impact. While technologies for warming are known for thousands of years, cooling technologies such as air-conditioning are still very expensive and complicated, which made them affordable only in developed countries in order to have them contribute to some economic growth, e.g. in Southern cities of the United States. Second, hot humid climate lowers the productivity of cattle (tsetse flies kill horses used for transport) and land (limiting agricultural production). Agricultural GDP per agricultural worker and latitude are positively correlated, controlling for productivity, farm machinery, fertilizer inputs and other variables.[746] Gallup[747] estimates the productivity loss due to tropical geography to lie between 30 and 50%. In turn, the limited agricultural output in the rural areas also constrains the size of cities and therefore the rate of technological progress.
- Tropical conditions make the exploration of minerals more difficult and costly. For example, most of the geophysical and geochemical exploitation techniques used to obtain knowledge on the geology of areas were developed for and tested in countries with moderate climate, not for extreme climates. Due to these restrictions, resource endowments at the land surface can be found, while hidden resources are more difficult to detect. Moreover, the productive period of agriculturally exploitable regions in the tropics is shorter than in regions with moderate climate, because of periods of drought followed by large rains (even floods) shortening the productive period.
- Infectious diseases such as Malaria pose a major burden to the economic development in affected regions. 90% of all Malaria cases (more than 1 million deaths a year) happen in Sub-Saharan Africa. Malaria is transmitted year-round via mosquitoes most common in the tropics. The malaria ecology index measures the susceptibility of a country's climate to mosquito breeding and is closely related to the actual incidence of malaria. Biologists have identified that malaria in Africa is more dangerous than in other parts of the world (e.g., India), because the spread of the disease is easier. This is due to the fact that the African type of mosquito bites humans more often than cattle.

---

[746] See Weil (2005), p. 445.
[747] See Gallup (1998).

- There are risks to the crop stemming from rapidly evolving and mutating "enemies" (parasites, insects, locusts, viruses, pests). Coffee rust eliminated the Arabica coffee industry in Sri Lanka, other examples include cloves in Zanzibar or cocoa in West Africa. The Philippines suffered from severe problems with diseases among new rice varieties. Environmental and agricultural projects in the tropics were often less successful than in more moderate climatic zones.[748]
- Infrastructure in climatically disadvantaged regions is more complicated, expensive and more difficult to sustain. Industrialized countries' goods must be adjusted to cope with local conditions. Examples of infrastructure needs include irrigation to overcome water scarcity, farming special soils, eradication of diseases and improved weather forecasting. However, infrastructural projects may have negative externalities on farmers and traders in other regions.[749]

- Impact on policy
  Negative geographic circumstances can lead to lower economic growth through policy shortcomings themselves. The idea is that geographic constraints can also result in countries being unresponsive for policy changes. One example is the difficulty in collecting taxes in rural areas. If both lower economic growth and unresponsive policies go hand in hand, a revenue-maximizing planner will set higher taxes and/or a higher level of protectionism, which generally reduces the growth rate even further. Thus, initial spatial disadvantages can lead to a permanent development path that is characterized by suboptimal policies. Moreover, studies on the impact of policy on growth must be carefully read according to the direction of causation, especially when techniques of cross-country regression analysis are involved. The simplified notion of Burnside and Dollar that good policies matter for economic growth might merely reflect the fact that these good policies are based on favorable initial geographic conditions, or put the other way around: Unfavorable geographic conditions do not allow for good policies. In this case, efforts to install "good policies" are short-lived and do not address the underlying causes.
- Impact on the size of governments
  On the European continent, a historical analysis reflects that the current European states have developed from a multitude of small political entities, in contrast to Asia. One could assume that a larger number of states in Europe also increased the potential for wars, which in fact did take

[748] See Kamarck (1976), p. 18 for more examples.
[749] See Rujis et al. (2004) on this thought.

place. But there was also a fierce competition among neighbors for innovation.[750] People in Europe could, at least to a certain degree, vote by their feet, if taxes or other burdens proved to be too high. Thus, there was something like a pressure for efficiency. Moreover, Europe had many "fertile islands" between unfertile regions, where settlers moved first. This led to nations (becoming the modern states) developing around these centers. The geographic diversity (mountains, channels, rivers) on close space proved to be an advantage for Europe and also influenced the political landscape.

Table 5.2. Geographical indices for selected regions

	Sub-Saharan Africa	Western Europe	East Asia	South Asia	Transition Economies	Latin America
Continent GDP per capita [$]	1,865	19,230	10,655	1,471	3,902	5,163
Total Population	580	383	1,819	1,219	400	472
Total Land Area [million km^2]	24	3	14	4	24	20
Land in tropics [%]	91	0	30	40	0	73
Population within 100 km of coast [%]	19	53	43	23	9	52
Population within 100 km of coast or river [%]	21	89	60	41	55	45
Land-locked population [%]	28	4	0	2	21	3
Distant to core market [km]	6,237	922	3,396	5,744	2,439	4,651
Coastal Density [pers./km^2]	40	109	381	387	32	52
Interior density [pers./km^2]	22	125	91	287	16	18

Source: Gallup et al. (1999), p. 66

A comparison of geographical indices for selected regions (see Table 5.2) reveals the following differences:

- Sub-Saharan Africa shows the highest concentration of land in the tropics (91%) and population concentrated in the interior of the country (28% landlocked population), the highest distance from destination markets (6237 km), small internal markets (low interior and low coastal density). These conditions are generally associated with low income levels.

[750] See Weil (2005), p. 438.

- Landlocked countries outside Western and Central Europe have a mean income per person of $1,771, non-European coastal countries: $5,567 (the difference in economic density is even stronger, because landlocked countries are more sparsely populated than coastal countries). Outside of Europe, there is no single high-income landlocked country: Nearly all landlocked countries outside Europe are poor.[751]
- Among the tropical countries, the simple 1995 average GDP per capita (PPP adjusted) is $3,326, among non-tropical countries it is $9,027.[752]
- Gallup et al. estimated the "value" of certain country characteristics in terms of forgiven GDP per capita, using a multiple regression estimate for 78 non-tropical countries. Average income per capita would be reduced by an estimated
  - $4,785 if a country were in the tropics,
  - $3,590 if it were in the Southern hemisphere,
  - $10,053 if it were socialist,
  - $5,190 if it were landlocked.
- Cities have historically developed near waterways or coastal areas. Africa is the continent with by far the lowest population within 100 km of coast or river (21%). One reason is that Africa's rivers are mostly not ocean-navigable.
- Countries within close proximity generally share more spillovers and trade more. Additionally, poor countries close to developed countries (low distance to core markets) will have an advantage over poor countries a great distance away (sub-Saharan Africa). Most poor countries are also located in a poor region. Geographic vicinity to other poor countries (that do not unfold demand for the neighbor country's goods) has a negative impact on the domestic growth rate.
- Calculating an index of geographical fragmentation,[753] Gallup et al. (2003) show that Latin America is more fragmented than any other region in the world, with Asia ranking second and Africa third.
- Redding and Venables detect that one quarter of Africa's poor export performance is accounted for by its internal geography and that a further quarter is explained by poor foreign market access.[754]

---

[751] In Europe, landlocked countries are Austria, the Czech Republic, Hungary, the Former Yugoslav Republic of Macedonia, Slovakia and Switzerland. The "richest" non-European landlocked countries are Botswana (with its diamond endowment) and Belarus.

[752] A country is defined as tropical if more than half of its area is within the geographical tropics.

[753] Geographical fragmentation is defined here as the probability that two individuals taken at random do not live in similar ecozones.

Empirical estimates on transport costs are rare, because international data is not easily available. Weil (2005) states that on average, each 1,000 kilometers of distance from the most developed regions (US, Europe, Japan) raises transport costs by one percentage point.[755] Another way of approximation is with the margin of cif and fob data,[756] which is estimated by IMF staff. These numbers indicate that the margin is much higher for less developed countries (19.5% for Sub-Saharan Africa, 4.9% for Europe, 9.8% for East Asia). A study by Radelet and Sachs confirms that countries with lower shipping costs have had statistically significant higher manufactured export growth.[757] One important implication is that countries with high transport costs (e.g., interior countries in Africa) were not able to copy the East Asian model of development through export promotion.

To conclude this section, some regions seem to face bad conditions for taking part in the international division of labor because of their inherent geographical conditions. The introduction of air transport and ways of communicating electronically or via satellite has reduced these disadvantages. Still, empirical evidence suggests that transportation costs are significantly higher in disadvantaged countries. While some point out the importance of investments in infrastructure, choosing better-suited export goods and fostering regional cooperation, others argue that some countries are indeed caught in a "geography trap". Similarly, the climatic conditions of disadvantaged regions demand not necessarily more, but more specific investments into infrastructure and health care in order to achieve the same "output", leading some researchers to the conclusion that certain poor countries are caught in a "climate trap".

Institutional heritage

According to the geography hypothesis, poor countries 500 years ago should also be poor now (and vice versa for rich countries), which is by no means the case. Another large branch of literature is thus concerned with the question how the evolution of institutions has impacted on economic

[754] See Redding and Venables (2003). Internal geography is measured using the proportion of the population close to the coast or navigable rivers. Foreign market access is defined as a country's location relative to sources of import demands.

[755] See Weil (2005), p. 435.

[756] cif = cost inclusive insurance and freight, fob = free on board (exclusive insurance and freight).

[757] See Radelet and Sachs (1998).

development.[758] More specifically in the context of low-income countries in Africa, Asia and Latin America, it is the adoption of different legal systems, property rights and land ownership that go back to distinct colonial structures and pre-colonial history. The creation of large empires yielded lower costs of transportation over long distances, introduced the rule of law, civil services and abolition of slavery and resulted in less conflicts and wars. However, the abandoning of colonialism resulted in high inequality and countless conflicts, caused by artificially drawn, ethnic-group splitting borders by the colonizers.[759]

European colonizers followed different colonial strategies: In some countries, they settled and created western style institutions, while in others they established institutions primarily extracting natural resources (Congo, Burundi, Ivory Coast). In many cases, existing autocratic structures were overtaken or power was shifted from educated local Africans to traditional "chiefs". The indirect ruling by very few officials from the colonizers' administration was incapable of controlling local authorities and their abuse of power. According to Acemoglu et al.,[760] Europeans based their decision whether to settle or to extract on environmental circumstances: In favorable regions they settled whereas in non-favorable regions, they extracted (often with the force of slavery). Later, favorable regions developed post-colonial governments that were more democratic compared to extractive regions where the elitist and autocratic structures remained. Another characteristic of European settlers is that they merely exerted (military) power on their colonies for control, but were not themselves the leading workforce to produce economic rents. European countries aimed to maximize the economic returns from their colonies and were not interested in the welfare of the colony itself. Following recent estimates, colonial heritage accounts for approximately 30% of the growth gap between the former colonies in Sub-Saharan Africa and other non-

[758] See Hall and Jones (1999) and Engerman and Sokoloff (2002) for a general review on the role of institutions on economic development. In order to measure the level of institutional development, a number of proxies and indices have been developed, including the rule of law (protection of individuals and property against violence, contract enforcement, property rights), political stability, government effectiveness, freedom, voice of the poor and accountability.

[759] See Easterly and Levine (1997). A different (reverse) understanding of the causes of African civil wars can be found in Elbadawi and Sambanis (2000) who argue that the relatively higher prevalence of war in Africa is not due to ethno-linguistic fragmentation of its countries, but rather to high levels of poverty, failed political institutions, and economic dependence on natural resources.

[760] See Acemoglu et al. (2002).

industrial countries.[761] In Africa, political arrangements with local powers were common to establish control, first at coastal areas, then over the inland. In these colonies, suffrage was restricted to Europeans, and expenditures on public services and education remained marginal, thus resulting in high levels of inequality. Such initial differences became persistent and shaped the economic development path. In India, for example, the British Empire (formerly: East India Company) invested heavily in railway tracks, but concentrated on those investments that helped to exploit Indian natural resources, as well as investments in supportive structures such as banking and services. These comparative advantages are still visible today. Simultaneously, the British crown protected the British textiles industry; investments in education and health for the large local population were neglected.

Colonial rulership left many countries with high levels of social inequality (some elitist institutions and structures alongside many poor people). Colonies in the Caribbean and Brazil developed especially high levels of inequality, because they heavily specialized in the production of some basic products (sugar, crops) on large slave plantations. Consequently, the population was dominated by a small European elite and characterized by a large share of un-free black workers. This has resulted in some scepticism towards open borders, trade, FDI, policy advice and technology from abroad. After liberalization, these countries aimed at strategies of self-induced, independent economic development, which proved to be less successful than more open policies. Also, a high level of inequality did not only affect aggregate savings and investment within these economies,[762] but also had an impact on the evolution of institutions and long-run development trajectories. Economies experiencing high inequality suffer from a lack of democratic institutions, investment in public goods and infrastructure, whereas in more homogenous (equal) countries, there is a stronger tendency to establish democratic institutions and public investment as well as securing property rights.

It has been shown by La Porta et al.[763] that a country's laws on creditor rights, shareholder rights and private property rights as well as a country's level of bank and stock market development depends on the origin of law. According to North (1988), Britain has better institutions than France, and British colonies have inherited these stronger institutions. Similarly, Stulz and Williamson[764] point out the superiority of British common law by em-

761 See Price (2003).

762 See Alesina and Rodrik (1994) as well as Persson and Tabellini (1994).

763 See La Porta et al. (1998).

764 See Stulz and Williamson (2003).

phasizing the Protestant instead of Catholic tradition. Legal origins have a different emphasis on private vs. state rights and the state influence on judiciary. English common law, for example, has evolved to protect private property owners against the Crown. French and German civil law, in contrast, stem from the 19th century and were initiated to strengthen state power and not individual rights. Another important characteristic is the ability of legal systems to adapt to changing conditions, mainly via the degree of jurisprudence, which affects effectiveness:

> "[T]he common law evolves efficiently as judges respond case-by-case to unforeseen and changing conditions […] and through repeated litigation efficient rules replace inefficient ones. […] Under Napoleonic legal doctrine, judges simply apply the law; judges do not interpret the law […]. Since Napoleonic legal doctrine did not work well in practice and is conflicted with France's long legal history, the French courts circumvented the doctrine. Unlike France, many French civil law colonies have been unable to shake off the shackles of the Napoleonic doctrine. [In contrast,] Germany accepted the need for jurisprudence and sought to create a responsive legal doctrine […] designed specifically to evolve with changing conditions."[765]

There is unity among economists that property rights are a decisive factor attributing to economic and institutional development.[766] In low-income countries, the majority of land occupied by the poor has unclear defined property rights, which is rooted in history. In Spanish America (Mexico and Peru and to a lesser extent Argentina, Uruguay and Costa Rica), routines of awarding the European elite with land claims (often rich in natural resources) resulted in uneven wealth distribution. In regions with relatively few Natives (New Zealand, Australia, Canada and the United States), the distribution of wealth was more equal. But still, the majority of European colonies were characterized, "primarily because of their factor endowments, by extreme inequality in the distribution of wealth, human capital and political influence."[767] Engerman and Sokoloff show that countries that began with a high level of inequality developed institutions manifesting these inequalities, resulting in a poor economic development in the long run.[768]

Colonizers' governments have pursued different policies regarding the distribution of publicly owned land to individuals, including pricing and

---

765 Beck et al. (2003), p. 655.

766 For a general overview on the importance of property rights, refer to Olson (1996), De Soto (2000) and North (1990).

767 Engerman and Sokoloff (2005), p. 3.

768 See Engerman and Sokoloff (1997, 2005).

minimum/maximum constraints. The United States managed to distribute its public land to a large number of small owners with the Homestead Act (1862), which allowed farm families to acquire land if they settled and worked the land. In South American countries, in contrast, public land was transferred to much larger private holdings, leaving the concentration of land ownership high. On the other hand, land redistribution without corresponding rural development expenditures may generate a large number of poor small farm holders. In fact, Latin American land redistribution has proven to be poverty generating rather than alleviating.[769]

Summing up the previous two sections, the geography vs. institutions debate is far from settled. Easterly and Levine[770] argue that measures of tropics, germs and crops explain cross-country differences in economic development through their impact on institutions. In a cross-country setting, after controlling for the impact of institutions, the two variables factor endowments and policies had no independent effect on country income levels. They conclude that "...contrary to a number of stories, [...] institutional quality seems to be a sufficient statistic for accounting for economic development."[771] In a reply, Sachs expands the composition of variables by the incident of malaria risk and shows that the null hypothesis of the Easterly/Levine paper may be readily rejected.[772] He also points out some econometrical issues.[773] In fact, he synthesizes that development processes are the outcome of complex interactions of institutions, policies, and geography.[774]

Socio-economic environment

Although postcolonial institutions in Asia and Africa developed from the constitutions of their former mother country, Go[775] asserts that imitation was not universal. At least in half of the independence constitutions, provisions for religion and ideologies ran counter to the constitutional model of the former mother country. Socio-economic factors seem to play a crucial role in post-colonial trajectories. The interdependencies between culture, society and economy lie at the heart of the literature on economic sociology. Potential factors causing and influencing regional (initial) inequalities

---

[769] See Thiesenhusen (1989).
[770] See Easterly and Levine (2002).
[771] See ibid., p. 33.
[772] See Sachs (2003b), p. 9.
[773] He criticizes the simplified usage of the "distance from the equator" variable as proxy for geography.
[774] See ibid., p. 9.
[775] See Go (2002).

include ethnicity, culture, social structure, levels of education, gender, propensity for entrepreneurial activity, traditions, behaviours and beliefs. In addition, factors such as personal dignity, personal safety or extent of participation in the society could be added. Clearly, a complete coverage of all socio-economic factors is beyond the scope of this chapter. The following facets will be highlighted:

- Values, traditions and beliefs
  Following the major ideas from institutional economics, incentives (e.g., secure property rights) determine economic performance. Rules, values and beliefs have a sizable impact on the institutional and economic structure and have the ability to provide incentives for economic development. The close interdependency between culture, institutions, and economy is documented by the importance of values such as job motivation, honesty and orientation towards the future. Culture is coined by common behaviour patterns and (historical) perceptions of a group of people. It is visualized by symbols, heroes and rituals.[776] Important elements of cultures are their ability to learn and diffuse knowledge. Although cultures inhabit a certain spatial dimension due to adaptation and problem-solving patterns to distinct environmental conditions (climate, natural resources, conquests, war), increased globalization (e.g., via migration) has reduced clear identifications and created more and more overlapping of values. Nevertheless, culture determines to a high degree the behaviour of market participants, their perceptions, their information and communication channels and their way of coping with uncertainties. The best known clustering approach of cultures has been introduced by Hofstede,[777] using the indices power distance, uncertainty avoidance, individualism, masculinity and long-term orientation in comparative studies. Similar indicators are used by Müller et al.[778] who use ethnolinguistic homogeneity/heterogeneity, family and kinship systems and male dominance as structural indicators for differentiating cultures.
- Ethnicity and religion[779]
  Ethnicity and religion, which influence societies and cultures, usually do not concur but fall apart with national borders. The two most difficult challenges in determining the impact of cultures is the missing willingness or ability to not measure another culture by one's own as well as its dynamics over time. Achievements of Western cultures such as liberal-

[776] See Hofstede (2001), p. 9.
[777] See ibid.
[778] See Müller et al. (1999). See also Gupta et al. (2002) for methodologies and findings in cultural clustering.
[779] This and the next section draw on Heiduk (2005), p. 97–100.

ism or capitalism are often applied as reference and universal norm for the optimal organization of society and economy. The "superiority" of protestant ethics goes back to the early 20th century works of Max Weber[780] who claimed that this ethic guaranteed the ability and eagerness to behave economically and individualistic in order to maximize welfare. Nevertheless, modern experiences such as the catching-up of some Asian economies provide evidence that different cultural values such as the principle of seniority, subordination and collectivism have been important pillars of an Asian way of economic success. Many Asian researchers point to the fact that it was exactly not the attempt to copy Western ways of economic development, but to search and find an own base for success built on an own local culture. More recent positions even postulate that Confucianism, until then regarded as hindering economic development, was in fact one engine of China's economic catch-up with its state-led development and hierarchical philosophy. In combination with colonialism, pre-existing local cultures and traditions were in some cases evaporated, in others mixed with Western styles resulting in new cultures. During the period of de-colonialization, a multitude of tribes and ethnical minorities was set free, which were then "officially re-organised" by colonial powers according to Western patterns. Easterly and Levine[781] have shown that a society exhibiting ethical conflicts is negatively correlated with economic growth. According to the authors, ethnic variety explains 35% of Africa's growth differential with the rest of the world and makes it nearly impossible to develop social cohesion necessary to build good institutions and democracy.[782] Measured by an index of ethnolinguistic fragmentation[783], Africa shows by far the highest value. Considering the mono- and polytheistic religions of African tribes, this high level of fragmentation rules out the development of strong economic and social order in Africa. At the same time, former colonies (and also other poor regions) are characterized by a large number of (historically grown) ethnic and merchant trading networks, of which one is often dominant in a poor region:

---

[780] See Weber (1980, 1993).

[781] Easterly and Levine (1995).

[782] Linder and Bächtiger (2005) have explored the conditions for democratization in 62 African and Asian countries between 1965 and 1995. They find that democratization is strongly related to favorable political and cultural factors, while economic factors have only limited effects. The index of power sharing was one of the strongest predictors for democratization.

[783] Gallup et al. (2003) define ethnolinguistic fragmentation as the probability that two persons taken at random speak different languages.

> „One ethnic group is usually prominent in business in a poor society. In pre-industrial Europe, it was the Jews. In East Africa, it's the Indians. (Indians own almost all businesses in Kenya, although they make up only 1 percent of the population.) In West Africa, it is the Lebanese. In southern Africa, it is whites and Indians. Among indigenous African groups, often one dominates trading – the Bamileke in Cameroon, the Luba in the Democratic Republic of the Congo, the Hausa in West Africa, the Igbo in Nigeria, and the Serahule in the Gambia."[784]

Such ethnic networks, various cultural/religious traditions (e.g., the Indian caste system) and a walling off to outsiders have also led to manifested inequalities.

- Social and cultural structure

  The structure of societies is grounded in cultural conditions and (economic) incentive systems. Studies distinguishing between individualistic and collectivistic societies have found that the former are organized more vertically and the latter more horizontally and that interactions within these systems have distinct features.[785] Individualistic societies of the middle ages (e.g., trading cities such as Florence) developed family enterprises and then stock exchanges, which again facilitated new organizational structures to conduct business, but also yielded higher income inequality. In contrast, collectivistic societies (e.g., Muslim Maghribi) were characterized by stronger inner unity, stability and equality.[786] Thus, long-term development trajectories seem to be sizably shaped by specific institutions whose characteristics result from specific cultural values and social structures. It seems reasonable to assume that institutions cannot be transferred from one society to the next, thereby expecting the same results, although various technological and economic developments allow for some degree of convergence of cultures, institutions and societies. Combining cultural and institutional economics, Leipold characterizes and compares various cultures according to their institutional structure (Table 5.3).[787]

---

[784] Easterly (2006), p. 83.

[785] See Greif (1994).

[786] Contracts were not the norm even in cross-border trade relations. Trust was created by reputation.

[787] The following explications stem from Leipold (2006).

Table 5.3. Characteristics of selected cultures

Culture	Dominance of institutional structure
African	Tribal bound
Chinese	Family and morally-ideological bound
Islamic	Religious bound
Russian	Informal and legally weak bound
American	Civil-religious and legal bound
German	Legal bound

Source: Leipold (2006)

To give an insight, the African, Chinese and Islamic culture will be taken as examples here, because many poor regions belong to these cultures.

- In most African countries, a sovereign order, at least according to a Western understanding does not exist. Politicians feel more obliged to family, tribe or their region of origin than to the state and there is no strict distinction between (town/state) authority and person in charge. Economic transactions in societies with tribal institutions and informal rules do not take place on efficient markets like in industrialized countries. "Rational decisions" are perceived differently. From the allotment of public contracts over hiring personnel in the public sector or private companies to the choice of suppliers and price discrimination: It is a (local) rational decision (and even expected in such societies) to favor close members of families or tribes. Social exclusion or loss of status would be the consequence otherwise.
- The Chinese culture is dominated by family values but is, in contrast to Africa, embedded into a social system of secular moral and ideological rules. Its historical origins are ancestor worship and a harmonic understanding of the world (unity of heaven, earth and human beings). The political, social and educational system was largely forged by Confucian thoughts, which on the one hand had a disintegrative effect because of its family focus and on the other hand an integrative effect with its moral and educational ideals. Concrete Confucian rules and norms were efficiency, loyalty, honesty, diligence and thrift, which all had a major impact on the development of a performance-related and autonomous economic activity. Chinese enterprises tend to be highly centralized and weakly formalized; the access and distribution of information serves as powerful instrument; high-ranked positions are granted to relatives; family clans and networks (guanxi) are primarily grounded in personal, emotional and trustworthy relationships. At the same time, there is a sense of social responsibility of individuals and a strong reliance in self-organization. Detailed legal systems imposed by outside (foreign) forces

were accepted only to very limited extent and Western attempts to teach China "Western legal values" may have produced more barriers than progress.

- Islamic culture
  It has been often claimed that the dominant Islamic religion leaves not much leeway for developing strong legal and social systems. While this may be indeed a relevant explanation for some Arab countries, the great diversity of Islamic countries and their mixture with other cultures pose major restrictions to such a generalization of the impact of Islamic culture. In fact, it is not religion per se but the derived structure of the political, legal and social order that is responsible for the legal uncertainty in Islam. The close concord of religion, state and law (unity of faith and reason) is founded in early Islamic history and goes back to the work of the prophet Mohammed.[788] The Islamic legal system, the Sharia, is dominated by criminal law derived from Koran and Sunna as the sources of the laws of God. Two distinct modern features of Islamic economic law are Zakat (almsgiving in the form of a social tax) and interest ban.[789] As a whole, the economic and legal systems in Islamic countries underlie strong religious and dogmatic restrictions, delaying the development of pluralistic values, rational recognitions, freedom of speech and democracy. Infidels can never have the same social status as believers. Not surprisingly, any attempts to combine Western ideologies (economic, political and social) with the closed-off Islamic culture were not successful.
- Education
  Colonial history of many LDCs has resulted in poor levels of education, because most colonial rulers did not pay much attention to educating the local workforce. And if so, a hybrid of vastly different educational systems, one of the enforced ideas of colonizers and one of formerly accepted native practices, was the result. A dual structure with some highly trained and many uneducated people dominated many educational systems. There were, however, discrepancies in colonial powers' educational investment patterns. British colonies invested more in education,

[788] The foundations of Islam by the prophet Mohammed have its roots in the rejection of polytheistic and deficient social order of tribes in the region around Mecca. Mohammed was not only a religious, but also a strong political leader: Beyond introducing a new monotheistic religion, he founded a new social order with moral and legal norms.

[789] Important modern substitutes applied to price capital are profit-sharing and mark-up pricing.

Spanish, Portuguese and French less.[790] In countries where colonization was abandoned first (Latin America), education developed better than in countries with late decolonization. Some countries were characterized by a mixture of two educational systems, one with colonial and one with a native background (e.g. India). Moreover, educational development in today's low-income countries differs from the path that developed countries took back then:

> "[o]ne of the characteristics of the educational systems in developing countries is that enrolment in secondary and higher education started increasing long before realization of universal primary education. In this respect, the educational performance of developing countries not only differs from Western development experience, but also from that of the late-developers Japan and the Soviet Union [...who] gave more priority to universal primary education."[791]

According to Thiong'o[792], colonial education affected the self-confidence of the natives and has created a wish to disassociate with native heritage. With decolonalization came a lack of identity. Post-colonial territories had to remove this sense of nothingness by boosting the identity of a liberated people and uniting formerly isolated individuals.

- Gender

  There is now a sizable literature on gender issues and the importance of female education for poverty reduction. Nearly all studies confirm the existence of an educational gender gap, which is greatest in the poorest countries. Women's enrolment in primary and secondary education is lower than that of men by at least 10 percentage points.[793] Educational discrimination against women increases social inequality and holds back economic development. Closing this gender gap is important, because the rate of return on women's education is higher than on men's and increasing women's education (especially basic education for girls) raises their productivity on the farm or in the factory and results in later marriage, lower fertility and improved child health and nutrition.[794] In many (Asian) low-income countries, however, the life of a boy is regarded ad-

[790] See Altbach (1982).
[791] Szirmai (2005), p. 238.
[792] See Thiong'o (1981).
[793] See Todaro and Smith (2006), p. 376.
[794] See ibid., p. 377.

vantageous to that of a girl, and the latter receive less schooling.[795] Governance in most low-income countries is still dominated by patrimony.

Conclusions

The last sections comprised a multitude of aspects influencing economic development. The complex conditions and circumstances under which low-income countries pursue their development strategies have been pointed out by concentrating on dissimilarities in natural resources, geographical conditions, institutional heritage and socio-economic factors, leading to some important conclusions. First and utmost, there is no single-cause explanatory factor; instead, it is the complex interdependency of societies, their cultural and institutional trajectories combined with distinct geographical conditions that all matter for economic development. Conquests, migration, intercultural and economic transactions have produced many unique development paths over time. A generalized one-fits-all strategy is likely to fail in diverse environments with fragmented societies. Max Weber was one of the first influential writers to point out that (policies based on) theories should give answers to concrete events and historical specificities. "For the knowledge of historical phenomena in their concreteness, the most general laws, because they are most devoid of content, are also the least valuable."[796] Walter Eucken[797] called it the Great Antinomy in his *Foundations of Economics*: The indispensable conflict between historical-cultural diversity in economic behavior and the desire of economists to find universally valid explanations. And following Friedrich August von Hayek,[798] the existence of functionally highly specialized societies is based on abstract and general (i.e. valid for everyone) rules, building the institutional prerequisites for the homo oeconomicus model of economists. But these prerequisites exist to a very different extent across cultures.[799]

Second, it must be doubted that poverty reduction strategies based on conditional clauses imposed from outside organizations will be trusted and thus executed ruthlessly, at least in post-colonial or Islamic low-income countries. The attempts to establish Western-like institutions and legal systems as well as giving policy recommendations have mostly failed. The

---

[795] In Asia, the gender ratio is remarkably reversed: For every 100 female persons, there are 110 male (reasons include female infanticide, selective abortion and poorer treatment). In China, this ratio has reached 116 to 100. In contrast, Africa shows a „normal" ratio of two percent more girls than boys.

[796] Weber (1949), p. 80.

[797] See Eucken (1950).

[798] See Hayek (1980).

[799] See Leipold (2006), p. 144.

present development in Africa is better characterized by a retraditionalization instead of Western modernization.[800] Similarly, the closedness and reform resistance of Islamic cultures and their distinct features of social and legal norms prohibit economic and political modernization. Emotionally-bound societies (family- and tribal-based) hinder market-based, anonymous economic relations to unfold, promote economic lethargy and rent-seeking and induce reciprocal actions, giving favors and result in nepotism. The often-heard notion that the right policy advice can transform entire countries into prospering market economies (for example, referring to the gradualism vs. big bang discussion in former socialist countries) does certainly not hold in poor regions with conditions described above. Detailed plans and conditional policy strategies led by international donors (many of them former colonizers) involving Poverty Reduction Strategy Papers, Comprehensive Development Frameworks, Country Assistance Strategies, Policy Framework Papers and Structural Adjustment Policies, just to name a few, seem to be overly optimistic regarding such a diversity of development trajectories. The following section will expand on the role of distinct poverty strategies and the role of development assistance under diverse conditions.

5.3 Region-specific conditions, poverty reduction and ODA

5.3.1 Is there a case for ODA in poverty reduction?

The preceding section has touched upon diverse regional conditions. International aid agencies plan to reduce poverty by "developing" low-income countries with standardized macroeconomic strategies. Throughout the last decades, such plans and conditional clauses have more or less failed. To the contrary, economies with high growth rates have had the lowest aid/GDP ratios. It seems that some (poor) countries entail conditions, be they geographical, political or socio-economic, that are inappropriate for economic progress. Any attempts to enforce poverty reduction via economic development in these countries with ODA have not proven to be a successful policy option. If this conclusion is taken one step further, it must be asked whether foreign financial assistance has any merits at all for poverty reduction. The simplest yet convincing arguments in favor are the large number of case studies in which aid has actually succeeded in improving the lives of the poor. The key is to find specific solutions for spe-

[800] See Chabal and Daloz (1999).

cific problems in regions with specific conditions. The objective is to identify solutions in which development assistance might actually have a positive, direct impact on the poor. Naturally, this task must be exemplifying and exploratory rather than exhaustive. Presenting detailed policy or (revised) strategy frameworks cannot be the right solution to counter this challenge. To conclude with Rebecca M. Blank:

> "The bottom line is that poverty is an extremely complex phenomenon. Even at a point in time and within the same region, low-income people may face very different constraints and be influenced and helped (or not) by very different policies. When poverty is viewed as a dynamic process, the analysis becomes even more difficult. Market expansion that helps one group over time may cause an increase in poverty among another group. Changes in the incentive structure of anti-poverty and development aid may promise long-term reductions among the poor but may actually increase economic need in the short run. Determining the appropriate policy for the appropriate place and time is no easy task."[801]

Aid programs are often designed to include a maximum number of beneficiaries/recipients, resulting in inefficient single but large anti-poverty programs. Smaller and more differentiated programs designed to suit different poor (young vs. elderly poor, rural vs. urban poor, chronic vs. transient) are likely to achieve better results.

> "At the macro level, approaches to poverty reduction are set out in Poverty Reduction Strategy Papers or equivalent documents written between 1999 and 2001, and the question that needs to be posed is whether these documents formulate the poverty reduction problem in a way that addresses the real barriers that rural citizens confront in their efforts to construct pathways out of poverty."[802]

Following this line of reasoning, macro-oriented PRSPs will not be used as a reference for policy suggestions here. Rather, the next sections present selected evidence in which ODA can actually directly lead to improved conditions of the poor: Differentiating between policies for different types of poverty (Sect. 5.3.2), rural poverty and agricultural productivity growth (Sect. 5.3.3), direct transfer schemes to the poor (Sect. 5.3.4) and fighting lethal diseases (Sect. 5.3.5). Wherever applicable, distinct features of Africa, Asia and Latin America are integrated into the analysis.

---

[801] Blank (2003), p. 459.

[802] Ellis and Freeman (2004), p. 23.

5.3.2 Poverty reduction according to different types of poverty

The overwhelming rhetoric incorporated in the MDG to halve global poverty gives rise to the suggestion that the nature of poverty is equal. "In particular, it encourages the conceptualization of the poor as a single homogenous group whose prime problem is low monetary income and has lead policy makers and their advisors to search for 'the policy' that increases the income of 'the poor'. However, different types of poverty have been identified in development economics. The three major distinctions are rural vs. urban poverty, permanent/chronic vs. transient/temporary poverty and (spatially) concentrated (pockets) vs. mass poverty. Much recent research is also devoted to female poverty ("gender and poverty"), which tends to be higher and more severe than that among males. There is much debate on the causes, processes and adequate policies for each type of poverty. This section will deal with chronic and transient poverty; the subsequent Sect. 5.3.3 addresses rural poverty and agricultural productivity growth.

Transient poverty delineates a person temporarily falling into state of poverty, e.g. due to shocks or unexpected crop failure. In contrast, chronic poverty describes situations in which income levels are consistently below the poverty line. In general, policies addressing basic human and physical assets are better suited to fight chronic poverty, whereas insurance-type assistance protecting the poor from shocks (credit schemes, buffer stocks) can help transient poor. But due to data limitations, it is difficult to obtain information whether individuals or households are actually transiently or chronically poor. Jalan and Ravallion[803] analyzed the determinants of transient and chronic poverty for rural China. Despite pinpointing some similarities among the two types of poverty (they are both reduced by greater command over physical capital and entail similar life-cycle effects), there are a number of differences:

- Smaller and better educated households have lower chronic poverty, which does not hold for transient poverty.
- Living in areas with better attainments in health and education reduces chronic poverty, but seems to be irrelevant to transient poverty.
- Higher foodgrain yields do not determine transient poverty, but are highly significant in reducing chronic poverty.

ODA to the poor should take into consideration these various types of poverty and finance projects accordingly. For transient poor, ODA could assist in buidlung up, maintaining and financing social safety nets. Further

---

[803] See Jalan and Ravallion (1998).

instruments include social grants, workfare and microcredit programs, which will be discussed in Sect. 5.3.4. In countries with a high share of chronic poverty, ODA should be disbursed to finance basic infrastructure and to reduce social exclusion.[804] A uniform strategy will not meet the needs of all poor people. Furthermore, in a condensed contemporary framework like the MDG with a severe pressure to drive down poverty headcounts, there may be incentives to direct attention towards those poor whose fate can be "relatively easily" avoided. This weighing up entails a normative challenge that is difficult to reconcile.

5.3.3 Rural poverty and agricultural productivity growth

Approx. two thirds of all poor earn their living from subsistence farming in rural areas and are engaged in agricultural and related activities. Including the poor engaged in minor services and those not directly living in urban areas, approx. 80% of the poor in Asia and Africa are located in rural areas, and about 50% in Latin America.[805] The agricultural sector in sub-Saharan Africa accounts for two thirds of the labor force, 35% of GNP and 40% of foreign exchange earnings.[806] Thus, any efforts to help the poor should begin in the agricultural sector.

Studies indicate that agricultural productivity growth has a substantial impact on poverty reduction, whereas productivity growth in industry and services has not.[807] Yet most of government expenditures in African and Asian low-income countries are still targeted towards the urban poor. In order to "develop" countries, structural transformation is regarded as pivotal and thus a large share of ODA is directed towards boosting the industry and service sector in low-income countries by introducing more capital-intensive technologies. This has been shown to have only limited or even negative effects on poverty reduction.[808] Instead, in order to reduce

[804] See Hulme (2003) on conceptualizing chronic poverty.

[805] See Todaro and Smith (2006), p. 225–226. Rural poverty as a percentage of the total poor (averaged 1991 to 2000) makes up the largest part for countries in Africa (e.g., Burkina Faso: 96%, Ghana: 80%) and Asia (Bangladesh: 82%, Thailand: 82%) and, although to a lesser extent, in Latin America (Guatemala: 81%, Panama: 66%).

[806] See Fulginiti et al. (2004).

[807] See Thirtle et al. (2003).

[808] See Datt and Ravallion (1996) for India and Warr (2001) for South East Asia. Timmer (1997) identifies a positive poverty reduction impact of growth in the manufacturing sector, but with increasing inequality, which is not the case for agricultural growth.

rural poverty, agricultural growth based on labor-intensive technologies is more effective, as the income of the (land- and capital-scarce) poor depends primarily on increased employment. Increased wages and income also raise demand for products, cut food prices and reduce migration to urban areas.[809] Datt and Ravallion[810] find that rural growth reduces poverty not only in the rural, but also in the urban sector, whereas urban growth has no impact on rural poverty. Gallup et al.[811] have analyzed the link between growth and poverty for different sectors and discover that a one per cent growth in agricultural GDP leads to 1.61% income increase of the poorest quintile. The elasticity values for the manufacturing sector (1.16%) and the services sector (0.79%) were significantly lower.

Despite the fact that agricultural productivity growth is important, there are restrictions to a generalization of the aforementioned findings. The first is the differentiation between different regional agricultural systems:[812]

- Latin America
  The Latin American agricultural system is characterized by a *Latifundio-Minifundio* dualistic pattern. Latifundios are large landholdings, controlling the majority of land in Latin America (1.3% of landowners hold 71.6% of land under cultivation) minifundios are the smallest agricultural units, leaving families barely enough land to cultivate.[813] Interestingly, small farms operate much more efficiently than large landholdings, which can be explained by the high share of under- or unutilized land and higher transaction costs (e.g., monitoring hired workers) in the latter. The vast differences of land concentration are empirically confirmed by Lorenz curves of agricultural land distribution, Gini coefficients and other indicators (see Table 5.4). In regions with such unequal land distribution, landowners prefer to use-capital-intensive goods instead of labor-intensive goods. If rural poverty nevertheless decreased in Latin America, it is due to migration to urban areas, thus urban poverty has grown instead. Agricultural productivity growth without land redistribution will have only limited effects on the poor in Latin America.

[809] See Mellor (2001). Empirical support is given by Datt and Ravallion (1998) for India.

[810] See Datt and Ravallion (1996).

[811] See Gallup et al. (1997).

[812] See Todaro and Smith (2006), p. 428ff.

[813] To be exact, a latifundio are farms large enough to provide employment for more than 12 people. Minifundios provide employment for no more than two workers. In between are family farms (2 to 4 people) and medium-size farms (4 to 12 people).

- Asia
  In contrast to Latin America's land abundance, it is the limited availability of arable land, high population growth and colonial history that has shaped Asian farming. More equal land distribution, but much higher population density led to fragmentation and subdivision of peasant land (see Table 5.4). Colonizers introduced private property ownership and reorganized the former informal, village-dominated agricultural structure into a system of landlords, tenant farmers and sharecroppers with some analogies to the Latin American type of patronage. Asian transformation to a commercial orientation was, earlier than in Africa, fostered because of rising food demand in the colonial powers. Also due to the powerful role of local moneylenders, Asian peasants steadily lost their economic status over time ("from small proprietors to tenant farmers and sharecroppers, then landless rural laborers, then jobless vagrants and finally migrant slum dwellers"[814]), leading to ever lower production and rising chronic poverty levels.
- Africa
  Africa's history and the availability of relative more unused land encouraged a subsistence pattern of agricultural activity. Sharecropping is virtually non-existent in Africa. Instead, African subsistence farming is dominant in the village community (farming under communal tenure). (Limited) excess of land allows shifting cultivation, made chemical fertilizers unnecessary (which is also one of the reasons why green revolution's impact in Africa was only partially effective) and "reduce[d] the value of land ownership as an instrument of economic and political power."[815] However, an increase in the cultivation of land (commercialization) was restricted by technology, cattle and other limitations, resulting in a relatively stable pattern of low agricultural productivity.

Hanmer and Naschold[816] show that the higher productivity in the primary sector in relation to the secondary sector, the higher poverty reduction, but that this result holds only for Africa and Asia, not for Latin America. Thirtle et al. provide further dissimilarities among regions, using a four equation, recursive causal chain model.[817] Investments in agricultural R&D have yielded high rates of return in Africa (22%) and Asia (30%), but not in Latin America (-10%). The per capita costs of poverty reduction are estimated at $180 in Africa and Asia and $21,470 in Latin America.

---

[814] Todaro and Smith (2006), p. 437.
[815] Ibid., p. 438.
[816] See Hanmer and Naschold (2001).
[817] See Thirtle et al. (2003).

Table 5.4. Distribution of farms and farmland in selected countries

Average country	Average farm size	Percentage of farm and farmland				Gini coefficient of land concentration	Percentage of tenanted area in total farmland		Percentage of share tenancy in tenanted land
		Below 5 hectares		Above 5 hectares					
		Farms	Area	Farms	Area		Pure tenancy	Total	
Asia									
Bangladesh	1.6	90.6	67.7	–	–	0.42	–	20.9	91.0
India	2.3	88.7	46.7	0.1	3.7	0.62	2.4	8.5	48.0
Indonesia	1.1	97.9	68.7	0	13.6	0.56	2.1	23.6	60.0
Nepal	1.0	97.2	72.1	0	0.8	0.56	1.5	13.2	48.3
Philippines	3.6	84.8	47.8	0.2	13.9	0.51	21.4	32.8	79.3
Thailand	3.7	72.3	39.4	0	0.9	0.45	6.0	15.5	29.0
Latin America									
Brazil	59.7	36.8	1.3	16.3	84.6	0.84	6.1	10.2	–
Costa Rica	38.1	48.9	1.9	14.5	79.7	0.82	1.2	9.0	9.4
Colombia	26.3	59.6	3.7	8.4	77.7	0.86	5.3	11.5	49.4
Peru	16.9	78.0	8.9	1.9	79.1	0.91	4.5	13.6	0
Uruguay	214.1	14.3	0.2	37.6	95.8	0.82	19.1	46.3	4.7
Venezuela	91.9	43.8	0.8	13.6	92.5	0.91	4.5	2.4	–

Source: Otsuka et al. (1992), p. 1972

Despite the different agricultural systems, a second factor is related to institutional development. Fulginiti et al.[818] differentiate between different colonies in Africa and find that former UK colonies exhibited significantly higher gains in agricultural productivity from 1960 to 1999 than former colonies from Portugal, French and Spain. They also identify military and ethnical conflicts to have a negative effect on agricultural productivity and the level of political rights and civil liberties to have a positive influence.

Third, green revolution of crop varieties and modern farming techniques have had a sizable influence in South East Asia, but only limited effect in Africa. Progress in agricultural production in various regions was very uneven. While East Asia and the Pacific enjoyed a 2.5 times increase in food production between from 1980 to 2000 (measured by the food production index), Latin America and Sub-Saharan Africa yielded much lower growth (1.5 times). Taking into consideration the population growth in the latter (75%), per capita food production actually steadily declined during that period.

Fourth and finally, family farming provides the focal point of living of the rural poor. Thus, any campaigns to transform the poor's way of life by introducing new technologies to cultivation or to start mass production do not only entail economic, but also socioeconomic and cultural implications for the peasants, which again vary across regions as derived earlier. Technological progress must be understood, adopted and also accepted.

To conclude, increasing agricultural-led productivity growth can be effective in some, not in all poor regions. The higher productivity gains in Africa and Asia may have their cause in the low initial level of productivity, which again has its roots in climatic conditions, lower productivity of cattle and land as pointed out in Sect. 5.2.2. Poverty reduction policies using foreign aid should take into consideration such biases. ODA could be disbursed as R&D research grants for developing specific technologies to increase agricultural productivity in poor regions, paying special attention to local agricultural conditions (soil erosion, acidity, salinity) and labor abundance. So far, most of the geophysical and geochemical exploitation techniques used to obtain knowledge on the geology of areas were developed for and tested in countries with moderate climate, not extreme climate. However, researchers have started to develop promising (bio)-technologies. One example is the German-Indian "Jatropha project": The Jatropha bush in India grows on desert soil, and the crop consists of fruits containing oil that can be used for bio diesel. Tests proved to be promising. More than 180 million ha of Indian land cannot be used for farming, but if only 20% of this area were used for Jatropha, up to 40% of India's diesel

[818] See Fulginiti et al. (2004).

demand could be satisfied. Furthermore, it improves the environment, because only the amount of CO_2 is produced that the crop has used initially. It is also cheaper than diesel imports.[819] Such projects should be explored more and could be financed with ODA grants. While this may not necessarily promote economic development in low-income countries, it is likely to reduce local poverty.

5.3.4 ODA subsidies to the poor

Direct subsidies to the poor have been shown to include certain advantages (higher risk-taking and economic activity, resolving market imperfections) and disadvantages (adverse incentives, administrative costs, leakage effects, dependencies). Strategies how to target direct subsidies were applying indicators or conditionality as well as community-based, self-selecting and geographical targeting which have been discussed in Sect. 4.3.7. Direct transfers can have a large and immediate effect on the poor if accurately designed. A crucial component is that careful evaluation and feedback loops (response by the poor) are embedded in these transfer programs. Exactly which subsidy programs are needed depend on the local conditions and needs of the poor; policies should be modified accordingly. Successful cases include:

- Conditional cash-transfer programs, i.e. cash transfers are conditioned to school attendance or visits to health centers (e.g. Bolsa Escola and Bolsa Alimentacao, Brazil or Familia en Acción, Colombia),
- Cash-for-education and nutrition programs (e.g. PROGRESA, Mexico),
- Subsidized food programs: Free school meals and preschool nutritional supplementation programs,
- Workfare programs (Food for Work and Food for Education Programs in Bangladesh, Maharashtra Employment Guarantee Scheme in India),
- Microfinance institutions giving small loans to the poor:
  There is a sizable literature on micro-finance in development economics, which shall not be reviewed here in detail. Although very successful forerunners such as Graheem Bank in Bangladesh are frequently cited, the positive impact of micro credits on the core poor is not undisputed. Montgomery and Weiss (2005) review the existing studies on microfinance institutions and conclude that, despite the enthusiasm among donors and politicians about them, the research on the channels, cost effectiveness and poverty focus remains ambiguous. Asian microfinance

[819] See Wagner (2005).

institutions seem to have a stronger poverty orientation than Latin American ones.

> "One of the most interesting generalizations to emerge from the microfinance and poverty literature is that the poorest of the chronic poor (the core poor) borrow essentially for protectional purposes given both the low and irregular nature of their income. This group, it is suggested, is too risk averse to borrow for promotional measures (that is for investment in the future) and therefore is only a very limited beneficiary of microfinance schemes (Hulme and Mosley 1996: 132)."[820]

The opening quote of Chap. 3 by Meghnad Desai, in which he calls for ways to give money directly to the poor, is not as exaggerated as it may sound. Hanlon cites two cases in Mozambique where such a direct transfer has been conducted efficiently via a cheque system. In the first case, 93,000 former fighters in Mozambique's civil war received $2 a week for about two-and-a-half years, at an administrative cost of only 5 per cent. The second case was a payment of $92 to 106,000 families affected by a flood in 2000, also with administrative cost of 5 percent.[821] Easterly[822] suggests testing more of such approaches, for instance development vouchers issued by aid agencies which the poor can bring into play for any use they want.

Another very promising project launched in 2002 is Globalgiving.com, which calls itself an online marketplace for international giving.[823] Potential donors can select from a list of projects (organized geographically or by subject) and then contribute financial resources via credit card, Paypal or stock transfer. The fully tax-deductible contributions directly support the entrepreneurial work of the project leaders.

However, it must be made clear again that these direct (consumption) subsidies are not the ultimate answer to long-term economic development, but may be part of an answer to reduce poverty.

5.3.5 ODA to fight infectious diseases

AIDS, Malaria and other infectious diseases are widespread and still growing in many low-income countries in Africa, Asia and Latin America. A number of international agencies have increasingly shifted their attention towards fighting these lethal diseases that spread across all political, eco-

---

[820] Montgomery and Weiss (2005), p. 6.

[821] See Hanlon (2004), pp. 182–185 for further details.

[822] See Easterly (2006), p. 378f.

[823] See www.globalgiving.com.

nomic and cultural borders. They include the WHO, UNAIDS, the World Bank and the Global Fund to Fight AIDS, TB and Malaria. For a variety of other diseases, vaccination campaigns and aid programs had quite some success, yet the number of new AIDS infections continues to grow to epidemic levels and the success in stopping them remains modest at best. At least part of this disappointing result can be traced back to the early years of these diseases, when the risks and potential infection rates were acknowledged by most agencies, but not (adequately) addressed. Collective responsibility to start early action failed. Since then, objectives to reduce infections and stop contagion have been repeatedly missed. The latest World AIDS Report published by the UN in May 2006 admitted that it failed on its objectives to reduce the new infection rate by 25%.

The recent development of a number of generic drugs to AIDS treatment has driven down prices to several hundred dollars annually per patient, but including all costs (testing, counceling, repeated treatment, refrigeration of drugs, treating side effects), treatment costs rose to $1,500 per patient annually. Compared with other diseases, which result in five to six times as many victims annually and are significantly easier to prevent (Malaria, TB), this cost is extremely high. ODA funds invested into prevention programs could assist in preventing many more infections in the future in a much easier process. However, according to the present allocation of the US Emergency Plan for AIDS Relief ($15 billion) and other contemporary AIDS relief programs, less than one fifth is spent on prevention, and more than 50 percent is spent on treatment. In general, the lobby for treatment is much more powerful than the lobby for prevention, with religious and ethical issues in developed and developing countries being major factors (many Africans do believe that AIDS is caused by witchcraft and therefore see no need for prevention; the religious right opposes free distribution of condoms, etc.). Donor countries' priority setting explains a major part of present allocation of limited funds. If there is a case for ODA resources to be expanded, it is likely to be for prevention and (then) treatment of infectious diseases. But to repeat, there are limits in scaling-up ODA disbursed to local governments (medicine is sold on black markets, corruption occuring in local health ministries).

5.4 Reforming ODA: Proposals and future research

There are many proposals to reform the present international system of ODA. They favor either more dirigiste plans or more market-oriented reforms. Meanwhile, as these positions continue to collide, it seems an urgent necessity to admit that an optimal, easy-to-reach solution (however defined) does not exist due to the complexity of the global poverty problem. This may bring about a renunciation of pursuing global plans of ending poverty. Once acknowledging the limits of global planning, second-best solutions and small step improvements that can have a direct and quick effect on alleviating poverty should be thought of. Although Jeffrey Sachs and William Easterly hold diametrically opposed positions about the right way forward, there is not so much distance between them on the obligation to start immediately with solutions (Sachs calls them Quick Wins, Easterly suggests to make incremental and specific tasks work). After all, there have been many successful aid projects.

Suggestions that can facilitate a change towards a more direct use of ODA for poverty reduction include:

- Promotion of understanding ODA as a subsidy
  In order to improve its poverty orientation, ODA should be looked upon as a mere subsidy to poor people. Nearly 50 years of experiences with foreign aid have provided enough evidence that aid does not possess the power to transform societies and compel them to economic development. Moreover, aid has been shown to have different characteristics than private capital and is of only limited use to fill financing gaps.
- Grants instead of loans and project instead of program aid
  Donors' tendency to provide increasingly more ODA grants instead of loans has already become visible since 2001. Global funds and foundations designed to address specific purposes of poor people primarily work with grants. This shift may also reduce the risk of future indebtedness. However, the trend to give more aid to (local) governments as budgetary assistance may only be justified if it is disbursed in poverty-reducing measures. Otherwise, project financing for specific tasks should dominate ODA.
- Shift from supply to demand focus
  The starting base for any poverty reduction strategy should be a thorough analysis of the local needs. Once identified, these demands are likely to require a financing solution, which, however, does not necessarily have to stem from foreign aid via complex allocation and disbursement channels. Only when the ability of ODA in reaching the poor as directly as possible can be confirmed, there is a case for giving ODA. In contrast, the slogan "halving poverty by doubling aid" does not seem to hold as constructive guideline for effective poverty reduction.
- Competitive advantages and accountabilities of aid agencies
  The heterogeneity of the institutional landscape, i.e. the multitude of beneficiaries and goals should be seriously addressed. This includes a

critical revaluation of the appropriateness of some multilateral institutions such as the IMF in the overall process of global poverty reduction and steps to delink the financing decision from the decision to allocate and utilize. Furthermore, it could be discussed in how far regional development banks could be given a stronger position to overcome regional cross-border externalities, coordinate infrastructural projects and deal with local and region-specific problems.

Global development institutions should carry out those tasks at which they perform best. Donors could also specialize according to different sectors (e.g., WHO in the health sector) and be held accountable for the results in its respective area of concern. Thus, it is not selectivity of countries, but selectivity of duties that could be part of future reform agendas. Admittedly, such reforms of global work share require much better communication, coordination and harmonization among donors. But here, the notion that good governance begins at home is not as far-fetched as it may seem.

6 Résumé

A detailed analysis of the entire ODA value chain (provision, allocation and utilization) comes to the conclusion that foreign aid has not the power to transform societies/governments and force economic development in recipient countries. Despite shortcomings rooted in the aid allocation and utilization process itself, it is the complexity of societies that does not allow for one-size-fits-all approaches still commonly prescribed by aid agencies. Thus measured by the objective to spur economic development of low-income countries, the recent aid optimism cannot be upheld upon closer scrutiny. Regardless of that, international and national aid agencies have laid out even more extensive and detailed plans and strategies than ever before, promising to halve poverty with increased quantities of aid, brought up in "innovative" ways. Catchy constructions such as pro-poor growth and country ownership as well as renaming old-fashioned IMF credit lines into poverty reduction facilities mask the fact that the poverty orientation of foreign aid has not significantly improved. PRSPs sound promising, but may fall into the same "conditionality trap" that SAPs did in the 1980s and 1990s. Donors' allocation policies involve so many annual reports, strategy papers and frameworks by so many different organizations that (even benevolent) recipient countries' governments must divert most of their scarce management resources in order to comply with the manifold conditions imposed therein, leaving not much left for tailored strategies concentrating on the local population. And in most countries ruled under poor governance, SAPs were so often repeated that they actually sustain these regimes and delayed or even prohibited reforms. Nevertheless, donors did not resolve the problem of conditionality but went over to prefer and select those recipients that do well in certain policy fields. So far, it remains an open question whether the poor will benefit from such a shift towards past performance indicators.

Despite these rather sobering results, aid can alleviate poverty. The top priority should be given to identifying the needs of the poor, taking into account their region-specific conditions. Thus, the present ODA provision focus – asking how much ODA is needed to achieve certain predefined goals – should be altered by asking what the poor actually need. Once this demand is known, solutions tackling these specific problems should be thought of. ODA may then contribute to reaching these goals, but should be understood as a subsidy attempting to assist the poor as directly as possible. Generalized poverty reduction strategies must be refined according to region-specific political, socioeconomic and geographic conditions, which are not embedded in current policy frameworks. Reasons for this lack may stem from the complexity of interdisciplinary research, the aspiration of economists to derive generalized findings valuable for all "clients" and the self-interest of aid agencies.

Naturally, it becomes difficult to derive and propose concrete measures once the overall conclusion is that a generalization of poverty reduction strategies is misdirected. However, some promising ideas exist. Among them, direct transfer schemes such as workfare programs, cash-transfer programs, subsidized food programs and social safety nets should deserve more attention in the future to give ODA a new poverty dressup. These measures should be adjusted according to the different causes and types of poverty. If such small-scale efforts prove to be effective (using evaluation and feedbacks by the locals), then and only then, a careful (not rapid) scaling-up of ODA should be considered. Nevertheless, much attention should be paid to the macroeconomic and non-economic side effects of large ODA increases.

Unfortunately, the immense interest in caring for the poor has become so widespread that any reductions in the current planning efforts by aid agencies would be probably regarded by the public as a lack of interest or step back. Furthermore, the lobby of the aid industry seems to be very strong. Not only more scientific research highlighting the advantages of markets over planning in the development processes of low-income countries seems appropriate, but also a realistic understanding and insight of donors that any of their efforts will not result in poverty elimination within the next decade or so. It should not be the ultimate goal to find an approach that works for all countries under all conditions. Such an approach is doomed to fail. Instead, the regional conditions should be evaluated more carefully in order to find out what works (under what circumstances) and what does not. Then, the question should be posed whether ODA can contribute to meet this goal. Following this understanding, the effectiveness of foreign aid is more likely to be improved by many household surveys carried out at the "clients" doorstep, each addressing specific problems of the local poor, than by extensive cross-country regression studies. While methodologists may find this dissatisfying, the poor may benefit more.

References

Acemoglu D, Johnson S, Robinson JA (2002) Reversal of fortune: geography and institutions in the making of the modern world income distribution. Quarterly Journal of Economics 117 : 1231–1294

Acemoglu D, Johnson S, Robinson JA, Thaicharoen Y (2002) Institutional causes, macroeconomic symptoms: Volatility, crises and growth. NBER Working Paper 9124, National Bureau of Economic Research, Cambridge MA

Acharya A, Fuzzo de Lima AT, Moore M (2006) Proliferation and fragmentation: Transaction Costs and the Value of Aid. The Journal of Development Studies 42 (1) : 1–21

Adam CS, Bevan DL (2003) Uganda – Aid, Public Expenditure, and Dutch Disease. Working Paper 184, The Centre for the Study of African Economies Working Paper Series, Oxford

Addison T, Chowdhury AR (2003) A Global Lottery and a Global Premium Bond. WIDER Discussion Paper 2003/80, World Institute for Development Economics Research, United Nations University, Helsinki

African Development Bank (2002) Achieving the Millennium Development Goals in Africa – Progress, Prospects, and Policy Implications. Global Poverty Report 2002, African Development Bank in Collaboration with the World Bank, Washington DC

Agence Francaise de Développement, Bundesministerium für Wirtschaftliche Zusammenarbeit und Entwicklung, UK Department for International Development, World Bank (2005) Pro-Poor Growth in the 1990s – Lessons and Insights from 14 Countries. Operationalizing Pro-Poor Growth Research Program, World Bank, Washington DC

Aghion P, Bolton P (1997) A Theory of Trickle-Down Growth and Development. Review of Economic Studies 64 : 151–172

Ahde M, Pentikäinen A, Seppänen J-M (2002) The Global Lottery. Proposal presented to the Office of President Ahtisaari, March 8, 2002, Ministry of Foreign Affairs of Finland, Helsinki

Ahluwalia MS, Chenery H (1974) A Model of Distribution and Growth. In: Chenery, Hollis et al. (eds), Redistribution with Growth, Oxford University Press, Oxford, pp 209–235

Aiyar S, Berg A, Hussain M (2005) The Macroeconomic Challenge of More Aid. Finance&Development : 28–31

Ajayi S, Khan MS (2000) External Debt and Capital Flight in Sub-Saharan Africa. International Monetary Fund, Washington DC

Akram T (2003) The international foreign aid regime: who gets foreign aid and how much? Applied Economics 35 : 1351–1356

Akyüz Y (2005) Reforming the IMF: Back to the Drawing Board. G–24 Discussion Paper 38, United Nations Conference on Trade and Development, Geneva

Albin A (2005) Innovative Entwicklungsfinanzierung – die International Finance Facility. Weltwirtschaftliche Lage und Perspektiven, Working Paper, July 2005, Kreditanstalt für Wiederaufbau (KfW), Frankfurt

Alesina A, Weder B (2002) Do Corrupt Governments Receive Less Foreign Aid? The American Economic Review 92 (4) : 1126–1137

Alesina A, Perotti R (1996) Income distribution, political instability, and investment. European Economic Review 40 (6) : 1203–1228

Alesina A, Rodrik D (1994) Distributive Policies and Economic Growth. Quarterly Journal of Economics 109 : 465–490

Amprou J, Guillaumont P, Guillaumont Jeanneney S (2005) Aid Selectivity According to Augmented Criteria. Working Paper 9, Agence Francaise de Dévéloppement, Paris

Amsden AH (1994) Why Isn't the Whole World Experimenting with the East Asian Model to Develop?: Review of the East Asian Miracle. World Development 22 (4) : 627–633

Amsden AH (1989) Asia's Next Giant: South Korea and Late Industrialization. Oxford University Press, New York

Anderson WHL (1964) Trickling Down: The Relationship Between Economic Growth and the Extent of Poverty Among American Families. Quarterly Journal of Economics 78 : 511–524

Andrews D, Lodewyk E, Powell R (2005) Ethiopia: Scaling up. Finance&Development 42 (3) : 32–35

Applegarth PV (2003) A Commentary on the Millennium Challenge Account. Africa Notes 17, May 2003, Center for Strategic and International Studies, Washington DC

Arslanalp S, Henry PB (2004) Helping the Poor to Help Themselves: Debt Relief or Aid. NBER Working Paper 10230, National Bureau of Economic Research, Cambridge MA

Arvin M, Rice J, Cater B (2001) Are there country size and middle-income biases in the provision of EC multilateral foreign aid? The European Journal of Development Research 13 (2) : 49–57

Aryeetey E (2005) A Development-Focused Allocation of the Special Drawing Rights. In: Atkinson, AB (ed) New Sources of development finance. A Study Prepared for the World Institute for Development Economics Research, United Nations University, Oxford University Press, Helsinki, pp 90–109

Aschinger G (1998) Die Tobin-Steuer: eine Möglichkeit zur Eindämmung der destabilisierenden Spekulation. Hamburger Jahrbuch für Gesellschafts- und Wirtschaftspolitik 1998 : 269–287

Ashoff G (2004) Donor Coordination: a Basic Requirement for More Efficient and Effective Development Cooperation. Briefing Paper 7/2004, German Development Institute, Bonn

Asian Development Bank (2003) Review of the Asian Development Bank's Poverty Reduction Strategy – Lessons and Issues. Progress Report, Asian Development Bank, Manila

Atkinson AB (1987) On the Measurement of Poverty. Econometrica 55 : 749–763

Auty RM (1997) Patterns of Development: Resources, Policy and Economic Growth. Edward Arnold, London

Azariadis C, Drazen A (1990) Threshold externalities in economic development. The Quarterly Journal of Economics 105 (2) : 501–526

Bacha EL (1990) A Three-Gap Model of Foreign Transfer and the GDP Growth in Developing Countries. Journal of Development Economics 32 : 279–296

Bacha EL (1984) Growth with Limited Supply of Foreign Exchange: A Reappraisal of the Two-Gap Model. In: Moshe S, Taylor L, Westphal LE (eds) Economic Structure and Performance – Essays in Honor of Hollis B. Chenery. Academic Press Inc, Orlando, pp 263–280

Bagci P, Perraudin W (1997) The Impact of IMF Programmes. Global Economic Institutions Working Paper 24 (March 1997), Global Economic Institutions Research Programme, London

Balassa B (1982) Structural Adjustment Policies in Developing Countries. World Development 10 (1) : 23–38

Bank for International Settlement (2005) Triennial Central Bank Survey: Foreign Exchange and Derivatives Market Activity in 2004. Bank for International Settlement, Basle

Barbone L, Forni L (2001) Market Based Debt Reduction Agreements: A Case Study on Mexican and Polish Brady Bonds. International Journal of Finance and Economics 6 : 115–126

Barro RJ (2000) Inequality and Growth in a Panel of Countries. Journal of Economic Growth 5 : 5–32

Barro RJ (1991) Economic Growth in a Cross Section of Countries. Quarterly Journal of Economics 106 : 407–443

Barro RJ, Lee JW (2003) IMF Programs: Who Is Chosen and What are the Effects. NBER Working Paper 8951, National Bureau of Economic Research, Cambridge MA

Barro RJ, Sala-i-Martin X (1995) Economic Growth, McGraw-Hill, New York

Baulch B (2004) Aid distribution and the MDG. CPRC Working Paper 48, Chronic Poverty Research Centre, Brighton

Baulch B (2003) Aid for the Poorest? – The distribution and maldistribution of international development assistance. CPRC Working Paper 35, Chronic Poverty Research Centre, Brighton

Baulch R, McCulloch N (2000) Tracking pro-poor growth. ID21 insights 31, Institute of Development Studies, Sussex

Beck T, Demirguc-Kunt A, Levine R (2004) Finance, Inequality, and Poverty: Cross-Country Evidence. NBER Working Paper 10979, National Bureau of Economic Research, Cambridge MA

Beck T, Demirguc-Kunt A, Levine R (2003) Law and Finance: why does legal origin matter? Journal of Comparative Economics 31 : 653–675

Bender D (1995) Außenhandel. In: Bender D et al. (eds) Vahlens Kompendium der Wirtschaftstheorie und Wirtschaftspolitik. Vol 2. 6th edn. Franz Vahlen, Munich

Berensmann K (2004) Neuere Vorschläge zur Erreichung von Schuldentragfähigkeit nach der HIPC-Initiative. Analysen und Stellungnahmen 6/2004, German Development Institute, Bonn

Berthélemy J-C (2006) Bilateral Donors' Interest vs. Recipients' Development Motives in Aid Allocation: Do All Donors Behave the Same? Review of Development Economics 10 (2) : 179–194

Berthélemy J-C, Tichit A (2004) Bilateral donors' aid allocation decisions – a three-dimensional panel analysis in: International Review of Economics and Finance 13 (3) : 253–274

Bértola L, Higachi H, Porcile G (2002) Balance-of-payments-constrained-growth in Brazil: a test of Thirlwall's Law, 1890–1973. Journal of Post-Keynesian Economics 25 (1) : 123–140

Besley T, Burgess R (2003) Halving Global Poverty. Journal of Economic Perspectives 17 (3) : 3–22

Beveridge WA, Kelly MR (1980) Fiscal Content of Financial Programs Supported by Stand-By Arrangements in the Upper Credit Tranches, 1969–78. IMF Staff Papers 27, 205–249

Beynon J (2003) Poverty Efficient Aid Allocations – Collier/Dollar Revisited. ESAU Working Paper 2 (November 2003), Overseas Development Institute, London

Bhaduri A, Skarstein R (1996) Short-period macroeconomic aspects of foreign aid. Cambridge Journal of Economics 20, 195–206

Bhagwati JN (1988) Poverty and Public Policy. World Development 16 (5) : 539–654

Bhagwati JN (1978) Foreign Trade Regimes and Economic Development, Anatomy and Consequences of Exchange Rate Control Regimes. Ballinger, Cambridge MA

Bhagwati JN (1958) Immiserizing growth: A Geometrical Note. Review of Economic Studies 3 : 201–205

Bhattacharya R, Clements B (2004) Calculating the Benefits of Debt Relief. Finance&Development 51 (4) : 48–50

Bibi S (2005) When is economic growth pro-poor? Evidence from Tunisia. Working Paper 05–22, Inter-university center on risk, economic policies and employment (CIRPEE), Montréal

Birdsall N (2000) The World Bank of the Future: Victim, villain, global credit union? Remarks at the conference Promoting dialogue: Global Challenges and Global Institutions, April 13, American University, Washington DC

Birdsall, N, Williamson J (2002) Delivering on Debt Relief: From IMF Gold to a New Aid Architecture. Institute for International Economics, Washington DC

Birdsall N, Ross D, Sabot R (1997) Education, growth and inequality. In: Birdsall N, Jasperson F (eds), Pathways to Growth: Comparing East Asia and Latin America. Inter-American Development Bank, Washington DC, pp 93–127

Birdsall N, Ross D, Sabot R (1995) Inequality and Growth Reconsidered: Lessons from East Asia. World Bank Economic Review 9 (3) : 477–508

Bitterman HJ (1973) The Refunding of International Debt. Duke University Press, Durham NC

Blanchard OJ, Weil P (2001) Dynamic Efficiency, the Riskless Rate, and Debt Ponzi Games under Uncertainty. Advances in Macroeconomics 1 (2) : 5–27

Blank RM (2003) Selecting Among Anti-Poverty Policies: Can an Economist be Both Critical and Caring? Review of Social Economy 61 (4) : 447–469

Bleijenberg AN, Wit RCN (1998) European Environmental Aviation Charge: Feasibility Study. Centre for Energy Conservation and Environmental Technology, Delft

Bliss F (2003) Alte Konzepte müssen angepasst werden – Die deutsche Beteiligung an den PRS-Prozessen. Entwicklung und Zusammenarbeit 44 (11) : 418–421

Bloom DE, Canning D, Sevilla J (2003) Geography and Poverty Traps. Journal of Economic Growth 8 : 355–378

Bloom DE, Sachs JD (1998) Geography, Demography and Economic Growth in Africa. Brookings Papers on Economic Activity 2 : 207–273

Boorman J (2001) Strengthening Country Ownership of Fund-Supported Programs. Report prepared by the Policy Development and Review Department, December 5, 2001, International Monetary Fund, Washington DC

Bourguignon F, Morrison C (1998) Inequality and Development: The Role of Dualism. Journal of Development Economics 57 (2) : 233–257

Bovenberg AL (1999) Green Tax Reforms and the Double Dividend: An Updated Reader's Guide. International Tax and Public Finance 6 : 421–443

Bowman MJ, Anderson AC (1963) Concerning the Role of Education in Economic Development. In: Geertz, Clifford (ed), Old Societies and New States. Free Press of Glencoe, New York : 247–279

Brainard L (2003) Compassionate Conservatism Confronts Global Poverty. The Washington Quarterly 26 (2) : 149–169

Brainard L, Driscoll A (2003) Making the Millennium Challenge Work for Africa. The Brookings Institution Policy Brief 123 : 1–8

Brainard L, Graham C, Purvis N, Radelet S, Smith GE (2003) The Other War – Global Poverty and the Millennium Challenge Account. Center for Global Development and Brookings Institution Press, Washington DC

Brandt Commission (1981) Das Überleben sichern – der Brandt-Report, Ullstein, Frankfurt/Main

Branson W, Hanna N (2000) Ownership and Conditionality. OED Working Paper 8, World Bank Operations Evaluation Department, Washington DC

Braudel F (1972), The Mediterranean and the Mediterranean World in the Age of Philip II. Harper and Row, New York

Bräutigam D, Knack S (2004) Foreign Aid, Institutions, and Governance in Sub-Saharan Africa. Economic Development and Cultural Change 52 (2) : 255–285

Brazilian Ministry of External Relations (2005) Joint statement by Brazil, Chile, France, Germany and Spain, February 11, 2005, Brasilia

Brockhagen D, Lienemeyer M (1999) Proposal for a European Levy to internalise External Costs of Climate Change. Centre for Energy Conservation and Environmental Technology, Delft

Brownbridge M (2004) Financing the Millennium Development Goals: Is more Public Spending the Best Way to Meet Poverty Reduction Targets? Health Policy and Development 2 (1) : 40–47

Bruno M, Ravallion M, Squire L (1998) Equity and Growth in Developing Countries: Old and New Perspectives on the Policy Issues. In: Tanzi V, Chu K-Y (eds), Income distribution and high growth, MIT Press, Cambridge MA

Bruns B, Mingat A, Rakotomalala R (2003) Achieving Universal Primary Education by 2015 – a Chance for Every Child. World Bank, Washington DC

Bruton HJ (1969) The Two Gap Approach to Aid and Development: A Comment. The American Economic Review 59 (3) : 439–446

Brzoska M (2004) Taxation of the global arms trade? An overview of the issues. Kyklos 57 (2) : 149–157

Buch CM, Kuckulenz A, Le Manchec MH (2002) Worker Remittances and Capital Flows, Kiel Working Paper 1130, Kiel Institute for World Economics, Kiel

Ales B, Hamann J (2003) Aid Volatility: An Empirical Assessment. IMF Staff Papers 50 : 64–89

Bull B, Boas M (2003) Multilateral Development Banks as Regionalising Actors: The Asian Development Bank and the Inter-American Development Bank. New Political Economy 8 (2) : 245–261

Bunte J, Gloede O, Trautfetter C (2004) The BOTOS-Approach – An Alternative Approach for Calculating and Achieving a Sustainable Debt Level of HIPC-Countries. Diskussionspapiere an der Universität Bayreuth 1 (5), Bayreuth

Burki J, Perry GE (1998) Beyond the Washington Consensus: Institutions Matter. World Bank, Washington DC

Burnham JB (1999) The IMF and the World Bank: Time to Merge. The Washington Quarterly 22 (2) : 101–111

Burnside C, Dollar D (2004) Aid, Policies and Growth: Reply. The American Economic Review 94 (3) : 774–780

Burnside C, Dollar D (2000) Aid, Policies and Growth. The American Economic Review 90, 847–868

Burnside C, Dollar D (1997) Aid, Policies and Growth, World Bank Policy Research Working Paper 1777, World Bank, Washington DC

Burnside C, Fanizza D (2004) Hiccups for HIPCs? NBER Working Paper 10903, National Bureau of Economic Research, Cambridge MA

Bush GW (2002) Millennium Challenge Account – A Presidential Initiative. August 2002, Washington DC

Caliari A (2003) The Millennium Challenge Account: Unlearning How to Make Aid Work? Center of Concerns Quarterly Newsletter 160, Center of Concern, Washington DC

Caplen B (2000) Paris Club comes under attack. euromoney magazine, September 2000 : 56–61

Cecil R (2001) Sovereignty, Automaticity and International Trust Funds: A Proposal for Implementation of Tobin-Style Taxes. Center for Environmental Economic Development (CEED), Arcata CA

Chabal P, Daloz J-P (1999) Africa Works: Disorder as political instrument. Indiana University Press, Oxford

Chami R, Fullenkamp C, Jahjah S (2003) Are Immigrant Remittance Flows a Source of Capital for Development? IMF Working Paper WP/03/189, International Monetary Fund, Washington DC

Chauvet L, Guillaumont P (2002) Aid and Growth Revisited: Policy, Economic Vulnerability, and Political Instability. Paper presented at the Annual Bank Conference on Development Economics, World Bank, Washington DC

Chenery HB, Strout A (1966) Foreign Assistance and Economic Development. The American Economic Review 56 : 679–733

Childers E, Urquhart B (1994) Renewing the United Nations System, Dag Hammarskjold Foundation, Uppsala

Chowdhury MB (2004) Resources Booms and Macroeconomic Adjustments in Developing Countries. Ashgate, Aldershot

Chowdhury AR (2001) External Debt and Growth in Developing Countries – A Sensitivity and Causal Analysis. WIDER Discussion Paper 2001/95, World Institute for Development Economics Research, United Nations University, Helsinki

Christaller W (1950) Das Grundgerüst der räumlichen Ordnung in Europa – Die Systeme der europäischen zentralen Orte. Kramer, Frankfurt/Main

Clark PB, Polak JJ (2002) International Liquidity and the Role of the SDR in the International Monetary System. IMF Working Paper WP/02/217, International Monetary Fund, Washington DC

Clemens MA, Kenny CJ, Moss TJ (2004) The Trouble with the MDG: Confronting Expectations of Aid and Development Success. Working Paper 40, Center for Global Development, Washington DC

Clemens M, Radelet S (2003) Absorptive Capacity: How much is too much, how long is long enough? Working Paper 23, Center for Global Development, Washington DC

Clements B, Gupta S, Pivovarsky A, Tiongson ER (2004) Foreign Aid: Grants versus Loans. Finance&Development 41 (3) : 46–49

Clements B, Bhattacharya R, Nguyen TO (2003) External Debt, Public Investment, and Growth in Low-Income Countries. IMF Working Paper WP/03/249, International Monetary Fund, Washington DC

Clunies-Ross A (2003) Resources for Social Development. Paper for the World Commission on the Social Dimensions of Globalization, International Labor Organization (ILO), Geneva

Coady D, Grosh M, Hoddinott J (2002) The Targeting of Transfers in Developing Countries: Review of Experience and Lessons. World Bank and International Food Policy Research Institute (IFPRI), Washington DC

Cohen D (2001) The HIPC Initiative, True and False Promises. International Finance 4 (3) : 363–380

Cohen D (1993) Low investment and Large LDC Debt in the 1980's. The American Economic Review 83 (3) : 437–449

Collier P (1999) Aid Dependency: A Critique. Journal of African Economies 8 (4) : 528–545

Collier P (1998) Aid and Economic Development in Africa. Centre for the Study of African Economies, University of Oxford

Collier P, Hoeffler A (2004) Aid, Policies and Growth in Post-Conflict Countries. European Economic Review 48 : 1125–1145

Collier P, Dollar D (2002) Aid Allocation and Poverty Reduction. European Economic Review 45 (1) : 1–26

Collier P, Dollar D (2000) Can the World Cut poverty in Half? How Policy Reform and Effective Aid Can Meet the International Development Goals. World Bank Policy Research Working Paper 2403, World Bank, Washington DC

Collier P, Dollar D (1999) Aid allocation and poverty reduction. Paper for the 1999 Annual Bank Conference on Development Economics, World Bank, Washington DC

Collier P, Dehn J (2001) Aid, shocks and growth. World Bank Policy Research Working Paper 2608, World Bank, Washington DC

Contreras D (2001) Economic growth and poverty reduction by region: Chile 1990-1996. Development Policy Review 19 (3) : 291–302

Cooksey B (2004) Elixir or poison chalice? The relevance of aid to East Africa. Paper presented at the 8th Asea Conference & Nairobi Stock Exchange Golden Jubilee, November 23–26, Nairobi

Corden W, Neary M and JP (1982) Booming Sector and De-Industrialization in a Small Open Economy. The Economic Journal 92 : 825–848

Craig D, Porter D (2003) Poverty Reduction Strategy Papers: A New Convergence. World Development 31 (1) : 53–69

Cuddington JT (1995) Analyzing the Sustainability of Fiscal Deficits in Developing Countries. World Bank Policy Research Working Paper 1784, World Bank, Washington DC

Culpeper R (1994) Regional Development Banks: Exploiting their Specificity. Third World Quarterly 15 (3) : 459–482

DAC (2005) Development Assistance Committee Glossary. OECD, Paris

Dagdeviren H, van der Hoeven R, Weeks J (2004) Redistribution does Matter: Growth and Redistribution for Poverty Reduction. In: Shorrocks, van der Hoeven A and R (eds) Growth, Inequality, and Poverty. Oxford University Press, Oxford New York : 125–153

Dalgaard C-J, Hansen H, Tarp F (2004) On the empirics of foreign aid and growth. The Economic Journal 114 : 191–216

Dalgaard C-J, Hansen H (2001) On aid, growth and good policies. Journal of Development Studies 37 (6) : 17–41

Dalmazzo A, de Blasio G (2003) Resources and Incentives to Reform: A Model and Some Evidence on Sub-Saharan African Countries. IMF Working Paper 86, International Monetary Fund, Washington DC

Dasgupta P, Ray D (1986) Inequality as a Determinant of Malnutrition and Unemployment. The Economic Journal 96 : 1011–1034

Datt G, Ravallion M (2002) Is India's Economic Growth leaving the poor behind? Journal of Economic Perspectives 16 : 89–108

Datt G, Ravallion M (1998) Farm productivity and rural poverty in India. Journal of Development Studies 34 (4) : 62–85

Datt G, Ravallion M (1996) How important to India's poor is the sectoral composition of economic growth? The World Bank Economic Review 10 (1) : 1–25

Davidson P (1997) Are Grains of Sand in the Wheels of International Finance Sufficient to do the Job When Boulders are Often Required? The Economic Journal 107 : 671–686

Dayton-Johnson J, Hoddinott J (2003) Aid, Policies, and growth, redux. Department of Economics at Dalhousie University Working Paper Series, Dalhousie University, Halifax (Canada)

Deen T (2004) U.N. to Put Global Taxes Center Stage. Inter Press Service, July 10, 2004

Deininger K, Squire L (1998) New Ways of Looking at old issues: Inequality and Growth. Journal of Development Economics 57 (2) : 259–287

Demery L, Walton M (1999) Are Poverty and Social Goals for the 21st century attainable? IDS Bulletin, Institute of Development Studies 30 (2) : 75–91

Demirguc-Kunt A, Detragiache E (1997) The Determinants of Banking Crises: Evidence from Industrial and Developing Countries. World Bank Policy Research Working Paper 1828, World Bank, Washington DC

Demombynes G, Özler B (2002) Inequality, Proper Crime, and Violent Crime in South Africa. World Bank Policy Research Working Paper 2925, World Bank, Washington DC

Desai M (2003) International Policies, Speaking at the Overseas Development Institute, June 18, 2003, London

Desai N (2003) An Innovative Source of Development Finance: The Carbon Tax. WIDER Angle 1 : 4–5

De Soto H (2000) The Mystery of Capital: Why Capitalism triumphs in the West and Fails Everywhere Else. Basic Books, London

Devarajan S, Miller MJ, Swanson EV (2002) Development Goals, History, Prospects and Costs. World Bank Policy Research Working Paper 2189, World Bank, Washington DC

Development Committee (2005) Note on the G8 Debt Relief Proposal – Assessment of Costs, Implementation Issues, and Financing Options. September 21, 2005, Development Committee (Joint Ministerial Committee of the Boards of Governors of the Bank and the Fund), Washington DC

Diamond J (1997) Guns, Germs, and Steel: The Fates of Human Societies. W.W. Norton, New York

Dicks-Mireaux L, Mecagni M, Schadler S (2000) Evaluating the Effect of IMF Lending to Low-Income Countries. Journal of Development Economics 61 : 495–526

Dijkstra G, Hermes N (2001) The Uncertainty of Debt Service Payments and Economic Growth of HIPCs: Is there a Case for Debt Relief? WIDER Discussion

Paper 2001/122, World Institute for Development Economics Research, United Nations University, Helsinki

Diwan RK (1968) A Test of the Two Gap Theory of Economic Development. Journal of Economic Development 4 (4) : 529–537

Dixit A (2003) Some Lessons from transaction-cost politics for less-developed countries. Economics and Politics 15 (2) : 107–134

Dixon JH, Hamilton K (1996) Expanding the Measure of Wealth. Finance&Development 12 : 15–18

Dollar D, Levin V (2004) The Increasing Selectivity of Foreign Aid, 1984-2002. World Bank Policy Research Working Paper 3299, World Bank, Washington DC

Dollar D, Kraay A (2002) Growth is good for the poor. Journal of Economic Growth 7 (3) : 195–225

Dollar D, Svensson J (2000) What explains the success of failure of Structural Adjustment Programmes? The Economic Journal 110 : 894–917

Domar ED (1946) Capital extension, rate of growth, and employment. Econometrica 14 : 137–147

Dorn JA, Hanke SH, Walters AA (1998) The Revolution in Development Economics. Cato Institute, Washington DC

Dornbusch R (1997) Cross-Border Payments Taxes and Alternative Capital-Account Regimes. In: International Monetary and Financial Issues for the 1990s, vol VIII, United Nations, New York : pp 27–35

Dornbusch R (1976) Expectations and Exchange Rate Dynamics. Journal of Political Economy 84 : 1161–1176

Dreher A (2004) IMF and Economic Growth: The Effects of Programs, Loans, and Compliance with Conditionality. Thurgauer Wirtschaftsinstitut Research Paper Series 1, Kreuzlingen (Switzerland)

Durbarry R, Gemmell N, Greenaway D (1998) New Evidence on the Impact of Foreign Aid on Economic Growth. CREDIT Research Paper 98/8, Center for Research in Economic Development and International Trade, Nottingham

Dutt AK (2002) Thirlwall's Law and uneven development. Journal of Post-Keynesian Economics 24 (3) : 367–390

Easterly W (2006) The White Man's Burden – Why the West's Efforts to aid the rest have done so much ill and so little good, Penguin Press, New York

Easterly W (2005) What did structural adjustment adjust? The association of policies and growth with repeated IMF and World Bank adjustment loans. Journal of Development Economics 76 : 1–22

Easterly W (2003) Can Foreign Aid Buy Growth? Journal of Economic Perspectives 17 (3) : 23–48

Easterly W (2001) IMF and World Bank Structural Adjustment Programs and Poverty. Paper presented at the NBER Conference on Management of Currency Crisis, March 28–31, 2001, Monterey

Easterly W (1999) How did highly indebted poor countries become highly indebted? Reviewing two decades of debt relief. World Bank Policy Research Working Paper 2225, World Bank, Washington DC

Easterly W (1997) The Ghost of Financing Gap – How the Harrod-Domar Growth Model Still Haunts Development Economics. World Bank Policy Research Working Paper 1807, World Bank, Washington DC

Easterly W (1993) How much do distortions affect growth? Journal of Monetary Economics 32 : 187–212

Easterly W, Levine R, Roodman D (2003) New Data, New Doubts: Revisiting "Aid, Policies, and Growth". NBER Working Paper 9846, National Bureau of Economic Research, Cambridge MA

Easterly W, Levine R (2002) Tropics, Germs, and Crops: How Endowments Influence Economic Development. NBER Working Paper 9106, National Bureau of Economic Research, Cambridge MA

Easterly W, Levine R (1997) Africa's Growth Tragedy: Policies and Ethnic Divisions. Quarterly Journal of Economics 112 (4) : 1203–1250

Easterly W, Levine R (1995) Africa's Growth Tragedy: A Retrospective, 1960-89. World Bank Policy Research Working Paper 1503, World Bank, Washington DC

Eberlei W (2003) Partizipation und Ownership in den PRS – Zu wenig Zivilgesellschaft, zu viel Weltbank. Entwicklung und Zusammenarbeit 11/2003 : 411–413

Eberlei W, Siebold T (2002) Armutsbekämpfung in Afrika: Neue Ansätze oder alte Konzepte? INEF Report 64, Institut für Entwicklung und Frieden, Duisburg

ECA (1999) The Economic Report on Africa. United Nations Economic Commission for Africa, Addis (Ethiopia)

Edgeworth FY (1894) The Theory of International Values. The Economic Journal 4 : 35–50

Edwards S (2003) Debt Relief and the Current Account: An Analysis of the HIPC Initiative. World Economy 26 (4) : 513–531

Edwards S (2002) Debt Relief and Fiscal Sustainability, NBER Working Paper 8939, National Bureau of Economic Research, Cambridge MA

Ehringfeld K (2003) Mexiko tilgt Brady-Bonds vor Fälligkeit. Handelsblatt, July 1, 2003

Eichengreen B, Tobin J, Wyplocz C (1995) Two Cases for Sand in the Wheels of International Finance. The Economic Journal 195 : 162–172

Eifert B, Gelb A (2005) Coping with aid volatility. Finance&Development 42 (3) : 24–27

Elbadawi IA (1999) External Aid: Help or Hindrance to Export Orientation in Africa? Journal of African Economics 8 : 578–616

Elbadawi IA, Sambanis N (2000) Why are there so many civil wars in Africa? Understanding and preventing violent conflict. Journal of African Economics 9 (3) : 244–269

Eliasson L, Turnovsky SJ (2002) Renewable Resources in an Endogenously Growing Economy: Balanced Growth and Transitional Dynamics. Central Bank of Iceland Working Paper 20, Central Bank of Iceland, Reykjavik

Ellis F, Freeman HA (2004) Rural Livelihoods and Poverty Reduction Strategies in Four African Countries. The Journal of Development Studies 40 (4) : 1–30

EMTA (2001) Burden-Sharing in 2001: Now Is the Time to Reform the Paris Club. Position Paper, February 13, 2001, Trade Association for the Emerging Markets, New York

Engerman SL, Sokoloff KL (2005) Colonialism, Inequality, and Long-Run Paths of Development. NBER Working Paper 11057, National Bureau of Economic Research, Cambridge MA

Engerman SL, Sokoloff KL (2002) Factor endowments, inequality and paths of development among New World Economies. Economia 3 : 41–109

Engerman SL, Sokoloff KL (1997) Factor endowments, institutions, and differential paths of growth among New World Economies. In: Haber SH (ed) How Latin America Fell Behind. Stanford University Press, Stanford CA : pp 260–304

Entwistle J, Cavassini F (2005) Country ownership: What does it really mean? PRS Implementation Series, World Bank, Washington DC

Esanov A, Raiser M, Buiter W (2001) Nature's blessing or nature's curse: the political economy of transition in resource-based economies. Working Paper 65, European Bank for Reconstruction and Development, London

Eucken W (1950) Die Grundlagen der Nationalökonomie, 6th edn. Springer, Berlin

European Commission (2005a) Annual Report 2004 on the European Community's Development Policy and the Implementation of External Assistance in 2004. European Commission, Brussels

European Commission (2005b) Accelerating progress towards attaining the Millennium Development Goals – Financing for Development and Aid Effectiveness. European Commission, Brussels

European Commission (2003) The consequences of enlargement for European development policy. European Commission, Brussels

European Commission (2002) Responses to the Challenges of Globalization: A Study on the International Monetary and Financial System and on Financing for Development. European Commission, Brussels

Fedelino A, Kudina A (2003) Fiscal Sustainability in African HIPC Countries: A Policy Dilemma? IMF Working Paper WP/03/187, International Monetary Fund, Washington DC

Federal Ministry for Economic Cooperation and Development (2003) Combating Poverty – Our Goals in the Regional Development Banks. Federal Ministry for Economic Cooperation and Development, Bonn

Federal Reserve Bank of Minneapolis (2003) Taking Food from Mouths? FedGazette, March 2003

Fekjoer HO (2002) Gambling as Taxation of the Poor. Paper presented at the EASG Conference, October 4, 2002, European Association for the Study of Gambling, Barcelona

Felix D, Sau R (1996) On the revenue potential and phasing in of the Tobin tax. In: Haq M, Kaul I, Grunberg I (eds) The Tobin Tax: Coping with financial volatility. Oxford University Press, New York

Fendel R, Stadtmann G (2003) Zur Durchführbarkeit einer Devisentransaktionssteuer – Anmerkungen zur Machbarkeitsstudie von Prof. Paul Bernd Spahn. Zeitschrift für Wirtschaftspolitik 52 (2) : 274–287

Feyzioglu T, Swaroop V, Zhu M (1996) Foreign Aid's Impact on Public Spending. World Bank Policy Research Working Paper, World Bank, Washington DC

Fields GS (2001) Distribution and Development. Russell Sage Foundation, New York

Fields GS (1980) Poverty, Inequality and Development. Cambridge University Press, Cambridge

Fischer F (2004) Weltbank und IWF zusammenlegen. Handelsblatt, June 17, 2004

Fischer S (1993) The Role of Macroeconomic Factors in Growth. NBER Working Paper 4565, National Bureau of Economic Research, Cambridge MA

Fischer S (1991) Growth, Macroeconomics, and Development. NBER Working Paper 3702, National Bureau of Economic Research, Cambridge MA

Fleck RK, Kilby C (2006) How do political changes influence US bilateral aid allocations? Review of Development Economics 10 (2) : 210–223

Forbes K (2000) A reassessment of the relationship between inequality and growth. The American Economic Review 90 : 869–897

Frankel JA (1996) How well do foreign exchange markets work? Might a Tobin tax help? In: Haq M, Kaul I, Grunberg I (eds) The Tobin Tax: Coping with financial volatility. Oxford University Press, New York : pp 41–81

Frenkel M, Hemmer HR (1999) Grundlagen der Wachstumstheorie. Vahlen, Munich

Führmann B (2003) Abkehr vom Washington Consensus? Die wirtschaftspolitische Strategie der Weltbank zur Armutsbekämpfung. INEF Report 71/2003, Institut für Entwicklung und Frieden, Duisburg

Fulginiti L, Perrin RK, Yu B (2004) Institutions and Agricultural Productivity in Sub-Saharan Africa. Agricultural Economics 31 (2-3) : 169–180

Furtado C (1961) Comments on Professor Rosenstein-Rodan's paper. In: Ellis HS, Wallich HC (eds) Economic Development for Latin America. Proceedings of a Conference held by the International Economic Association, Macmillan, London : pp 67–73

G8 (2005) The Gleneagles Communiqué, G8, Gleneagles

Gaiha R (2003) Are Millennium Development Goals of Poverty Reduction Useful? Oxford Development Studies 31 (1) : 61–84

Gallup JL (1998) Agricultural Productivity and Geography. HIID Working Paper, Harvard Institute for International Development, Cambridge MA

Gallup JL, Gaviria A, Lora E (2003) Is Geography Destiny? Lessons From Latin America. Inter-American Development Bank, Washington DC

Gallup JL, Sachs JD, Mellinger AD (1999) Geography and economic development. NBER Working Paper 6849, National Bureau of Economic Research, Cambridge MA

Gallup JL, Radelet S, Warner A (1997) Economic growth and the income of the poor. CAER II Discussion Paper 36, Harvard Institute for International Development, Cambridge MA

Galor O, Weil DN (2000) Population, technology, and Growth: From Malthusian Stagnation to the Demographic Transition and Beyond. The American Economic Review 90 (4) : 806–828

Ghosh AR, Wolf H (1998) Thresholds and context dependence in growth. NBER Working Paper 6480, National Bureau of Economic Reseach, Cambridge MA

Gibson CC, Andersson K, Ostrom E, Shivakumar S (2005) The Samaritan's Dilemma: The Political Economy of Development Aid. Oxford University Press, Oxford

Gillis M, Perkins DH, Roemer M, Snodgrass DR (1983) Economics of Development. WW Norton & Company, New York London

Go J (2002), Modeling the State: Postcolonial Constitutions in Asia and Africa. Southeast Asian Studies 39 (4) : 558–583

Gong L, Zou H-F (2001) Foreign Aid Reduces Labor Supply and Capital Accumulation. Review of Development Economics 5 (1) : 105–118

Gottschalk R (2000), Growth and Poverty Reduction in Developing Countries: How Much External Financing Will be Needed in the New Century? Working Paper, Institute of Development Studies, University of Sussex, Sussex

Grahl J, Lysandrou P (2003) Sand in the wheels or spanner in the works? The Tobin tax and global finance. Cambridge Journal of Economics 27 : 597–621

Greeley M (2001) Pro-Poor Growth: a Review of Three Issues Informing the Current Policy Agenda. In: Middleton N, O'Keefe P, Visser R (eds) Negotiating Poverty – New Directions, Renewed Debate. Pluto Press, London, chapter 5

Greene J, Villanueva D (1991) Private Investment in Developing Countries: An Empirical Analysis. IMF Staff Papers 38 (1) : 33–58

Greif A (1994) Cultural Beliefs and the Organization of Society: A Historical and Theoretical Reflection on Collectivist and Individualist Societies. Journal of Political Economy 102 : 912–950

Griffin K (1970) Foreign Capital, Domestic Savings and Economic Development. Bulletin of the Oxford Institute of Economics and Statistics 32 : 99–112

Griffin K, Enos J (1970) Foreign Assistance: Objectives and Consequences. Economic Development and Cultural Change 18 : 313–327

Grossman GM, Helpman E (1994) Protection for Sale. The American Economic Review 84 : 833–850

Guillaumont P, Chauvet L (2001) Aid and Performance: A Reassessment. Journal of Development Studies 37 (6) : 66–87

Gunning JW (2000) The Reform of Aid: Conditionality, Selectivity and Ownership. Paper presented at the conference Aid and Development, January 21–22, Stockholm

Gunter BG (2001) Does the HIPC Initiative Achieve its Goal of Debt Sustainability? WIDER Discussion Paper 2001/100, World Institute for Development Economics Research, United Nations University, Helsinki

Gupta S, Clements B, Inchauste G (2004) Helping Countries Develop: The role of fiscal policy. International Monetary Fund, Washington DC

Gupta V, Hanges PJ, Dorfman P (2002) Cultural Clusters: Methodology and Findings. Journal of World Business 37 : 11–15

Gwatkin DR (2002) Who Would Gain most from Efforts to Reach the Millennium Development Goals for Health? Nutrition and Population Discussion Paper, December 2002, World Bank, Washington DC

Gylfason T (2000) Resources, Agriculture, and Economic Growth in Economics in Transition. Kyklos 53 (4) : 545–579

Gylfason T (1998) Understanding Economic Growth. SNS Förlag, Stockholm

Hadjimichael MT, Ghura D, Muhleisen M, Nord R, Ucer EM (1995) Sub-Saharan Africa: Growth, Savings and Investment, 1986–1993. Occasional Paper 118, International Monetary Fund, Washington DC

Hakura DS, Nsouli SM (2003) The Millennium Development Goals, the Emerging Framework for Capacity Building, and the Role of the IMF. IMF Working Paper WP/03/119, International Monetary Fund, Washington DC

Hall RE, Jones CI (1999) Why do some countries produce so much more output per worker than others? Quarterly Journal of Economics 114 : 83–116

Handelsblatt (2004) Brasilien zahlt richtungweisende zehnjährige Anleihe Dollar-Anleihe zurück, May 6, 2004

Hanley E (2002) Thinking and doing things about poverty II: the poverty reduction strategy process in Africa. Progress in Development Studies 2 (1) : 47–51

Hanlon J (2004) It is Possible to Just Give Money to the Poor. In: Pronk, JP et al. (eds) A Debate on Aid. Blackwell Publishing, Malden MA : pp 181–189

Hanmer L, Naschold F (2001) Attaining the International Development Targets: Will Growth be Enough? Paper presented at the UNU/WIDER Development Conference on Growth and Poverty, May 25–26, 2001, Helsinki

Hanmer L, de Jong N, Kurian R, Mooij J (1999) Are the DAC targets achievable?: Poverty and human development in the year 2015. Journal of International Development 11 (4) : 547–563

Hansen H, Tarp F (2001) Aid and growth regressions. Journal of Development Economics 64 (2) : 547–570

Hansen H, Tarp F (2000) Aid and growth regressions. CREDIT Research Paper 00/07, Centre for Research in Economic Development and International Trade, Nottingham

Hansen H, Tarp F (1999) Aid effectiveness disputed. CREDIT Research Paper 99/10, Centre for Research in Economic Development and International Trade, Nottingham

Haq M, Kaul I, Grunberg I (1996) The Tobin Tax: Coping with financial volatility. Oxford University Press, New York

Harrod RF (1939) An essay in dynamic theory. The Economic Journal 49 : 14–33

Hayek von FA (1980) Recht, Gesetzgebung und Freiheit, Vol 1: Regeln und Ordnung. Wilhelm Fink Verlag, München

Heiduk G (2005) Außenwirtschaft – Theorie, Empirie und Politik der interdependenten Weltwirtschaft. Physica, Heidelberg

Heller PS (2005) Making Aid Work. Finance&Development 42 (3) : 9–15

Heller PS, Gupta S (2002) Challenges in Expanding Aid Flows. Finance&Development 39 (2) : 40–43

Henke H, Boxill I (2000) The Asian Model in Crisis and the Transferability of Development Experiences. In: Henke H, Boxill I (eds) The End of the 'Asian Model'. John Benjamins Publishing Company, Amsterdam

Herfkens E (2005) Die Millenniumsziele gehören auf die Straße. Entwicklung&Zusammenarbeit 46 (3) : 96–97

Hermle R, Gad G (2005) Stagnation oder Aufbruch? – Eine Bewertung des UN „Millennium+5" Gipfels aus entwicklungspolitischer Sicht. Paper published September 30, 2005, Verband Entwicklungspolitik Deutscher Nichtregierungsorganisationen e.V. (VENRO), Bonn

Hibbs DA, Olsson O (2003) Geography, biogeography, and why some countries are rich and others are poor. Working Paper in Economics 105, Department of Economics, Göteborg University, Göteborg

Hirsch B (1980) Poverty and Economic Growth: Has Trickle Down Petered Out? Economic Inquiry 18 : 151–158

Hirschman AO (1958) The Strategy of Economic Development. Yale University Press, New Haven

Hjertholm P (1999) Analytical History of Heavily Indebted Poor Country (HIPC) Debt Sustainability Targets. Development Economics Research Group (DERG), Institute of Economics, University of Copenhagen, Copenhagen

Hjertholm P, Laursen J, White H (1998) Macroeconomic Issues in Foreign Aid. Paper presented at the conference Foreign Aid and Development: Lessons of Experience and Directions for the Future, October 9–10, 1998, Institute of Economics, University of Copenhagen, Copenhagen

HM Treasury (2005) International Finance Facility Proposal. September 2005, Department for International Development, London

HM Treasury (2003a) International Finance Facility. January 2003, Department for International Development, London

HM Treasury (2003b) Why we need an International Finance Facility. Department for International Development, London

HM Treasury (2003c) Doubling Aid to Halve Poverty. Press Conference 09/09, January 23, 2003, Department for International Development, London

Hofstede G (2001) Culture's Consequences, 2nd edn. Sage Publications, Thousand Oaks

Hulme D (2003) Conceptualizing chronic poverty. World Development 31 (3) : 403–423

Hulme D, Mosley P (1996) Finance against poverty. Routledge, London

Hussain MN (2001) "Exorcising the ghost": an alternate model for measuring the financing gap in developing countries. Journal of Post Keynesian Economics 24 (1) : 89–124

Hussain MN (1997) Financial Liberalization, Currency Substitution and Investment: The Case of Egypt. African Review of Money Finance and Banking 1997 (1/2)

Hutchison MM (2001) A Cure Worse Than The Disease? Currency Crises and the Output Costs of IMF-Supported Stabilization Programs. NBER Working Paper 8305, National Bureau of Economic Research, Cambridge MA

IFFIm (2005) International Financing Facility for Immunization. IMMIm, Internet: http://www.iffim.com
IIF (2004) Debt restructuring clubs – The London Club. The Institute of International Finance, Internet: http://www.iif.com/ipi/sovereign.quagga
IMF (2005a) Factsheet: Special Drawing Rights (SDR). International Monetary Fund, Washington DC
IMF (2005b) The Multilateral Debt Relief Initiative (MDRI) – A Factsheet. December 2005, International Monetary Fund, Washington DC
IMF (2004) Evaluation of the IMF's Role in Poverty Reduction Strategy Papers and the Poverty Reduction and Growth Facility. Independent Evaluation Office, International Monetary Fund, Washington DC
IMF (2003) Gold in the IMF: A fact sheet. September 2003, International Monetary Fund, Washington DC
IMF (2002) Review of the Poverty Reduction Strategy Paper (PRSP) Approach: Main findings. International Monetary Fund, Washington DC
IMF (2001a) Involving the Private Sector in the Resolution of Financial Crises – The Treatment of the Claims of Private Sector and Paris Club Creditors – Preliminary Considerations. Report prepared by the Policy Development and Review Department, International Monetary Fund, Washington DC
IMF (2001b) Public Information Notice 1/28. March 21, 2001, International Monetary Fund, Washington DC
IMF (2000a) IMF Lending to poor countries – How does the PRGF differ from the ESAF? IMF Issues Brief 01/06
IMF (2000b) Do we need a HIPC Initiative for domestic debt? IMF Survey : 255–257
IMF and IDA (2005) Heavily Indebted Poor Countries (HIPC) Initiative – Status of Implementation. International Monetary Fund, Washington DC
IMF and World Bank (2004) Debt Sustainability in Low-Income Countries – Proposal for an Operational Framework and Policy Implications. International Monetary Fund and World Bank, Washington DC
IMF and World Bank (2001a) 100% Debt Cancellation? A Response from the IMF and the World Bank. Issues Brief 01/07
IMF and World Bank (2001b) The Challenge of Maintaining Long-Term Debt Sustainability. Progress Report presented to the Development Committee and the IMFC, International Monetary Fund and World Bank, Washington DC
Iqbal Z (1995) Constraints to the Economic Growth of Pakistan: A Three-Gap Approach. Pakistan Development Review 34 : 1119–1133
Islam MN (2003) Political Regimes and the Effects of Foreign Aid on Growth. Journal of Developing Areas 37 (1) : 35–53
Jakobeit C (2001) Alternative Quellen der Entwicklungsfinanzierung. In: Betz J, Brühne S (eds) Neues Jahrbuch Dritte Welt – Entwicklungsfinanzierung. Leske+Budrich, Opladen : pp 67–80
Jalan J, Ravallion M (1998) Determinants of Transient and Chronic Poverty: Evidence from Rural China. World Bank Policy Research Working Paper 1936, World Bank, Washington DC

Jha R (2002) Innovative Sources of Development Finance – Global Cooperation in the Twenty-first Century. WIDER Discussion Paper 2002/98, World Institute for Development Economics Research, United Nations University (also published in: World Economy 27 : 193–214)

Johnson OEG (2005) Country Ownership of Reform Programmes and the Implications for Conditionality. G–24 Discussion Paper Series 35, UNCTAD, Geneva

Johnson JH, Wasty SS (1993) Borrower Ownership of Adjustment Programs and the Political Economy of Reform. World Bank Discussion Paper 199, World Bank, Washington DC

Jones S, Riddell R, Kotonglu K (2004) Aid Allocation: Managing for Development Results and Difficult Partnerships. Paper prepared for the DAC Learning and Advisory Process on Difficult Partnerships, Oxford Policy Management, Oxford

Kaiser J (2001) Debt management a la Louis XVI – A short Promenade through the Programme and Practice of the Paris Club. Paper prepared for Jubilee 2000, Internet: http://www.jubilee2000uk.org

Kakwani N, Son H (2002) Pro-poor growth: Concept, Measurement, and Application. Unpublished document, University of New South Wales, Sydney

Kakwani N, Pernia EM (2000) What is Pro-poor growth? Asian Development Review 18 (1) : 1–16

Kaldor N (1956) Alternative theories of distribution. Review of Economic Studies 23 (2) : 83–100

Kamarck AM (1976) The Tropics and Economic Development – A provocative inquiry into the poverty of nations. John Hopkins University Press, Baltimore London

Kampffmeyer T, Taake HH (1999) Die Verschuldung der Entwicklungsländer. Analysen und Stellungnahmen 2/99, German Development Institute, Bonn

Kanbur R, Sandler T (1999) The Future of Development Assistance: Common Pools and International Public Goods. ODC Policy Essay 25, Overseas Development Council, Washington DC

Kappel R, Lay J, Steiner S (2005) Uganda: No More Pro-poor Growth? Development Policy Review 23 (1) : 27–53

Kaufman D, Kraay A (2002) Governance indicators, aid allocation, and the Millennium Challenge Account. Unpublished working paper, World Bank, Washington DC

Kenen P (1996) The Feasibility of Taxing Foreign Exchange Transactions. In: Haq M, Kaul I, Grundberg I (eds) The Tobin Tax: Coping with Financial Volatility. Oxford University Press, New York and Oxford : pp 109–128

Kersting S, Riedel D (2005) Eichel and Bundesbank uneins über Goldverkäufe des IWF. Handelsblatt, April 5, 2005

Killick T, Gunatilaka R, Marr A (1998) Aid and the Political Economy of Political Change. Routledge, London New York

Klasen S (2005) Economic Growth and Poverty Reduction: Measurement and Policy Issues. Paper prepared for POVNET for the Work Program on Pro Poor Growth, Göttingen

Klasen S (2003) In Search of The Holy Grail: How to Achieve Pro-Poor Growth? In: Kolstad, I, Tungodden B, Stern N (eds) Towards Pro Poor Policies. Proceedings from the ABCDE Europe Conference, Washington DC

Klugman J (2004) Overview. In: World Bank (ed) PRSP Sourcebook. World Bank, Washington DC

Knack S (2001) Aid dependence and the quality of governance: Cross-country empirical tests. Southern Economic Journal 68 (2) : 310–329

Knack S, Rahman A (2004) Donor Fragmentation and Bureaucratic Quality in Aid Recipients. World Bank Policy Research Working Paper 3186, World Bank, Washington DC

Kraay A (2006) When Is Growth Pro-Poor? Evidence from a Panel of Countries. Journal of Development Economics, forthcoming. (also published as World Bank Policy Research Working Paper 3225, World Bank, Washington DC)

Kraay A, Raddatz C (2005) Poverty Traps, Aid and Growth. World Bank Policy Research Working Paper 3631, World Bank, Washington DC

Krueger A (1985) The experiences and lessons of Asia's super-exporters. In: Krueger A, Ossa F (eds) Export-oriented Development Strategies. Westview Press, Boulder CO

Krugman P (1991) Increasing returns and economic geography. Journal of Political Economy 99 : 484–499

Krugman P (1989) Differences in income elasticities and trends in real exchange rates. European Economic Review 33 : 1031–1046

Krugman P (1988) Financing vs. Forgiving a Debt Overhang. NBER Working Paper 2486, National Bureau of Economic Research, Cambridge MA

Kuck A (1998) Strukturanpassungsprogramme auf dem Prüfstand – Zur Theorie der Stabilisierungs- Wachstums- und Verteilungswirkungen von IWF- und Weltbankprogrammen am Beispiel Sub-Sahara-Afrikas. S+W Steuer- und Wirtschaftsverlag, Berlin

Kuroda H (2000) The Role of Regional Development Bank in the 21st Century. Speech delivered at ADB Headquarters, Mandaluyong City, December 21, 2000, Asian Development Bank

Kuznets S (1955) Economic Growth and Income Inequality. The American Economic Review 45 : 1–28

Lahiri S, Raimondos-Møller P (2000) Lobbying by ethnic groups and aid allocation. The Economic Journal 110 : 62–79

Lal D (1998) Unintended Consequences – The Impact of Factor Endowments, Culture, and Politics on Long-Run Economic Performance. MIT Press, Cambridge MA London

Landau J-P (2004) Action Against Hunger and Poverty. Report of the Technical Group on Innovative Financing Mechanisms, September 2004, French Ministry of Foreign Affairs, Paris

Langhammer RJ (2002) Halving Poverty by Doubling Aid: How Well Founded is the Optimism of the World Bank? Kiel Working Paper 1116, Kiel Institute for World Economics, Kiel

La Porta R, Lopez-de-Silanes F, Shleifer A, Vishny RW (1998) Law and Finance. Journal of Political Economy 106 (6) : 1113–1155

Lee DHK (1957) Climate and Economic Development in the Tropics. Greenwood Press, Westport CT

Leibenstein H (1957) Economic Backwardness and Economic Growth. Wiley, New York London

Leipold H (2006) Kulturvergleichende Institutionenökonomik. Lucius&Lucius, Stuttgart

Leipziger D, Fay M, Wodon Q, Yepes T (2003) Achieving the Millennium Development Goals – The Role of Infrastructure. World Bank Policy Research Working Paper 3163, World Bank, Washington DC

Lensink R, White H (1998) Does the Revival of International Private Capital Flows mean the End of Aid?: An Analysis of Developing Countries' Access to Private Capital. World Development 27 : 1221–1234

Lewis WA (1984) Development Economics in the 1950s. In: Meier G, Seers D (eds) Pioneers in Development. Oxford University Press, Oxford : pp 121–137

Lewis WA (1978) The Evolution of the International Economic Order. Princeton University Press, Princeton NJ

Lewis WA (1976) Diffusion of Development. In: Wilson T, Skinner A (eds) The Market and the State. Clarendon Press, Oxford : pp 135–163.

Lewis WA (1954) Economic Development with Unlimited Supplies of Labor. Manchester School of Economics and Social Studies 22 : 139–191

Li H, Zou H (1998) Income Inequality is not harmful for growth: Theory and evidence. Review of Development Economics 2 (3) : 318–334

Limao N, Venables AJ (2001) Infrastructure, geographical disadvantage, transport costs, and trade. World Bank Economic Review 15 : 451–479

Linder W, Bächtiger A (2005) What drives democratisation in Asia and Africa? European Journal of Political Research 44 : 861–880

Loayza N, Raddatz C (2005) The composition of growth matters for poverty alleviation. Unpublished working paper, World Bank, Washington DC

Lopez JH (2004a) Pro-Poor growth: a review of what we know (and of what we don't). Unpublished working paper, World Bank, Washington DC

Lopez JH (2004b) Pro-growth, pro-poor: Is there a trade-off? Paper prepared for the Pro-poor growth program, World Bank, Washington DC

Lopez JH, Serven L (2004) The mechanics of the poverty-growth-inequality relationship. Unpublished working paper, World Bank, Washington DC

Lösch A (1962) Die räumliche Ordnung der Wirtschaft, 3rd edn. Fischer, Stuttgart

Lucas RE (2002) Lectures in Economic Growth. Harvard University Press, Cambridge MA

Luke DF (2003) Rethinking the Poverty Reduction Strategy Paper (PRSP) as an Instrument for Mainstreaming Trade Capacity Development: a Note. In: OECD (2003) Trade Capacity Building: Experiences in an African Context. OECD, Paris : pp 67–68

Macdonald R, Hoddinott J (2004) Determinants of Canadian bilateral aid allocations: humanitarian, commercial or political? Canadian Journal of Economics 37 (2) : 294–312

Maizel A, Nissanke M (1984) Motivation for aid to developing countries. World Development 12 : 879–900

Maligalig DS (2003) Measuring the Millennium Development Goals Indicators. Paper presented at the Concluding Workshop RETA 6007: Enhancing Social and Gender Statistics, June 24–27, 2003, Bangkok

Manne AS (1963) Key Sectors of the Mexican Economy, 1960–1970. In: Manne AS, Markowitz HM (eds) Studies in Process Analysis. John Wiley and Sons, New York

Martens J (2005) Der Report des UN-Millenniumprojekts: Moskitonetze gegen die Armut. Informationsbrief Weltwirtschaft & Entwicklung, Februar 2005 : 1–2

Martens B, Mummert U, Murrell P, Seabright P (2002) The Institutional Economics of Foreign Aid. Cambridge University Press, Cambridge

Mascarenhas R, Sandler T (2005) Donors' Mechanisms for Financing International and National Public Goods: Loans or Grants? World Economy 28 (8) : 1095–1117

Mavrotas G (2003) The U.K HM Treasury-DFID Proposal to Increase External Finance to Developing Countries: The International Finance Facility. Paper presented at the WIDER Conference on Sharing Global Prosperity, September 6–7, 2003, World Institute for Development Economics Research, United Nations University, Helsinki

Maxwell S (2005) The Washington Consensus is Dead! Long Live the Meta-Narrative! Working Paper, January 2005, Overseas Development Institute, London

Maxwell S, Engel P (2003) European Development Cooperation to 2010. ODI Working Paper 219, Overseas Development Institute, London

McGillivray M (2006) Aid allocation to fragile states. WIDER Discussion Paper 2006/01, World Institute for Development Economics Research, United Nations University, Helsinki

McGillivray M (2005) What determines African bilateral aid receipts? Journal of International Development 17 (8) : 1003–1018

McGillivray M (2004) Descriptive and prescriptive analyses of aid allocation: Approaches, issues, and consequences. International Review of Economics and Finance 13 (3) : 275–292

McGillivray M (2003) Modelling Aid Allocation – Issues, Approaches and Results. WIDER Discussion Paper 2003/49, World Institute for Development Economics Research, United Nations University, Helsinki

McGillivray M, Oczkowski E (1992) A two-part sample selection model of British bilateral foreign aid allocation. Applied Economics 24 : 1311–1319

McKinley RD, Little R (1977) A Foreign Policy Model of US Bilateral Aid Allocation. World Politics 30 (1) : 58–86

McKinnon RI (1964) Foreign exchange constraints in economic development. The Economic Journal 74 : 388–409

McNeill WH (1963) The Rise of the West: A History of the Human Community. University of Chicago Press, Chicago

Mellor JW (2001) Faster, More Equitable Growth – The Relation between Growth in Agriculture and Poverty Reduction. Agricultural Policy Development Project, Research Report 4, Cambridge MA

Meltzer AH (2000) Report of the International Financing Institution Advisory Commission, Washington DC

Mende A, Menkhoff L (2003) Tobin Tax Effects Seen from the Foreign Exchange Market's Microstructure. International Finance 6 (2) : 227–247

Menkhoff L, Michaelis J (1995) Steuern zur Begrenzung unerwünschter Währungsspekulation. Aussenwirtschaft 50 (3) : 443–462

Mesjasz C (2000) Reorganization of Commercial Debt: Negotiations between Poland and the London Club (1981-1994). In: Kremenyuk V, Sjöstedt G (eds) International Economic Negotiation: Models versus Reality. Edward Elgar, Cheltenham Northampton MA : pp 143–166

Michaelowa K (2002) The Political Economy of the Enhanced HIPC Initiative. HWWA Discussion Paper 161, Hamburg Institute of International Economics, Hamburg

Michalopoulos C (1975) Production and Substitution in Two-Gap Models. Journal of Development Studies 11 (4) : 343–356

Micklewright J, Wright A (2005) Private donations for economic development. In: Atkinson AB (ed) New Sources of development finance. World Institute for Development Economics Research, United Nations University, Helsinki, Oxford University Press : pp 132–155

Millennium Challenge Corporation (2004) Report on the Criteria and Methodology for Determining the Eligibility of Candidate Countries for the Millennium Challenge Account in FY 2004. Millennium Challenge Corporation, Washington DC

Montgomery H, Weiss J (2005) Great Expectations: Microfinance and Poverty Reduction in Asia and Latin America. ADB Institute Research Paper Series 63, Asian Development Bank, Tokyo

Moreira SB (2003) Evaluating the Impact of Foreign Aid on Economic Growth. Paper presented at the 15th Annual Meeting on Socio-Economics, June 26–28, 2003, Aix-en-Provence

Mosley P (1987) Overseas Aid and Its Defence and Reform. Wheatsheaf Books, Brighton

Mosley P, Hudson J, Verschoor A (2004) Aid, Poverty Reduction and the 'New Conditionality'. The Economic Journal 114 : 217–243

Moss T (2005) Ten Myths of the International Finance Facility. Working Paper 60, Center for Global Development, Washington DC

Moss T, Subramanian A (2005) After the Big Push? Fiscal and Institutional Implications of Large Aid Increases. Working Paper 71, Center for Global Development, Washington DC

Müller H-P, Kock Marti C, Seiler Schiedt E, Arpagaus B (1999) Atlas of precolonial societies: Cultural heritage and social structures of African, Asian and Melanesian countries. Reimer, Berlin

Murphy KM, Shleifer A, Vishny RJ (1989) Industrialization and the Big Push. Journal of Political Economy 97 (5) : 1003–1026

Myrdal G (1984) International Inequality and Foreign Aid in Retrospect. In: Meier GM, Seers D (eds) Pioneers in Development. Oxford University Press, Oxford

Ndikumana L (2004) Additionality of debt relief and debt forgiveness, and implications for future volumes of official assistance. International Review of Economics and Finance 13 : 325–340

Ndung'u NS, Odedokun M, Amani HKR, Msutze A, Gilbert C, Tabova A (2004) Long-Term Debt Sustainability in Low-Income Countries: The HIPC Initiative Revisited. Commonwealth Economic Paper Series, Economic Affairs Division of the Commonwealth Secretariat, London

Nelson R (1956) A Theory of the Low-Level Equilibrium Trap in Underdeveloped Economies. The American Economic Review 66 : 894–908

Neumayer E (2005) Is the Allocation of Food Aid Free from Donor Interest Bias? Journal of Development Studies 41 (3) : 394–411

Neumayer E (2003a) Do Human Rights Matter in Bilateral Aid Allocation? A Quantitative Analysis of 21 Donor Countries. Social Science Quarterly 84 (3) : 650–666

Neumayer E (2003b) The Determinants of Aid Allocation by Regional Multilateral Development Banks and United Nations Agencies. International Studies Quarterly 47 (1) : 101–122

Nissanke M (2005) Revenue Potential of the Tobin Tax for Development Finance: A Critical Appraisal. In: Atkinson AB (ed) New Sources of Development Finance. Oxford University Press, New York : pp 58–89

Nissanke M, Ferrarini B (2001) Debt Dynamics and Contingency Financing – Theoretical Reappraisal of the HIPC Initiative. WIDER Discussion Paper 2001/139, World Institute for Development Economics Research, United Nations University, Helsinki

Nkusu M (2004) Aid and the Dutch Disease in Low-Income Countries: Informed Diagnoses for Prudent Prognoses. IMF Working Paper WP/04/49, International Monetary Fund, Washington DC

Nnedu I (2005) Regional Development Banks: Stepping Out of the Shadows – The African Development Bank. Economic Justice News 8 (1) (Online version)

North DC (1990) Institutions, Institutional Change and Economic Performance. Cambridge University Press, Cambridge

North DC (1988) Institutions, economic growth, freedom: an historical introduction. In: Walker MA (ed) Freedom, Democracy and Economic Welfare. Fraser Institute, Vancouver

Norton SW (2002) Economic Growth and Poverty: In Search of Trickle-Down. Cato Journal 22 (2) : 263–275

Nunnenkamp P (2001) Was bringt ein Entschuldungsprogramm für hochverschuldete arme Länder? ifo Schnelldienst 54 (1)

Nunnenkamp P (2005a) Targeting Aid to the Needy and Deserving: Nothing but Promises? Discussion Paper, January 2005, Kiel Institute for World Economics, Kiel

Nunnenkamp P (2005b) Mehr ist nicht genug: Wirksame Entwicklungshilfe für Afrika? Kiel Working Paper 1239, Kiel Institute for World Economics, Kiel

Nurkse R (1953) Problems of Capital Formation in Underdeveloped Countries. Basil Blackwell, Oxford

Nyoni TS (1998) Foreign Aid and Economic Performance in Tanzania. World Development 26 : 1235–1240

Obstfeld M, Rogoff K (1998) Foundations of International Economics, 3rd reprint. MIT Press, Cambridge MA

OECD (2005a) OECD/DAC statistics. OECD, Paris.

OECD (2005b) 2004 Development Co-operation Report 6 (1), OECD, Paris

OECD (1996) Shaping the 21st Century: The Contribution of Development Cooperation. OECD, Paris

Okun AM (1975) Equality and Efficiency. Brookings Institution, Washington DC

Olson M (1996) Distinguished Lecture on Economics in Government. Big Bells Left on the Sidewalk: Why Some Nations are Rich, and Others Poor. Journal of Economic Perspectives 10 (2) : 3–24

Otsuka K, Chuma H, Hayami Y (1992) Land and labor contracts in agrarian economies: Theories and facts. Journal of Economic Literature 30 : 1965-2018

Ottaviano GIP, Puga D (1997) Agglomeration in the global economy: A survey of the 'new economic geography'. Centre for Economic Performance Discussion Paper 356, London

Papanek GF (1973) Aid, Foreign Private Investment, Savings and Growth in Less Developed Countries. Journal of Political Economy 81 : 120–130

Paris Club (2003) Description of the Paris Club, Paris Club, Internet: http://www.clubdeparis.org

Patomäki H, Denys LA (2002) Treaty on Global Currency Transactions Tax. Draft version, January 24, 2002, Network Institute for Global Democratization, Helsinki

Paul E (2002) The Poverty Reduction Strategy Paper (PRSP): Incarnation of a new development aid paradigm or a SAP sub-product? Review of the PRSP process in Benin. Paper presented to the International Conference Africa and the Development Challenges of the New Millennium, April 23–26, 2002, Third World Network Africa and the Council for the Development of Social Research in Africa, Accra

Pearson LB (1969) Partners in Development. Report of the Commission on International Development, New York

Perkins DH (1994) There are at least three models of East Asian Development. World Development 22 (4) : 655–661

Perotti R (1996) Growth, Income Distribution and Democracy. Journal of Economic Growth 1 : 149–187

Perraton, J (2003) Balance of Payments Constrained Growth and Developing Countries: an examination of Thirlwall's hypothesis. International Review of Applied Economics 17 (1) : 1–22

Persson T, Tabellini G (1994) Is Inequality Harmful for Growth? The American Economic Review 84 : 600–621

Pettifor A, Greenhill R (2003) Debt Relief and the Millennium Development Goals. Background paper for the Human Development Report 2003, United Nations Development Programme, New York

Poston M, Conway T, Christiansen K (2003) The Millennium Development Goals and the IDC: driving and framing the Committee's work. Report commissioned by the IDC, January 17, 2003, Overseas Development Institute, London

Powell R (2003) Debt Relief, Additionality, and Aid Allocation in Low-Income Countries. IMF Working Paper WP/03/175, International Monetary Fund, Washington DC

Powell R (2000) Debt Relief for Poor Countries. Finance&Development 37 (4) : 42–45

Price G (2003) Economic Growth in a Cross-section of Nonindustrial countries: Does Colonial Heritage Matter for Africa? Review of Economic Development 7 : 478–495

Priewe J (2005) Verhängnisvolle Einigkeit. Entwicklung&Zusammenarbeit 1 : 22–25

Pronk JP (2001) Aid as a Catalyst. Development and Change 32 (4) : 611–629

PRSA (2003) The Global Poll: Multinational Survey of Opinion Leaders 2002. Report prepared for the World Bank, Princeton Survey Research Associates, Washington DC

Przeworski A, Vreeland JR (2000) The Effect of IMF Programs on Economic Growth. Journal of Development Economics 62 : 385–421

Quah DT (1997) Empirics for Growth and Distribution: Stratification, Polarization, and Convergence Clubs. Journal of Economic Growth 2 : 27–59.

Radelet S (2004) Qualifying for the MCA: An Update. Working Paper, Center for Global Development, Washington DC

Radelet S (2003a) Will the Millennium Challenge Account be Different? The Washington Quarterly 26 (2) : 171–187

Radelet S (2003b) The Millennium Challenge Account: Transforming U.S. Foreign Assistance Policy? Working Paper, Center for Global Development, Washington DC

Radelet S (2003c) Bush and Foreign Aid. Foreign Affairs 82 (5) : 104–117

Radelet S, Lucas S, Bhavnani R (2004) A Comment on Country Selection. Paper prepared for the MCA Threshold Program, October 2004, Center for Global Development, Washington DC

Radelet S, Sachs J (1998) Shipping costs, Manufactured Exports, and Economic Growth. Paper presented at the 1998 AEA meetings, Chicago

Rahman A (1968) Foreign Capital and Domestic Savings: A Test of Haavelmo's Hypothesis with Cross-Country Data. Review of Economics and Statistics 50 (1) : 137–138

Ranaweera T (2003) Foreign Aid, Conditionality and Ghost of the Financing Gap: A Forgotten Aspect of the Aid Debate. World Bank Policy Research Paper 3019, World Bank, Washington DC

Ranis G (1996) On fast-disbursing policy-based loans. Background paper prepared for the Task Force on the United States and Multilateral Development Banks, Center for Strategic and International Studies, Washington DC

Ranis G (2004) Arthur Lewis' Contribution to Development Thinking and Policy. Paper prepared for the conference The Lewis Model After 50 Years: Assessing Sir Arthur Lewis's Contribution to Development Economics and Policy, July 6-7, 2004, Manchester

Ratha D (2003) Workers' Remittances: An Important and Stable Source of External Development Finance. In: World Bank (ed) Global Development Finance 2003, World Bank, Washington DC : pp 157–175

Ravallion M (2004a) Pro-Poor Growth: A Primer. World Bank Policy Research Working Paper 3242, World Bank, Washington DC

Ravallion M (2004b) Globalization and Poor People: The Debate and Evidence. Second Annual Max Corden Lecture, March 4, 2004, Melbourne

Ravallion M (2003a) The Debate on Globalization, Poverty and Inequality: Why Measurement Matters. World Bank Policy Research Working Paper 3038, World Bank (also published in: International Affairs 79 (4) : 739–753)

Ravallion M (2003b) Targeting Transfers in Poor Countries: Revisiting the Tradeoffs and Policy Options. CPRC Working Paper 26, Chronic Poverty Research Centre, World Bank, Washington

Ravallion M (2001) Growth, Inequality, and Poverty: Looking Beyond Averages. World Bank Policy Research Paper 2558, World Bank, Washington DC

Ravallion M (1997) Can High Inequality Developing Countries Escape Absolute Poverty? Economics Letters 56 : 51–57

Ravallion M (1995) Growth and Poverty: Evidence for Developing Countries in the 1980s. Economics Letters 48 : 411–417

Ravallion M (1992) Does Undernutrition Respond to Incomes and Prices? Dominance Tests for Indonesia. World Bank Economic Review 6 (1) : 109–124

Ravallion M, Chen S (2003) Measuring pro-poor growth. Economics Letters 78 : 93–99

Ravallion M, Datt G (1999) When is growth pro-poor? World Bank Policy Research Working Paper 2263, World Bank, Washington DC

Ravallion M, Datt G (1996) How important to India's Poor is the sectoral composition of economic growth? World Bank Economic Review 10 (1) : 1–25

Rector R, Lauder WF (1995) America's Failed $5.4 Trillion War on Poverty. The Heritage Foundation, Washington DC

Redding S, Venables AJ (2003) Geography and Export Performance: External Market Access and Internal Supply Capacity. NBER Working Paper 9637, National Bureau of Economic Research, Cambridge MA

Reddy S, Heuty A (2004) Achieving the Millennium Development Goals: A Review and a strategy. Draft 2.3, April 4, 2004, Bureau for Development Policy, United Nations Development Programme, New York

Reinhardt GY (2006) Shortcuts and Signals: An Analysis of the Micro-level Determinants of Aid Allocation, with Case Study Evidence from Brazil. Review of Development Economics 10 (2) : 297–312

Reinhart VR (2000) How the Machinery of International Finance Runs with Sand in its Wheels. Review of International Economics 8 (1) : 74–85

Reisen H (2004) Innovative Approaches to Funding the Millennium Development Goals. OECD Policy Brief 24, OECD, Paris

Reno RA (1997) Gambling and the Poor. Palmetto Family Council, Columbia SC

Rieffel L (2003) Restructuring Sovereign Debt: The Case for Ad Hoc Machinery. The Brookings Institution Press, Washington DC

Rieffel L (2002) A Note on the International Debt Commission. March 31, 2002, Washington DC

Rodrik D (2001) The Global Governance of Trade as if Development Really Mattered. Background Paper to the UNDP project on Trade and Sustainable Human Development, October 2001, United Nations Development Programme, New York

Rodrik D, Subramanian A, Trebbi F (2002) Institutions rule: The primacy of institutions over integration and geography in economic development. IMF Working Paper 2/189, International Monetary Fund, Washington DC

Rogerson A (2005) Aid Harmonisation and Alignment: Bridging the Gaps between Reality and the Paris Reform Agenda. Development Policy Review 23 (5) : 531–552

Rojas-Suarez L (2002) International Standards for Strengthening Financial Systems: Can Regional Development Banks Address Developing Countries Concerns? Paper prepared for the Conference on Financing for Development: Regional Challenges and the Role of Regional Development Banks, February 19, 2002, Institute for International Economics, Washington DC

Rosenstein-Rodan P (1984) Natura Facit Saltum: Analysis of the Disequilibrium Growth Process. In: Meier GM, Seers D (eds) Pioneers in Development. Oxford University Press, Oxford : pp 207–221

Rosenstein-Rodan P (1961) Notes on the Theory of the 'Big Push'. In: Ellis HS, Wallich HC (eds) Economic Development for Latin America. Proceedings of a Conference held by the International Economic Association, Macmillan, London : pp 57–67

Rosenstein-Rodan P (1943) Problems of Industrialization of Eastern and South-Eastern Europe. The Economic Journal 53 : 202–211

Rostow WW (1960) The Stages of Economic Growth: A Non-Communist Manifesto. Cambridge University Press, Cambridge

Round JI, Odedokun M (2004) Aid effort and its determinants. International Review of Economics and Finance 13 : 293–309

Rujis A, Schweigman C, Lutz C (2003), The impact of transport- and transaction-cost reductions on food markets in developing countries: evidence for tempered expectations for Burkina Faso. Agricultural Economics 31 (2-3) : 219–228

Sachs JD (2005) Millennium Development Compact. The Millennium Project, Washington DC

Sachs JD (2003a) Institutions Matter, but Not for Everything – The role of geography and resource endowments in development shouldn't be underestimated. Finance&Development 6 : 38–41

Sachs JD (2003b) Institutions don't rule: Direct effects of geography on per capita income. NBER Working Paper 9490, National Bureau of Economic Research, Cambridge MA

Sachs JD (2000) The Charade of Debt Sustainability. Financial Times, September 17, 2000

Sachs JD (1986) The debt overhang problem of developing countries. Contribution at the conference in memorial to Carlos Diaz-Aljandro, August 1986, Helsinki

Sachs JD (1984) Theoretical issues in international borrowing. Princeton Studies in International Finance 54, Princeton University, Princeton NJ

Sachs JD, Warner A (1995) Natural resource abundance and economic growth. NBER Working Paper 5398, National Bureau of Economic Research, Cambridge MA

Sackey HA (2001) External Aid Flows and the Real Exchange Rate in Ghana. AERC Research Paper 110, African Economic Research Consortium, Nairobi

Sahn DE, Stifel DC (2003) Progress toward the Millennium Development Goals in Africa. World Development 31 (1) : 23–52

Sandmo A (2003) Environmental Taxation and Revenue for Economic Development. WIDER Discussion Paper 2003/86, World Institute for Development Economics Research, United Nations University, Helsinki

Sanford JE (2004) IMF Gold and the World Bank's Unfunded HIPC Deficit. Development Policy Review 22 (1) : 31–40

Sanford JE (2002) World Bank: IDA Loans or IDA Grants? World Development 30 (5) : 741–762

Sauer C, Gawande K, Li G (2003) Big Push industrialization: some empirical evidence for East Asia and Eastern Europe. Economics Bulletin 15 (9) : 1–7

Savvides A (1992) Investment Slowdown in Developing Countries during the 1980s: Debt Overhang or Foreign Capital Inflows. Kyklos 45 (3) : 363–378

Schabbel C (2001) Die osteuropäischen und ostasiatischen Länder auf dem Weg in die Weltwirtschaft: Ein Vergleich der Strategien und Entwicklungsmuster. Ausgewählte Volkswirtschaftliche Diplomarbeiten des Fachbereichs Wirtschaftswissenschaft der Gerhard-Mercator-Universität Duisburg 35, Duisburg

Schmidt R (1999) A feasible foreign exchange transaction tax. The North-South Institute, Ottawa

Schneider AK (2003) Zwischen Armutsorientierung und Stabilitätssicherung – PRS als Fortsetzung der Strukturanpassungsprogramme? Entwicklung und Zusammenarbeit 11 : 414–417

Schöb R (2003) The Double Dividend Hypotheses of Environmental Taxes: A Survey. CESifo Working Paper 946, CESifo, Munich

Schweinberger AG, Lahiri S (2006) On the provision of official and private foreign aid. Journal of Development Economics 80 (1) : 179–197

Sen AK (2001) Addressing Global Poverty. In: The Economist (ed), The World in 2002. RAC Publishing, London

Sen AK (1997) Poverty and Famines. Clarendon Press, Oxford

Sen AK (1976) Poverty: An ordinary approach to measurement. Econometrica 44 : 219–231
Shams R (1999) Entwicklungsblockaden: Neuere theoretische Ansätze im Überblick. In: Lemper A, Sell A, Wohlmuth K (eds) Berichte aus dem Weltwirtschaftlichen Colloquium der Universität Bremen 62, Institute for World Economics and International Management, Bremen
Sharpe S, Wood A, Wratten E (2005) U.K.: More Country Ownership. Finance&Development 42 (3) : 36–38
Shikwati J (2006) Fehlentwicklungshilfe – Mit eigenständigen Lösungen kann Afrika eine neue Rolle spielen. Internationale Politik 61 (4) : 6–15
Shin J-S (2005) The future of development economics: a methodological agenda. Cambridge Journal of Economics 29 : 1111–1128
Shorrocks A, van der Hoeven R (2004) Introduction. In: Shorrocks A, van der Hoeven R (eds) Growth, Inequality, and Poverty – Prospects for Pro-Poor Economic Development. Oxford University Press, New York
Shultz GP (1998) Merge the IMF and World Bank. The International Economy, January/February : 14–16
Siebold T (1995) Die soziale Dimension der Strukturanpassung – eine Zwischenbilanz. INEF Report 13/1995, University of Duisburg-Essen, Duisburg
SIPRI (2004) SIPRI Yearbook 2004 – Armaments, Disarmament, and International Security, 35th edn. Oxford University Press, Stockholm
Snape RH (1978) Effects of mineral development on the economy. Australian Journal of Agricultural Economics 21 : 147–156
Soete L (1999) Reaction to European Commission, DG XIII, Bit Tax Proposal Analysis. Internet: http://www.merit.unimaas.nl/cybertax/response.html
Solimano A (2003) Remittances by Emigrants – Issues and Evidence. WIDER Discussion Paper 2003/89, World Institute for Development Economics Research, United Nations University, Helsinki
Son HH (2004) A note on pro-poor growth. Economics Letters 82 : 307–314
Son HH, Kakwani N (2004) Economic Growth and Poverty Reduction: Initial Conditions Matter. Working Paper 2, International Poverty Centre, United Nations Development Programme, New York
Soros G (2002) George Soros on Globalization. Public Affairs, Oxford
Spahn PB (2002) Zur Durchführbarkeit einer Devisentransaktionssteuer. Report for the Bundesministerium für Wirtschaftliche Zusammenarbeit und Entwicklung, Bonn
Stallings B (2004) Financial Liberalization, Crisis, and Rescue: Lessons for China from Latin America and East Asia? Working Paper 32, presented at the 2004 LAEBA Annual Conference, December 2–4, 2004, Beijing
Stambuli PK (1999) Paris Club Debt Relief, Multilateral Frameworks and Implications for Poor Country debt. Pre-doctoral research paper, Department of Economics, University of Surrey
Stiglitz JE (2003) How to Reform the Global Financial System. Harvard Relations Council International Review 25 (1) : 54–59
Stiglitz JE (2002) Globalization and its discontents. W.W. Norton&Company, New York London

Stiglitz JE (1998) More Instruments and Broader Goals: Moving toward the Post-Washington Consensus. World Institute for Development Economics Research, 1998 Annual Lecture, January 7, 1998, United Nations University, Helsinki

Strauss J (1986) Does better nutrition raise farm productivity? Journal of Political Economy 94 : 297–320

Stulz R, Williamson R (2003) Culture, openness, and finance. Journal of Financial Economics 70 (3) : 313–349

Svensson J (2000) Foreign Aid and Rent-Seeking. Journal of International Economics 51 (1) : 437–461

Svensson J (1999) Aid, growth and democracy. Economics and Politics 11 (3) : 275–297

Tavares J (2003) Does Foreign Aid Corrupt ? Economics Letters 79 (1) : 99–106

Taylor L (1994) Gap models. Journal of Development Economics 45 : 17–34

Taylor L (1991) Foreign Resource Flows and Developing Country Growth. World Institute for Development Economics Research, United Nations University, Helsinki

Taylor L (1990) A Three-Gap Model. In: McCarthy DF (ed) Problems of Developing Countries in the 1990s. World Bank, Washington DC : pp 55–90

The Global Fund (2004) The Global Fund. Internet: http://www.theglobalfund.org

Thiele R (2005) Aid Allocation and Aid Effectiveness. In: Ahrens H (ed) Development Cooperation – Evaluation and New Approaches. Schriften des Vereins für Socialpolitik, Gesellschaft für Wirtschafts- und Sozialwissenschaften, Neue Folge Band 308, Duncker&Humblot, Berlin : pp 39–48

Thien E (2003) International Finance Facility – Versuch einer Securitization künftiger Entwicklungshilfebudgets. Die Bank, September 2003 : 635–637

Thiesenhusen WC (1989) Searching for Agrarian Reform in Latin America. Unwin Hyman, Winchester

Thiong'o NW (1981) Decolonising the Mind: The Politics of Language in African Literature. Heinemann, Portsmith NH

Thirlwall AP (1979) The Balance of Payments Constraint as an Explanation of International Growth Rate Differences. Banca Nazionale del Lavoro Quarterly Review 128 : 44–53

Thirlwall AP, Hussain MN (1982) The Balance-of-Payments Constraint, Capital Flows and Growth Rate Differentials Between Developing Countries. Oxford Economic Papers 34 (3) : 498–509

Thirtle C, Lin L, Piesse J (2003) The Impact of Research Led Agricultural Productivity Growth on Poverty in Africa, Asia and Latin America. World Development 31 (12) : 1959–1975

Thomas V, Evans A, Mensah M, Dabelstein N (2002) Panel Discussion: Evaluation Perspectives on Poverty Reduction. In: World Bank (2001) Evaluation and Poverty Reduction – World Bank on Evaluation and Development. World Bank, Washington DC : pp 51–61

Thorbecke E (2000) The development doctrine and foreign aid 1950–2000. Routledge, London New York

Thornton JR, Agnello RJ, Link CR (1978) Poverty and Economic Growth: Trickle Down Peters Out. Economic Inquiry 16 : 385–394

Thünen JH von (1826) Der isolierte Staat in Beziehung auf Landwirtschaft und Nationalökonomie, 4th edn. Fischer, Stuttgart

Timmer CP (1997) How well do the poor connect to the growth process? CAER II Discussion Paper 17, Harvard Institute for International Development, Cambridge MA

Timmer CP (1988) The Agricultural Transformation. In: Chenery HB, Srinivasan TN (eds) Handbook of Development Economics 1. North Holland, Amsterdam

Tobin J (1996) Prologue. In: Haq M, Kaul I, Grunberg I (eds) The Tobin Tax: Coping with financial volatility. Oxford University Press, New York : pp ix–xviii

Tobin J (1978) A Proposal for International Monetary Reform. Eastern Economic Journal 4 : 153–159

Tobin J (1974) The New Economics One Decade Older. The Eliot Janeway Lectures on Historical Economics in Honour of Joseph Schumpter, Princeton University Press, Princeton NJ

Todaro MP (1997) Economic Development. Addison-Wesley, Reading MA

Todaro MP, Smith SC (2006) Economic Development, 9th edn. Addison-Wesley, Reading MA

Tornell A (1990) Real vs. Financial Investment: Can Tobin Taxes Eliminate the Irreversibility Distortion? Journal of Development Economics 32 : 419–444

Torsvik G (2005) Foreign economic aid: should donors cooperate? Journal of Development Economics 77 : 503–515

UN (2002) Report of the International Conference on Financing for Development 2002, United Nations, New York

UN (2001) Report of the High-Level Panel on Financing for Development, United Nations, New York

UN (2000) A Better World for All. Oxford University Press, New York

UN (1999) Human Development Report 1999, Oxford University Press, New York

UNAIDS (2006) 2006 report on the global AIDS epidemic. UNAIDS, Geneva

UNDP (2003) Human Development Report 2003. Oxford University Press, New York Oxford

UNDP (2002) Peer Review System. National Human Development Report Unit, United Nations Development Programme, New York

UNDP et al. (1998) Implementing the 20/20-Inititative – Achieving universal access to basic social services, United Nations Development Programme, New York

UNESCAP (2002) Economic and Social Survey of Asia and the Pacific 2002. United Nations Economic and Social Commission for Asia and the Pacific, Bangkok

United Nations Millennium Project (2005) Investing in Development – A Practical Plan to Achieve the Millennium Development Goals. Earthscan, New York

Uppal R, Van Hulle C (1997) Sovereign debt and the London Club: A precommitment device for limiting punishment for default. Journal of Banking and Finance 21 : 741–756

Vásquez I (2003) The New Approach to Foreign Aid – Is the Enthusiasm Warranted? Foreign Policy Briefing 79, Cato Institute, Washington DC

Vellutini C (2003) Capital mobility and underdeveloped traps. Journal of Development Economics 71 : 435–462

Voivodas CS (1973) Exports, Foreign Capital Inflow and Economic Growth. Journal of International Economics 3 : 337–349

Wagner F (2005) Biodiesel-Produktion in der Wüste. Handelsblatt, June 24, 2005

Wagner N, Kaiser M, Beimdiek F (1983) Ökonomie der Entwicklungsländer. Gustav Fischer Verlag, Stuttgart

Wahl P (2005) International Taxation – Regulating Globalisation, Financing Development. World Economy, Ecology, and Development e.V. (WEED), Berlin

Warr P (2001) Poverty Reduction and Sectoral Growth: Evidence from South East Asia. Paper presented at the WIDER Development Conference on Growth and Poverty, World Institute for Development Economics Research, United Nations University, Helsinki

Watts HW (1968) An Economic Definition of Poverty. In: Moynihan DP (ed) On Understanding Poverty. Basic Books, New York

Weber A (1909) Über den Standort der Industrien – Erster Teil: Reine Theorie des Standorts. JCB Mohr, Tübingen

Weber M (1993) Die protestantische Ethik und der „Geist“ des Kapitalismus, based on the first edn in 1904/05. Hanstein Verlagsgesellschaft, Bodenheim

Weber M (1980) Wirtschaft und Gesellschaft: Grundriss der verstehenden Soziologie, 5th and revised edn. JCB Mohr, Tübingen

Weber M (1949) The Methodology of Social Sciences. Free Press, Glencoe

Wehrheim M, Schmitz T (2003) Devisentransaktionssteuer – Historische Entwicklung und kritische Würdigung. Wirtschaftswissenschaftliches Studium 32 (11) : 649–653

Weil DN (2005) Economic Growth. Addison-Wesley, Boston

Weisskopf TE (1972) The Impact of Foreign Capital Inflow on Domestic Savings in Underdeveloped Countries. Journal of International Economics 2 (1) : 25–38 (reprinted in: Dutt AK (2001) The Political Economy of Development. Edward Elgar, Cheltenham)

White H, Anderson EA (2001) Growth vs. Redistribution: Does the Pattern of Growth Matter? Development Policy Review 19 (3) : 267–289

Wieczorek-Zeul H (2005) Abschied von alten Dogmen. Entwicklung&Zusammenarbeit, Januar 2005 : 12–15

Williamson J (2000) What Should the World Bank Think about the Washington Consensus? The World Bank Research Observer 15 (2) : 251–264

Williamson J (1990) What Washington Means by Policy Reform. In: Williamson J (ed) Latin American Adjustment: How Much Has Happened? Institute for International Economics, Washington DC

Winter-Nelson A (1995) Natural resources, National Income, and Economic Growth in Africa. World Development 23 (9) : 1507–1519
Wolfensohn JD, Bourguignon F (2004) Development and Poverty Reduction – Looking Back, Looking Ahead. World Bank, Washington DC
World Bank (2006a) 2006 World Development Indicators. World Bank, Washington DC
World Bank (2006b) Poverty reduction strategies. World Bank, Washington DC
World Bank (2005a) Global Data Monitoring Information System. World Bank, Washington DC
World Bank (2005b) Global Development Finance 2005 – Meeting the Needs of Poor Countries. World Bank, Washington DC
World Bank (2005c) Country ownership. World Bank, Washington DC
World Bank (2004a) From Adjustment Lending to Development Policy Lending: Update of World Bank Policy. Operations Policy and Country Service, World Bank, Washington DC
World Bank (2004b) The Poverty Reduction Strategy Initiative – An Independent Evaluation of the World Bank's Support through 2003. World Bank Operations Evaluation Department, World Bank, Washington DC
World Bank (2004c) Global Development Finance 2004. World Bank, Washington DC
World Bank (2002a) The Financial Impact of the HIPC Initiative. World Bank, Washington DC
World Bank (2002b) The Role and Effectiveness of Development Assistance: Lessons from World Bank Experience. Research Paper from the Development Economics Vice Presidency, World Bank, Washington DC
World Bank (2000a) Social Dimension of Adjustment Programs. A submission to the World Summit for Social Development Five-Year Review, June 2000, World Bank, Washington DC
World Bank (2000b) World Development Report: Attacking Poverty. Oxford University Press, New York
World Bank (1999) World Development Indicators. World Bank, Washington DC
World Bank (1998) Assessing Aid: What Works, What Doesn't, and Why. Oxford University Press, New York
World Bank (1993) The East Asian Miracle: Economic Growth and Public Policy. World Bank Policy Research Report, Oxford University Press, New York
World Bank (1990) World Development Report: Poverty. Oxford University Press, New York
World Bank (1980) Annual Report 1980. World Bank, Washington DC
World Bank and IMF (2005) Global Monitoring Report 2005 – MDG: From Consensus to Momentum. World Bank and IMF, Washington DC
Younger S (1992) Aid and the Dutch Disease: Macroeconomic Management When Everybody Loves You. World Development 20 (11) : 121–125
Zafar A (2004) What happens when a country does not adjust to terms of trade shocks? The case of oil-rich Gabon. World Bank Policy Research Working Paper 3403, World Bank, Washington DC

Zee HH (2000) Retarding Short-Term Capital Inflows Through Withholding Tax. IMF Working Paper WP/00/40, International Monetary Fund, Washington DC
Zheng B (1993) An Axiomatic Characterization of the Watts Index. Economics Letters 42 : 81–86